"Writing a book about the Revelation of Jesus Christ, as given to the Apostle John, is a courageous and consuming task. Recommending such a book may require almost as much courage, but I am glad to do so because I have great confidence in Pastor Keinath's careful walk with the Lord and the integrity and excellence of his scholarship. You will be richly nourished as you tread the holy ground of this study on the apocalyptic drama that promises a special blessing to those who read it."

DR. DAVID E. SCHROEDER
President, Pillar College
Former President, Philadelphia Theological Seminary
Former President, Nyack College and Alliance Theological Seminary

"Rev. Dr. Thomas Keinath has contributed to the theological world an exceptionally well-written, pragmatic and insightful look at the first seven chapters of the book of Revelation. Dr. Keinath, a pastor for 37 years, begins the preface with 'I am a pastor—it is not what I do; it is who I am.' With this underpinning, Pastor Keinath exegetically examines every verse and amply sprinkles in practical applications. He writes from the perspective that 'the book of Revelation may well be the single most important book of the Bible.' He concludes his exegetical study with an inimitable theological overview of eleven major doctrines as found in Revelation."

DR. WAYNE R. DYER
Vice President Strategic Alliances, Pillar College

"This is a thought-provoking and spiritually impactful book by Dr. Tom Keinath. I find this work to be both an academic and inspirational devotional, a book that everyone should have on their shelf."

REV. DAVID S. KIM, M. DIV.
(PRINCETON THEOLOGICAL SEMINARY)
President, University of Valley Forge

"This work is truly a biblical masterpiece on the Book of Revelation. Written from the perspective of a pastor, teacher, and theologian, this is by far one of the best, thought-provoking, deep, and understandable studies I have ever read on the subject. Here is a must-have resource for every Christian and pastor who wants to understand the Book of Revelation."

DR. RICHARD MARTINEZ
General Director & Dean, New Jersey District School of Ministry (A/G)
Senior Pastor, Community Gospel Church; Northvale, New Jersey

"In perilous times people need understanding, a compass, and hope. Tom Keinath, with the skill of a scholar, the heart of a pastor, and the zeal of a missionary carefully enlightens readers to the important messaging of the Book of Revelation. This commentary is historically reliable and a balanced guide for our present times."

REV. CARL COLLETTI, M.A.
Former District Superintendent, New Jersey Assemblies of God

CONQUEST & GLORY

A Pastor's Journey Through
THE BOOK OF REVELATION

Volume 1

Biblical Insights & Life Application
from Chapters 1-7

· · · · ·

A Theological Overview with
Textual Concordance

Rev. Thomas W. Keinath, M.A., D.Min.

EQUIP PRESS

Colorado Springs

CONQUEST & GLORY

A Pastor's Journey Through
THE BOOK OF REVELATION
—Volume 1—

Published by Equip Press
5550 Tech Center Drive
Colorado Springs, CO 80919

Printed in the United States of America

First Edition: 2018
Conquest & Glory: A Pastor's Journey Through the Book of Revelation /
    Rev. Thomas W. Keinath, M.A., D.Min.
Paperback ISBN: 978-1-946453-37-2
eBook ISBN: 978-1-946453-38-9

Lovingly Dedicated to My Parents,

Rev. David L. and Margaret H. Keinath,
who taught me a love for God's Word from my earliest memories.

Dad,
you have always lived with the humility and compassion of Christ.

Mom,
"Then I heard a voice from heaven say,
'Write this: Blessed are the dead who die in the Lord from now on.'
'Yes,' says the Spirit, 'they will rest from their labor,
for their deeds will follow them.'"
(REVELATION 14:13)

Table of Contents

Volume 1

Section 1:
An Introduction to the Book of Revelation

Section 2:
Biblical Insights and Life Application from Chapters 1-7

Section 3:

A Theological Overview of the Book of Revelation with
Textual Concordance and Summary Statements

Preface

I am a pastor—it is not what I do; it is who I am. To shepherd God's people is the call on my life, known from my earliest memories. As a pastor, it is my greatest honor to nurture, to protect, and to guide those whom the Chief Shepherd has entrusted to my care. The congregation I have pastored now for the last seventeen years, and which I have served additionally as an associate pastor for many more, is Calvary Temple International Assembly of God in Wayne, New Jersey. Our church family is a multi-campus, multi-cultural, and multi-generational evangelical, Spirit-filled body of believers. On any given weekend, many hundreds from the most densely populated center in the nation join with believers from rural outskirts and suburban communities to worship and to grow in the Word with spiritual passion. Business people, tradesmen, professionals, homemakers, and those on their way out of homelessness all love to be in God's presence together. It really is amazing!

One of the highlights and greatest joys of my thirty-seven years of full-time ministry has been the clear leading of the Lord to preach, verse by verse, through the entire Book of Revelation. In January of 2013, I went into this nearly eleven-month journey with rather strong apprehension. "Will I be able to relate one of the more challenging books of the Bible to the real-life concerns of our congregation today?" "Will we continue to see the altars filled with people seeking more of Jesus?" "Will people still respond to a salvation call?" "Will they understand what I'm saying?" "Will I understand what I'm saying?" "Will we lose people whose 'cup of tea' is not prophecy?" "Will people stay focused in one book of the Bible month after month—and the Book of Revelation at that?"

It is now five years later and I can say with all my heart, looking back and looking forward, how blessed we are to obey Jesus! I am a changed man, having revisited with fervor and joy this incredible book of the Bible. Our church is a changed church. Our church has grown … in every way. In fact, during the preaching of these messages we planted two new churches in two northern New Jersey cities.

As I completed that preaching series, the Lord laid yet another radical idea upon my heart. I was soon to write a book based in part on what I had preached. So, here I am saying that as a pastor it is my intention to "keep it real" as I present this study. And nothing could be more real—Jesus is coming back soon! Very soon! Therefore, the pastor side of me will aim to bring devotional inspiration from every passage of Revelation in the Life Application sections of this book.

I am also a teacher—it is not what I do; it is who I am. Since early in ministry, I have found a special joy in teaching the Word, along with various courses of study, within a classroom setting. Here, I have been blessed to bring instruction in venues ranging from seminary, college, and churches to numerous conferences in the U.S. and overseas. Yet, above all, I have enjoyed teaching as I preach expositorily and textually from my own "sacred desk." Thus, in this book the teacher side of me will delve exegetically into every verse of Revelation, alongside related Scripture, within the Biblical Insight sections of this study. Additionally, over many months, what began with the need to organize verses according to doctrinal topics grew into an extensive textual concordance with an accompanying theological overview. I pray that this addition to volume one will be a helpful tool to the serious student of the Word.

At the beginning of this project, I was blessed to invest two weeks on a life-altering tour through the areas of the Seven Churches of the Revelation in Turkey, eight days on the Island of Patmos, and quick stops in Corinth and Athens, Greece. I will need the rest of my days on this earth to process it all, for it was on this journey that I came under the conviction that the Book of Revelation may well be the single most important book of the Bible. While I understand that some ministry colleagues might not choose to express their appreciation for Revelation with such confidence—and some would disagree altogether—I will begin to explain my personal reasoning within the introduction to this book.

But first, I will draw upon the insight of a gentleman, Saki, who along with his wife Suzi graciously provided my accommodations while staying on the Island of Patmos. In hearing that my purpose in visiting their picturesque and deeply religious gem of the Aegean Sea was to begin the writing of a book on Revelation, he resolutely commented, "This book is not all about destruction, it is about hope."

So, here we go on the hope-filled journey of a lifetime! Here, in what has become to me the pinnacle of the Word of God, we will discover God's "wrap-up" of all the major and supporting doctrines of the Bible: the Deity of Jesus, the Trinity of God, Heaven and Hell, the Rapture and the Tribulation, the Millennial Reign of Christ, the Times of the Gentiles, Armageddon, the Judgments, the Resurrection of the righteous and the wicked, the Heavenly Jerusalem, and so many more. Here, we will meet characters like riders on horses, a great red dragon, beasts, horns that speak, and a "Scarlet Woman." Here, we will encounter the unparalleled and ultimate Conquest and Glory of Jesus, the King of all kings and Lord of all lords!

Thomas Keinath

"From the Cave of the Apocalypse"

The view from this cave is spectacular. From here—alone with God—a man is able to see so far. From here, if a man ... or a church will listen, they can hear so deeply.

For the man John, advanced in years, a proven apostle of the Faith now exiled and alone, this cave would have been a welcomed shelter from torrential rain or blazing sun. Today, a Greek Orthodox chapel with arched doorways and vaulted ceilings surrounds and protects this grotto. Outside, a sign on the approach to the monastery that keeps these grounds welcomes guests with one simple request for quiet reverence.

In John's day, there were no ornate brass lamp stands along the wall, nor the three-tiered candelabra hanging from the ceiling off to my left. There were no silver oil lamps like those suspended in front of me from brass rods fastened to the stone interior. This once-secluded refuge now welcomes pilgrims from all over the world. Even local residents come here for prayer vigils and religious services led by priests dressed in flowing black robes with grayish beards and gentle demeanors.

Immediately beyond the mouth of the cave and the stone chapel which encloses it, the terrain drops abruptly, eighty or so feet to a pleasant valley below. From there, a hill slopes steeply to the right; another smaller hill rises gradually just to the left. Between these two, the valley plain stretches out perhaps a half-mile or so toward the bluish-green shoreline of the Aegean Sea. I see it all through a simple window. Stone walls—hundreds of them—run through this valley, sometimes parallel, sometimes less descript. The hill to the right is more perfectly patterned, though most of the boundary walls are overtaken by an abundance of lush, green ground cover. A tiny white chapel, one of over 400 that dot this island, sits quietly on the middle of this hillside; at the top stand three stone windmills, situated like sentinels guarding the valley below. Serenity has met promise.

In John's day, there was no fortressed monastery—built in his honor a thousand years later—just a short-but-vigorous climb up the hill directly behind the cave. Nor was the beautiful and historic village of Chora that encircles the monastery even in existence. And though there is evidence of an ancient harbor off to the left of the valley below, the weekly flow of vacationing tourists into the port of Skala in our day was inconceivable back then.

In the distance, I hear the hammer of a workman in the valley. A rooster occasionally crows and a dog is barking just now. At determined times, the clarion bells from the ancient monastery tower ring out with varying tones, filling the valley and village, like they have for hundreds of years. Now, in has walked the caretaker; his electric vacuum seems so much out of place.

John would not have heard any of this. But he would hear what few men on this side of glory have ever heard. He would hear the audible voice of God—sometimes still as a whisper, sometimes as thunderous as many waters. If the historical record is true, there were no trees, palm or any other, on ancient Patmos. Known only as a Roman penal colony for the most incorrigible, the only vegetation was scrub brush, growing in between the harsh, rocky terrain. But John, while still in mortal body, would have seen the peaceful shore of Heaven … a vision few on this side of glory have ever seen.

There is a hewn niche in the corner along the base of the wall, not far from where I am sitting. Tradition says John would rest his head there. Another smaller notch is carved into the wall just above it. It is said that here John would place his hand to lift himself up. Oh, there is nothing innately sacred about a cave in the side of a hill. But, there are places where God and man choose to meet. And somehow, this place is different.

A light breeze is blowing and the day has started with heavy clouds; the temperature is cool by local standards. It is winter in Patmos, January 18, 2014, and few visitors are on the island. Even the caretaker is gone now and it is quiet again.

I am glad to be alone this morning. Sitting here, I tell you with tears, nothing has been more important to me than the close presence of Jesus. I want to be like John, near to the Master's side; I want to rest my head upon His chest. I want to say to all the world, I am the one "whom Jesus loves."

Some things are very different about this cave in our day. But other things—the more important things—have never changed, nor will they until John's vision is fulfilled. A young couple has walked in just now; they are reverent and quiet. Seated on a bench in front of me, she whispers out a prayer from her heart in her native language. A priest has just arrived as well. Though focused upon his sacred duties of preparing this chapel for worshipers later in the day, he looks up occasionally with a smile, silently acknowledging that he knows why we are here.

I am overcome with emotions.

The view from the Cave of the Apocalypse is spectacular. From here, alone with God, a man is able to see so far. From here—or anywhere alone with Jesus—if a man … or a church will listen, really listen, we can all hear so deeply.

Thomas Keinath

SECTION 1

An Introduction to the Book of Revelation

Author and Authenticity

John, son of Zebedee and one of the original apostles, is believed to be the writer of the Book of Revelation, as well as the Gospel of John and the three Letters of John, by most, yet not all, evangelicals today. Employing the disciplines of lower criticism, which is most concerned with the preservation and transmission of the biblical text, many scholars are convinced that the John who identifies himself by name in Revelation 1:1, 4, 9; 21:2 (*Textus Receptus*); and 22:8 is none other than John the beloved apostle (John 20:2; 21:7, 20). As will be seen, this was also the prevailing belief of the vast majority of Church leaders and theologians for the first several centuries of the Church. By contrast, the largely secular and often anti-supernatural approach of higher criticism, which is most concerned with investigating the origination and sources behind the biblical texts, generally rejects the Johannine authorship of all five of these books of the Bible. Here, with little exception, rationalism is the rule and any thought of divine revelation is dismissed out of hand.

In laying the groundwork for the divine inspiration of the Apostle John's writings, it is first important to note that there is prolific early, external evidence for his authorship of the Gospel of John. In circa A.D. 180, Church Father and apologist Irenaeus states, "Afterwards, John, the disciple of the Lord, who also had leaned upon His breast, did himself publish a Gospel during his residence at Ephesus in Asia" (*Against Heresies*, Book 3, Chapter 1.1).[1] This is significant, since we know from early historian and Christian polemicist Bishop Eusebius (c. A.D. 260-340) that Irenaeus (A.D. 130-202) was the student of Polycarp (A.D. 69-155), who was himself the student of the Apostle John (*Church History*, Book 5, Chapter 20.6).[2] Eusebius also writes (in his *Church History*, Book 6, Chapter 14.5-7) that Clement of Alexandria (A.D. 150-215) affirmed John as the writer of the Gospel of John with these words, "But, last of all, John, perceiving that the external facts had been made plain in the Gospel, being urged by his friends, and inspired by the Spirit, composed a spiritual Gospel."[3]

We find the same support for the apostle's authorship of the Gospel of John in the writings of two early theologians, Tertullian (c. A.D. 160-225)—in his *Against Marcion*, Book 4, Chapter 5[4]—and Origen (A.D. 185-254)—in his *Commentary on the Gospel of John*, Book 1, Chapter 6.[5] Furthermore, the earliest known list of the books of the New Testament, the *Muratorian Canon* (c. A.D. 180-190) states that,

> John, one of the disciples, wrote the Fourth Gospel. When his fellow disciples and the bishops urged him to do so, he said, "Join me in fasting for three days, and then let us relate to one another what shall be revealed to each." The same night it was revealed to Andrew, one of the apostles, that John should write down everything in his own name, and they should all revise it.[6]

Coming later, but of no less significance, are the words of Augustine (A.D. 354-430) in His *Consensus of the Gospels* (Book 1, Chapter 4.7), "But John, on the other hand, had in view that true divinity of the Lord in which He is the Father's equal, and directed his efforts above all to the setting forth of the divine nature in his Gospel in such a way as he believed to be adequate to men's needs and notions."[7]

As there is clear, early allusion to the Apostle John's authorship of the fourth Gospel, there is likewise substantial, early external evidence for his authorship of the Book of Revelation. Justin Martyr (A.D. 100-165), in his *Dialogue with Trypho* (Chapter 81), states: "And further, there was a certain man with us, whose name was John, one of the apostles of Christ, who prophesied, by a revelation that was made to him, that those who believed in our Christ would dwell a thousand years in Jerusalem; and that thereafter the general, and, in short, the eternal resurrection and judgment of all men would likewise take place."[8] Later, Irenaeus writes the following: "John also, the Lord's disciple, when beholding the sacerdotal and glorious advent of His kingdom, says in the Apocalypse: [...]"; he then extensively quotes from and comments upon the text of the Book of Revelation (*Against Heresies*, Book 4, Chapter 20.11).[9] Tertullian also affirms the Apostle John as author with these words, "We have also churches which are nurselings of John's: for although Marcion disallows his Apocalypse, yet the succession of their bishops, when traced back to its origin, will be found to rest in John as originator" (*Against Marcion*, 4.5).[10] Again, in his treatise *On Modesty* (Chapter XIX—*Objections from the Revelation and the First Epistle of St. John Refuted*), while quoting from the Apocalypse, Tertullian attributes the authorship of Revelation to the Apostle John as he states, "I am content with the fact that, between apostles, there is a common agreement in rules of faith and of discipline."[11]

Critical to the certainty of the Apostle John's authorship of Revelation is that he indeed was exiled to the Island of Patmos; again, there exists a great amount of factual ancient testimony. Once more, Tertullian writes in his *On Prescription Against Heretics 36*, "How fortunate is that church upon which the apostles poured their whole teaching together with their blood, where Peter suffered like his Lord, where Paul was crowned with John's death, where the apostle John, after he had been immersed in boiling oil without harm, was banished to an island."[12] Origen, too, adds (in his *Commentary on Matthew* 16.6), "A Roman emperor, as tradition teaches, banished John into the island of Patmos for the testimony which he bore to the word of truth; and John himself bears witness to his banishment."[13] In the third century, theologian Hippolytus of Rome (A.D. 170-235) then states the following in his *Treatise on Christ and Antichrist 36,* "For he sees, when in the isle Patmos, a revelation of awful mysteries, which he recounts freely, and makes known to others. Tell me, blessed John, apostle and disciple of the Lord, what didst thou see and hear concerning Babylon? Arise, and speak; for it sent thee also into banishment."[14] Onward into the fourth century A.D., Eusebius (in his *Church History*, Book 3, Chapter 18.1-5) informs us that John's exile came during the reign of Emperor Domitian (r. A.D. 81-96).[15]

Likewise, important to the Apostle's authorship of Revelation is that John had a ministry relationship with the churches and locales of western Asia Minor in the last quarter of the first century A.D. This is necessary, in consideration of the Spirit's direction to address the book, "To the seven churches in the province of Asia: [...]" (Revelation 1:4) and the Spirit's instruction to, "Write on a scroll what you see and send it to the seven churches: [...]" (1:11). That John was well known to especially the church in Ephesus and to the region of the seven churches is again well-documented. Theologian Clement of Alexandria (A.D. 150-215), in his essay, *Who Is the Rich Man That Shall Be Saved? 42*, testifies that following the death of Domitian, John was released from exile and did return to Ephesus where he ministered until his natural death in circa A.D. 100. He writes,

> [...] listen to a tale, which is not a tale but a narrative, handed down and committed to the custody of memory, about the Apostle John. For when, on the tyrant's death, he returned to Ephesus from the isle of Patmos, he went away, being invited, to the contiguous territories of the nations, here to appoint bishops, there to set in order whole Churches, there to ordain such as were marked out by the Spirit.[16]

Church Father Irenaeus, in his *Against Heresies* (Book 3, Chapter 3.4), tells both of a report he received from Bishop Polycarp concerning the character of John and that the apostle lived permanently in Ephesus during the reign of Emperor Trajan (r. A.D. 98-117).

> There are also those who heard from him that John, the disciple of the Lord, going to bathe at Ephesus, and perceiving Cerinthus within, rushed out of the bath-house without bathing, exclaiming, "Let us fly, lest even the bath-house fall down, because Cerinthus, the enemy of the truth, is within." [...] Then, again, the Church in Ephesus, founded by Paul, and having John remaining among them permanently until the times of Trajan, is a true witness of the tradition of the apostles.[17]

Likewise, Eusebius (in his *Church History*, Book 3, Chapter 23.1, 2) again confirms that John,

> [...] the one whom Jesus loved, was still living in Asia, and governing the churches of that region, having returned after the death of Domitian from his exile on the island. And that he was still alive at that time may be established by the testimony of two witnesses. They should be trustworthy who

have maintained the orthodoxy of the Church; and such indeed were Irenæus and Clement of Alexandria.[18]

In the subsequent sections of this same book and chapter, Eusebius tells with great detail the story of John's merciful, compassionate, and successful evangelistic appeal to a young man who had turned from the faith to a lifestyle of thievery (here, Chapter 23.17-19):

> 17. But John, forgetting his age, pursued him with all his might, crying out, 'Why, my son, dost thou flee from me, thine own father, unarmed, aged? Pity me, my son; fear not; thou hast still hope of life. I will give account to Christ for thee. If need be, I will willingly endure thy death as the Lord suffered death for us. For thee will I give up my life. Stand, believe; Christ hath sent me.'

> 18. And he, when he heard, first stopped and looked down; then he threw away his arms, and then trembled and wept bitterly. And when the old man approached, he embraced him, making confession with lamentations as he was able, baptizing himself a second time with tears, and concealing only his right hand.

> 19. But John, pledging himself, and assuring him on oath that he would find forgiveness with the Saviour, besought him, fell upon his knees, kissed his right hand itself as if now purified by repentance, and led him back to the church. And making intercession for him with copious prayers, and struggling together with him in continual fastings, and subduing his mind by various utterances, he did not depart, as they say, until he had restored him to the church, furnishing a great example of true repentance and a great proof of regeneration, a trophy of a visible resurrection.[19]

Of further great value to understanding the heart and mind of John while ministering through to the hour of his death are the words of Saint Jerome (A.D. 347-420) in his commentary on Galatians. While observing Galatians 6:10, he writes,

> The blessed John the Evangelist, who remained in Ephesus to an advanced age and could scarcely be carried to the church with the help of his disciples. At each assembly, he used to say no more than this: "Little children, love one another!" Eventually, the disciples and brethren who were present grew tired of always hearing the same thing, and said, "Master, why do you keep on saying this?" He replied with a sentiment worthy of John: "Because it is a precept of the Lord [i.e., Jesus], and it is sufficient if this alone is done."[20]

As concerns John's death and burial in Ephesus, Eusebius (*Church History*, Book 3, Chapter 31.3) quotes these words of Polycrates (c. A.D. 130-196), bishop of Ephesus (in his *Epistle to Victor*), "[…] and moreover John, who was both a witness and a teacher, who reclined upon the bosom of the Lord, and being a priest wore the sacerdotal plate. He also sleeps at Ephesus."[21] In a later, but reliable, statement from theologian and historian Jerome (A.D. 347-420) (*Lives of Illustrious Men*, Chapter 9), we find further indication of the events surrounding John's exile, his writing of the Revelation, his return to Ephesus, and the year of his death,

> In the fourteenth year, then after Nero Domitian having raised a second persecution he was banished to the island of Patmos, and wrote the *Apocalypse,* on which Justin Martyr and Irenæus afterwards wrote commentaries. But Domitian having been put to death and his acts, on account of his excessive cruelty, having been annulled by the senate, he returned to Ephesus under Pertinax and continuing there until the time of the emperor Trajan, founded and built churches throughout all Asia, and, worn out by old age, died in the sixty-eighth year after our Lord's passion and was buried near the same city.[22]

Having established that the commonly held position of Church leaders and theologians through the first three centuries of the Church was in support of the Apostle John's authorship under divine inspiration, it must be noted that a limited, but significant, divergence from this view rose in the third and fourth centuries A.D. Initially, and most notably, this came through the opinion of Dionysius (c. A.D. 200-c. 265), Bishop of Alexandria. While claiming to admire the book of Revelation and while accepting its canonicity, he yet rejected its apostolic authorship in favor of one John the Presbyter, Bishop of Hierapolis. This he based in part on his assessment of the language and style of the Revelation. Eusebius (*Church History*, Book 7, Chapter 25, *The Apocalypse of John*, Section 26) quotes Dionysius as writing, "[…] I perceive, however, that his dialect and language are not accurate Greek, but that he uses barbarous idioms, and, in some places, solecisms."[23] (To this charge, many conservative scholars have given a fairer treatment in light of the unique circumstances surrounding John's reception of the Apocalypse and the question of whether John wrote with or without the assistance of an amanuensis.[24]) Additionally, Dionysius denied that the Apostle would have identified himself by name; here, he is quoted again by Eusebius (*The Apocalypse of John*, Sections 7-8):

> 7. Therefore that he was called John, and that this book is the work of one John, I do not deny. And I agree also that it is the work of a holy and inspired man. But I cannot readily admit that he was the apostle, the son of Zebedee, the brother of James, by whom the Gospel of John and the Catholic Epistle were written.

8. For I judge from the character of both, and the forms of expression, and the entire execution of the book, that it is not his. For the evangelist nowhere gives his name, or proclaims himself, either in the Gospel or Epistle.[25]

Certainly, it would have been best for Dionysius and those influenced by him to have adhered to his very own instruction concerning the Revelation, as follows (*The Apocalypse of John*, Sections 4-5):

4. But I could not venture to reject the book, as many brethren hold it in high esteem. But I suppose that it is beyond my comprehension, and that there is a certain concealed and more wonderful meaning in every part. For if I do not understand I suspect that a deeper sense lies beneath the words.

5. I do not measure and judge them by my own reason, but leaving the more to faith I regard them as too high for me to grasp. And I do not reject what I cannot comprehend, but rather wonder because I do not understand it.[26]

That Dionysius was amongst the leadership of the Alexandrian School of Theology (in North Africa) during the third century—an institution that championed the allegorical interpretation of the Scriptures—is, no doubt, central to his rejection of the apostolic authority of Revelation. It is possible, as some scholars hold, that relegating the Apocalypse to a less authoritative intention served to diminish the importance of some of its prophecies. Amongst these was the teaching of the Millennial Reign of Christ (Revelation 20:1-6), the literal fulfillment of which the Alexandrian School strongly rejected. Nevertheless, though the external evidence is overwhelming for the Apostle John's authorship, many scholars still follow the sentiments of Dionysius.

Having looked at the external evidence, we must also consider the internal evidence, which strongly supports John, the son of Zebedee and the writer of the fourth Gospel, as the writer of the Book of Revelation. Most apparent is the author's overt submission of his name; three times we read "I, John" (1:9; 21:2 [*Textus Receptus*]; and 22:8; cf. 1:1, 4). In consideration of the prolific use of the Old Testament in the Revelation, the author's Jewish heritage is suggested as well. Further, John's historic and biblical apostolic relationship to the churches of Asia Minor would certainly position him to be the "servant" (1:1) whom Jesus would choose to communicate His Word "To the seven churches in the province of Asia" (1:4 and verse 11).

While some scholars are quick to point out stylistic differences between John's Gospel and the Revelation, these may certainly be attributable to the author's intent and the distinct nature of each type of literature, if not also the passing of time. What is indisputable, however, is the thematic relationship between all of John's writings. Is not John's consistent message concerning such truths as spiritual light and darkness;

spiritual sight and blindness; belief and unbelief; eternal life and eternal damnation; signs from Heaven; an overcoming, victorious life in Christ; etc., prolific in all of his writings? And are we not compelled in both Gospel and Apocalypse to gaze upon the Word of God, the Lamb of God, and Heaven's King?

Continuing to survey the internal evidence for apostolic authorship, it is clear that the writer of both Gospel and Apocalypse was a deeply devoted believer in Jesus, fully convinced that the Christian faith would soon triumph over the demonic forces at work in the world. And what more do we know of John, the Beloved disciple? He was the youngest son of Zebedee (Matt. 4:21) and Salome. Interestingly, a comparison of Gospel accounts gives strong evidence that John was a first cousin to Jesus, their mothers evidently being sisters. Matthew 27:55-56 states that amongst those present at the crucifixion "watching from a distance ... were Mary Magdalene, Mary the mother of James and Joseph, and the mother of Zebedee's sons." The parallel account in the synoptic Gospel of Mark (15:40) states that "Some women were watching from a distance. Among them were Mary Magdalene, Mary the mother of James the younger and of Joseph, and Salome." (These same three are noted together again in Mark 16:1.) John (19:25) gives further clarification by stating that, "Near the cross of Jesus stood his mother, his mother's sister, Mary the wife of Clopas, and Mary Magdalene." If this line of reasoning is correct, then the Apostle John was also cousin to John the Baptist, whose mother Elizabeth was Mary's cousin. This may also shed light on Christ's willingness to commend the support of his own mother to John as He breathed out His last (John 19:26-27).

We know, too, that John was a fisherman, along with his father Zebedee, his brother James, and their business partners Peter and Andrew, operating together from the northern shore of the Sea of Galilee. The success of their business is evident inasmuch as they were able to hire additional help (Mark 1:20). While we know for certain that Andrew and Peter were from Bethsaida (John 1:44), we can only assume that John and his family resided nearby. It is commonly held that the unnamed disciple of John the Baptist, along with Andrew in John 1:35, was the Apostle John. This is upheld by the detail of "about the tenth hour" as the time that they met Jesus and heard him say, "Come and you will see" (John 1:39). John then followed Jesus in this first phase of the disciples' call for a period of approximately four months, during which time he was witness to the power of Jesus through such miracles as the turning of water into wine (John 2:9, 11) and to the uniqueness of His mission through such words as, "My food is to do the will of him who sent me and to finish his work" (John 4:34).

After returning to their fishing nets for approximately two months, John, along with his brother and colleagues, were called again, this time to continuous discipleship (Matt. 4:18-22; Mark 1:16-20; Luke 5:1-11). In this second phase of their calling, John and James responded to the words, "Come, follow me" as they "immediately [...] left the boat and their father and followed him" (Matt. 4:19, 22). Further hearing the word, "from now on you will catch men" (Luke 5:10), they were suddenly brought into the front lines of Christ's ministry. For approximately the next ten months, John and the others underwent intensive training as Jesus sought to make them mature in their faith and bold in their ministry. This was the season for developing character and skills for the sake of the Kingdom as the Master Discipler modeled the way.

The third season of the disciples' call may be identified as the "Come and be with Me" phase based on Mark 3:13-19 (cf. Luke 6:12-16). At this time, the Twelve, now specifically named, were appointed to proclamation and demonstration of the Gospel. A careful study reveals that for the next twenty months, Jesus led John and the other disciples through teaching, modeling, delegating, and supervising as a repeated pattern. Together, this small group formed the epicenter for ministry to the multitudes and to individuals. The parallel passages of Matthew 10:1ff; Mark 6:7-13; and Luke 9:1ff, speak of the more specific and formal call to apostleship and the commencement of actual direct ministry which followed several months after the initial commission of Mark 3. From this point on, the disciples, empowered with the authority of Christ's name, often ministered apart from the immediate presence of Jesus and gave leadership to the Seventy as well (Luke 10:1ff). At the close of this season of discipleship, Jesus announced that all true disciples must continue to carry on the future work of the Kingdom—now to extend to every nation until His return.

Along with James and Peter, John was part of the inner core of Christ's disciples (Mark 5:37; 13:3; 14:31; Matt. 17:1; Luke 8:51; 22:8); such intimacy and trust is mirrored in John's self-identification as "the disciple whom Jesus loved" (John 13:23; 19:26; 20:2; 21:7, 20). We see the nearness of his heart to Jesus again as he sat next to his Master during their last supper together (John 13:23) and also in his courageous appearance, alone of all the Twelve, at the foot of the cross, near to Mary (John 19:25-27). And we cannot forget that he, outrunning Peter, was the first to arrive at the empty tomb after Mary's report (John 20:2-8).

Though it is difficult to support the commonly held belief that John was the youngest of the disciples, it is accurate to say that he was quite young, perhaps even a teenager at the time he first heard the call of Jesus. We may gather this: from the lateness of his writings, which commonly date to the later part of the first century A.D.; from the insistence of his mother to promote his and his brother's place in Christ's Kingdom (Matt. 20:20-21; Mark 10:35-37; unlikely if they were matured adults); and, from the fact that Zebedee was still an active fisherman in a day when life expectancy was rarely over the age of forty-five. It is also most likely that John was younger than his brother James, since nearly every one of twenty references to the two lists James first, and often John is listed as "his brother." It is also safe to say that Jesus nicknamed John and James "Boanerges" (meaning "Sons of Thunder"; Mark 3:17) because of their sometimes-misplaced prophetic zeal (Luke 9:54-56; Mark 9:38), if not also because of their youthful energy.

Later, we read in the Scriptures that John became a great leader in the early Church (Gal. 2:9). Long established in his heart and mind, he had been an eyewitness to Christ's miracles, His transfiguration, His crucifixion, and His resurrection. He, too, had received His commission and had watched His ascension in glory. And with other faithful seekers, John was present to receive the outpouring of Christ's Spirit in the Upper Room at Pentecost. It is no wonder, then, that John was the Lord's choice vessel to "write" and "send" this glorious message from His throne. And here, in Christ's full and final Revelation, all earlier revelations entrusted to John would find their pinnacle.

Place, Date, and Occasion of Writing

In the previous section, numerous early sources were cited to support the position that the Apostle John wrote the Book of Revelation while exiled on the Island of Patmos by Emperor Domitian (A.D. 81-96). Since John was released from his banishment shortly after the death of Domitian, it is commonly held that John wrote the Apocalypse in approximately A.D. 95. Amongst the earliest and most reliable witnesses to this fact is the testimony of apologist Irenaeus (A.D. 130-202), who writes of the timing of the apostle's reception of Revelation, "For that was seen no very long time since, but almost in our day, towards the end of Domitian's reign" (*Against Heresies*, Book 5, Chapter 30.3).[27] Church Father Victorinus of Pettau (d., c. A.D. 304), who wrote the earliest known commentary on Revelation (believed written in the last quarter of the third century) also speaks of this dating. Commenting on Revelation 10:11 he writes:

> [...] because when John said these things he was in the island of Patmos, condemned to the labour of the mines by Cæsar Domitian. There, therefore, he saw the Apocalypse; and when grown old, he thought that he should at length receive his quittance by suffering, Domitian being killed, all his judgments were discharged. And John being dismissed from the mines, thus subsequently delivered the same Apocalypse which he had received from God.[28]

Theologian and historian Jerome (c. 347–420) likewise echoes this dating in his *Against Jovinianus*, Book 1, Chapter 40.26 (A.D. 393), where he states, "a prophet, for he saw in the island of Patmos, to which he had been banished by the Emperor Domitian as a martyr for the Lord, an Apocalypse containing the boundless mysteries of the future."[29]

Those commentators who are given to a preterist view (see Four Primary Views below) prefer an earlier dating for the writing of Revelation. Holding to A.D. 68 or 69, this school of thought applies the cataclysmic events of the Apocalypse to the destruction of Jerusalem in A.D. 70. For preterists, their only appeal to early external evidence comes from the alleged claim of Papias, Bishop of Hierapolis, namely, that John and his brother James were martyred at the hands of the Jews before A.D. 70.[30] While the exact dates of the birth and death of Papias are unknown, it is believed that his writings date to around the turn of the first century.[31] But here is where the testimony of Papias is to be questioned, since all we know of his writings is by reference—and that uncomplimentary—contained in the records of Eusebius in the fourth century. Of Papias he writes (*Church History*, Book 3, Chapter 39.11, 13): "The same writer gives also other accounts which he says came to him through unwritten tradition, certain strange parables and teachings of the Saviour, and some other more mythical things." [...] "For he appears to have been of very limited understanding, as one can see from his discourses."[32] And here is irony, for while preterists firmly deny any allusion to a literal Millennial Reign in Revelation 20, Eusebius (in Book 3, Chapter 39.12) goes on to say of Papias' writings (while insinuating his error):

> To these belong his statement that there will be a period of some thousand years after the resurrection of the dead, and that the kingdom of Christ will be set up in material form on this very earth. I suppose he got these ideas through a misunderstanding of the apostolic accounts, not perceiving that the things said by them were spoken mystically in figures.[33]

Conservative scholarship, then—based upon the solid testimony of many early Church Fathers—has strong reason to hold that the Apostle John wrote the Book of Revelation during the middle of the last decade of the first century A.D. while banished (a common Roman punishment) to the Island of Patmos. This he did as an elderly man, after having received a personal revelation of his Resurrected Lord and a strong mandate along with detailed prophetic insights from the Holy Spirit.

Though descriptions of Patmos have often pictured this volcanic island as desolate and barren, reliable archeology has proven that Patmos during the Roman Empire was important to ancient communication and trade and that it was a significant center for the pagan worship of Artemis, Apollo, and Aphrodite. "First-century Patmos, with its natural protective harbor, was a strategic island on the sea lane from Ephesus to Rome. A large administrative center, outlying villages, a hippodrome (for horse racing), and at least three pagan temples made Patmos hardly an isolated and desolate place!"[34] Excavations also include an acropolis at the center of the crescent shaped island, as well as ancient cemeteries and fortresses. Nevertheless, there is much evidence that Patmos in John's day was in decline and was known primarily as a place of exile for Roman convicts. While the severity of John's incarceration is uncertain, historical evidence suggests that his sojourn there lasted only between one and two years.

Purpose, Theme, and Recipients

Since John wrote and sent the Revelation under the directive of the Holy Spirit, it is best to find the purpose for this book within the will of God, the divine Author, rather than within the will of the apostle, the human writer. Knowing the hostility and aggression of the Roman government against the Church during much of the first century and beyond, it is easy to understand how the Holy Spirit would use this message to affirm and strengthen the faith of believers in that early day. Still, as inspired Scripture, that same encouragement continues to be present for Christians from that day till this.

But the Book of Revelation also evidences warnings and correction to believers, individually and corporately of all ages, who may be tempted to conform to the standards of the world. Contained in this unfolding revelation is direct exhortation from Him who knows His Church best; straightforward warning of coming judgment upon the disobedient; and, vivid glimpses into the eternal blessings promised to the righteous—all of which sounds a wakeup call to the Church.

Though supportive themes may be found in Revelation ranging from God's verdict and final judgment upon spiritual darkness to God's reward upon the righteous, the most prominent theme of Revelation is the glorious and ultimate victory of Jesus, Heaven's King! (For a fuller treatment of the theological themes of Revelation, see below: A Theological Overview of the Book of Revelation with Textual Concordance and Summary Statements.)

Without question, the first and most immediate recipients of the Book of Revelation were the believers of the late first and early second century Church. John is instructed to record what he sees and hears and to send this record, "To the seven churches in the province of Asia" (1:4, 11). Based on this instruction and upon early Church record, we are certain that this Revelation was circulated through these particular churches and eventually many other local churches.

From the perspective of many centuries of Church history, several differing approaches have been taken to the reading and receiving of the Book of Revelation. Some have found a message only for those seven, original, historic first century local churches. Here, Jesus is addressing, solely, real issues that were present in these real churches.

Other students of the Bible find in Revelation a message for the entire corporate Church, since, though the seven churches of Asia were not necessarily the most influential churches of their day, they certainly were remarkably representative of the character and condition of churches throughout the nearly 2,000 years of Church history. This view builds upon the significance of the number "seven" as a number of completeness to the Jewish mind. If the seven churches represent the totality of the visible Church, then the "what is now" of Revelation 1:19 speaks to the varying conditions of the Church of all times in all places. (As will be seen below, the historic approach to the Book of Revelation applies the messages to the seven churches as representative of clear and direct messages to seven successive Church periods down through history.)

Still another approach to reading and receiving the messages to the seven churches sees a much more personal and individual application. Emphasis is placed here upon the words of Jesus in Revelation, "He who has an ear, let him hear" (repeated with each of the seven messages) and the opening words found in 1:3, "Blessed is the one who reads the words of this prophecy." Compare also the personal call of Christ in Revelation 3:5: "The one who is victorious will, like them, be dressed in white. I will never blot out the name of that person from the book of life, but will acknowledge that name before my Father and his angels."

While these several approaches to reading and receiving may seem narrow in view, they are not necessarily mutually exclusive. There is every reason to find that these early messages to seven very real first century churches may also speak with great relevance to believers, corporately and individually, from the first century to the last century before the Second Coming of Jesus. In fact, is that not how most believers read and receive the balance of the New Testament?

Theological Considerations in Interpreting the Book of Revelation

The Inspiration of the Book of Revelation

Before a serious study of the Book of Revelation can be undertaken, several areas of theological interest must be addressed. Most foundational of these is the matter of divine inspiration. To those who dismiss the idea of God's direct intervention in the writing of Revelation, the book at best holds some intrigue as a rich sample of ancient, apocalyptic writing. To be clear, that is not the position of this author. In agreement with the prevailing position of the early Church Fathers and in alignment with conservative scholarship today, the conviction and position of this study is that the Book of Revelation is one of the sixty-six divinely inspired books of the canon of Scripture.

The Bible's own claim that "All Scripture is God-breathed and is useful for teaching, rebuking, correcting and training in righteousness" (2 Timothy 3:16) is captured in the phrase "verbal plenary inspiration." The term "verbal" affirms that God chose to use words and language as a tool or vehicle to reach humanity with His personal revelation. Since God ordained the resource of language, He is certainly able to use it for His purposes as He chooses. "Plenary," meaning "full" or "complete," affirms that every word of the original writings was used exactly as God intended in order to express His revelation. "Inspiration," the English translation of *theopneustos*—literally, "God-breathed"—indicates God's direct and personal involvement in giving us the Scriptures, including the Book of Revelation.

In bringing us His Word, God used the personalities of many writers from a wide range of backgrounds and experiences. Serving under the Divine Author's anointing, these human writers were shielded from all error and all sin in what they wrote. (God's superintendency assures that we can have confidence in the inerrancy of the autographs, i.e., the original texts of the Scriptures.) In a similar way that an artisan creates a stained-glass picture, God perfectly colored, shaped, and positioned the lives of the biblical writers such that, once the light of His anointing shone through, a beautiful and revealing image would perfectly emerge.

Certainly, in the breathing forth of the Word of God, the Holy Spirit impressed, directed, and led the writers in their sacred work. It is wrong to say that God did *not* use the human personalities of these writers. However, it is also wrong to say that human personalities overruled or overshadowed the work of the Holy Spirit in the process of writing the Scriptures. Truly, God in His great wisdom and authority remained above the vehicles of language and personalities, using both to His glory. Now, as concerns the writing of the Book of Revelation, what has been said of all the inspired biblical writers and texts is certainly also true of the Apostle John and of The Apocalypse.

Revelation as Apocalyptic Literature

By its very name, "Revelation"—*apokalypsis* (meaning a "revelation," "unveiling," or "disclosure")—is identified with the ancient genre of literature called "apocalyptic." Though this Jewish and early Christian literary form flourished in the years between 200 B.C. and A.D. 150, a period known for its crushing religious persecution, apocalyptic elements were included much earlier in the inspired writings of the biblical prophets, primarily Isaiah (Chapters 24-27), Ezekiel (Chapters 37-39), Daniel (Chapters 2, 7-12), Joel (Chapter 3), and Zachariah (Chapters 9-14). Apocalyptic elements may be found in New Testament passages as well, such as in the Olivet Discourse of Matthew 24 (par. Mark 13 and Luke 21), the Parable of the Sheep and the Goats in Matthew 25:31-46, and Paul's description of the overthrow of "the man of lawlessness" in 2 Thessalonians 2:1-12.

Generally described, apocalyptic style was intentionally spiritual, esoteric, and mysterious, claiming divine messages often delivered by angelic visitations, visions, and dreams. To validate these messages, pseudonymity (meaning, "falsely named") was employed as contemporary writers placed their "revelations" in the mouths of supposed ancient Old Testament saints (such as Enoch, Abraham, Moses, and Isaiah). The focus of apocalyptic literature was always eschatological, that is, with a focus upon the future end of time. This present evil age was viewed with pessimism while the age to come, introduced by the advent and triumph of the Messiah, was viewed with great optimism. With this came the forecast of divine judgment, the Resurrection, and eternity. While anticipating the ultimate victory of God and His coming Kingdom, apocalyptic literature gave much attention to the "cosmic dualism" between good and evil, and specifically, God's righteousness and Satan's rebellion and leadership of this present evil age. Finally, this genre also made great use of symbolism through images, personalities, animals, and numbers.

Yet there is a marked difference between canonical apocalyptic writing, including the Book of Revelation, and non-canonical apocalyptic literature. Most importantly and exclusively, biblical apocalyptic writing is closely related to biblical prophetic literature, and this may be seen in several ways.[35] In both biblical apocalyptic and prophetic literature, we do not find the more open-ended dualism of non-canonical apocalyptic writings; rather, God's power is supreme and His victory is final. Canonical apocalyptic writing is also clearly not pseudonymous, assuming the position of conservative scholarship. As with all biblical prophecy, so it is in the Apocalypse that John as the writer clearly identifies himself as the immediate recipient and messenger of God's revelation. He writes what he personally has received and experienced, not vicariously through another.

Additionally, in contrast to the usual otherworldly focus of extra-biblical apocalyptic literature, biblical apocalyptic literature is also quite focused upon the circumstances of God's people in this present age. For instance, Revelation starts early with messages addressed to seven contemporary, localized churches. Here, the concerns, judgments, and determinations of God pertain just as much to the present conditions and activities of these churches and their constituents as to their future destiny.

We must also not miss the fact that extra-biblical apocalyptic writings have a strong orientation to Jewish nationalism, while biblical apocalyptic writings—especially those of the New Testament—address and apply their messages to followers of God and His Messiah throughout the world (cf. Rev. 5:6, 9-10; 7:9; 10:11; 14:6). Noticeably, the most important distinction of New Testament apocalyptic style—as seen in the Matthew 24, Mark 13, and Luke 21 and the entirety of Revelation—is the affirmation of the deity and ultimate victory of Jesus as the Messiah of the world.

Approaching Revelation Hermeneutically and Exegetically

Bible students and scholars often speak of two complementary disciplines in the study of Revelation (in fact, of all inspired Scripture), namely, hermeneutics and exegesis. The discipline of hermeneutics, which deals with principles of interpretation, is concerned in part with *how* we interpret the Scriptures. Important to hermeneutics will be a recognition and appreciation for the uniqueness of different types of literary genre. In the Bible, these include law, history, wisdom, poetry, narrative, gospel, epistles, prophecy, and apocalyptic. It is this last classification, the unique style of communication through apocalyptic literature, which must guide our study of the Book of Revelation. In part, this directs that the message we seek will be related from God to man through the use of symbolism to a degree not common to ordinary speech, whether in that ancient day or in our contemporary day.

The central question, then, asked through hermeneutics is this: Must we relegate the meaning of these symbols (let alone the visions and mysteries which accompany them) to allegory, which portrays lofty but general ideas; or, may we find indications in the text of certain, critical, and real historical events and of real people? To the conservative student of the Word, who determines to seek the literal and plain meaning of a text when at all possible, this becomes the challenge of Revelation.

Once we determine *how* we must approach the text hermeneutically, we may proceed with the actual work of interpretation. Here, we come to exegesis, meaning, "to lead or draw out of," which calls for the discovery of the true meaning of a text through objective analysis. Also described as biblical exposition, exegetical study involves a careful examination of the applicable rules of grammar and syntax and of the historical and cultural backgrounds, which together shape the meaning of the text. Within this commentary those sections marked "Biblical Insights" will employ exegetical study. For the student of Revelation, the ultimate goal of studying each passage will be to understand what the biblical text meant in its original context to its original readers. Once this is discovered, we may then with confidence move from exposition to inspiration. Joining exegetical work with hermeneutical principles, those sections marked "Life Application" will propose significance and relevance for our lives today.

Four Primary Views to Understanding the Meaning of Revelation

Before interpretation of Revelation begins, it is helpful to know that devoted Christians from varying backgrounds (as well as scholars and students with more secular interests) hold to four basic, yet vastly differing, views of the interpretation and even the appreciation of the Book of Revelation. This has been true historically, and it is true around the world still today. While I must be gracious toward those who differ with the interpretation I bring in this book—and, I do find some elements of truth in what other views maintain—I will not say that one's choice of theological approach is actually just that, his or her choice. Whether speaking hermeneutically or devotionally, I cannot accept that God intended to give us this inspired apex of His Word only to leave its interpretation up to "a personal matter of opinion." Truly, "God means what He says, and He says what He means."

The first view to be examined is that of the preterist (referring to that which is past in time). Here, Revelation is understood entirely in terms of past history. The messages to the seven churches contained in Chapters 2 and 3 directly address the actual conditions found within the specifically named local congregations of that day. The subsequent chapters of Revelation, then, symbolically describe the conflict historically present during the Jewish Revolt against the Roman occupation of Judaea in A.D. 66-70 and the eventual total destruction of Jerusalem by the Romans in A.D. 70. (Notably, this same context is attributed by preterists to the entirety of the words of Jesus spoken in the Olivet discourse of Matthew 24.) This interpretation extends to all of the symbolic language and imagery of the book, including the seal, trumpet, and bowl judgments and to each of the personages described. In short, the primary value of Revelation to the preterist is as symbolic history during a time of extreme turmoil for the Jewish nation and the early Church.

Some called "full preterists" follow this interpretation of past, symbolic fulfillment through to the last chapters of Revelation. To them, as far as this apocalyptic book is concerned, we are now living in the eternal state John described as "the new heavens and the new earth." Still, there are "partial preterists" who find fulfillment of Chapters 20-22 in the future General Resurrection and Judgment at the final return of Christ. Yet, to these preterists the biblical writer's only reason for an allusion to that future day was for the purpose of encouraging the beleaguered saints of his own day.

Disputed by non-preterists, the preterist view claims the support of theologians as early as the fourth century A.D. Nevertheless, both sides agree that this view was only fully developed by the Spanish Jesuit Luis del Alcázar (1554–1613) during the Roman Catholic Counter Reformation. Against the prevailing evidence, then, it remains that all preterists argue for a date of writing well before the destruction of Jerusalem in A.D. 70.[36] Yet, if this claim is in error, their position falls apart.

A second view in interpreting Revelation is the idealist view. Rather than symbolic history, the idealist approaches the Book of Revelation as pure allegory. The writer's intent is to bring a symbolic picture of the ageless struggle, both broadly between good and evil (or righteousness and unrighteousness) and more specifically, between Christianity and the pagan world system. The symbolic details of Revelation are not to be applied to actual, specific historic events or to certain personages; they are to be applied to the abstract idea of righteousness ultimately triumphing over the abstract idea of unrighteousness. Believers of all ages may then, through the reading of this book, be encouraged that their suffering will certainly and finally be vindicated.[37]

Such a "spiritualizing" of the message of Revelation was first held by the early Church Father Origen (A.D. 185-254) of the Alexandrian school of theology in ancient Egypt, well known for its allegorical approach to the Scriptures, generally. Subsequently, Saint Augustine of Hippo (A.D. 354-430) gave further support to this view, which certainly contributed in making this the prominent interpretive approach to Revelation for the next one thousand years. The greatest strength of the idealist view, however long it has been held, becomes its greatest weakness. Though it speaks a spiritual message to Christians of all times, it promotes a very subjective approach to interpretation rather than seeking the intended meaning of the author. Such an intention of real historic fulfillment is found as early as Revelation 1:1, "to show his servants what must soon take place."

A third view of the interpretation of Revelation is that held by the historicist. Along with the preterist, the historicist approaches the Book of Revelation as symbolic history, but here is where the two part ways. The historicist finds fulfillment of the symbolic events, imagery, and personages of Revelation far beyond A.D. 70, pertaining to all of the history of the Church (and usually the Western Church) extending from John's day on Patmos to the end of the Church age at the return of Christ.

Down through the centuries, the historicist approach has been used to apply, in sequence, the symbols, imagery, and personages of Revelation to a wide range of actual, historic events, movements, and individuals. Commonly, historicists find a broad overview of seven periods or eras of Church history in the messages to the seven churches in Chapters 2-3. From the Reformers to the older commentators to many present-day evangelicals, the symbolic history indicated in the remaining chapters has been specifically applied to a wide variety of events. These have included: the collapse of the Roman Empire; the rise of the Roman Catholic Church and the papacy; the Islamic invasions; world conflicts ranging from the French Revolution to the 20th century wars; and world leaders from Charlemagne to Napoleon to Hitler. While the applications vary, historicists agree that John wrote prophetically and symbolically of Church history from his day to the end of days.

A review of the historicist approach from the 14th through 19th centuries demonstrates a reader-centered interpretation producing a very wide-ranging and far-reaching application of the symbolic language of Revelation. Since coming into prominence during the Protestant Reformation, and being held by all of the major reformers, it is clear that the historicist view tends to interpretations that fit the day in which the interpreter lives and that almost exclusively address conditions in the Western Church.[38] This begs the question of relevance for believers in the early Church and later for the Church universal. In part, this may account for the waning popularity of this view over the last 100 years.

The fourth and final major approach to interpreting the Book of Revelation is the futurist view. Most notably, this view takes a literal interpretation and employs the customary use of language, the accepted rules of grammar, and the known context of history in order to seek the plainest meaning evident to both the first century recipient and all subsequent readers. While not discounting the figurative and symbolic nature of apocalyptic literature, the futurist finds real meaning and literal significance within those symbols and imagery.[39]

While the handling of the first three chapters of Revelation by futurists varies— ranging from a more or less preterist view to a historicist view—the handling of Chapters 4-22 is more consistently applied to Last Days events. Specifically, these events connect to the Second Coming of Christ in His final conquest and glory. Differing strongly from the preterist and idealist schools of thought, the futurist finds in the Book of Revelation a literal Tribulation lasting seven years (correlating to Daniel's "seventieth week" [Dan. 9:24-27]) and a literal Battle of Armageddon culminating with the visible Revelation of Jesus Christ. Also unique to the futurist view is the belief in a literal Millennial Reign of Christ over the earth according to Revelation 20.

The futurist interpretation extends to the Olivet Discourse; to the apocalyptic messages of the Book of Daniel (though the past history of the Babylonian, Medo-Persian, Roman, and Greek Empires is also there in view); and to many of the prophecies of the Major and Minor Prophets. Though futurists will differ in their application of the messages to the seven churches, and also in how far they distinguish between Israel and the Church in the Apocalypse, all futurists do agree that the book's principle aim is to prophetically forecast God's plan for the culmination of redemptive history. To objections that the futurist view makes the message of Revelation irrelevant to its early recipients, at least apart from Chapters 2-3, we need only remember that the prophets of the Old Testament consistently related their contemporary message to the future events accompanying the Day of the Lord.[40]

It is the assertion of futurists that many of the Church Fathers articulated a premillennial view and a literal interpretation of Revelation, and that this predominant view was only called into question by the allegorical method made popular by the Alexandrian school in the third and fourth centuries.[41] Today, the futurist view is commonly held by conservative scholars and students of the Word of God.

Unique Characteristics Witnessing to the Inherent Importance of the Revelation

What is contained within a two-thousand-year-old book—revealed to an exiled elderly man on a relatively tiny, despised island—that demands our undivided attention on one hand, while offering unparalleled hope for the believer on the other? To this question we find in Revelation certain distinctive characteristics that establish its uniqueness within the canon of inspired Scripture and affirm that it cannot—it must not—be ignored. Nine of the most prominent of these are as follows:

1. Jesus himself, His deity and His power, is the primary focus of this entire Revelation.
2. Here is the only New Testament book that contains a promise of blessing for its reader and adherent (see 1:3).
3. The worship of God is prevalent throughout the Revelation, even in the midst of judgment.
4. The Revelation contains more references and allusions to the Old Testament—no less than 400—than any other New Testament book.
5. The largest part of Revelation is concerned with divine judgments outlined through a series of seven seals, trumpets, and bowls.
6. Here, every major biblical theme finds its fulfillment and culmination. In effect, the Book of Revelation is by God's design the Epilogue of the Bible, His very Word. (See below, A Theological Overview of the Book of Revelation with Textual Concordance and Summary Statements.)

7. Likewise, in Revelation all of the great prophetic themes of Scripture are consummated, including God's plan for His Church, the resurrection and glorification of all true believers, the Great Tribulation, the triumph of the Kingdom of Light over the kingdom of darkness, and God's judgment of the nations. It is in knowing the appointment this earth has with an all-powerful God that we find growing incentive and encouragement toward righteousness (cf. 2 Peter 3).

8. In the Book of Revelation John speaks of receiving multiple visions from four differing vistas, i.e., from the Island of Patmos (1:9-3:22); from Heaven (4:1-16:21); from a desert (or wilderness) (17:1-21:8); and from a mountain (21:9-22:6).

9. In keeping with the genre of apocalyptic literature, Revelation makes great use of symbolism through numbers (primarily "seven"), colors, and animated characters, both human and animal. Consider alone the many "sevens" in the Book of Revelation:

- Seven Churches (1:4, 11, 20)
- Seven Spirits (1:4; 3:1; 4:5; 5:6; best understood as the Seven-Fold Spirit of God)
- Seven Golden Lamp Stands (1:12, 20; 2:1)
- Seven Stars (1:16, 20; 2:1; 3:1)
- Seven Seals (5:1, 5; 6:1)
- Seven Horns and Seven Eyes (5:6)
- Seven Angels (8:2, 6; 15:1, 6-8; 16:1; 17:1; 21:9)
- Seven Trumpets (8:2, 6)
- Seven Thunders (10:3, 4)
- Seven Crowns (12:3)
- Seven Heads (12:3; 13:1; 17:3, 7, 9)
- Seven Plagues (15:1, 6, 8; 21:9)
- Seven Golden Bowls (15:7; 16:1; 17:1; 21:9)
- Seven Hills (17:9)
- Seven Kings (17:10)

Truly the message of Revelation is timeless for the corporate Church and for every individual believer of every time and in every place. All the more is our privilege—we, who live in the days just before the final conquest and glory of our Lord.

Introduction Notes

1. Philip Schaff, ed., "ANF01. The Apostolic Fathers with Justin Martyr and Irenaeus," *Christian Classics Ethereal Library* 13 July 2005 <www.ccel.org/ccel/schaff/anf01. ix.iv.ii.html>.

2. Philip Schaff, ed., "NPNF2-01. Eusebius Pamphilius: Church History, Life of Constantine, Oration in Praise of Constantine," *Christian Classics Ethereal Library* 13 July 2005 <www.ccel.org/ccel/schaff/npnf201.iii.x.xxi.html>.

3. Schaff

4. Ernest Evans, ed. and trans., "Tertullian: Adversus Marcionem (1972)," *The Tertullian Project* 8 Dec. 2001 <www.tertullian.org/articles/evans_marc/evans_marc_00index. htm>.

5. Kevin Knight, ed., "Commentary on the Gospel of John (Book I)," CHURCH FATHERS: *Commentary on John, Book I (Origen)*, New Advent, 2009 <www.newadvent.org/fathers/101501.htm>.

6. Peter Kirby, ed., "The Muratorian Fragment," *Early Christian Writings* 4 Apr. 2018 <www.earlychristianwritings.com/text/muratorian-metzger.html>.

7. Philip Schaff, ed., "NPNF1-06. St. Augustine: Sermon on the Mount; Harmony of the Gospels; Homilies on the Gospels," *Christian Classics Ethereal Library* 13 July 2005 <www.ccel.org/ccel/schaff/npnf106.vi.iv.iv.html>.

8. Peter Kirby, ed., Justin Martyr, "Saint Justin Martyr: Dialogue with Trypho (Roberts-Donaldson)." *Early Christian Writings* 4 Apr. 2018 <www.earlychristianwritings. com/text/justinmartyr-dialoguetrypho.html>.

9. Schaff, "ANF01."

10. Evans, "Tertullian."

11. Philip Schaff, ed., "ANF04. Fathers of the Third Century: Tertullian, Part Fourth; Minucius Felix; Commodian; Origen, Parts First and Second," *Christian Classics Ethereal Library* 1 June 2005 <www.ccel.org/ccel/schaff/anf04.iii.viii.xix.html>.

12. S. L. Greenslade, ed., Tertullian, "Tertullian: The prescriptions against the heretics," trans. by Greenslade, 1956, *Early Latin Theology, Library of Christian Classics V (1956)*, 19-64, 11 May 2001 <www.tertullian.org/articles/greenslade_prae/ greenslade_prae.htm>.

13. Paton J. Gloag, *Introduction to the Johannine Writings* (London: James Nisbet & Co., 1891) 57.

14. Philip Schaff, ed., "ANF05. The Extant Works and Fragments of Hippolytus. Part II—Dogmatical and Historical; Treatise on Christ and Antichrist," *Christian Classic Ethereal Library* 1 June 2005 <http://www.ccel.org/ccel/schaff/anf05.iii.iv.ii.i.html>.

15. Philip Schaff, ed., "NPNF2-01. Eusebius Pamphilius: Church History, Life of Constantine, Oration in Praise of Constantine," *Christian Classics Ethereal Library* 13 July 2005 <www.ccel.org/ccel/schaff/npnf201.iii.viii.xviii.html>.

16. Kevin Knight, ed., "Who is the Rich Man That Shall Be Saved?" *CHURCH FATHERS: Who is the Rich Man That Shall Be Saved? (St. Clement of Alexandria)*, New Advent, 2009 <www.newadvent.org/fathers/0207.htm>.

17. Schaff, "ANF01."

18. Schaff, "NPNF2-01."

19. Schaff

20. John R.W. Stott, *The Epistles of John: Tyndale New Testament Commentaries* (Grand Rapids: Eerdmans, 1964) 49.

21. Schaff, "NPNF2-01."

22. Philip Schaff, ed., "NPNF2-03. Theodoret, Jerome, Gennadius, & Rufinus: Historical Writings," *Christian Classics Ethereal Library* 1 June 2005 <www.ccel.org/ccel/schaff/npnf203.v.iii.xi.html>.

23. Schaff, "NPNF2-01."

Eusebius's fuller quotation of Dionysius from Chapter 25, Sections 24-27 follows:

24. "Moreover, it can also be shown that the diction of the Gospel and Epistle differs from that of the Apocalypse.

25. For they were written not only without error as regards the Greek language, but also with elegance in their expression, in their reasoning, and in their entire structure. They are far indeed from betraying any barbarism or solecism, or any vulgarism whatever. For the writer had, as it seems, both the requisites of discourse—that is, the gift of knowledge and the gift of expression—as the Lord had bestowed them both upon him.

26. I do not deny that the other writer saw a revelation and received knowledge and prophecy. I perceive, however, that his dialect and language are not accurate Greek, but that he uses barbarous idioms, and, in some places, solecisms.

27. It is unnecessary to point these out here, for I would not have any one think that I have said these things in a spirit of ridicule, for I have said what I have only with the purpose of showing clearly the difference between the writings."

24. For instance, John Walvoord writes, "Impartial scholarship has admitted that there are expressions in the book of Revelation which do not correspond to accepted Greek usage, but this problem is not entirely confined to the book of the Bible. Conservative scholarship has insisted that infallibility in divine revelation does not necessarily exclude expressions which are not normal in other Greek literature and that such instances do not mar the perfection of the truth that is transmitted. [...] some of the supposedly bad grammar in Revelation was used in contemporary Koine literature, as is revealed by discoveries in the Papyri." John Walvoord, *The Revelation of Jesus Christ* (Moody Press: Chicago, 1966) 11.

    Additionally, in his *"Introduction to the Book of Revelation—Section II, Who Wrote It?"*, Steve Gregg writes, "In answer to these things, defenders of the apostolic authorship, however, point out that John is described in Acts 4:13 as 'unschooled' and may have been incapable of writing cultured Greek. The other writings of John may owe their polished style to the use of an amanuensis (a secretary, not available on Patmos, where Revelation was written), or to the editorial involvement of the elders of the Ephesian church, where John spent his final years. Alternately, Revelation's poor style may be accounted for by John's haste to write down visions as they occurred or by his excited mental state." Steve, Gregg, ed., *Revelation. Four Views. A Parallel Commentary* (Nashville: Thomas Nelson Publishers, 1997)

    Of note is this comment by Mark Powell in his *Introducing the New Testament*, "[...] supporters of apostolic authorship think that the differences (literary and theological) between Revelation and John's Gospel can be attributed to the diverse circumstances under which the books were composed. John's Gospel was produced under controlled and ideal conditions; the apostle may have used a secretary (as Paul did for his letters), or he may have written only an early draft that later was expanded and edited. Revelation, by contrast, perhaps preserves the apostle's unedited work, possibly produced while he was in an ecstatic state." Mark Allan Powell, Authorship of Revelation, Introducing the New Testament (*Baker Academic*, 2009) <assets.bakerpublishinggroup.com/processed/esource-assets/files/556/original/hyperlink-29-03.pdf?1375210704>.

25. Schaff, "NPNF2-01."

26. Schaff

27. Peter Kirby, ed., "Irenaeus of Lyons," *Irenaeus of Lyons, Against Heresies/Adversus Haereses, Book 5 (Roberts-Donaldson translation)* 2017 <www.earlychristianwritings.com/text/irenaeus-book5.html>.

28. Philip Schaff, ed., "ANF07. Fathers of the Third and Fourth Centuries: Lactantius, Venantius, Asterius, Victorinus, Dionysius, Apostolic Teaching and Constitutions, Homily," *Christian Classics Ethereal Library* 1 June 2005 <www.ccel.org/ccel/schaff/anf07.vi.ii.x.html>.

[29.] Philip Schaff, ed., "NPNF2-06. Jerome: The Principal Works of St. Jerome," *Christian Classics Ethereal Library* 13 July 2005 <www.ccel.org/ccel/schaff/npnf206. vi.vi.I.html>.

[30.] A.T. Robertson brings this insight, "In the ninth century lived Georgius Hamartolus, and a MS. of his alleges that Papias says that John the son of Zebedee was beheaded by the Jews and there is an extract in an Oxford MS. of the seventh century which alleges that Papias says John and James were put to death by the Jews. On the basis of this slim evidence some today argue that John did not live to the end of the century and so did not write any of the Johannine books. But a respectable number of modern scholars still hold to the ancient view that the Apocalypse of John is the work of the Apostle and Beloved Disciple, the son of Zebedee." Archibald Thomas Robertson *Word Pictures in the New Testament. VI* (Nashville: Broadman, 1933) 272-273.

[31.] Irenaeus (A.D. 130-202), the student of Polycarp, in his *Against Heresies* (Book 5, Chapter 33.4) gives us insight here: "And these things are borne witness to in writing by Papias, the hearer of John, and a companion of Polycarp, in his fourth book; for there were five books compiled (συντεταγμένα) by him." Schaff, "ANF01."

[32.] Schaff, "NPNF2-01."

[33.] Schaff

[34.] Gordon Franz, "The King and I: Exiled To Patmos, Part 2," *Associates for Biblical Research* <www.biblearchaeology.org/post/2010/01/28/The-King-and-I-Exiled-To-Patmos-Part-2.aspx#>. (First Published in the Fall 1999 edition of Bible and Spade magazine).

[35.] A distinction is clear, however, between the messages of the Old Testament prophets, which were usually spoken first and then written, and apocalyptic messages, which were normally only written.

[36.] Christian apologist Dr. Patrick Zukeran raises strong argument against the preterist claim that Revelation was symbolically fulfilled in the destruction of Jerusalem in A.D. 70 with these words: "…the events described in Jesus' Olivet Discourse and in Revelation 4-19 differ in several ways from the fall of Jerusalem. One example is that Christ described his return to Jerusalem this way: '[A]s lightning that comes from the east is visible even in the west, so will be the coming of the Son of Man' (Mt. 24:27). Preterists believe this refers to the Roman army's advance on Jerusalem. However, the Roman army advanced on Jerusalem from west to east, and their assault was not as a quick lightning strike. The Jewish war lasted for several years before Jerusalem was besieged, and the city fell after a lengthy siege. Second, General Titus did not set up an 'abomination of desolation' (Mt. 24:15) in the Jerusalem Temple. Rather, he destroyed the Temple and burned it to the ground. Thus, it appears the preterist is required to allegorize or stretch the metaphors and symbols in order to find fulfillment of the prophecies in the fall of Jerusalem." Patrick Zukeran, "Four Views of Revelation," *Probe for Answers* 26 Dec. 2016 <www.probe.org/four-views-of-revelation/>.

37. Evangelical scholar Dr. Robert Mounce summarizes the idealist view stating, "Revelation is a theological poem presenting the ageless struggle between the kingdom of light and the kingdom of darkness. It is a philosophy of history wherein Christian forces are continuously meeting and conquering the demonic forces of evil." Robert H. Mounce, *The Book of Revelation: The New International Commentary on the New Testament.* (Grand Rapids: Eerdmans, 1977)

38. Commenting on the historicist view, Dr. John Walvoord makes this observation: "As many as fifty different interpretations of the book of Revelation therefore evolve, depending on the time and circumstances of the expositor." Walvoord 19.

39. "Symbols, figures of speech and types are all interpreted plainly in this method, and they are in no way contrary to literal interpretation. After all, the very existence of any meaning for a figure of speech depends on the reality of the literal meaning of the terms involved. Figures often make the meaning plainer, but it is the literal, normal, or plain meaning that they convey to the reader." Charles Ryrie, *Dispensationalism* (Chicago: Moody Publishers, 2007) 91.

40. Speaking of the "dynamic tension" often found in prophetic writing between "the events of the present and the immediate future, and the ultimate eschatological event," George Eldon Ladd comments, "… The two are often blended together in apparent disregard for chronology, for the same God who acts in the imminent historical judgment will also act in the final eschatological judgment to further his one redemptive purpose." [...] "Thus, while the Revelation was primarily concerned to assure the churches of Asia of the final eschatological salvation at the end of the age, together with the judgment of the evil world powers, this had immediate relevance to the first century. For the demonic powers which will be manifested at the end in the great tribulation were also to be seen in the historical hatred of Rome for God's people and the persecution they were to suffer at Rome's hands." George Eldon Ladd, *A Commentary on the Revelation of John.* (Grand Rapids: Eerdmans, 1972) 13.

41. "And Augustine set the standard for most catholic exegesis in the West when he surrendered the millenarian interpretation of Revelation, to which he had held earlier, in favor of the view that the thousand years of that text referred to the history of the church." Jaroslav Pelikan, "The Emergence of the Catholic Tradition (100-600)," *The Christian Tradition: A History of the Development of Doctrine, Vol. 1.* (Chicago: University of Chicago Press, 1975) 127.

SECTION 2

Biblical Insights and Life Application from Chapters 1-7

Revelation 1:1-8

The Revelation Sent from the Throne of God

Introduction to Revelation 1:1-8

From the beginning of this captivating message from God through His servant John, the Book of Revelation engages its readers with three distinct objectives. The first is that those who read, listen, and accept its words by faith would receive spiritual insights and understanding of truths past, present, and future. As God Himself oversaw and breathed out to John each and every word contained in this book, He also used those words to paint pictures and to present symbols. While the tendency is for words to change in meaning over time, pictures and symbols are uniquely well-suited to carry spiritual truths across both cultures and generations.

A second objective in respect to John's readers is that this same spiritual insight and understanding would ignite intrigue and anticipation toward the current and future hope of the believer. Revelation from start to finish engages the reader with intensely vivid images of entities, known and unknown, both heavenly and hellish. Situations and events, too, are disclosed that stagger the imagination. In this way, God is intentional to evoke a strong response toward that which He blesses and that which He curses; and in all, He is clear in His call to renewed repentance, faith, faithfulness, and enduring trust.

John's third objective in writing is that the people of God would be encouraged with a great sense of His protection and providence. Only a careless reading will miss this. The believing Jew of the early Church, already learned in the Scriptures, would take great comfort in the weaving of over 400 Old Testament allusions into the tapestry of God's plan for the ages. Likewise, the new believer with non-Jewish roots would be persuaded to rest in the One who eternally speaks with unquestioned and final authority.

The Prologue—1:1-3

[1] The revelation from Jesus Christ, which God gave him to show his servants what must soon take place. He made it known by sending his angel to his servant John, [2] who testifies to everything he saw—that is, the word of God and the testimony of

Jesus Christ. [3] Blessed is the one who reads aloud the words of this prophecy, and blessed are those who hear it and take to heart what is written in it, because the time is near.

Biblical Insights

"The Revelation" is to be received from God Himself as just that, as "revelation" (Greek, ἀποκάλυψις, *apokalypsis,* hence our "apocalypse"), meaning an unveiling or uncovering. In the case of this greatest of all unveilings, the word also means a manifestation and an appearance. No doubt, the Apostle John's use of the word *apokalypsis* includes the idea of a truth revelation hidden for a time as "mystery" by God not *from* us but *for* us, His servants. This is the connection made also by Paul in Romans 16:25, "in keeping with the revelation of the mystery hidden for long ages past" (cf. Eph. 1:17; 3:3 and Col. 1:26-27). In fact, the Apostle Paul had been given his own "revelation" of the preeminence of Jesus Christ (2 Cor. 12:1-7; Gal. 1:12). So, here John joins with the earlier writings of Paul in saying that God has graciously chosen to pull away the veil of ignorance, even darkness, to show us the Light of who Jesus really is.

By definition, the apocalyptic literature we have existent today from antiquity typically employs figurative language and vivid symbols to present to the faithful— and to hide from the oppressor—the real situation behind the apparent (see Introduction—Revelation as Apocalyptic Literature). Commonly, this genre of literature envisions the eventual destruction of the wicked and of wickedness, the ultimate victory of God's righteousness and of His righteous people, and a final catastrophic end to this present world. Far from allegory, the imagery of John's use of apocalyptic form represents real entities and real events, not merely ideas about them. In fact, such looming realities and continuing relevance is the strength behind this literary appeal.

Revelation or apocalyptic literature was a familiar and flourishing genre to the Jews in the last two centuries B.C. and the first century A.D. However, the writing and use of both Judaic and Christian apocalyptic literature was known even as far as the closing years of the Middle Ages. As concerns the Bible, the books of Revelation and Daniel are apocalyptic in their entirety, while some Old Testament prophetic books such as Isaiah, Ezekiel, Joel, and Zechariah also contain certain apocalyptic passages. In all or in part, the intention of such unveiling of things once hidden is charged with Messianic expectation for the near and distant future.

So, what is it in John's Revelation that sets it apart from all other apocalyptic writings? Simply, yet profoundly, this: In John's own words, this is "The Revelation" exclusively "from Jesus Christ" (*Iēsou Christou,* dative case indicating "from," "of," or "by") in the sense that since the Revelation belongs to Him, He is the one doing the revealing (Rev. 1:1). But this grammatical form can also mean that He is the very object being revealed, i.e., that the Revelation is "about" Him. Both meanings are permissible and both are supported in other passages. Just as clear, then, is that God the Father is the One who gave this Revelation to Jesus to give to us. The reader is confronted with this all-important truth again in 19:10b, "Worship God! For it is the Spirit of prophecy who bears testimony [*martyria*, 'witness'] to Jesus." (Here "spirit" [*pneuma*] clearly speaks of the purpose, disposition, and aim of prophecy, captured in the New Living Translation, "For the essence of prophecy is to give a clear witness for Jesus.") Therefore, in light of Revelation's over 400 allusions from the Old Testament, scores of parallels to New Testament passages, and thematic alignment with 65 other books woven together with the "scarlet thread" of redemption, this *"Apokalypsis"* and its biblical counterparts stand above all others.

John saw himself and us as God's "servants" (doulois). Though by definition *doulos* (singular) clearly means a position of humble servitude, the New Testament use also implies the idea of free will in serving Christ (cf. 1 Cor. 7:22-23; Rom. 6:16-18). Yet we must also remember that by grace, Christ views us no longer as disadvantaged "servants," but as privileged "friends" who are welcomed to receive revelation from the Father through the Son, "for everything that I learned from my Father I have made known to you" (John 15:14-15).

Given to us from the Father through the Son is "what must soon take place" (1:1). Some reading this insist that all that John writes would only have immediate and contemporary fulfillment in his day "because the time is near" (1:3), but that is saying more than what is called for. (A review of this preterist position can be found in the Introduction—Four Primary Views.) The phrase translated as "must soon" is the dative of *en tachos*, meaning "in or with swiftness" or "with speed." This same phrase is commonly translated "quickly" or "quick" in Acts 12:7 and 22:18 and "speedily" (NKJV, ESV, RSV) or "quickly" (NIV and NLT) in Luke 18:8. From *tachos* we derive "tachometer," which helps us to understand that once these events begin, they will come with acceleration. In our day, we can truly say that the signposts of prophecy are spaced more closely and that they are coming toward us more rapidly than ever before.

Now, this Revelation received from the Father through and about His Son has been delivered by the first of many messenger angels John would encounter (all of whom, it will be made clear in 19:10, are distinct from the eternal, divine Son). And to this Revelation, John "testifies to everything he saw—that is, the word of God and the testimony of Jesus Christ" (1:2). What John has recorded for us is what "he saw" through many visions he would receive (4:1, 3; 5:1, 2, 6; 7:1, 9; 8:2; 9:17, etc.). And what he saw is the "Word" belonging to and carrying the authority of Almighty God and the "testimony" (*martyria*, of which more will be said in v. 9), again, belonging to and carrying the authority of Jesus Christ.

A three-fold blessing is now spoken, the first of seven blessings altogether in this book (1:3; 14:13; 16:15; 19:9; 20:6; 22:7; 22:14). "Blessed" or "happy" (*makarios*) is the same encouragement pronounced by Jesus in the Beatitudes of Matthew 5 and Luke

6. That "one" is blessed implies both a personal and corporate right to this book, a privilege denied by many leaders of the visible Church for most of 2,000 years of Church history. "Blessed" is the one "who reads aloud" (*anaginōskō*), which implies a reading aloud both privately (cf. Acts 8:28, 30, 32) and publicly (cf. Luke 4:1; Acts 13:27; Col. 4:16) in order to gain accurate knowledge. "Blessed" also "are those who hear [*akouō*] it," which implies throughout the New Testament active and attentive listening (cf. Matt. 7:24, 26; 11:15; Rom. 10:14, 18). Further, "blessed" are those who "take to heart [*tēreō*] what is written in it," which implies care in keeping, guarding, and observing God's Word.

"What is written" for us to heed is contained here in "prophecy" (*prophēteia*) (v. 3), which, by definition, is the "*forth*-telling" of the will of God, and by biblical use also the "*fore*-telling" of the will of God yet to be realized. All the more we must read aloud, hear actively, and keep diligently "because the time"—here, *kairos*, used of God's specific, opportune season—"is near"; it is *eggys,* i.e., imminent, near, and soon to come to pass (cf. Matt. 24:32-33; Phil. 4:5; Rev. 22:10).

Life Application

Is this book about captivating future events and intriguing key players in the end-time drama? Yes, it is! But the Revelation contains so much more than Last Days insights. These many prophecies are all seen in relationship to who Jesus is, the true Source of the promised blessing to the reader. Everything here speaks of His presence and power, His great love and sacrifice, even of His enemies and His complete and final victory over everything dark in this world. Crucial to our understanding of God's intention in giving us this book are the words of an angelic messenger to John in 19:10, "Worship God! For the testimony of Jesus is the spirit of prophecy."

With Jesus as the focal point, God has also chosen to bring culmination to every major biblical theme in this closing book of the New Testament. In a very real sense, minus the Book of Revelation, God's people would be left without His final word on what He says we must know for now and eternity. In short, Revelation is the Bible's Epilogue, God's "wrap-up." Summed up in Jesus, as we witness His mission and ministry completed and affirmed throughout God's creation, all that was promised and prophesied in ages past now finds its ultimate fulfillment. For those who know Jesus and love Jesus, our future is Jesus!

Having said this, it is important to recognize that Revelation was never meant to stand alone; it cannot be properly understood without the teachings and perspective of the balance of inspired Scripture. Interestingly, not one personality, world system, or major world event makes its debut in the Book of Revelation. Whether speaking of high ranking angels, the three entities of the satanic trinity, the Great Tribulation, a false church, or the Babylon world system, all this and much more are foreseen in earlier prophetic writings. (The only exception to this may be the "twenty-four elders" and the "four living creatures"; yet, as will be seen, even these are representative of the people of God and of angelic entities already introduced in Scripture.)

God loved John so much that He wanted him to see His Son for Who He really is. And so, God loves you as well, since it was given to John "to show his servants"—you and me—"what must soon take place." Yet, there are those in and out of the visible Church who ignore and brush off every promise and every warning concerning the soon return of the Lord in His glory. The apostle Peter definitely saw our day when he wrote, "Above all, you must understand that in the last days scoffers will come, scoffing and following their own evil desires. They will say, 'Where is this "coming" he promised?'" (2 Peter 3:3-4a). We might expect this from the world, but saddest of all is to hear believers carelessly say of the Revelation of Jesus, "This has no relevance to my life." Subtler is the complaint, "Preachers have been talking about the signs of the times for years, but life still goes on." To this Peter continues, "But do not forget this one thing, dear friends: With the Lord a day is like a thousand years, and a thousand years are like a day" (2 Peter 3:8). What is time to eternal God?

According to Albert Einstein's Theory of Relativity, time increasingly slows down as an object nears the speed of light (that's about 186,300 miles/second, or for the race car enthusiast, 700 million miles/hour), a phenomenon he called "time dilation." (And though debated and in theory only, when that object meets the speed of light, to that object time stands still.) So, what is time to God, the very One who spoke light into being? Because He Himself is not subject to time—yet uses time to advance His will—we have His Word, "The Lord is not slow in keeping his promise, as some understand slowness. Instead he is patient with you, not wanting anyone to perish, but everyone to come to repentance" (2 Peter 3:8-9).

John's Greetings and Hymn of Praise—1:4-6

[4] John, To the seven churches in the province of Asia: Grace and peace to you from him who is, and who was, and who is to come, and from the seven spirits before his throne, [5] and from Jesus Christ, who is the faithful witness, the firstborn from the dead, and the ruler of the kings of the earth. To him who loves us and has freed us from our sins by his blood, [6] and has made us to be a kingdom and priests to serve his God and Father—to him be glory and power for ever and ever! Amen.

Biblical Insights

The author of "The Revelation" is God Himself, every word breathed out by His Spirit. The writer he breathed through was a man greatly loved by Jesus, namely John. A full presentation and overview of John's life and ministry, and the evidence that this John is indeed the apostle who also wrote the Gospel of John and the Epistles of First, Second, and Third John, can be found in the Introduction—Author and Authenticity of this study.

Under the Spirit's anointing, John addresses this revelation "To the seven churches in the province of Asia." Without question these were seven real church congregations, comprised of the entirety of believers located in seven ancient cities, all lying in relatively close proximity in the most western part of Asia Minor (modern day Turkey). In the Book of Acts, we read that Paul was present in the city of Ephesus, the first of the seven churches to be addressed, near to the coast of the Aegean Sea. Though his first visit there, conducted during his Second Missionary Journey, was brief (Acts 18:19-21), he returned for a longer stay during his Third Missionary Journey. We read of Paul's ongoing ministry there in 19:10-12, "This went on for two years, so that all the Jews and Greeks who lived in the province of Asia heard the word of the Lord. God did extraordinary miracles through Paul, so that even handkerchiefs and aprons that had touched him were taken to the sick, and their illnesses were cured and the evil spirits left them." Again, we see the advance of the Gospel throughout this region in 19:20, "In this way the word of the Lord spread widely and grew in power." Acts 20:31 then indicates that Paul's influence within Ephesus was for three years in all. In light of what Luke records here, it is very possible that the seven churches to which John writes were first established through the ministry of Paul and his ministry associates. More will be said of each of these seven as they are specifically addressed in Revelation 2 and 3.

John begins his greeting with two words, "grace" (*charis*, undeserved loving-kindness and favor) and "peace" (*eirēnē*, rest and calm assurance that comes from a harmonious relationship with God). Though both of these can be given and received on a human level, John is clear that the blessings he desires for his readers comes from all three persons of the Trinity.

The Father first is described as the One "who is, and who was, and who is to come." He is the One who revealed Himself to Moses as the "I am who I am" (Exod. 3:14), the timeless and self-existent One, the One who lives in eternal "nowness." But "grace" and "peace" is also sent "from the seven spirits before His throne" (v. 4; see also 4:5 and 5:6). Since there is only one Spirit of God according to Ephesians 4:4, this can only apply to the "seven-fold" manifested ministry of the Spirit of God "sent out into all the earth" (Rev. 5:6). This same idea—which may by use of the number seven speak of the Spirit's completeness of ministry—is captured in Isaiah 11:2 and Zechariah 4:2, 6, 10.

Still, John sees "grace" and "peace" proceeding "from Jesus Christ, who is the faithful witness" (v. 5). Here John most likely has in mind Christ's witness of the Father. One of many passages in the Gospel of John that demonstrate this witness is found in John 14:8-9. To Philip's request to "show us the Father and that will be enough for us," Jesus replied, "Don't you know me, Philip, even after I have been among you such a long time? Anyone who has seen me has seen the Father. How can you say, 'Show us the Father'?"

Jesus is next described as "the firstborn from the dead." A basic understanding of the use of the word "firstborn" (*prōtotokos*) in the New Testament will answer to the hasty and cultic claim that Jesus evidently is not eternal, that He was rather created, and that He is therefore not divine. While it is true that Jesus was in His human nature born of Mary, "and she gave birth to her firstborn [*prōtotokos*], a son" (Luke 2:7), this term was also regularly used in the ancient world to indicate rulership and preeminence. In the Old Testament Scriptures, we see this idea in God's words through Jeremiah, "I am Israel's father and Ephraim is my first born" (31:9), when in fact Manasseh was the older of Joseph's two sons, not Ephraim. In much the same way in modern English we call the wife of the president the "first lady," not because of her age, but because of her position of prominence.

In Colossians 1:15, Paul says of Jesus in His eternal nature, "The Son is the image of the invisible God, the firstborn over all creation." This means that He is above all and superior to all of creation inasmuch as He has produced all of creation, as is also made clear in verse 16. (See also John 1:3; 1 Corinthians 8:6; Ephesians 3:9; and Hebrews 1:2.) Colossians 1:18 goes on to state that Jesus is, as John agrees in Revelation 1:5, "the beginning and the firstborn from among the dead, so that in everything he might have the supremacy." His Lordship is proven by the fact that He was the first to be resurrected into a new, glorified, immortal, and incorruptible body; that is, He was not raised from the dead into a mortal body once again as were all others raised before Him.

Three other New Testament verses also proclaim the supremacy of Jesus through the use of the word *prōtotokos*. In Romans 8:29, Paul states that Jesus is "the firstborn among many brothers and sisters," demonstrating his Lordship within the Church. The writer of Hebrews also proclaims the preeminence of Jesus by saying, "when God brings his firstborn into the world, he says, 'Let all God's angels worship him'" (1:6) and that believers in Jesus comprise "the church of the firstborn, whose names are written in heaven" (12:23).

Carrying further this idea of supremacy, John now identifies Jesus as "the ruler of the kings of the earth" (v. 5). Though the rule and realm of Christ's Kingdom will be realized in all the earth in association with His Second Coming (Rev. 11:15; 12:10; 17:14; and 19:16), John also sees His rule as a present reality, here grammatically tied to His faithful witness and resurrection established in His First Coming.

Remember again that this is "the Revelation of Jesus Christ," the fullness of who He is and the fullness of what He has and will accomplish before the end of time. To the three-fold identity John gives us here in v. 5, he will yet add that Jesus is the First and the Last, the Beginning and the End, the Alpha and Omega (1:17; 21:6; 22:13); the Head of the Church (2:1-3:22); the Lion of the Tribe of Judah, the root of David (5:5); the Lamb (5:6, 12, 13); the Bridegroom (19:7-9); the King of Kings (19:16); the Lord of Lords (19:16); and, the Judge (19:11-15).

Having honored the Godhead in his greeting, John now bursts into a hymn of praise to Jesus. While scholars differ over the best ancient texts and versions of the New Testament to be used here—the KJV and NKJV reading, "him who loved us" and the NASB, NIV, and NLT reading, "him who loves us"—we can be thankful that both are true. Romans 5:8 sheds further light here; "But God demonstrates his own love for us in this: While we were still sinners, Christ died for us." We rejoice with John and Paul that the same love of God that caused Jesus to shed His blood for us once and for all on the cross is also now an ongoing, present reality in the life of the believer. And while the blood that reconciles us to God assures us of His love, it also "has freed [*lusanti*, 'having loosed or released'] us from our sins." This, the first of several references to the shedding of the blood of the Lamb in the Revelation (5:6, 9; 7:14; 12:11; 13:8), reminds us that the song of the Redeemed will forever fill Heaven with praise to God the Father for the blood of His Son.

Set free from our sins by Christ's blood, we are now able to fulfill our greatest calling as "a kingdom and priests to serve his God and Father" (v. 6; and Rev. 5:10). The Apostle Peter captures both aspects of our high calling through Christ's anointing in 1 Peter 2:9a, "But you are a chosen people, a royal priesthood, a holy nation, God's special possession." As citizens of Heaven, we have inherited our place in the Kingdom of God. While the realm of that Kingdom fills our hearts in this present world, the realm of the Kingdom of which we eternally belong will also fill the entire world in the age to come as we rule and reign with Christ (cf. Gen. 49:10; Isa. 9:6; 25:6-8; Zech. 14:9; Matt. 13:43; 19:28; Luke 19:11; 22:29-30; 2 Tim. 2:12; Rev. 2:26-27; 11:15; 20:6; etc.). To the royal nature of our position and service in and through Christ, both Peter and John add the priestly nature.

The Old Testament tells us about a large family line of priests, descendants of Levi, who God raised up over a period of hundreds of years to do a very special work unto the Lord. Amongst the ancient people of Israel, there was perhaps no greater privilege than to be a priest who ministered unto the Lord in the tabernacle, and later the temple. What many students of the Bible miss is that God had also placed a special calling to priestly ministry upon the whole nation of Israel. Consider the words of the Lord through Moses, "Now therefore, if you will indeed obey My voice and keep My covenant, then you shall be a special treasure to Me above all people; for all the earth is Mine. And you shall be to Me a kingdom of priests and a holy nation" (Exodus 19:5-6, NKJV). However, when this privileged heritage was forfeited by Israel through disobedience, it was consequently passed upon all those who were redeemed by God through the blood of the New Covenant. This day of the Messiah was foreseen by Isaiah, "And you will be called Priests of the Lord, you will be named ministers of our God" (Isaiah 61:6). Indeed, as John affirms in verse 6, one of the greatest privileges the Church has today is to be a spiritual priesthood unto God: "[…] you also, like living stones, are being built into a spiritual house to be a holy priesthood, offering spiritual sacrifices acceptable to God through Jesus Christ" (1 Peter 2:5).

With this John ends his opening hymn of praise, "to him be glory and power for ever and ever! Amen." His praise is directed "to him," that is to Jesus (Rev. 4:9; 5:13;

7:10; cf. Jude 25) in the sense of recognizing and honoring Him for who He is and what He has so greatly accomplished. Glory (*doxa*) is derived from *dokeō*, meaning, "to be of opinion, think, suppose" and "to seem" (Vine). From this it can be said that God's glory is the honor that comes in seeing Him for who He really is. Mirroring the song that arises before the Throne of God and of the Lamb out of all creation (Rev. 5:13), John adds to God's eternal glory His eternal "power" (*kratos*, meaning, power, might, and dominion).[1] This he seals with the first of nine utterances of "amen" in this Revelation (also 1:7, 18; 3:14; 5:14; 7:12; 19:4; 22:20, 21). Originating from the Hebrew "*amen*," this word has become a universal statement of affirmation, meaning "so let it be" or "may it be fulfilled" when uttered at the end of a prayer or statement. More will be said when in Revelation 3:14 the name "Amen" is attributed to Jesus (2 Cor. 1:20).

Life Application

Within the opening words of the Revelation, John's heart is filled with praise to God for His loving, loosing, and lifting ministry toward his children. This amazing love will soon be declared in His care for the Church; John will see Him—and so will we—glorious beyond human words, walking in the midst of us. John will hear Him—and so will we—lovingly saying what needs to be said to those He claims as His own. But above all, Christ's loving ministry is first and foremost demonstrated in his will-ingness and power to loose us from our sins. John's revelation will take us there into the throne room where angels and creation itself sustain the new song, which rises from the hearts of the redeemed. Forever and ever, we will never forget the blood that has torn down every wall and bridged every chasm to bring us into the presence of the One who loves us best.

But before we are given a new view of Jesus, John announces that we have been lifted, distinguished amongst all the peoples of the earth. We are a royal priesthood! No, the New Testament knows nothing of a closed, elite group of priests based upon one's family line. Nor does it pronounce even once a call for the blood of animals. There is only one great High Priest and there is only one spotless Lamb of God. But there does remain in Christ a Church-wide office to be filled—there is "a priesthood" open to all believers.

Just as Jesus has and continues forever to fulfill the office of the High Priest, we now and forever fulfill the calling of "Priests of the Lord [...] ministers of our God" (Isaiah 61:6). As priests unto God we are called to worship the Lord (Ps. 54:6; Rom. 12:11; Heb. 13:15; 1 Pet. 2:5). As priests unto God we are called to pray and intercede for others (Acts 4:29-31; 1 Tim. 2:1-2; Heb. 4:16; Rev. 8:3-5)—here we reflect back upon Aaron, then high priest, who bore the names of the twelve sons of Israel upon his shoulders (Exod. 28:9-12). Yet, ultimately, we take our lead from our Great High Priest, Jesus, who intercedes for us forever (Heb. 7:25). As priests unto God we are also called to have compassion upon the needs and burdens of others (1 Thess. 2:8-9; 3:12-13; Rom. 15:16)—again we reflect upon Aaron, who bore the names of the sons of Israel over his heart (Exod. 28:29-30). Once more, we know no greater than Jesus, moved with compassion for us (Heb. 2:17-18 and 4:15).

His Coming is Announced—1:7-8

[7] "Look, he is coming with the clouds," and "every eye will see him, even those who pierced him"; and all peoples on earth "will mourn because of him." So shall it be! Amen. [8] "I am the Alpha and the Omega," says the Lord God, "who is, and who was, and who is to come, the Almighty."

Biblical Insights

The eternal power and glory that John has just recognized in the present will be seen universally in the future. "Look" (*idou*, derived from *eidon* "to see") is a strong call to attentiveness found over 200 times in the New Testament, including twenty-nine times in Revelation. Jesus will not and cannot be ignored nor missed! Various words are used in the New Testament to describe His public, visible return to the earth. Though John uses the common word for His "coming" (*erchomai*) here (cf. Matt. 24:46 and Mark. 8:38), the word *parousia*, meaning, "presence, coming, or advent" is also used of the visible return of Christ in Matthew 24:3; 24:27, 37, 39; 1 Thessalonians 3:13; 2 Thessalonians 2:8; and 2 Peter 3:4. But be careful to note that this same word is also used for the "coming" of the Lord specifically for His Church (1 Cor. 15:23; 1 Thess. 2:19; 4:15; 5:23; 2 Thess. 2:1; James. 5:7, 8; 1 John 2:28). The ability for "*parousia*" to serve for the "coming" of the Lord at different times for different purposes is evidenced further in 2 Peter 3:12—"looking for and hastening the coming [*parousia*] of the day of God, because of which the heavens will be dissolved, being on fire, and the elements will melt with fervent heat?" (NKJV). Paralleled to "the day of the Lord" in 3:10, Peter looks beyond the Tribulation and Millennial Reign of Christ to see the "*parousia*" "of the day of God."

Speaking clearly of His public, visible return to earth, John sees Him "coming with the clouds" in direct fulfillment of the message of the angels at Christ's ascension (Acts 1:10-12). His return in the clouds, the fact that "every eye will see him," and that "all peoples on earth 'will mourn because of him'" aligns completely with Jesus' own words. We read in Matthew 24:30, "Then will appear the sign of the Son of Man in heaven. And then all the peoples of the earth will mourn when they see the Son of Man coming on the clouds of heaven, with power and great glory" (par. Mark 13:26; Luke 21:27), and again in Matthew 26:64b, "From now on you will see the Son of Man sitting at the right hand of the Mighty One and coming on the clouds of heaven" (par. Mark 14:62). See also Christ's words in Matthew 24:26-27 concerning the visibility of His return.[2]

With this announcement, John also focuses upon the Jewish nation with the words, "even those who pierced him." This identity is further evidenced when compared with the message of Zechariah (12:10), "And I will pour out on the house of David and the inhabitants of Jerusalem a spirit of grace and supplication. They will look on me, the one they have pierced, and they will mourn [*caphad*] for him as one mourns [*caphad*] for an only child, and grieve bitterly [*marar*] for him as one grieves [*marar*] for a firstborn son." Interestingly, the Septuagint translates the Hebrew word for "mourn" [*caphad*] with forms of the same Greek word *koptō*—a strong and expressive word indicating wailing, even "beating the breast, as a token of grief" (Vines)—used by John here in v. 7 and by Jesus in Matthew 24:30 for "mourn." Nevertheless, there is an apparent difference to be found. While it is clear that gentiles who survive until the visible return of Christ will "mourn" under the heavy wrath of God (Rev. 6:15-17; cf. 2 Thess. 1:7-8), Zechariah indicates that the Jews will "mourn," "grieve," and "weep[ing]" when given "a spirit of grace and supplication" in remembrance of their long-standing rejection of Jesus (12:10-14; 13:6). Furthermore, at the time of this sadness God will come to the final rescue of Judah and Jerusalem (Zechariah 12:2-9); "On that day I will set out to destroy all the nations that attack Jerusalem" (12:9). Jeremiah too foretold both the terror and the mercy that would be Israel's in the days before Christ's return, (30:7) "How awful that day will be! No other will be like it. It will be a time of trouble for Jacob, but he will be saved out of it." (See also Matthew 23:39 and Romans 11:25-26.) Finally, to strengthen the certainty of this coming encounter, John adds to his "amen" the affirmative "so shall it be!" [*nai*] (14:13; 16:7; 22:20).

The warning spoken by the Spirit through John is now underscored by three authoritative names of God. Before the first of these, John uses the copula "I am" (*ego eimi*), which reminds the reader of the seven "I am" statements of John's Gospel (6:35; 8:12; cf. 9:5; 10:7, 9; 10:11, 14; 11:25; 14:6; 15:1, 5). However, John's use of "I am" in those passages and here in verse 8 is followed by a predicate (subject complement). In these cases, theological significance (i.e., a statement of deity) is conveyed more so by pattern and by context. More distinct is Jesus statement in John 8:58b, "before Abraham was born, I am!"[3] Here, *ego eimi* stands without a predicate and is a clear claim to divinity, grammatically and as evidenced by the reaction of those who opposed Him. In this case, we see a direct association with the Septuagint's (Greek) translation of the Hebrew *ehyeh-asher-ehyeh* (English transliteration YHVH) as *ego eimi* (cf. Exod. 3:14; Deut. 32:39; Isa. 41:4; 43:10). Thus, the deity John reveals here in v. 8 is found in the names that follow.

Alpha and Omega are the first and last letters of the Greek alphabet, which speaks of God's eternality here and in 1:11 (in the Received Text); 21:6 and 22:13. Supporting this truth is the phrase "the beginning and the end" which follows here in v. 8 in some texts and versions and also consistently in 21:6 and 22:13.[4] (See also "the first and the last" in 1:17 and 22:13.)

To the question of whether the One introducing himself as "the Lord God, 'who is, and who was, and who is to come" is Jesus or the Father, it can only be concluded that often in the Revelation (as elsewhere in the Word of God) what can be said of the Father can also be said of the Son (cf. Isa. 9:6; John 10:30; 14:9-11, etc.). As we have already seen, Jesus is clearly speaking in 22:13 where we again read, "I am the Alpha and the Omega, the First and the Last, the Beginning and the End." While the Father is clearly the One "who is, and who was, and who is to come" in 1:4 and in 4:8, there is stronger evidence in 11:17 that "the One who is and who was" is Jesus, who has "begun to reign." Finally, there will be no doubt by the end of the Revelation that both the Father and the Son together are "the Almighty."[5]

Life Application

As a young boy, the question of who actually crucified Jesus impacted and intrigued me as I watched the classic 1960 British film, *Hand in Hand*. In the story, two young children, Michael, a nine-year-old Catholic boy and Rachel, a seven-year-old Jewish girl, become best of friends, despite the prevailing prejudice of the world around them. Their religious differences don't seem to matter until a biased classmate convinces Michael that "the Jews killed Christ." The plot thickens and their friendship is strained and tested when the young man rushes to their clubhouse and angrily confronts Rachel with the charge, "You killed Jesus!" Shocked at the accusation, she innocently replies, "I don't even know Jesus." The lessons they learn from there and the friendship that endured through adventure and near tragedy won the film the Golden Globe award for "Best Film Promoting International Understanding."

Better than this film for the promotion of understanding is the work of the Spirit through His Word. Truth be known, each and every one of us is blameworthy for His nailed pierced hands—"There is no difference between Jew and Gentile, for all have sinned and fall short of the glory of God" (Romans 3:22b-23). But praise God, every one of us may be freed from our sins and guilt through those same nailed pierced hands—"and all are justified freely by his grace through the redemption that came by Christ Jesus" (v. 24).

And now the universal call goes out to be ready for the Savior's Return. "Look, he is coming with the clouds, and every eye will see him." When Jesus returns at the end of the horrific events soon to be revealed, He will be seen and known by all—"and all the peoples of the earth will mourn because of him." In that day Jesus will come "in flaming fire taking vengeance on those who do not know God" (2 Thessalonians 1:8). "See, the Lord is coming with thousands upon thousands of his holy ones" (Jude 14). What the world ignores and rejects so lightly, they should dread so soberly.

How different is the story surrounding the return of Jesus for those who do know Him, to those who cannot wait to see Him! To us, the soon coming of the Lord is an event beyond words. Titus speaks for every true believer, "while we wait for the blessed hope—the appearing of the glory of our great God and Savior, Jesus Christ," (2:13). Paul agrees that we are those "who have longed for his appearing" (2 Timothy 4:8). As believers, we await "being gathered to him" (2 Thessalonians 2:1) when "we who are still alive and are left will be caught up together with them in the clouds to meet the Lord in the air" (1 Thessalonians 4:17).

While those who are ready for the Return of the Lord will soon be seen in this Revelation standing before the Throne of Almighty God, John's early warning here in v. 7 is toward those who are not ready, who are not waiting. "Be warned!" John cries, "He is coming with the clouds" just like He said. He is coming with judgment upon humanity's rebellion against a holy God. He is coming to deliver the only destiny left to those who have rejected His mercy and grace. He is coming to make good on His words, "If anyone is ashamed of me and my words in this adulterous and sinful genera-tion, the Son of Man will be ashamed of them when he comes in his Father's glory with the holy angels" (Mark 8:38).

How great is the Almighty, whom John recognizes throughout this book with the loftiest of names ever spoken or written. He is greater than we have understood Him to be, far greater than we have allowed Him to be to us. The "I am" of Moses' revela-tion (Exod. 3:14) is now the "I am" of John's Revelation. To this he adds, "the Alpha and Omega," "who is, and who was, and who is to come" (1:8; cf. 1:17; 21:6; 22:13). He is the Self-Existent One, Who always has been; He is the One Who never began, and Who will never end. He is the Self-Sufficient One, Who knows no lack and knows no limit.

And how wonderful to know that what is said of our all-sufficient Father is said of His all-sufficient Son. Seven times in seven ways we have already known the soon-coming "I Am" through John's earlier words in his Gospel record. There, Jesus speaks to those who are empty inside, "I am the bread of Life." To all who have lost their way, "I am the Light of the world." To all who need protection, "I am the door of the Sheep." To all who need to be rescued and held, "I am the Good Shepherd." To all who look death in the face, "I am the Resurrection and the Life." To all who need an answer to life's toughest questions, "I am the Way, the Truth, and the Life." To all who have come to the end of their own strength, "I am the True Vine."

How wonderful to know this timeless and eternal One as our very own! And the greater you choose to know Him, the greater you will know Him. And the greater you know Him, the greater you will love Him.

Chapter 1A Notes

1. Charles Spurgeon wrote, "Again, if we truly say, 'To him be glory and dominion,' then *we must give him dominion over ourselves*. Each man is a little empire of three kingdoms—body, soul, and spirit—and it should be a united kingdom. Make Christ king of it all. Do not allow any branch of those three kingdoms to set up for itself a distinct rule; put them all under the sway of your one King." (As quoted by David Guzik) David Guzik, "Study Guide for Revelation 1 by David Guzik," *Blue Letter Bible* 2017 <www.blueletterbible.org/Comm/guzik_david/StudyGuide2017-Rev/Rev-1.cfm?a=1168006>.

2. 1:7—For correlation with Daniel's vision of "one like the son of man, coming with the clouds of heaven" (Daniel 7:13), see comments under Revelation 5:6-7.

3. Early Church Father John Chrysostom (ca. 349-407) taught the following in his 55th Homily on John: "But wherefore said He not, Before Abraham was, 'I was' (εγω ἦν), instead of 'I Am' (εγω ειμι)? As the Father uses this expression, I Am (εγω ειμι), so also does Christ; for it signifies continuous Being, irrespective of all time. On which account the expression seemed to them to be blasphemous." Kevin Knight, ed., "Homily 55 on the Gospel of John," *CHURCH FATHERS: Homily 55 on the Gospel of John (Chrysostom)*, New Advent, 2009 <www.newadvent.org/fathers/240155.htm>.

4. "In Greek thinking, 'the beginning and the end' indicated the eternity of the highest god, and that idea is reflected in the biblical image." Leland Ryken, et al., eds. *Dictionary of Biblical Imagery* (Westmont, Illinois: Inter-Varsity Press, 1998) 445.

5. As Jesus is the subject in 1:7, it is fitting that following John's greeting and expressed praise Jesus now proceeds to introduce His own Revelation.

Revelation 1:9-20

John's Vision of the Voice

Introduction to Revelation 1:9-20

John had been so near to Jesus during His earthly ministry. By birth, he was Christ's first cousin; by calling, he was part of the inner core of Christ's closest followers. He was, in humble terms, "the disciple whom Jesus loved" (John 13:23; 19:26; 20:2; 21:7, 20). Even at the cross, John was entrusted with the care of Mary, Jesus' mother. A first-hand witness to Christ's countless miracles, he was also present at His transfiguration, His crucifixion, His resurrection, and His ascension. John was there as the resurrected Lord breathed out His regenerating Spirit (John 20:22), and again he was there in the Upper Room when Jesus sent His Spirit's fullness. Yet, after all of these inconceivable blessings, Jesus had reserved still more for John.

According to tradition and historical commentary, by the end of the first century A.D. all of the original twelve apostles (Matthias having replaced Judas)—with the exception of the Apostle John—had been martyred following their widespread missionary work.[1] Of the martyrdom of Peter and Paul and the miraculous survival of John, Church Father Tertullian records: "How happy is its church, on which apostles poured forth all their doctrine along with their blood! where Peter endures a passion like his Lord's! where Paul wins his crown in a death like John's where the Apostle John was first plunged, unhurt, into boiling oil, and thence remitted to his island-exile!"[2] Yet again, the Spirit of God had reserved still more for John.

Victoriously eluding death, John was then banished to the Island of Patmos, a virtual Alcatraz in that ancient day. According to Roman historian and senator Tacitus (*Annals* 3.68; 4.30; 15.71), the Roman government used various islands in the Aegean Sea as penal colonies, prisons without walls reserved for the worst of political dissidents.[3] Specifically, one of these expatriates was John; but he was no criminal. Strong early record tells that this apostle, now well into his nineties, was exiled to Patmos during the fourteenth year of Emperor Domitian's reign (A.D. 95).[4] There on this rocky island, John was abandoned to God alone; and there the Spirit pulled back the curtain on eternity and opened his eyes to a full revelation of the Risen King ... in all His resplendent glory.

John Hears a Voice Like a Trumpet—1:9-11

[9] I, John, your brother and companion in the suffering and kingdom and patient endurance that are ours in Jesus, was on the island of Patmos because of the word of God and the testimony of Jesus. [10] On the Lord's Day I was in the Spirit, and I heard behind me a loud voice like a trumpet, [11] which said: "Write on a scroll what you see and send it to the seven churches: to Ephesus, Smyrna, Pergamum, Thyatira, Sardis, Philadelphia and Laodicea."

Biblical Insights

While John was well-known to the Church as one of the Twelve and as an "elder" (2 John 1; 3 John 1), he seeks here only to be thought of as a Christian "brother" and "companion" (*sygkoinōnos*, a co-participant) with them (cf. 1 Cor. 9:23; Phil. 1:7).[5] He had been and he was then a sharer with them in "suffering" (*thlipsis*) for Jesus. This word often translated as "tribulation," "trouble," or "trials" carries the idea of being pressed in upon. On the evening before the cross, John had heard Jesus speak this word when he said, "I have told you these things, so that in me you may have peace. In this world you will have trouble [*thlipsis*]. But take heart! I have overcome the world" (John 16:33). Paul would later use the verbal form of this word to say, "We are hard pressed [*thlibō*] on every side, but not crushed; perplexed, but not in despair" (2 Corinthians 4:8). To be sure, it would be through the pressing in of persecution that kingdom blessings and realities would come. "We must go through many hardships [*thlipsis*] to enter the kingdom of God" was the message of Paul and Barnabas to recent believers, "[…] strengthening the disciples and encouraging them to remain true to the faith" (Acts 14:22).

Since the Kingdom of God was and is both a present and future reality for the believer, a truth that is made all the clearer in this Revelation, John also shares with his readers in their "patient endurance" (*hypomonē*), that is, their steadfast perseverance while under persecution, which comes through faith in the Kingdom's King. The words of Paul again lend support, "But if we are to share his glory, we must also share his suffering" (Romans 8:17, NLT).

Now an aged man, John was ordered by Roman decree—but led by the hand of God—to the barren island of Patmos. It is a relatively small landmass amongst many others that rise from the Aegean Sea, lying just thirty-six miles offshore of ancient Asia Minor and modern-day Turkey. Ten miles long and six miles wide at its furthest points, Patmos is shaped roughly like a "c." For many centuries before and after John's stay there, the island has been inhabited and subjugated to a vast array of cultures and political rule.[6] In John's day the island was under Roman control.

While John was sent to Patmos as an enemy of Rome, he was not there for sedition or espionage against the state as were others who worked in the quarries alongside him.[7] John's only "crime" was that he was a faithful minister of the Word of God and a faithful witness (*martys*) for Jesus. John was not reserved in proclaiming his own firsthand "testimony" (*martyria*) of the incarnate Jesus in such passages as 1 John 1:2, "The life appeared; we have seen it and testify [*martyreō*] to it, and we proclaim to you the eternal life, which was with the Father and has appeared to us" (cf. 1 John 4:14). The importance of what one has seen or heard or knows to be true concerning Jesus is emphasized again and again throughout John's writings. See John 1:8, 15, 34; 4:39; 5:31-39; 12:17; 15:27; 21:24; 1 John 5:9-10; Rev. 2:13; 11:3; 17:6; 22:16, 20.

The first of many visions came to John while he was "in the Spirit." While all true believers have the Holy Spirit dwelling within them (Rom. 8:9; 1 Cor. 3:16), this full phrase, meaning literally, "I came to be in the Spirit," refers to a special experience through the moving of the Spirit upon John. This same phenomenon of being carried by the Spirit will mark other visions within the Revelation as well (4:2; 17:3; 21:10). (More will be said of the additional marker "after this" [Rev. 4:1, etc.].) A supernatural encounter with the Holy Spirit accompanied with prophetic revelation was also the experience of Isaiah (Isa. 6), Ezekiel (Ezek. 2:2; 3:12, 14; 11:1; 37:1; etc.), Zechariah (Zech. 1:8-21; 2; 3; 4; 5; 6:1-8), Peter (Acts 10:11-16) and Paul (Acts 22:17-21). In fact, the Bible also abounds with accounts of prophetic dreams and visions that came to God's people, including Abraham, Jacob, Joseph, Solomon, the Major and Minor Prophets, Mary and Joseph, the women at Christ's empty tomb, the prophet Ananias, and the centurion Cornelius.

John tells us that this divine encounter took place "on the Lord's Day." The word "Lord's" (*kyriakos*) here is an adjective in the sense of belonging to or relating to the Lord; its only other use is in 1 Corinthians 11:20, "the Lord's supper." Much debate surrounds John's use of this phrase. Some hold that John is referring to the first day of the week, Sunday. Though Scripture does offer limited reference to the gathering together of New Covenant believers on the first day of the week (Acts 20:7; 1 Cor. 16:2), nowhere else in Scripture is Sunday called "the Lord's day" as it is commonly called today.[8] However, this doesn't dismiss altogether the possibility that John may well have been speaking of Sunday. There is, in fact, strong extra-biblical, historical evidence that early Christians did refer to the first day of the week, the day of Christ's resurrection, as "the Lord's day." And if this be the case, it may well have come in protest of the common secular use of *kyriakos* ("lord's") when referring to "imperial" government and the naming of the first day of the month "Emperor's Day."[9]

Another view is that John's use of "the Lord's day" means that he was lifted by the Spirit into the prophetic "Day of the Lord," a phrase used many times in the Old Testament to describe the entire Last Days period of God's judgment and His sovereign rule (cf. Isa. 2:12; 13:6, 9; Jer. 46:10; Ezek. 13:5; 30:3; Joel 1:15; 2:1, 11; 3:14; Amos 5:18, 20; Obad. 1:15; Zeph. 1:7, 14; Zech. 14:1). Though not in the same adjectival form as in Revelation 1:10, the phrase "the day of the Lord" referring to the same future period is also found in the New Testament (1 Cor. 5:5; 2 Cor. 1:14; 1 Thess.

5:2; 2 Pet. 3:10). While both interpretations of "the Lord's Day" are permissible, it is not reasonable to think that John would have received this entire revelation of multiple visions all within the duration of one Sunday. On the other hand, the case could be made that John had been lifted by the Spirit in a way that transcended time.

Now as John's divine encounter began, he heard behind him "a loud voice like a trumpet," clear and distinct from Heaven. The instruction was given to, "Write on a scroll what you see and send it to the seven churches: to Ephesus, Smyrna, Pergamum, Thyatira, Sardis, Philadelphia and Laodicea" (v. 11). These are the seven churches already spoken of in 1:4, seven real congregations with real issues and real promises, located in seven cities well known to John. The messages John will soon hear from Jesus for His Church are contained in Chapters 2-3. That John is to write "on a scroll" (*biblion*; a book as John would have known it) what he "sees" probably refers to the entirety of this Revelation contained in multiple visions. That this book is to be "sent" lets us know that God would also deploy others to circulate this book to those seven original churches and beyond.

Because Jesus loves the Church, John was in God's timing released from Patmos; and in his hands went a scroll to be delivered to the Church. And unrolling that scroll, the Church in city after city would read its opening words, "The Revelation of Jesus Christ." Without question, these words alone would have excited the hearts of those early Christians! Surely, these words alone would have brought the immediate encouragement they needed since in these words was the message that King Jesus lives and reigns forever and that He—and not Rome's Caesar—held their future in His hands.

It should be noted that the King James and New King James versions include in verse 11 the phrase, "'I am the Alpha and the Omega, the First and the Last,' and," based upon the Received Text. The importance of the title "the Alpha and the Omega" has been addressed under 1:8 and will be again under 21:6 and 22:13. We will also see the title "the First and the Last" in 1:17; 2:8; and 22:13. The application of these titles to Christ Jesus—who is "before all things" (Colossians 1:17)—is abundantly clear in view of all these verses together.

Life Application

John's humility is heard in the words, "I, John, your brother and companion." While some men boast in their titles and their accomplishments, John kept his heart bowed low before the Lord. And if there was any sense of superiority in his miraculous deliverance from death, it never shows in these self-effacing words. No, just the opposite!

There had been a day long before when John and his brother James did see the Kingdom of God as an opportunity for upward mobility.

'Teacher,' they said, 'we want you to do for us whatever we ask.' 'What do you want me to do for you?' he asked. They replied, 'Let one of us sit at your right and the other at your left in your glory.' 'You don't know what you are asking,' Jesus said. 'Can you drink the cup I drink or be baptized with the baptism I am baptized with?' 'We can,' they answered. Jesus said to them, 'You will drink the cup I drink and be baptized with the baptism I am baptized with, but to sit at my right or left is not for me to grant. These places belong to those for whom they have been prepared' (Mark 10:35b-40).

Calling the disciples together, Jesus turned their indiscretion into a teaching moment,

You know that those who are regarded as rulers of the Gentiles lord it over them, and their high officials exercise authority over them. Not so with you. Instead, whoever wants to become great among you must be your servant, and whoever wants to be first must be slave of all. For even the Son of Man did not come to be served, but to serve, and to give his life as a ransom for many (vv. 42-45).

Jesus' words now defined John's very life; a servant heart was the measure of his own greatness. The growing revelation of Christ's love was now interwoven with a growing revelation of His glory, with still more to come. Christ's words, all of them, had come to pass. Even in his later years he was drinking "the cup" of "suffering," drawing ample strength from Jesus to "patiently endure" for the Kingdom's sake.

And what was true for John is often true for us. This most incredible encounter with Jesus and most breathtaking of revelations of His beauty and power could not have happened at a time nor place more difficult than where John now found himself. But a "Patmos" experience—a place of outward struggle, yet inward surrender—may be the very season of our most glorious victory.

John's Vision of the Voice—1:12-20

[12] I turned around to see the voice that was speaking to me. And when I turned I saw seven golden lampstands, [13] and among the lampstands was someone like a son of man, dressed in a robe reaching down to his feet and with a golden sash around his chest. [14] The hair on his head was white like wool, as white as snow, and his eyes were like blazing fire. [15] His feet were like bronze glowing in a furnace, and his voice was like the sound of rushing waters. [16] In his right hand he held seven stars, and coming out of his mouth was a sharp, double-edged sword. His face was like the sun shining in all its brilliance. [17] When I saw him, I fell at his feet as though dead. Then he placed his right hand on me and said: "Do not be afraid. I am the First and the Last. [18] I am the Living One; I was dead, and now look, I am alive for ever and ever! And I hold the keys of death and Hades. [19] "Write, therefore, what you have seen, what is now and what will take place later. [20] The mystery of the seven stars that you saw in my right

hand and of the seven golden lampstands is this: The seven stars are the angels of the seven churches, and the seven lampstands are the seven churches.

Biblical Insights

So vibrant and powerful was the sound of the voice of Jesus, that John "turned around to see" the voice. Before he could receive what was being said, John had to "see" who was saying it. Clearly, the Lord stood behind John while he was already "in the Spirit" (v. 10). Though this common word for "to see" (*blepō*) can be used, as can our English word, for mental vision as well as physical, there is every reason to accept that John saw this vision of the glorified Jesus with his natural eyesight.

What John now saw "in the Spirit" brought to him a four-fold glorious revelation of Christ's presence. At first, the Spirit revealed His voice; John had heard this voice before. It was human enough and familiar enough, yet this was no ordinary voice. Nearly eighty years before, John had heard this voice speak to waves and winds, and they became still. He had heard this voice speak to demons and they screamed in terror. He had heard this voice speak to dead people and they came back to life. But John had never heard that same familiar voice quite like he heard it that day. At first the voice was as "loud" (*megas*; even, "great" or "mighty") and powerful as the crisp, unmistakable blast of "a trumpet." Momentarily, that same voice would come thundering "like the sound of rushing waters" (v. 15). This was the voice that had called the universe into existence and that would someday call John's body from its grave.

Having turned to see the voice behind him, John "saw" (*eidon*) before him "seven golden lampstands." These "seven" were different from the seven-branched single lampstand instructed by God for the tabernacle in Exodus 25:31-40 (cf. 1 Kings 7:49; Zech. 4:2). Nevertheless, like the lampstand in the tabernacle and Solomon's Temple, these were "golden," which in Revelation is a symbolic or real reflection of the glory of God's presence. The appearance of blazing oil-fed lamps or pots placed on top of stands would have been well understood by John, but it was Jesus himself who would explain (in verse 20) "the mystery" of these seven lampstands; "the seven lampstands are the seven churches" (already introduced in 1:4 and 11). The assumed presence of oil in these lamps is symbolic of the Holy Spirit's presence in the Church. That Jesus was "among the lampstands" may be an allusion to the ministry of the Old Testament Aaronic priests, who were responsible to inspect the oil in the seven lamps held by the lampstand to ensure that they kept burning. In fulfillment of the typology, Christ stands in the midst of His Church to inspect us.[10]

With this, John now receives a second revelation of Christ's presence, namely of His appearance. To the apostle, Jesus seemed to be "someone like," that is, resembling "a son of man" (see also 14:14). It cannot be said that Jesus is "someone like" "the son of man" since he is, in fact, that one; and so, the definite article "the" is missing here. Rather, John is describing Christ's resemblance to our humanity. When Jesus used the title "the Son of Man" for Himself (eighty-two times in the Gospels) the definite article was used, since He is the one and only. Though an apparent term of identity with our humanity, the title is much more than that in the Gospels and again here. John is identifying this Jesus as the Jewish Messiah, the all-superior, divinely anointed "man" of Daniel 7:13. Moreover, this entire Revelation will proceed to declare that Jesus is in fact the One to whom the Father will give "authority, glory and sovereign power" so that "all nations and peoples of every language worshiped him. His dominion is an everlasting dominion that will not pass away, and his kingdom is one that will never be destroyed" (Daniel 7:14).

John saw Him, "dressed in a robe reaching down to his feet." This was the ancient clothing of a man of great dignity and authority, often worn by priests and kings. The "golden sash around his chest" is an allusion to the fine belt worn by the high priest (Exodus 39:29). In Exodus 28:5, we read that God instructed Moses to have Israel's artisans "use gold, and blue, purple and scarlet yarn, and fine linen" in the weaving of "sacred garments" for Aaron, their first high priest, and his priestly sons (v. 4). It seems evident, then, from a comparison of Exodus 39:3 and 39:29, that thin strands or threads of finely cut gold were woven into the sash, as was the case with all of the priestly garments. How important then is the appearance of Christ wearing a sash made entirely of gold. Furthermore, while common men wore a belt of cloth or leather around their waste, Jesus is seen wearing one of gold, placed high around his "chest," further identifying Him as our Great High Priest (Heb. 4:14-16; 7:23-28; 8:1-2).[11]

As the revelation of Christ's appearance continues, John describes the Resurrected Lord's visible attributes. That the "hair on his head was white like wool, as white as snow," is a symbol of His purity and wisdom and not of the passing of time since Jesus in his divine essence and glorified humanity is timeless. That His "eyes were like blazing fire" speaks of His penetrating, searching judgment, like the colloquialism, "he looked right through me" (also 2:18 and 19:12; cf. Heb. 4:13). Now John sees that Christ's feet "were like bronze glowing in a furnace," His own wisdom and holiness establishing His feet as the "Judge of the Living and the Dead" (Acts 10:42; 2 Timothy 4:1). Though the word for "bronze" is uncertain and found only here and in 2:18 in the NT;, it is best understood as a shiny and refined bronze-like metal that was seen as if burning in a kiln or oven.[12] Christ's righteous judgment, then, is seen in both the refined metal and in the fire. Note that John describes resemblance to "wool," "snow," "fire," and "bronze" as a means of putting the awesome nature of what he saw into words. Note also the direct parallel to the words Daniel used to describe the presence of God the Father in Daniel 7:9 and of the messenger angel that was sent from God's presence in Daniel 10:6.

Again, by analogy, John describes the voice of Jesus as being "like the sound of rushing waters" (also 14:2; 19:6). "Rushing" here is more properly "many" (*polys*), which may be better captured as the sound of many rivers or even "much," as the roar of the ocean (as in the NLT). With this picture, John describes deity, just as Ezekiel had heard "the voice of the Almighty" (Ezek. 1:24; 43:2).

On into verse 16, John saw a "sharp double-edged sword" proceeding "out of his mouth." John's word for "sword" here is *rhomphaia* (and in 2:12, 16; 6:8 [though there of "Death" and "Hell" personified]; 19:15, 21). Though this word may also refer to a spear or javelin, its further description as "double-edged" (*distomos*) and its Old Testament Hebrew counterpart *chereb* (used of divine judgment [Deut. 32:41, 42; Ps. 7:12; Isa. 34:5, 6; 66:16] and used messianically [Ps. 45:3]) certainly identifies this instrument as a long and heavy sword. The much more common New Testament word for "sword" is instead *machaira,* indicating a shorter sword, dagger, or even a large knife (Matt. 10:34; 26:47, 51, 52, 55; John 18:10, 11; Rom. 8:35; 13:4, etc.). In Ephesians 6:17 and Hebrew 4:12 this latter word is used to describe the Word of God. In light of the additional uses of *rhomphaia* in Revelation, what John now saw issuing from the mouth of Jesus was the sword of judgment, comfort to the righteous, but terror to the wicked.[13] Again, in this metaphor John is describing deity in the appearance of Jesus.

Completing the revelation of Christ's appearance to John, he proclaims that, "His face was like the sun shining in all its brilliance" (v. 16). The glorious light of the Messiah had long been the hope of Israel, prophetically seen by Balaam (Num. 24:17), David (2 Sam. 23:4), Hosea (6:3), Malachi (4:2), and Isaiah (9:2). John declared, "In him was life, and that life was the light of men" (John 1:4). Paul announced, "For God, who said, 'Let light shine out of darkness,' made his light shine in our hearts to give us the light of the knowledge of the glory of God in the face of Christ" (2 Cor. 4:6). Of His own glory, Jesus proclaimed for all to hear, "I am the light of the world. Whoever follows me will never walk in darkness, but will have the light of life" (John 8:12). What John saw, he describes more literally as light as bright as "the sun shining in its power" (*dynamis*), causing him most likely to shield his eyes. In contrast, while Jesus was still in His pre-Resurrection human body, the radiating glory of His divine essence (Col. 2:9) had been hidden from the physical eyes of those who saw Him. On only one occasion, and that by divine privilege, was Christ's inner core of disciples permitted to see His glory as He was "transfigured" before them. Of this Matthew writes, "His face shone like the sun, and his clothes became as white as the light" (Matthew 17:2; par. Mark 9:2-3). But what was once revealed to Peter, James, and John through these awe-inspiring encounters, will soon be the eternal blessing of all those who stand before Him in Heaven. As John assured the Church in 1 John 3:2, "But we know that when Christ appears, we shall be like him, for we shall see him as he is."

Along with the glorious revelation of Christ's voice and of His appearance came a third revelation, namely, of the Risen Christ's possession. John writes, "In his right hand he held seven stars" (v. 16). What Jesus himself will call a "mystery" (*mystērion*)—a hidden or secret matter revealed at the will of God (Rev. 10:7; 17:5, 7; cf. Col.

3:4-11)—is made clear in verse 20b, "The seven stars are the angels of the seven churches." In the New Testament, an "angel" (*aggelos*) most often refers to one of the countless ancient, created spirit beings—whether holy and heavenly (Matt. 18:10; Luke 1:11; Acts 12:7; Rev. 7:1, 2, 11) or rebellious and fallen (Matt. 25:41; 2 Pet. 2:4; 2 Cor. 11:14 [of Satan himself]; 12:7; Jude 1:6). Yet, an "angel" (*aggelos*) may also refer to a human messenger sent by God (Matt. 11:10; Luke 7:27; 9:52; Mark 1:2) or by another (Luke 7:24; James 2:25). Whether an "angel," then, is supernatural or human is completely dependent upon the context. Here, it is most likely that the "seven angels" in Christ's hand are the spiritual leaders, namely, the earthly pastors of the "seven churches" already introduced (v. 4 and 11). If this is so, then the messages directed to each of the churches and the Revelation in its entirety were entrusted to these seven leaders (2:1, 8, 12, 18; 3:1, 7, 14).[14]

That these are metaphorically called "stars" (1:16, 20) may refer to their responsibility to reflect the Light of Jesus amongst His people, as should also all believers (cf. Phil. 2:15; and see Matt. 5:14; Eph. 5:8).[15] Nevertheless, some have found in the imagery of the "stars" a reference to the heavenly spirit beings, "angels," which are given assignment over these local churches. This could receive only weak support from the following references, which use the word "star" as a metaphor for angelic spirit beings, but primarily fallen (Job 38:7; Isa. 14:12; cf. Rev. 12:3-4 with 7-9). Favoring the view that these "angels" or "messengers" are the human leaders commissioned to the seven churches, it is important, then, to see that they are possessed by the "right hand" of Jesus, a picture of His favor (Ps. 16:11; Gal. 2:9), sustenance (Isa. 41:10), protection (Ps. 18:35; John 10:28), and guidance (Ps. 139:10). In this regard, we are blessed as His people to know that when he holds the leaders of the Church in His hands, He holds us all. Furthermore, it will be seen in Chapters 2-3 that though these churches were far from faultless, He still possessed them by His hand. He had not cast them away! Praise God that He forever possesses and forever holds on to those He calls His own.

To complete this glorious four-part revelation of the presence of Jesus, the Spirit now reveals to John the Risen Christ's touch. This glorious encounter with the Son of God was so powerful that the finiteness of John's being could not endure. The disciple who often had expressed his coveted closeness to Jesus in His earthly ministry, now humbly writes in retrospect, "When I saw him, I fell at his feet as though dead" (v. 17). We may compare this response before the overwhelming glory to the experiences of others, such as Abraham (Gen. 17:3), Manoah and his wife (Judg. 13:20), Ezekiel (Ezek. 3:23; 43:3; 44:4), Daniel (Dan. 8:17; 10:8-9, 15-17), and Peter, James, and John (Matt. 17:6).

Reviving his chosen servant, Jesus first touched John with "his right hand," again an indication of favor and protection. But with this, Jesus also touched John with His words, "Do not be afraid." John had heard those words from His Lord before (Matt. 10:26; 17:7; Luke 12:32; John 6:20; 14:27). And as he would write, or perhaps had already written, John was convinced of this, "There is no fear in love. But perfect love drives out fear, because fear has to do with punishment" (1 John 4:18). Jesus wanted his child to know Him as "The First and the Last" (cf. 2:8 and 22:13). A comparison of 1:8, 1:11 (in the Received Text, see above), and 22:13 makes clear that Christ is avowing His deity in this title. He is the eternal One—equal in being with God the Father—as in Isaiah 44:6, "I am the first and I am the last; apart from me there is no God" (cf. 48:12). For John, a child of the Living God through His Son Jesus Christ, a guilty fear would have no place.

Still claiming deity, Jesus spoke comfort to John as "the Living One" (Josh. 3:10; Jer. 10:10). Indeed, Jesus is Life Himself (John 5:26; 14:6) and the giver of Life (1:4; 10:10). Through His atoning work at Calvary, Jesus could say, "I was" or literally, "I became dead."[16] Many years before, John had been privileged to say with the other disciples that they had looked upon the Resurrected Lord (John 20:25). Yet, Jesus invites him again to see the proof of His resurrection—"now look [*idou*; cf. 1:7; 3:20; 16:15; 22:7, 12], I am alive for ever and ever! [lit. 'unto the ages of the ages,' a structure that indicated indefinite duration in ancient Greek]."

In Christ's death, He "disarmed the powers and authorities, he made a public spectacle of them, triumphing over them by the cross" (Colossians 2:15). Hebrews 2:14 adds, "that by his death he might break the power of him who holds the power of death—that is, the devil—and free those who all their lives were held in slavery by their fear of death." But it was in His resurrection that the full implications of Christ's death are ministered to His children (Rom. 4:25; 1 Pet. 1:3; 3:18). Through both His death and His resurrection, the life-giving Jesus "holds" (in the sense of possesses) the "keys" (here, symbolic of authority) of "death" and "Hades" (the realm of the dead). He is Victor over "death" in both its physical (1 Cor. 15:55) and spiritual (Rev. 20:6) dimensions. He is also Victor over "Hades" (corresponding to the Old Testament "Sheol")— the current dwelling of the wicked dead (Luke 16:23; Rev. 20:13-14) and the former dwelling of the righteous dead up until the resurrection and successive ascension of Jesus (cf. Eph. 4:8, "He led captivity captive"; 1 Cor. 15:55, "O Hades, where is your victory?"; 2 Cor. 5:8, "to be away from the body and at home with the Lord"). It is evident that the triumphant removal of the righteous dead out of Hades and into Heaven was signified in the event which Matthew reports (27:52-53) "the bodies of many holy people who had died were raised to life. They came out of the tombs, and after Jesus' resurrection they went into the holy city and appeared to many people."[17]

The injunction to "write," spoken in v. 11 before Christ's glorious appearance, is now repeated to John, as it will be many times within this Revelation. (See the introductory words to each of the seven churches in Chapters 2-3, as well as 14:13; 19:9; 21:5.) In fact, the importance of the "written" nature of the "words of this prophecy" is presented from the outset (1:3). As was already seen, blessings would come through this written word in the providence of God. It seems clear, then, that all that is written at the command of God is certain and established now and forevermore. This holds true whether John writes concerning the seven-sealed Book of Redemption "with writing on both sides" (5:1); of the names written in or absent from "the book of life" (13:8; 17:8; 20:12, 15; 21:27); of those who have "his Father's name written on their foreheads" (14:1); of the horrible name written on the forehead of "babylon the great" (17:5); or, above all, of the written, sacred name of "the King of Kings and Lord of Lords" (19:12, 16). Even the closing words of this book strongly emphasize that only what has been revealed by God in this Revelation is certain and blessed, while every attempt to add to or to take away from its writings is cursed (22:18, 19). Only once will John be prohibited from writing what he sees and hears (10:40).

What John is to write is "what you have seen, what is now and what will take place later" (v. 19). Those who hold to a futuristic view of Revelation generally agree that this instruction forms a clear, three-part overview of this prophecy. John's immediate encounter with the glory of the risen Jesus forms "what you have seen." "What is now" will be contained in Christ's inspection and assessment of the seven churches found in Chapters 2 and 3. "What will take place later" fills up the future events contained in Chapters 4-22. Thus, John's present vision of Jesus, together with the messages to the seven churches (which in themselves carry timeless truths), will usher him into his vision of eternity ahead. In this way, we are reminded that the prophecy is one, that the plan of the Father is all encompassing, and that the presence of Jesus transcends all time.

Life Application

God has spoken and He has spoken through His Son. And, to those who will listen, what God began to speak through His Son, He is still speaking with authority today. To hear the voice of Jesus is to hear the voice of the Living God. In fact, so direct—so filled with personality and power—was the voice of God to John, that he confessed, "I turned around to see the voice that was speaking to me." John's encounter tells us that we will never be blessed by the "what" of what God is saying until we receive with humility the "Who" of the Voice which is speaking.

There is a Voice that speaks like no other voice to the human soul. There is a Voice that speaks from Heaven, timeless and all knowing. Though there are so many voices contending to be heard in this noisy world, there remains one Voice Who calls the listening heart away from the confusion of it all. This is the Voice that pierces the darkness like a trumpet and rushes in to silence every argument. This is the Voice of the Word of God. If our greatest need had been for more intelligence, the Father would have sent us the ultimate scientist. If our greatest need had been for increased wealth, He would have sent us a world-class economist. If our greatest need had been for unending pleasure, He would have sent a performer extraordinaire to entertain us. But in His perfect wisdom, our Father knew that our greatest need was simply to hear His Voice; so, He sent us the revelation of His Word.

What you and I must know more than anything else in this world is a fresh, personal revelation of Jesus! In fact, our single greatest human need is to see Him, the Living Word of God, for Who He really is. And, never will a true unveiling of Jesus in His glory be received apart from the anchor of the written Word of God. How incredible it is then that we may know the very same Resurrected Lord who announced to John, "I am the Living One; I was dead, and now look, I am alive for ever and ever!" (1:18).

But how can we answer the skeptic who rejects or questions the legitimacy of the Bible's account of the life and mission of Jesus? Can any evidence be produced that could help them to question their doubts? In fact, there are a number of early, reliable sources outside of the Bible that verify much of what the Word states about the historic Jesus. One of the most important of these is a statement made by the Romano-Jewish scholar and historian Flavius Josephus (A.D. 37-100). At roughly the same time that John was on the island of Patmos, Josephus wrote the following words in his monumental work entitled *Antiquities of the Jews* (Book 18, Chapter 3, Section 3).

Now, there was about this time Jesus, a wise man, if it be lawful to call him a man, for he was a doer of wonderful works, a teacher of such men as receive the truth with pleasure. He drew over to him both many of the Jews and many of the Gentiles. He was [the] Christ. And when Pilate, at the suggestion of the principal men amongst us, had condemned him to the cross, those that loved him at the first did not forsake him; for he appeared to them alive again the third day, as the divine prophets had foretold these and ten thousand other wonderful things concerning him. And the tribe of Christians, so named from him, are not extinct at this day.[18]

Not as favorable are the references to Jesus and to first century believers made by Publius Cornelius Tacitus (A.D. 56-117), a Roman senator and historian. In his work entitled *Annals* (Book 15, Chapter 44), he wrote the following about the aftermath of the six-day fire that burned much of Rome in A.D. July 64 (which most historians attribute to Nero himself):

But all human efforts, all the lavish gifts of the emperor, and the propitiations of the gods, did not banish the sinister belief that the conflagration was the result of an order. Consequently, to get rid of the report, Nero fastened the guilt and inflicted the most exquisite tortures on a class hated for their abominations, called Christians by the populace. Christus, from whom the name had its origin, suffered the extreme penalty during the reign of Tiberius at the hands of one of our procurators, Pontius Pilatus, and a most mischievous superstition, thus checked for the moment, again broke out not only in Judaea, the first source of the evil, but even in Rome, where all things hideous and shameful from every part of the world find their centre and become popular. Accordingly, an arrest was first made of all who pleaded guilty; then, upon their information, an immense multitude was convicted, not so much of the crime of firing the city, as of hatred against mankind. Mockery of every sort was added to their deaths. Covered with the skins of beasts, they were torn by dogs and perished, or were nailed to crosses, or were doomed to the flames and burnt, to serve as a nightly illumination, when daylight had expired.[19]

From the first century A.D. comes another historic report about Jesus drawn from official Jewish court documents. A large number of ancient manuscripts were translated and compiled in a work called *The Archko Volume; or, the Archeological Writings of the Sanhedrim and Talmuds of the Jews* (1896). Also contained on its title page are the words, "These are the official documents made in these courts in the days of Jesus Christ." Contained in a fascinating section entitled "Chapter V: Gamaliel's interview with Joseph and Mary and others concerning Jesus" (pp. 92-93), are the following words about Jesus:

I asked him to describe this person to me, so that I might know him if I should meet him. He said: 'If you ever meet him [Jesus] you will know him. While he is nothing but a man, there is something about him that distinguishes him from every other man. He is the picture of his mother, only he has not her smooth, round face. His hair is a little more golden than hers, though it is as much from sunburn as anything else. He is tall, and his shoulders are a little drooped; his visage is thin and of a swarthy complexion, though this is from exposure. His eyes are large and a soft blue, and rather dull and heavy. The lashes are long, and his eyebrows very large. His nose is that of a Jew. In fact, he reminds me of an old-fashioned Jew in every sense of the word. He is not a great talker, unless there is something brought up about heaven and divine things, when his tongue moves glibly and his eyes light up with a peculiar brilliancy; though there is this peculiarity about Jesus, he never argues a question; he never disputes. He will commence and state facts, and they are on such a solid basis that nobody will have the boldness to dispute with him. Though he has such mastership of judgment, he takes no pride in confuting his opponents, but always seems to be sorry for them. I have seen him attacked by the scribes and doctors of the law, and they seemed like little children learning their lessons under a master. His strongest points are in the spiritual power of the law and the intentions of the prophets. The young people tried to get him to take a class of them and teach them; but he utterly refused.' This Jew is convinced that he is the Messiah of the world.[20]

But wait! Neither these nor ten thousand other ancient records of the historic Jesus will ever move a resistant heart into the Kingdom of God. In fact, the wisdom of the Holy Spirit through the words of Paul settles the matter of any pursuit of Jesus that is empty of faith: "So we have stopped evaluating others from a human point of view. At one time, we thought of Christ merely from a human point of view. How differently we know him now!" (2 Corinthians 5:16, NLT).

To see Jesus—even the Resurrected Jesus—"from a human point of view," has never engaged the full reality of Who He is. How is it that so many who had been privileged to walk closely with Jesus, still did not see Him "differently?" Consider that even on the morning of His Resurrection, Jesus appeared to Mary Magdalene. At first "she did not realize that it was Jesus," "thinking he was the gardener" (John 20:14, 15). It was only when He spoke her name that her eyes of faith were opened, and only then did she run with the news, "I have seen the Lord!" (20:18). Later that day, He appeared to two followers who walked together; knowing Him only "from a human point of view," they were filled with sadness. Though the Resurrected Lord appeared to them, "they were kept from recognizing him" (Luke 24:16). Only when He sat with them and gave thanks in prayer and broke bread with them—only then, as faith rose, "their eyes were opened and they recognized him" (24:31).

Onward, though the news quickly spread to the eleven disciples, at first, they too doubted the reports—"When they heard the news that Jesus was alive [...] they did not believe it" (Mark 16:11). So dim was their vision, that Jesus "rebuked them for their lack of faith and their stubborn refusal to believe" (v. 14). And wasn't it only at the sight and touch of the nail marks in Christ's hand that Thomas' weak faith was strengthened? And wasn't it only when Jesus countered his wavering convictions with, "Stop doubting and believe," that Thomas freely confessed, "My Lord and my God!" (John 20:27-28). Sadly, even after these amazing encounters, His closest followers still often saw Him only "from a human point of view." Appearing on the shore, He called to seven who were weary from a failed night of fishing, "but the disciples did not realize that it was Jesus" (John 21:4).

To be sure, it is possible to know all about Him, even to be on the receiving end of so many of His blessings, and yet still not to see Jesus for who He really is—the glorious Risen King. It has been said that, "A great deal of what we see depends on what we're looking for." If in Jesus we wish to see only a passing historic figure, Satan will be glad to accommodate.[21] Or, if in Jesus we are looking to find merely a sacred and devout man, then man-made religion will fill the need. But, if with eyes of faith and hearts of passion we pursue only the beautiful One whose face shines "like the sun shining in all its brilliance," whose feet burn with holiness "like bronze glowing in a furnace," and whose voice resonates "like the sound of rushing waters," then the Spirit of our Father will reveal to us His Son.

To be clear, what you and I need more than anything else is a fresh, personal revelation of Jesus! And how do you see Him today? If only through the eyes of history, or only through the eyes of a parent or a spouse, or only through the eyes of a relationship you used to have with Jesus, then know that God in Heaven has so much more for you. Our Father wants you and me, just like John, to receive a revelation of what the Risen Savior looks like now—through the eyes of our hearts.

Chapter 1B Notes

1. "Meanwhile the holy apostles and disciples of our Saviour were dispersed throughout the world. Parthia, according to tradition, was allotted to Thomas as his field of labor, Scythia to Andrew, and Asia to John, who, after he had lived some time there, died at Ephesus." Philip Schaff, ed., "NPNF2-01. Eusebius Pamphilius: Church History, Life of Constantine, Oration in Praise of Constantine," *Christian Classics Ethereal Library* 13 July 2005 <www.ccel.org/ccel/schaff/npnf201.iii.viii.i.html>.

2. Peter Kirby, ed., "Tertullian—The Prescription Against Heretics," trans. Peter Holmes, *Tertullian (Roberts-Donaldson)* 2017 <www.earlychristianwritings.com/text/tertullian 11.html>.

3. Peter Kirby, ed., The Annals of Tacitus, "Cornelius Tacitus." *Early Christian Writings* 2017 <www.earlychristianwritings.com/text/annals.html>.

4. See Introduction—Author and Authenticity above for prolific historical evidence of John's exile on Patmos.

5. That John writes "I, John" here and in 22:8 is likely an overt assertion of his authority as Christ's messenger. A.T. Robertson points out that, "In apocalyptic literature the personality of the writer is always prominent to guarantee the visions (Dan. 8:1; 10:2)." A.T. Robertson, *The Revelation of John. Word Pictures in the New Testament, Vol. VI* (Nashville: Broadman, 1933) 289.

6. Throughout the centuries, occupation of Patmos has come at the hands of the Greek, Roman Byzantine, and Ottoman Empires, Italy, and Nazi Germany. See also Introduction—Place, Date, and Occasion.

7. Victorinus of Pettau (A.D. b. 250, d. 303), who wrote the first commentary on the Book of Revelation, writes at Revelation 10:11, "He says this, because when John said these things he was in the island of Patmos, condemned to the labour (sic) of the mines by Caesar Domitian. There, therefore, he saw the Apocalypse; and when grown old, he thought that he should at length receive his quittance by suffering, Domitian being killed, all his judgments were discharged. And John being dismissed from the mines, thus subsequently delivered the same Apocalypse which he had received from God, [...]" Philip Schaff, ed., "ANF07. Fathers of the Third and Fourth Centuries: Lactantius, Venantius, Asterius, Victorinus, Dionysius, Apostolic Teaching and Constitutions, Homily," *Christian Classics Ethereal Library* 1 June 2005 <www.ccel. org/ccel/schaff/anf07.vi.ii.x.html>.

8. Church Father, Ignatius (A.D. 35-108) in his Epistle to the Magnesians, Chapter 9, writes, "If, therefore, those who were brought up in the ancient order of things have come to the possession of a new hope, no longer observing the Sabbath, but living in

the observance of the Lord's Day, on which also our life has sprung up again by Him and by His death [...]." Kevin Knight, ed., "The Epistle of Ignatius to the Magnesians," *CHURCH FATHERS: Epistle to the Magnesians (St. Ignatius)*, New Advent, 2009 <www.newadvent.org/fathers/0105.htm>.

Church Father Justin Martyr (c. A.D. 100 – 165) in his *First Apology*, Chapter 67. *Weekly Worship of the Christians* writes, "But Sunday is the day on which we all hold our common assembly, because it is the first day on which God, having wrought a change in the darkness and matter, made the world; and Jesus Christ our Saviour on the same day rose from the dead. For He was crucified on the day before that of Saturn (Saturday); and on the day after that of Saturn, which is the day of the Sun, having appeared to His apostles and disciples, He taught them these things, which we have submitted to you also for your consideration." Philip Schaff, ed., "ANF01. The Apostolic Fathers with Justin Martyr and Irenaeus," *Christian Classics Ethereal Library* 13 July 2005 <www.ccel.org/ccel/schaff/anf01.viii.ii.lxvii.html>.

In the *Didache*, also known as *The Teaching of the Twelve Apostles* (dated to the late first century A.D.), are recorded these words in Section 14, "On every Lord's Day— his special day—come together and break bread and give thanks, first confessing your sins so that your sacrifice may be pure." Philip Schaff, ed., "The Teaching of the Twelve, Commonly Called the Didache," *Christian Classics Ethereal Library* 1 June 2005 <www.ccel.org/ccel/richardson/fathers.viii.i.iii.html>.

9. Theologian Gustav Adolf Deissmann (1866-1937) writes the following, "On collecting the examples known to me some time ago, I said that this name, formed probably after some Hellenistic model was analogous to the Primitive Christian 'Lord's Day' as a name for Sunday. But the more I regard this detail in connexion(sic) with the great subject of 'Christ and the Caesars,' the more I am bound to reckon with the possibility that the distinctive title 'Lord's Day' may have been connected with conscious feelings of protest against the cult of the Emperor with its 'Emperor's Day.'" Gustav Adolf Deissmann, *Light from the ancient East—the New Testament Illustrated by Recently Discovered Texts of the Graeco-Roman World* (London: Hodder & Stoughton, 1910).

10. Commentator David Guzik writes, "The light doesn't come from the lampstands. The light comes from the oil lamps themselves. The stands merely make the light more visible. Therefore, the lampstands are a good picture of the church. We don't produce the light, we simply display it." He then goes on to quote theologian Adam Clark (1760—1832), "A lamp is not *light in itself*, it is only the *instrument* of dispensing light, and it must receive both *oil* and *fire* before it can dispense any; so, no Church has in itself either *grace* or *glory*, it must receive all from Christ its head, else it can dispense neither light nor life." David Guzik, Introduction, A Vision of Jesus, "Study Guide for Revelation." *Blue Letter Bible* <www.blueletterbible.org/Comm/archives/guzik_david/studyguide_rev/rev_1.cfm>.

11. The Jewish historian, Flavius Josephus (A.D. 37-100), being himself of priestly descent, writes (the following description of the priestly garments, "The high priest is indeed adorned with the same garments that we have described, without abating one; only over these he puts on a vestment of a blue color. This also is a long robe, reaching to his feet, […], and is tied round with a girdle, embroidered with the same colors and flowers as the former, with a mixture of gold interwoven." Flavius Josephus, Concerning the Garments of the Priests, and of the High Priest, "Josephus: The Complete Works. Antiquities of the Jews." *Christian Classics Ethereal Library* 21 Apr. 2011 <www.ccel.org/ccel/josephus/complete.ii.iv.vii.html>.

12. Scholar A.T. Robertson, drawing from the 10th century Byzantine Suidas Lexicon, describes this "bronze" as "an *elecktron* (amber) or a compound of copper and gold and silver." Robertson 292.

13. However, some have found an allusion here to the sword of Christ's chastening within the visible church. Theologian Stanley Horton comments, "It may be that the sword also speaks of reproof and punishment to the churches, judgment beginning in the house of God (1 Peter 4:17)." Stanley M. Horton, *The Ultimate Victory—An Exposition of the Book of Revelation* (Springfield, MO: Gospel Publishing House, 1991) 33.

14. Scholar John Walvoord states, "These messengers were probably the pastors of these churches or prophets through whom the message was to be delivered to the congregation." John F. Walvoord, *The Revelation of Jesus Christ* (Chicago: Moody, 1966) 53.

15. Again Walvoord writes, "As the churches were to emit light as a lampstand, the leaders of the churches were to project light as stars." Walvoord 45.

16. The verb here—*egenomen*, the aorist middle indicative of *ginomai,* "to become"— stands in stark contrast to Christ's eternality.

17. As the only reference to this event, many questions, if not quandaries, come to mind, e.g., were these raised into their natural bodies like Lazarus, only to die physically a second time, or were they raised at the point and as a result of the power of Christ's resurrection into their glorified bodies, only to ascend to Heaven at the point of Christ's ascension? Commentator David Guzik writes, "It is better to understand that Matthew intended us to see that the earthquake happened on the day Jesus was crucified. Then, on the day He was revealed as resurrected, the radiating power of new life was so great that it resuscitated some of the righteous dead."

   Guzik then quotes Charles Spurgeon, "These first miracles wrought in connection with the death of Christ were typical of spiritual wonders that will be continued till he comes again—rocky hearts are rent, graves of sin are opened, those who have been dead in trespasses and sins, and buried in sepulchers of lust and evil, are quickened, and come out from among the dead, and go unto the holy city, the New Jerusalem." Guzik, Jesus' Trial, Death, and Burial, "Study Guide for Matthew 27 by David Guzik." Blue Letter Bible 2010 <www.blueletterbible.org/Comm/ archives/guzik_david/studyguide_mat/mat_27.cfm>.

18. Josephus, Flavius. Concerning Christ, et al., "Josephus: The Complete Works." *Christian Classics Ethereal Library* 21 Apr. 2011 <www.ccel.org/ccel/josephus/complete.ii.xix.iii.html>.

19. Alfred John Church and William Jackson Brodribb, eds., "Cornelius Tacitus, The Annals," *Perseus Digital Library*, 2017 <www.perseus.tufts.edu/hopper/text?doc=Pers eus%3Atext%3A1999.02.
0078%3Abook%3D15%3Achapter%3D44>.

20. W.D. Mahan. ed., McIntosh and Twyman, trans., Genoa, Italy, *The Archko Volume; or, the Archeological writings of the Sanhedrim and Talmuds of the Jews.* From manuscripts in Constantinople and the records of the Senatorial Docket taken from the Vatican of Rome. Second edition, (Philadelphia: Antiquarian Book Company, 1896).

21. The great orator and pastor Charles Spurgeon, shared these profound words, "The great fault of many professors is that Christ is to them a character upon paper, certainly more than a myth, but yet a person of the dim past, an historical person who lived many years ago, and did most admirable deeds, by which we are saved, but who is far from being a living, present, bright reality. Many think of Jesus as gone away, they know not where, and He is little more actual and present to them than Julius Caesar or any other remarkable personage of antiquity. We have a way, somehow, a very wicked way it is, of turning the facts of Scripture into romances, exchanging solidities for airy notions, regarding the august sublimities of faith as dreamy, misty fancies, rather than substantial matters of fact. It is a grand thing personally to know the Christ of God as a living existence, to speak into His ear, to look into His face, and to understand that we live in Him, and that He is always with us, even to the end of the world." Charles H. Spurgeon, "John's First Doxology," *Charles H. Spurgeon Sermons* 2017 <ssca.virtuebible.com/volume_29/1749-johns-first-doxology/>.

CHAPTER 2

Revelation 2:1-29

Words from the One Who Knows Us Best — Part 1

Introduction to Revelation 2:1-29

As noted in 1:19, Revelation follows a three-part outline. Having recorded the four-fold glorious revelation of Christ's presence, filling up "what you have seen," John now records through the Spirit "what is now." Here, Jesus speaks directly to seven real and prominent churches (1:4, 11), which were well established by the time of this writing, and which, no doubt, were well-known to John. Contained in Chapter 2, then, are messages to the first four of these seven churches located in the ancient and influential cities of Ephesus, Smyrna, Pergamum, and Thyatira. Together with the remaining three, these cities were laid out along what appears on a map as an inverted "u" within the region of Asia Minor, and all of them within one long modern-day's drive. Interestingly, in the ancient world these seven cities were positioned along a Roman postal circuit. A parallel can be seen, inasmuch as John's order of addressing these seven follows in geographical order from the southwestern start of this inverted "u" northward and then southward to the southeastern ending of this "u." Possibly then, it can be said that John and his associates carried "God's mail" along this ancient postal route.

In the modern world, the counterparts to all seven of these ancient cities continue to be strong population centers in western-most Turkey, though for the most part their names have changed. Furthermore, the existing ruins of the seven ancient cities, lying within or near to the contemporary cities, do vary in measure, Ephesus, Pergamum, and Sardis being the best preserved.

Now it needs to be understood that students of the Bible generally acknowledge three primary ways of reading and receiving the messages of Jesus to these seven churches. (These three are addressed within the larger context of the Four Primary Views to Understanding the Meaning of Revelation in the Introduction to this study.) The first approach is to see a message directly and specifically addressed to the real issues of each of these first century local churches. In fact, some scholars find that every detail of John's record speaks to situations known in each church and in each locale of that day.

A second approach is to see that these relevant messages to very real churches speak also to the entire Church of Jesus Christ in every part of Church history. Thus, what was true of them by principle and application is still true 2,000 years later to us. It should be noted that while the seven churches of Revelation 2 and 3 were not the most influential of all local churches of that day, they certainly were remarkably representative of the issues of the Church at large. It is also reasonable to find in the number "seven"—to the Jewish mind, a number of completion—a means of representing and speaking to all local churches everywhere at all times. This view is strengthened by Christ's own seven-fold appeal at the conclusion of each message, "He who has an ear, let him hear what the Spirit says to the churches." "He" generically includes all who would read this prophecy; and in this way, we are all to receive not only through one church, but also through the messages to the "churches" plural. Furthermore, Jesus' own words in Revelation 3:5 reinforce this view by identifying a group of listeners who are distinct from the remnant of Sardis, the original recipients. "*The one*," in future days, "who is victorious will, *like them*, be dressed in white" (italics added).

Still a third approach to reading and receiving the messages to the seven churches is to view them as seven successive eras within the span of Church history, from the early Church to the Church just before the return of Christ. Thus, though these ancient churches were real, they were more so to be viewed as symbolic and prophetic of conditions and events in future periods of Church history. Following this view, many students of the Word find strong parallel in the details contained in the words of Jesus—both in commending and correcting—applied first to the ancient churches and then more fully to the historic situations of later Church periods. While many who approach the entirety of Revelation as futurists also take this historical approach to the seven messages, we must all be careful to not allow our subjectivity to strain the interpretation and application.

Trusting the Holy Spirit, who is faithful and able to speak "to the churches" then and now, we must be reminded that it is Jesus, the Head of the Church, who is seen "among the lampstands" (1:13). He is the One who inspects and assesses the Church, because He is the One Who knows us best. It should be noted that with little exception the messages to each of the seven churches follow a clear pattern of words of affirmation and encouragement followed by words of correction and warning, which then is followed by words of blessing and promise.

The Message to the Church in Ephesus—2:1-7

[1] "To the angel of the church in Ephesus write: These are the words of him who holds the seven stars in his right hand and walks among the seven golden lampstands. [2] I know your deeds, your hard work and your perseverance. I know that you cannot tolerate wicked people, that you have tested those who claim to be apostles but are not, and have found them false. [3] You have persevered and have endured hardships for my name, and have not grown weary. [4] Yet I hold this against you: You have forsaken the love you had at first. [5] Consider how far you have fallen! Repent and do the things you

did at first. If you do not repent, I will come to you and remove your lampstand from its place. [6] But you have this in your favor: You hate the practices of the Nicolaitans, which I also hate.[7] Whoever has ears, let them hear what the Spirit says to the churches. To the one who is victorious, I will give the right to eat from the tree of life, which is in the paradise of God.

Biblical Insights

Background Information

The ancient city of Ephesus, located in the westernmost part of Asia Minor, was situated on the Cayster River near to where it emptied into the Aegean Sea.[1] In John's day, Ephesus was a large and influential city of about 250,000 residents, serving as the economic and religious center of the district of Lydia and of the entire Roman province of Asia. For this reason, its citizens boasted in her wealth and luxury. But to her shame, this center for the worship of the Greek goddess Artemis (known as Diana to the Romans) was infested with idol worship and sexual perversion.[2] To worship Artemis, the goddess of the hunt, wild animals, virginity, and childbirth was to engage in prostitution. Insight to the hold those demonic powers associated with the worship of Artemis had upon Ephesus is presented by Luke in Acts 19:23-28, 34-35:

> About that time there arose a great disturbance about the Way. A silversmith named Demetrius, who made silver shrines of Artemis, brought in a lot of business for the craftsmen there. He called them together, along with the workers in related trades, and said: 'You know, my friends, that we receive a good income from this business. And you see and hear how this fellow Paul has convinced and led astray large numbers of people here in Ephesus and in practically the whole province of Asia. He says that gods made by human hands are no gods at all. There is danger not only that our trade will lose its good name, but also that the temple of the great goddess Artemis will be discredited; and the goddess herself, who is worshiped throughout the province of Asia and the world, will be robbed of her divine majesty.' When they heard this, they were furious and began shouting: 'Great is Artemis of the Ephesians!' [. . .] But when they realized he was a Jew, they all shouted in unison for about two hours: 'Great is Artemis of the Ephesians!' The city clerk quieted the crowd and said: 'Fellow Ephesians, doesn't all the world know that the city of Ephesus is the guardian of the temple of the great Artemis and of her image, which fell from heaven?'

Luke also provides understanding of the role of Ephesus as a center for occult practice in Acts 19:19, "A number who had practiced sorcery brought their scrolls together and burned them publicly. When they calculated the value of the scrolls, the total came to fifty thousand drachmas." In stark contrast, God showed forth His authority there with extraordinary miracles, healings, and deliverances (v. 11).

Words of Affirmation and Encouragement—2:1-3, 6

It is to this Ephesian church, which sought to please God in the midst of dismal paganism, that Jesus said, (v. 1) "These are the words of him who holds the seven stars in his right hand [...]." The word for "holds," here, *krateo,* speaks of holding firmly, a stronger word than *echon* (from *Herecho,* to have), which John uses for "held" in 1:16. In a day when even Christians were tempted to fear the crushing grip of Rome and of its emperor, Jesus speaks with reassuring words, in effect, "I hold your leadership and I hold you in the right hand of my favor and protection." And, in a day when believers were hated and misrepresented everywhere, Jesus speaks with calming words, "I walk in your midst." To the Ephesian church, Jesus speaks as their Sovereign Lord.

As was explained from the last verse of Chapter 1, John was directed to write this message "to the angel of the church in Ephesus," namely the pastor or another appointed leader of this local church. Though we cannot be certain of the identity of this "angel," we do know that the Apostle Paul had founded this church several decades before (Acts 18:19-21; 19:1-11) and that his ministry was followed by such outstanding ministers as Priscilla and Aquila; Apollos; Gaius and Aristarchus; other elders; and finally, Timothy (Acts 18:19-28; 19:29; 20:17 and 1 Tim. 1:3). Broadening the appeal and application of this message, Jesus also reminds this church that He holds all "seven stars in his right hand" and "walks among" all "seven golden lamp-stands." They, like we, were not alone in this world.

With all authority, Jesus begins to speak with affirmation and encouragement, "I know your deeds, your hard work and your perseverance." Seven times the Head of the Church will declare, "I know" (2:9, 13, 19; 3:1, 8, 15), using the word *oida,* which speaks of God's complete and full knowledge (as compared to *ginosko,* which would indicate knowledge learned progressively).[3] "Deeds" (*erga,* works, activities) here refers to the spiritual accomplishments of these believers. "Hard work" (*kopon,* labor, toil) then refers to the intensity of their service for the Lord, which was fulfilled with "perseverance" (*hupomonēn*), a patient endurance under pressure and despite hardships. The Lord's commendation of the Ephesian church is similar to the commendation of the Spirit through Paul to the Thessalonian church where all three words, *ergon, kopos,* and *hupomone* are combined in 1 Thessalonians 1:3. Closely related is the promise given to every believer in Hebrews 6:10, "God is not unjust; he will not forget your work and the love you have shown him as you have helped his people and continue to help them."

It is also to this church's credit that they could not "tolerate" (from bastazō, in the sense of support) "wicked" (*kakos,* morally evil) people. Outside the church was grievous paganism; inside the church was insidious heresy. Jesus himself warned of false teachers and false prophets who would come in amongst the flock as "ferocious wolves" (Matt. 7:15-16). Paul later spoke the following directly to the Ephesian elders thirty years before this Revelation was written, "I know that after I leave, savage wolves will come in among you and will not spare the flock" (Acts 20:29). In the same way that Paul had earlier encountered them in the city of Corinth (2 Cor. 11:5, 13-15; 12:11), these false ministers in Ephesus now attempted to cover their lies under the self-appointed title of "apostle." But these were "tested" (from *peirazō*, in the sense of "try" and "prove"; cf. 2 Cor. 13:5) and found to be false. John would himself write generally to the Church, "Dear friends, do not believe every spirit, but test [here, *dokimazō*, in the sense of "prove," "examine," or "discern"] the spirits to see whether they are from God, because many false prophets have gone out into the world" (1 John 4:1).

In v. 6, as an extension of Christ's affirmation, we read of one specific heretical group that had troubled the Ephesian church, "But you have this in your favor: You hate the practices of the Nicolaitans, which I also hate." Only here and in Christ's message to the church in Pergamum, which was rebuked for having those who held to their teaching (2:15), is reference to the Nicolaitans found in the Bible. Extra-biblically, we have the assertions of several Church Fathers that this false movement was founded by Nicolaus, the proselyte of Antioch, one of the seven first deacons listed in Acts 6:5.[4]

What both Christ and the Ephesian church continue to "hate" (abhor and detest; and again, in 2:15) are the "practices" (*erga*, "works," in the sense of their actions) of the Nicolaitans. Opinion about what these heretics taught and lived out generally follows along two lines of thought (though it is quite possible that both assertions could be true of this same group). The first approach finds evidence toward an oppressive clerical hierarchy in the meaning of the name "Nicolaitans" built upon *nikaō*, meaning, "to conquer" and *laos*, meaning, "the people."[5]

A second approach builds upon the movement's likely relationship to "Nicolas from Antioch, a convert to Judaism" (Acts 6:5) with an emphasis on his non-Jewish roots. Raised a gentile in a pagan world, he would have been well familiar with the immoral practices and occult activity of his surroundings.[6] Again, some Early Church Fathers indicate that this same deacon had fallen back into a compromised life, actually teaching the poisonous lie that active participation in sin—which then would have involved sexual immorality and idolatry—is totally compatible with faith in Christ.[7] Additional strength to this view comes in light of the fact that Jesus himself would soon relate the "teaching" (or "doctrine") of the Nicolaitans with that of Balaam (2:14), "who taught Balak to entice the Israelites to sin so that they ate food sacrificed to idols and committed sexual immorality." (It is also interesting that the only two cities Jesus associated with the Nicolaitans, i.e., Ephesus and Pergamum, were two of the most influentially pagan cities of Asia Minor.) To this heresy and vice, the Early Church Council in Jerusalem had long before given clear warning as recorded in Acts 15:20.

Christ's words of affirmation and encouragement to the Ephesian church are completed with verse 3. Under the heavy hand of persecution and the steady barrage of temptation to conformity, God's people had "persevered" (from *bastazō*, "to bear, to carry," [cf. v. 2]). They had carried those burdens that attend Christ's call, for He had told them, "And whoever does not carry their cross and follow me cannot be my disciple" (Luke 14:27). They had also "endured hardships," more literally, they "continued in patience" (*hypomonē*); as in v. 2, they were holding up under trials. This they did for the sake of Christ's name, while not growing "weary" through it all. They had gladly received Christ's invitation, "Come to me, all you who are weary and burdened, and I will give you rest" (Matthew 11:28). In all, they were careful to follow Paul's instruction: "Let us not become weary in doing good, for at the proper time we will reap a harvest if we do not give up" (Galatians 6:9; cf. 2 Thess. 3:13).

Words of Correction and Warning — 2:4-5

The church in Ephesus had believed rightly and acted rightly, but over time the flame of their spiritual fervor had died down. So Jesus, Who has absolute and complete knowledge of the individual and corporate heart, now speaks correction to His people, "You have forsaken ['actively left'] the love you had at first" (cf. Mark 12:30 and 1 John 4:7-10, 19-21). No one knew better than the Baptizer himself that this church had been birthed in Pentecostal fire (Acts 19:1-6). Yet now, the backslidden state of this second generation of believers was prevalent enough for the One who "walks among the seven golden lampstands" to say, "Yet I hold this against you" and, "Consider [lit. 'continue to remember'] how far you have fallen [*ekpiptō*, as also in Gal. 5:4 and 2 Pet. 3:17]."[8]

How sad that Jesus not only saw the unfaithfulness of that ancient day, but also of our current day when He warned, "Because of the increase of wickedness, the love of most will grow cold" (Matthew 24:12). But the converse is also true to the glory of God; both then and now, "he who stands firm to the end will be saved" (24:13). Praise God that Christ "is able to keep you from falling away ['stumbling'] and will bring you with great joy into his glorious presence without a single fault" (Jude 24, NLT).

Christ's corrective for their spiritual cooling off is clear: "repent" (aorist active imperative of *metanoeō* [here in 2:5 twice and in 2:16, 21, 22; 3:3, 19]). Literally, Jesus commands, "change your mind now!" And then, "do [again, aorist active imperative of *poieō*] the things you did at first." (The prayerful words of Paul for this church— which had at first moved in their first love for Christ in response to His great love for them—are brought to mind from Ephesians 1:15-19.) Jesus pleads in effect, "first change your mind, then change your ways." To refuse repentance and renewal leaves only one equally clear alternative. "If you do not repent, I will come to you ['quickly' (*tachei*) is included here in the Textus Receptus] and remove your lampstand from its place." What a terrible thought, that Jesus would, because of their rejection of Him corporately or individually, no longer walk in their midst. Yet, so it is when the love of God is replaced by a compromising love for this world (1 John 2:15; 5:21).

Words of Blessing and Promise—2:7

What is spoken to the Church at large and to the local church then and now is also spoken to the individual in the word "whoever." "To hear" (also 2:11, 17, 28; 3:3, 6, 13, 22) implies faith and obedience on the part of each reader, as in 1:3, "who hear it and take to heart what is written in it." We have heard these words from Jesus before in Matthew 11:15; 13:9, 43; Mark 4:9, 23; and Luke 8:8; 14:35. Now filling up His eternal position as anointed Prophet, Priest, and King, He speaks to His Church from Heaven by His Spirit with great assurance of hope (John 14:26; 16:7-15).

The promise given from the beginning of this revelation—"Blessed is the one who reads aloud the words of this prophecy" (1:3)—will in these seven messages unfold with multifaceted blessings from God. "To the one who is victorious" indicates the continuous victory of the true believer. An overcoming life of faith, which conquers over the flesh, the spirit of this world, and the kingdom of darkness (cf. 1 John 2:16-17; 5:4-5; and also Rom. 8:37) is grounded in *nikaō* ("to overcome, to conquer") so common in John's writings (John 16:33; 1 John 2:13-14; 4:4; 5:4-5; Rev. 2:11, 17, 26; 3:5, 12, 21; 5:5; 12:11; 15:2; 17:14; 21:7; etc.).

To those who are victorious through their faith in Jesus, He "will give the right to eat from the tree of life" (2:7; 22:14). This physical tree with spiritual and eternal implications is first seen in Genesis 2:9 positioned in the middle of the Garden of Eden along with the tree of the knowledge of good and evil. To be clear, Adam and Eve were welcomed to eat of the Tree of Life, which would have actuated God's provision of immortality, the blessing of living eternally in wholeness of life—spirit, soul, and body—in close relationship with God. It was rather the tree of the knowledge of good and evil that was forbidden to them, which represented in the act of eating the prideful will of self, rebelling against God's authority and declaring themselves independent. Genesis 2:16-17 states, "And the Lord God commanded the man, 'You are free to eat from any tree in the garden; but you must not eat from the tree of the knowledge of good and evil, for when you eat of it you will surely die'." More insight into the consequences of their disobedience is then spelled out in Genesis 3:22, "And the Lord God said, 'The man has now become like one of us, knowing good and evil. He must not be allowed to reach out his hand and take also from the tree of life and eat, and live forever'." Paul, by the Spirit in Romans 5:12-19, is clear in identifying Adam's sin—and our evidential co-participation in his sin ("because all sinned" [v. 12])—as the source of death, physically and spiritually.

Our sin had not destroyed the Tree of Life; it had only placed it beyond our reach. Its fuller and final location is now declared at the end of the Bible! The Tree of Life "is in the paradise of God." "Paradise," originally a Persian word, meant to the Jewish mind the "garden" of God. (See also Luke 23:43 and 2 Corinthians 12:2, 4.) No more just the temporary, intermediate residence of the righteous dead, "paradise" in the Book of Revelation indicates our eternal residence in the "third Heaven," the very dwelling place of God. In fact, John will later (22:2) describe in detail this tree that brings eternal abundance and healing. (Ezekiel [47:1-5] had already seen this blessing prophetically.) And so here Jesus promises to His victorious children that all lost through sin is now rediscovered by faith. Victoriously in Jesus alone, we have found the reversal of the curse, forgiveness, and restoration!

Life Application

Of the modern-day locations of the seven churches of the Revelation, Ephesus by far offers the greatest historic record. Each week, tourists by the thousands trek the several miles of Roman roads, still paved with slabs of marble and lined with full and partial marble columns.[9] Remarkably preserved and conspicuously situated is the Great Theatre, capable of holding 24,000 spectators. Clearly evident along the semi-circular auditorium are deep ravines, which once caught the flowing blood of gladiators and slain believers.[10] Yet, the once great Imperial Rome that ruled the ancient world with an iron fist in John's day is no more. Empty are its temples and its "love houses" where sexual immorality interlaced pagan religion with pagan debauchery. Empty is the Library of Celsus, where once countless scrolls of vain philosophies lined its ornate shelves. These ruins testify to the brevity, if not the futility, of humanity's best-laid plans when absent of God's approval.

Within a short walk is the alleged tomb of John the Revelator. It is said that from his nearby home he could hear the cheering Roman crowds, who found a depraved satisfaction in watching the gruesome and savage executions of his brothers and sisters in Christ. Within a short drive, hidden away high on the other side of a nearby mountain is a dwelling which many religionists and scholars believe to be the ancient home of Mary, the mother of Jesus. Secluded and protected, John honored the last words of his Master, and first cousin, to care for His own mother.

The Ephesian church is the first to hear Jesus say, "I know." He walks in the midst of His Church; He speaks to His own; and He knows us best. The words of Samuel come to mind, "The Lord does not look at the things people look at. People look at the outward appearance, but the Lord looks at the heart" (1 Samuel 16:7). To be sure, Jesus did not find a country club attitude in the believers of Ephesus. They were ardent in their service for the Lord; they persevered and held up despite the strong pressure to crack under the weight of unthinkable persecution. Nor did they compromise what was happening inside their own ranks; they were diligent to protect pure doctrine. Every indication was that they were on fire for Jesus. But things were changing, and it was breaking the heart of God.

"First love" love tends to be very expressive love and very extravagant love. It is the deep, fiery love that we had when we first believed—when our world changed and our hearts were free in Jesus. It is the devoted love that makes and takes every opportunity to commune in prayer and in His Word. But could anything be worse than to hear Jesus say, "You don't love me like you used to"? As if He pleads, "Don't you remember what we had together; have you already forgotten how your heart soared in my love!" "You used to be like Mary, but now you seem so much more like Martha." What could be worse than to hear our Bridegroom say, "You have forsaken your first love"? If the words, "You don't love me like you used to" are the wake-up call that can save an earthly marriage, then to hear this word from Jesus is the wake-up call that can save your eternity.

Brother, sister, He knows us best; and He knows the danger of a drifting heart! Be on your guard; every demon in hell and the spirit of this world wants to make a pass at you! So, when the world wants to court you, you answer back, "My heart belongs to another!" And may the call of Jesus resonate in the heart of the Church of any age in any place, which has become a sub-culture instead of a counter-culture, which settles for vain acceptance instead of impassioned influence.

And some today as in John's day will hear Jesus calling. Some will remember, repent, and return to their first love. These have always been the winners in God's book; these are the overcomers! These are the lovers of God who are led back to the Garden of God's presence. These are the partakers of His life. "I will give the right to eat from the tree of life, which is in the paradise of God." What a far different picture is this garden now than it was back in the day when humanity's rebellion drove us out of reach of the Tree of Life. What less could God do with a renegade pair than to keep them—and us—from the unthinkable and the impossible, from rotting on the vine?

When I was a kid, growing in my side yard were two very tall, mature pear trees. Thinking back, the memory of those trees is bitter sweet. It's not that my family didn't enjoy juicy pears; it's that those trees were so productive that we had more pears than we could eat or even give away by the bags full. The bitter reality (as I remember it) was that pears by the hundreds would fall to the ground only to rot there, to the delight of a small army of squirrels and swarms of yellow jacket bees. But here's the lesson that lives on in my mind: you will never find a tree loaded with rotten fruit! No, first the fruit falls from the tree, and then in that place—removed from the tree—it rots.

In guarding the way to the Tree of Life from rebellious humanity, God was saying, "I will not put my seal of approval on your spiritual rottenness. If you choose to live rotten lives, then you're going to fall from the spiritual and eternal blessings of this Tree, namely, immortality, eternal wholeness of life—spirit, soul, and body—in unbroken intimacy with your God." The timeless message of separation from the Tree of Life is unchanging. To be sure, sin will always place the blessings of God beyond the reach of rebellion!

But praise God, if turning from God costs us everything, turning back to God through His Son restores everything! A world of change has come to the winners who follow the Revelation of Jesus. In this new Garden view (Rev. 2:7 and 22:1-3), the curse is lifted and death has forever lost its grip. Here a pure river flows again, and wherever it flows everything lives. Amazingly, in this reinstated Garden, the Tree of Life has been multiplied; in fact, here we will find "a great number of trees on each side of the river" (Ezekiel 47:7). In this restored Paradise, the trees are laden down with an abundant supply of life-giving food, trees that never stop bearing fruit, trees so powerful that even their leaves provide healing.

And to the one who might dare say, "But John and Ezekiel were looking down the road; I need a now experience," the promise to the overcomer is a present revelation. What will be true of Heaven then has already been planted in us now—in fact, the Life of Jesus is already taking root. Listen to ancient Solomon speak under the Spirit's anointing of the now reality of life in Jesus. Wisdom is "a tree of life to those who embrace her" (Proverbs 3:18); righteousness too is "a tree of life" (11:30). To the overcomer now, hope in the heart is "a tree of life" (13:12) and "a tree of life" (15:4) is the source of healing words.

Real winners have embraced the central, timeless message of this Revelation. Real living is the fruit of a personal relationship with the Son of man; it's about Jesus planted right in the center of your life, His life becoming yours!

The Message to the Church in Smyrna—2:8-11

[8] "To the angel of the church in Smyrna write: These are the words of him who is the First and the Last, who died and came to life again. [9] I know your afflictions and your poverty—yet you are rich! I know about the slander of those who say they are Jews and are not, but are a synagogue of Satan. [10] Do not be afraid of what you are about to suffer. I tell you, the devil will put some of you in prison to test you, and you will suffer persecution for ten days. Be faithful, even to the point of death, and I will give you life as your victor's crown.[11] Whoever has ears, let them hear what the Spirit says to the churches. The one who is victorious will not be hurt at all by the second death.

Biblical Insights

Background Information

Nearly forty miles north of Ephesus was located Smyrna, modern day Izmir, Turkey's third largest city with over three million inhabitants. In John's day, the city was already an influential and prosperous harbor city of over 100,000 citizens. Its idyllic location along the sea, surrounded by hills and dotted with groves of trees, inspired the ancient Smyrnaeans to stamp on some of their coins the motto "First of Asia in Beauty and Size."[11] But the city's beauty was only outward, for Smyrna was permeated with pagan worship and allegiance to a pantheon of gods and goddesses. Along its "Golden Street" alone were temples dedicated to Zeus, Apollo, Aphrodite, Asklepios, and Cybele Sipylene, the mother goddess. Still another temple was built in honor of Emperor Tiberius, reflecting the city's close alliance with Rome.

Unlike our biblical knowledge of the founding of the church in Ephesus, the New Testament is silent about the founding of the church in Smyrna. Yet, knowing that Paul ministered in nearby Ephesus for three years (Acts 20:31), it is highly probable that he personally, or through his ministry partners, had brought spiritual influence to the city. While we don't know with certainty the one whom John addresses as "the angel of the church in Smyrna," we do know that the city's most recognized church leader and martyr was Bishop Polycarp (A.D. 69 – c.156). That he was himself a student of the Apostle John gives weight to this idea.

Words of Affirmation and Encouragement — 2:8-10a

Reminiscent of Christ's earlier words to John in Revelation 1:17, Jesus presents Himself to the church in Smyrna as the "First and the Last," the timeless and self-existent One. And again, as in 1:18, He is also the resurrected Lord. Some Bible students have found a parallel in the history of the city itself. More than four hundred years after being destroyed and demoralized, Smyrna experienced a rebirth as a Greek metropolis in 290 B.C. Whether the parallel was intended or not, the restoration and hope of the believer is infinitely greater through Christ's victory over death itself.

It is more likely that Christ intended His proclamation as the One "who died and came to life again" as a glorious and triumphal indictment against the gross spiritual darkness of the city. We can find parallel in His declaration in Matthew 16:18, "the gates of Hades will not overcome [His church]," which He spoke near to the pagan "Gate of Hell" shrine in Caesarea Philippi. Darkest in the paganism of Smyrna was the mystery cult worship of Dionysus, the god of wine. In part, the veneration of this demonic entity was intended to celebrate the alleged bestial side of man. The "worship" of Dionysus involved ecstatic and unbridled orgies and live sacrifices, both animal and human, and with this often cannibalism. Most blasphemous of all was the annual ritual, which re-enacted the supposed life, death, burial, descent into the underworld, and resurrection of Dionysus. Those priests who officiated were given crowns for their identity with their god.

As in 2:2, the Risen and triumphant Jesus has full and complete knowledge of His Church. The One who himself had become "poor" (*ptōcheia*) for us (2 Cor. 8:9) sees both the pressing "afflictions" (*thlipsis*) of their persecution and the abject "poverty" (*ptōcheia*) which it was causing them.[12] Nevertheless, Jesus declares them to be "rich" (*plousios*), here meaning that they were wealthy in spiritual virtues. The promise of "spiritual wealth" is widespread in the New Testament (cf. Luke 12:21; Rom. 10:12; 2 Cor. 6:10; 8:2, 9; 1 Tim. 6:18; Jas. 2:5; and Rev. 3:18). How completely opposite will be Christ's disclosure of the spiritual condition of the church in Laodicea (3:17)!

Jesus also knows the "slander" (*blasphēmia*), literally the blasphemy or defamatory speech, coming from those "who say they are Jews." History tells us that the large Jewish population of Smyrna, in their rejection of Jesus, often incited violence against and brought false accusations against believers. But the Word of God claims that these are Jews, in name only, for "A person is not a Jew who is one only outwardly, [...] No, a person is a Jew who is one inwardly [...]" (Romans 2:28-29; cf. Gal. 6:15). With the same indictment that Jesus once spoke to the unbelieving Jews who reviled Him—"You belong to your father, the devil" (John 8:44)—He now speaks against those who persecute His Church. These, He says, "are a synagogue of Satan" (cf. 3:9). The slandering nature of the Devil (*diabolos*, meaning "false accuser") himself will be seen in 12:9-10.

And here we must remember the martyrdom of Polycarp in approximately A.D. 156. At a time when Smyrna was committed to emperor worship, this great Church leader refused to participate in the annual ritual of offering a pinch of incense on the altar in adoration of Caesar. This act and the confession that "Caesar is Lord" would assure good standing; but Polycarp would not! *The Martyrdom of Saint Polycarp* (c. A.D. 160), an early and reliable account of the execution of this great Bishop and also of other believers in Smyrna, gives amazing insight into the circumstances surrounding his death and of his unbending faithfulness toward God and God's unbounded grace toward him in the hour of his sufferings. Here we read:

(Chapter 5) And while he was praying, it so happened, three days before his arrest, that he had a vision and saw his pillow blazing with fire, and turning to those who were with him he said, 'I must be burned alive.'

(Chapter 9) But as Polycarp was entering the arena, a voice from heaven came to him, saying, 'Be strong, Polycarp, and play the man.' No one saw the one speaking, but those of our people who were present heard the voice. And when finally, he was brought up, there was a great tumult on hearing that Polycarp had been arrested. Therefore, when he was brought before him, the proconsul asked him if he were Polycarp. And when he confessed that he was, he tried to persuade him to deny [the faith], saying, 'Have respect to your age'—and other things that customarily follow this, such as, 'Swear by the fortune of Caesar; change your mind; say, "Away with the atheists!"' But Polycarp looked with earnest face at the whole crowd of lawless heathen in the arena, and motioned to them with his hand. Then, groaning and looking up to heaven, he said, 'Away with the atheists!' But the proconsul was insistent and said: 'Take the oath, and I shall release you. Curse Christ.' Polycarp said: 'Eighty-six years I have served him, and he never did me any wrong. How can I blaspheme my King who saved me?'

(Chapter 12) When this was said by the herald, the entire crowd of heathen and Jews who lived in Smyrna shouted with uncontrollable anger and a great cry: 'This one is the teacher of Asia, the father of the Christians, the destroyer of our gods, who teaches many not to sacrifice nor to worship.'

We also learn in Chapter 13 that the unbelieving Jews were not only complicit with his death, but that they, on the Sabbath, carried the wood for the pyre.[13]

As Polycarp's martyrdom would demonstrate, Jesus warns these first century believers that the pressure of persecution they now face would soon grow worse. The word for the "suffering" they will increasingly endure is *paschō*, the same as used of the passionate suffering of Christ (Acts 1:3). On the basis of four truths, Jesus then encourages them not to fear. First, though the Devil himself is behind this oppression, these hardships will serve "to test" (*peirazō*, "to try, test, or prove") them. Even imprisonment and death will provide opportunities to prove the quality of their faith and devotion to Christ. (For the advantage of proven faith, see Romans 5:3-5; 2 Corinthians 13:5; Hebrews 11:17, 37; and 1 Peter 1:7.) Jesus himself has both endured this "test" (Matthew 4:1, 3) and is able to help us when we too are tested (1 Corinthians 10:13; Hebrews 2:18; 4:15).

A second word of encouragement through persecution is that their suffering would come only for a defined period of time, i.e., "ten days." While it is clear that these are not literal days, some scholars have claimed that these refer to ten specific and extended periods of persecution under successive Roman emperors. But this is questionable and includes some persecutions already having taken place. It is more likely that Jesus intends that they know that the days of their suffering, while intense, will be limited.[14]

Words of Blessing and Promise—2:10b-11

A third truth about their suffering continues to provide encouragement. To this Church, along with the church in Philadelphia, comes no rebuke, no words of correction, as it came to all the others. Rather we now hear a promised reward to these who may even die for their faith. The believers' "faithfulness"—actively trusting God and passively being trustworthy (the second is indicated by the grammar here)—is expressed toward Christ himself. His word to Paul through Ananias was, "I will show him how much he must suffer for my name" (Acts 9:16). In return He would give these martyrs "the crown of life." Unlike a king's royal diadem, this crown (*stephanos*) was well known in the Greek athletic world as the wreath (of ivy, laurel, or others) given to winners. (See *stephanos* also in 1 Corinthians 9:25; 1 Thessalonians 2:19; 2 Timothy 4:8; James 1:12; 1 Peter 5:4; and Revelation 3:11.) It is clear that the various rewards associated with the believer's crown—such as righteousness, glory, and rejoicing—all accompany our incorruptible, eternal life found only in Jesus. Even in death these faithful believers will be presented the "victors crown."[15]

Again, the One who walks amongst the lampstands of His Church calls His followers both corporately and individually to actively "hear" with faith and obedience what the Spirit is speaking (2:7). To those who receive His Word as "overcomers" (*nikaō*) or "victors" still a fourth word of blessing, promise, and encouragement comes to these persecuted saints. Even in the face of physical death, they will not be "hurt" (*adikeō,* or "harmed," as in Luke 10:19) "by the second death." As in Revelation 20:6, this is the reward of the righteous who follow the Lamb of God; they will not die spiritually, nor will they find condemnation before the "great white throne" of God's judgment (20:11) as will unbelievers (20:14; 21:8). And so we remember the words of Jesus to Martha in the very face of her brother's death, "I am the resurrection and the life. The one who believes in me will live, even though they die; and whoever lives by believing in me will never die. Do you believe this?" (John 11:25-26).

Life Application

The very name "Smyrna" means myrrh, one of the leading exports of this ancient harbor city on the Aegean Sea. Beginning as mere tree sap, myrrh oozes as a gummy resin from a particular species of trees still found today throughout the Middle East and Northern Africa. Once processed, myrrh was greatly valued throughout the world as a perfume, incense, and even as a medicine.

Scripture itself places high value on myrrh. First in importance, it was to be an essential ingredient in the sacred anointing oil used in the worship of God in the tabernacle (Exod. 30:23). As a perfume, myrrh is referenced seven times in the Song of Solomon (1:13; 3:6; 4:6, 14; 5:1, 5, 13). Before presentation to her royal husband, Esther herself fulfilled a beauty regiment including "six months with oil of myrrh" (Esther 2:12). Even the coming Messiah is expected as a victorious Bridegroom whose "robes are fragrant with myrrh" (Psalm 45:8). In New Testament times, myrrh's great worth is seen as it was presented, along with gold and frankincense, by wise men from the East to the Christ child. And, as an antiseptic, ancient Jews also used myrrh in embalming their dead, as did Joseph of Arimathaea and Nicodemus with the body of Jesus (John 19:38-40).

However, we cannot miss a deeper meaning in the words Jesus chose to speak to the believers of Smyrna, the city of myrrh, and through them to us. Just as myrrh is obtained through the wounding of a thorny tree, which commonly grows in rocky, dry soil, so something very precious would rise from the wounds of His followers—"I know your afflictions and your poverty." While Smyrna means "myrrh," its root Hebrew meaning is "bitter." Bitter is the taste of the oily resin that flows when the bark is caused to bleed, but fragrant is its smell; and, sweet-scented are its leaves when they are crushed.

The suffering of those who even today are despised, slandered, imprisoned, tortured, and even put to death is not in vain! There are those who choose to say, "I want to know Christ—yes, to know the power of his resurrection and participation in his sufferings, becoming like him in his death" (Philippians 3:10). The Spirit of God testifies that the Father received the love of Christ, which took Him to the cross for us, "as a fragrant offering and sacrifice to God" (Ephesians 5:2). Becoming "like him in his death" the sacrifices of those who obey and endure for the cause of Christ are also remembered as a sweet-smelling fragrance before the Lord—"For we are to God the pleasing aroma of Christ among those who are being saved and those who are perishing" (2 Corinthians 2:15; see also Phil. 4:18).

Though for Christ's sake we are considered "foolish," "weak," "lowly," "despised," and of no significance (1 Cor. 1:27-28), Jesus considers us "rich!"—gloriously rich in His mercy, grace, power and love (Eph. 2:4, 7; 3:16-19). His message to the faithful has not changed, "Do not be afraid of what you are about to suffer" (Rev. 2:10). If in this life the enemies of Christ threaten your outward comfort, job security, at times even your physical wellbeing, then remember your victor's crown! They cannot take that away! What is it to you that in their ignorance they call you "loser"? Your God has crowned you a winner! And if in this life they inflict pain and even death, then remember the gift of eternal life. They cannot take that away! "Precious in the sight of the LORD is the death of his faithful servants" (Psalm 116:15), "absent from the body," but "present with the Lord" (2 Corinthians 5:8). If death comes, it has lost its sting (1 Cor. 15:55)! For the believer, it is merely the "first" death, physical in nature alone; and even that has been "swallowed up in victory" (15:54). It is not the "second," spiritual, death, which is the eternal destiny of the wicked. No! On the authority of the One "who died and came to life again" and of His Spirit Who still speaks to His Church, "The one who is victorious will not be hurt at all by the second death" (cf. Matt. 10:28).

The Message to the Church in Pergamum—2:12-17

[12] "To the angel of the church in Pergamum write: These are the words of him who has the sharp, double-edged sword. [13] I know where you live—where Satan has his throne. Yet you remain true to my name. You did not renounce your faith in me, not even in the days of Antipas, my faithful witness, who was put to death in your city—where Satan lives. [14] Nevertheless, I have a few things against you: There are some among you who hold to the teaching of Balaam, who taught Balak to entice the Israelites to sin so that they ate food sacrificed to idols and committed sexual immorality. [15] Likewise, you also have those who hold to the teaching of the Nicolaitans. [16] Repent therefore! Otherwise, I will soon come to you and will fight against them with the sword of my mouth. [17] Whoever has ears, let them hear what the Spirit says to the churches. To the one who is victorious, I will give some of the hidden manna. I will also give that person a white stone with a new name written on it, known only to the one who receives it.

Biblical Insights

Background Information

Some sixteen miles inland from the Aegean Sea and seventy miles north of Smyrna, the ancient city of Pergamum (also known as Pergamon) was situated on a large hill overlooking the fertile Caicus River Valley. Its very name meant "height" or "elevation" from a root word meaning "a fortified structure" or "tower." Unlike Ephesus and Smyrna, the city was known much more for its political influence than its commercial dealings. During the times of the Greek Empire, Pergamum had been the capital city of the Hellenistic Attalid dynasty of kings and of the Kingdom of Pergamum. However, the political future of the city thoroughly changed in 133 B.C. when the last Attalid king, Attalus III, having no successor, bequeathed his kingdom and capital city to the Roman Empire, apparently to avoid civil war. For the next 106 years, until the reign of Caesar Augustus in 27 B.C., Pergamum served, then, as the capital of the Roman province of Asia.

In John's day, this great Roman city was known as a leading center for religion, art, and education, with a population of 150,000. Built during the Attalid dynasty was the immense altar of Zeus, the king of the gods, situated high upon the acropolis of Pergamum. Adjacent was the distinguished Temple of Athena, the goddess of wisdom and warfare, as well as the Temple of Dionysus, the god of wine and revelry, and the precipitous 10,000-seat Theatre of Pergamum. Not long after John's death would also be erected here a majestic marble temple built in honor of the Roman Emperor Trajan.

Upon this acropolis was additionally located the great Library of Pergamum (built in the second century B.C. by King Eumenes II [d. 160 B.C.]), which was reputed to contain 200,000 volumes (second only to the library in Alexandria), later to be given as a gift by the Roman General Anthony to the Egyptian Queen Cleopatra. Contemporary to the founding of this library was the development of parchment (namely, calf, sheep, or goat skin) as a writing material, an alternative to the more costly papyrus, which was imported from Egypt. In fact, the very word "parchment" was derived from the Latin *Pergamena charta*, "paper of Pergamum."

On the valley floor, just west of the acropolis of Pergamum, was the sprawling Sanctuary of Asclepius, the Greek god of medicine and healing, which functioned as both spa resort and therapeutic center (dating back to the early fourth century B.C.). Here patients were directed to sleeping rooms or dormitories, providing "incubation," during which healing was expected through appearances of Asclepius and through dreams, which the next morning were reported to and interpreted by priests. Supposedly based upon these revelations, cures for sicknesses and injuries were then prescribed. These might involve any combination of the following: visits to the sacred water and mud baths; gymnasium exercise; special diets; the drinking of sacred water; the administering of medicinal herbs; study in the library; or even music therapy in the theatre. These healing arts attributed to the god Asclepius were often represented by a physician's staff with a snake wrapped around it (a symbol which has carried into modern day medicine). It is not surprising then that non-venomous snakes, in themselves a symbol of regeneration to the Greeks, were often released to crawl freely throughout the dormitories of the Asklepion.

Words of Affirmation and Encouragement—2:12-13

As with Smyrna the Bible does not reference the founding of the church in Pergamum nor does it describe its spiritual condition other than through John's reference here amongst the seven churches. However, again as with Smyrna, it is probable that the church was planted through the ministry of the Apostle Paul and his associates on his Third Missionary Journey (Acts 19:10). Yet we do not know with certainty the leader whom John addresses as "the angel of the church in Pergamum" (v. 12; see note under 1:20).

To this church Jesus presents himself as the "one who has the sharp, double-edged sword," as He had earlier revealed himself to John (1:16). Again, this is best seen as a long and heavy sword (*rhomphaia*), the "double-edged" Word of God (Eph. 6:17 and Heb. 4:12), which brings comfort to the righteous and terror to the wicked (Rev. 2:16; 19:15, 21). As the Word of God, the sword's "double-edged" nature may speak of its ability to bring salvation (or even chastening) to those who embrace Jesus and condemnation to those who reject Him. Certainly, we must keep the recipient of the Word of God in view according to context. To believers in Pergamum, the Word brings correction, but to unbelievers (as in 19:15 and 21) it can only speak of eternal judgment. It may also be that John's repetitive use of the definite article—"the sword," "the double-edged," "the sharp"—stands to emphasize the thoroughness of Christ's dealings, whether toward His children or His enemies.

To the faithful believers in Pergamum, Jesus says, "I know where you live."[16] "Live" (*katoikeō*) here carries the idea of settling down or dwelling. Despite increased persecution, these faithful believers were not running from the hostility, which Jesus described as "where Satan has his throne," an apt title in light of the pervasiveness of idolatry in this city. (Some students of the Word associate this phrase directly with the altar of Zeus, while others see it relating to the snake cult of Asclepius.) This prevalent evil is re-emphasized with the phrase "where Satan lives [again, *katoikeō*]." Yet despite all this pressure and opposition, Jesus is able to say to the church in Pergamum as a whole, "you remain true to my name" (NKJV, NASB, and ESV, more literally, "you hold fast," here, the present active indicative of *krateō* [cf. 2:25 and 3:11]). These believers continued to hold fast to the name of Jesus, which speaks of His person and His ministry. They also did not "renounce" (*arneomai*, "deny" or "reject") their faith, which had its focus in Christ, literally, "my faith."

One of their own brothers, who had already stayed true even unto death, was Antipas (perhaps a contraction of Antipater, his name then meaning "like a father" or "in place of a father"). Though Christian tradition, issuing first from Eastern Orthodoxy, holds that Antipas was the first Bishop of Pergamum and that he was appointed by John, he is referenced only here in the New Testament. What we know for sure is that he is called "my faithful witness" by Jesus. This is a remarkable acclamation in consideration that the phrase is used in this Revelation additionally only of Jesus himself (1:5, 3:14). Again, while tradition holds that Antipas was executed by being incinerate within a hollow bronze bull, we know only from the Word that he was "put to death" in Pergamum before this writing. It is in this passage, along with Stephen's martyrdom in Acts (7:54-60; 22:20), that we begin to see the common word for "witness" (*martys*; cf. Acts 1:8, 22) extended to include, if not imply, suffering unto death for Christ's sake (also 2:10; 6:11; 13:10, 15).

Words of Correction and Warning—2:14-16

As with the church in Ephesus, Jesus now must temper His commendation with rebuke, "I have a few things against you" (cf. 2:4). Christ's identity of the "some" who were "among" that church does not imply that they were indeed true believers, only that they were known to be in within their company (cf. 2 Tim. 2:20; 1 John 2:19). While true believers continued to "hold fast" (*krateō*) to the name of Jesus, others were falsely "holding" (present participle of *krateō*) "to the teaching of Balaam."

There is no question as to the complaint of the Lord here. What is told in detail in Numbers 22-25 is here briefly summarized. Though Balaam had been gifted by God to speak prophetically, Balak (then king of Moab) was still able to bribe him with wealth and promotion. (In rebuking the greed and deceit of false teachers, Peter exposes those who "follow the way of Balaam son of Beor, who loved the wages of wickedness" [2 Peter 2:15; and cf. "Balaam's error" in Jude 11]). And though, under this delusion, Balaam attempted to speak curses over Israel, the anointing of God caused him to speak only blessings (Num. 23-25). Nevertheless, with calculated rebellion Balaam finally advised the king on how to subdue the Israelites; he "taught Balak to entice [ballō skandalon] the Israelites to sin." Most versions more literally translate ballō skandalon ("a trap," "snare," or "stumbling block") as "to put [or cast] a stumbling block." We know from Numbers 25:1-3 that the men of Israel "began to indulge in sexual immorality with Moabite women, who invited them to the sacrifices to their gods. The people ate and bowed down before these gods." Remarkably, we then learn from Numbers 31:16 that this scheme to compromise and then overthrow Israel, came at "Balaam's advice."

Now in first century Pergamum, where civic life so interlocked with pagan religion, believers needed to make active decisions toward living a life above reproach. It was one matter to eat in one's own home meat purchased from the public market, even with the knowledge that this meat often had first been offered in sacrifice to idols in pagan temples. As a matter of Christian liberty, Paul had written, "Eat anything

REVELATION 2:1-29 **95**

purchased in the meat market without raising questions of conscience, for 'The earth is the Lord's, and everything in it'" (1 Corinthians 10:25-26). Yet, it was a far different matter for a believer to accept an invitation to, or to regularly frequent, those public events often held in heathen temples. Such festivities always centered upon heathen, false deities and did also often involve sexual immorality. Now as a matter of warning against compromise, Paul again wrote (10:18-21):

> Consider the people of Israel: Do not those who eat the sacrifices participate in the altar? Do I mean then that a sacrifice offered to an idol is anything, or that an idol is anything? No, but the sacrifices of pagans are offered to demons, not to God, and I do not want you to be participants with demons. You cannot drink the cup of the Lord and the cup of demons too; you cannot have a part in both the Lord's table and the table of demons.

To strengthen their resolve and to follow their convictions, Christians could also invoke the decision of the First Council of the Church held in Jerusalem in A.D. 49-50 and recorded in Acts 15:20, 29: "You are to abstain from food sacrificed to idols, from blood, from the meat of strangled animals and from sexual immorality. You do well to avoid these things."

Nevertheless, some in the visible church of Pergamum not only embraced the world's invitations to be present in the midst of what constituted idolatry and prostitution, but justified this poor judgment by placating it with their heretical doctrine— "the teaching of Balaam." With the word "likewise," Jesus directly associates this false teaching with "the teaching of the Nicolaitans" (v. 15). These false believers, too, attempted to justify their compromised lifestyles by claiming that faith in Christ and participation in sin was totally compatible. What the Ephesian church would not tolerate, some in Pergamum would not renounce (see notes under 2:6).

It is important next to note that Christ's warning to "repent" (*metanoeō*; lit. "change of mind"; cf. 2:5) comes to the entire church in Pergamum, as was clear from verse 14, "Nevertheless, I have a few things against you: There are some among you [...]." Further warning continues in verse 16 as he addresses the church at large as "you" and the offending party as "them"—"I will soon come to you and will fight against them." This should come as no surprise, "For it is time for judgment to begin with God's household" (1 Peter 4:17). The same warning came earlier to the church in Corinth, which sanctioned, by their apathy and silence, illicit immorality within their community of faith. By the Spirit, Paul had written in 1 Corinthians 5:1-2, 5:

> It is actually reported that there is sexual immorality among you, and of a kind that even pagans do not tolerate: A man is sleeping with his father's wife. And you are proud! Shouldn't you rather have gone into mourning and

have put out of your fellowship the man who has been doing this? [...] hand this man over to Satan for the destruction of the flesh, so that his spirit may be saved on the day of the Lord.

Knowing that sin was infiltrating that local church, Paul continued (verses 6-7a), "Your boasting is not good. Don't you know that a little yeast leavens the whole batch of dough? Get rid of the old yeast, so that you may be a new unleavened batch—as you really are." The Spirit's final word speaks to every local church that would walk honorably before the Lord, "[...] it certainly is your responsibility to judge those inside the church who are sinning" (1 Corinthians 5:12b, NLT).

Without corporate repentance, Jesus declares that He will "soon come to you" (cf. 2:5; 3:11; 22:7, 12, 20). This "coming" is in judgment upon the unrepentant within the Church, for Christ "will fight against them," a strong word, *polemeō* ("to fight or make war"). As already revealed in 1:16 and 2:12, the unrepentant will be judged with the sword of His Word (19:15, 21). Justly, those who hold to Balaam's teaching will receive Balaam's reward (cf. Josh. 13:22). (Compare also Paul's words in 1 Corinthians 3:17, "If anyone destroys God's temple, God will destroy that person; for God's temple is sacred, and you together are that temple.")

Words of Blessing and Promise—2:17
Now for the third time the Priestly Jesus, who knows His Church best, speaks by His Spirit from Heaven (see notes under 2:7). Those who faithfully listen and obey His words live in a position of "victory" (from *nikaō*) or "overcoming." In his Gospel, John had already recorded Christ's promise of an overcoming life for those who place their faith in Him (John 16:33). His first letter, as well, affirms this sure victory through faith (1 John 5:4; cf. 2:13, 14; 4:4).

To these overcomers Jesus pledges, "I will give some of the hidden manna." As one of the hundreds of Old Testament allusions in Revelation, we are reminded of the manna that God sent to sustain the Israelites in the wilderness (Exod. 16:4-31; Deut. 8:3, 16; Ps. 78:24-25). We read also that Aaron concealed an omer of this manna in a golden jar within the Ark of the Covenant (Exod. 16:33-34; Heb. 9:4). Ancient Jewish tradition further maintained that, in advance of Nebuchadnezzar's destruction of Jerusalem, the prophet Jeremiah hid the Ark in a sealed cave where it would be held safely till the final days when Israel is restored (cf. 2 Macc. 2:5-8; 2 Bar. 29:8). But to those who know Christ, the promise is much greater, for Christ himself is our fresh manna. "For the bread of God is he who comes down from heaven and gives life to the world. [...] Then Jesus declared, 'I am the bread of life. He who comes to me will never go hungry, and he who believes in me will never be thirsty" (John 6:33, 35).

Promised to the faithful believer is also "a white stone with a name written on it." Obscure in meaning today, this was well understood in John's day since several uses are known from this ancient period. Amongst these uses, white stones were given to victors of the ancient sporting games, granting them special privileges and access. White stones, engraved with the invitee's name, were also used to allow access as a guest to special events, such as to a banquet. Perhaps most importantly, white stones and black stones were used in ancient courts of law. While a black stone placed by a judge indicated guilt, a white stone was the sign of acquittal. Knowing that the righteous have been given "a name better than sons and daughters" (Isaiah 56:5; cf. 62:2) and that this name has been "written in Heaven" (Luke 10:20), it is this last application which seems to suit this passage best.

What a blessing it must have been to these believers in Pergamum, who found themselves surrounded by a pagan world rife with demonic secrets and dark mysteries, that the Righteous Jesus had given them a name "known only to the one who receives it." But there is also merit in the position that the "new name" written and known so personally is none other than Jesus' own name entrusted to every believer. Revelation 3:12b and 19:12b would lend credence to this interpretation (cf. 22:4). In both cases, what intimacy, what assurance, and what victory every faithful believer can know even in the midst of prevalent hardship for the Gospel's sake.

Life Application

"I know where you live." Whether residing in first century Pergamum or 21st century America, we can find comfort and assurance in hearing Jesus say that He knows the world in which we live. If believers in ancient Pergamum were surrounded by a prideful and boastful society, so are we today. If their world was diseased with immorality and wickedness, so is ours. If those early Christians were pressured to conform to a culture, so opposite the Kingdom of God, then so are we. But still Jesus says, "I know where you live"; "I understand your trials and I know about your temptations—and in all this you can know that 'my grace is sufficient for you, for my power is made perfect in weakness'" (2 Corinthians 12:9).

Portions of ancient Pergamum have been so well preserved that it is not hard to imagine this city in the height of its influence within the Roman Empire. Standing atop its sprawling acropolis and looking down upon its modern counterpart of Bergama, it is not hard to imagine the pride and boast of its ancient citizens. After all, there is much in her history, which testifies to human achievements. Here was the second greatest library in the world and the invention of parchment. Here was engineering brilliance, which built a 10,000-seat theatre into the side of a mountain and ornate marble statues and columns by the thousands. Here in the valley below was the Asklepion, a therapeutic center that staked its own claim in the history of medical arts and science.

But while walking these ancient grounds it is not hard to understand why Jesus Himself said, "I know where you live—where Satan has his throne." Wickedness and carnality was prevalent in this city whose centerpiece of social and religious life was the colossal and exquisite altar of Zeus, king and father of the gods, built high upon its acropolis. Nearby this place of sacrifice, two other temples had been consecrated to the dominant mythical deities Athena, Zeus's daughter and the goddess of wisdom, civilization, and strategic war and Dionysus, Zeus's son and the god of ritual madness and religious ecstasy.

Satan does not yet live in hell; he has not yet been thrown into the abyss nor has he yet found his place of final damnation in the Lake of Fire (Rev. 20:1-3; 10). According to this very Revelation, to this day he finds his headquarters in "the second heavens" (12:3, 7-13; cf. Eph. 2:1-2; 6:12). By the very words of Jesus, "Satan lives" in a wicked city like ancient Pergamum or for that matter any place on the earth today, which boasts in its immorality and resists the witness of God's Spirit.

Sadly, in this wicked city "the god of this world" (2 Cor. 4:3-4) was successful in placing a veil of deception over many even within the visible church in Pergamum. Finding entrance as "an angel of light" (2 Cor. 11:14), Satan was able to sow a perverted message into the church. The "teaching of Balaam" and "the teaching of the Nicolaitans" both enticed weak followers to compromise their faith. Some who were recognized as being in the church had returned to their former lives of idolatry and immorality. Some refused "to say 'No' to ungodliness and worldly passions, and to live self-controlled, upright and godly lives in this present age" (Titus 2:12). Some had exchanged "faith and a good conscience" for a lifestyle which caused their walk with Jesus to be "shipwrecked" (1 Tim. 1:19). Sadly, some people even today who are "Christian" in name only will seek out a teaching and its teachers who affirm their compromised lifestyle. It remains true in every age: our morality will shape our theology!

But praise God for the victory that belongs to those who remain faithful to the Lord Jesus. These are the overcomers who know Him as their Bread of Life. These are the ones whose spiritual supply will never be depleted. In a world infiltrated by dark and shadowy enticements, Jesus says to His own, "You're not missing a thing." To those the world has "blackballed"—to those the world calls "foolish," "weak," "lowly," and "despised" (1 Cor. 1:27)—Jesus speaks forgiveness, acceptance, favor, and exaltation.

The Message to the Church in Thyatira—2:18-29

[18] "To the angel of the church in Thyatira write: These are the words of the Son of God, whose eyes are like blazing fire and whose feet are like burnished bronze. [19] I know your deeds, your love and faith, your service and perseverance, and that you are now doing more than you did at first. [20] Nevertheless, I have this against you: You tolerate that woman Jezebel, who calls herself a prophet. By her teaching she misleads

my servants into sexual immorality and the eating of food sacrificed to idols. [21] I have given her time to repent of her immorality, but she is unwilling. [22] So I will cast her on a bed of suffering, and I will make those who commit adultery with her suffer intensely, unless they repent of her ways. [23] I will strike her children dead. Then all the churches will know that I am he who searches hearts and minds, and I will repay each of you according to your deeds. [24] Now I say to the rest of you in Thyatira, to you who do not hold to her teaching and have not learned Satan's so-called deep secrets, 'I will not impose any other burden on you, [25] except to hold on to what you have until I come.' [26] To the one who is victorious and does my will to the end, I will give authority over the nations—[27] that one 'will rule them with an iron scepter and will dash them to pieces like pottery'—just as I have received authority from my Father. [28] I will also give that one the morning star. [29] Whoever has ears, let them hear what the Spirit says to the churches.

Biblical Insights

Background Information

Forty miles southeast of Pergamum and nearly fifty miles inland from the Aegean Sea is the ancient city of Thyatira, modern day Akhisar. Archeology and history tells of this vicinity's long and varied cultural past with settlements reaching back as early as 3,000 B.C. During the neo-Hittite kingdom of Lydia (mid. seventh-mid. sixth century B.C.), local residents knew the city as "Pelopia." The Persians then ruled this area from the middle of the sixth century B.C. With the later conquest of Alexander the Great (356 B.C.-323 B.C.), the city became a Macedonian colony. It was only then, in c. 300 B.C., that it was renamed "Thyatira" by King Seleucus I Nicator (311-280 B.C.) at which time it served as a military base within the Seleucid Empire. In c. 190 B.C. the city was brought under Roman control as it remained through John's day when it was situated within the province of Lydia, close to the border of Mysia.

Thyatira's location upon the extensive Lycus River Valley and at the juncture of main roads leading to Pergamum, Sardis, and Smyrna positioned her as a leading trade center for many centuries. Ancient inscriptions indicate that the city was known for its many artisan and trade guilds, which included dyers; those who worked with wool, linen, and leather; as well as tanners, potters, bakers, bronze-smiths, and copper-smiths.[17] Yet, despite its cultural diversity and commercial significance, Thyatira was still the smallest of the seven host cities addressed in the Revelation. How ironic it is then that the church in this city received the lengthiest letter from the Lord.

It is also important to note the one additional reference to Thyatira in the Bible. In Acts 16:14 we read, "One of those listening was a woman from the city of Thyatira named Lydia, a dealer in purple cloth. She was a worshiper of God. The Lord opened her heart to respond to Paul's message." Though she shared her name with her own place of origin (which in itself could indicate her status as a servant), there are also examples of the given name "Lydia" amongst noblewomen of that day.[18] The fact that Paul and his company were invited to the home of Lydia "and the members of her household" (Acts 16:15) most likely indicates that she was a woman of means and influence, quite possibly a successful business woman.[19] While no reference is made in Scripture to evangelistic or church planting efforts in Thyatira, it is altogether possible that Lydia was somehow influential in bringing the Gospel to her home town. Sadly, many years later, Jesus would speak a stinging rebuke to an absolutely different type of influential woman and to her followers within that city's church.

Words of Affirmation and Encouragement—2:18-19

This message sent "to the angel of the church in Thyatira" (see notes under 1:20 and 2:1) contains one of the strongest reprimands amongst the seven. It is understandable then that to this church Jesus presents Himself as "the Son of God" (only here in Revelation, but see Matt. 27:43; John 5:25; 19:7; cf. Matt. 11:27). Although son-ship with God is known in the Bible to imply spiritual adoption (cf. 1 Chron. 17:13; Hosea 11:1) and to indicate Christ's Messiah-ship (cf. Ps. 2:7; John 20:31), Jesus' use of this title here is certainly an assertion of His own Deity.[20] He continues to declare His divine nature with intensity of language similar to John's description of the priestly Jesus in 1:14-15. That His "eyes are like blazing fire" once again speaks of His penetrating and searching judgment. That His "feet are like burnished bronze" once again speaks of His absolute holiness, which positions Him as "the Judge of the Living and the dead" (Acts 10:42; 2 Tim. 4:1; 1 Pet. 4:5).

Now with a word of affirmation, Jesus is fully knowledgeable (again *oida*, as in all seven letters) of this church's admirable traits, presented in verse 19. "Deeds" (*ergon*, as in Rev. 2:2) are those good and righteous actions for which believers have been created (Eph. 2:10; 4:12; Col. 1:10; 3:17). Furthermore, Jesus says that these works have grown over time; "you are now doing more than you did at first." The church of Thyatira was active for Christ's honor. And, as Hebrews 6:10 promises, Jesus had not forgotten; "God is not unjust; he will not forget your work and the love you have shown him as you have helped his people and continue to help them."

Continuing, "love" (*agape*) is that selfless and enduring affection demonstrated perfectly in God for His people (Rom. 5:8; 8:39) and produced freely in His people by His Spirit (Gal. 5:22). "Faith" (*pistis*) can refer both to conviction (or belief) and to faithfulness, its conclusion; most likely both are meant here. Added to these qualities Jesus acknowledges in these believers their "service" (*diakonia*, "ministry"; cf. 1 Cor. 12:5; 16:15; 2 Cor. 8:4) and their "perseverance" (*hypomonē*; "steadfastness," "patience"; cf. Rev. 1:9; 2:2, 3; 3:10). Within this Revelation, both "faithfulness" and "perseverance" will be essential to the believer's final victory over spiritual darkness (13:10; 14:12).

Words of Correction and Warning—2:20-25

Despite His words of affirmation for these believers, Jesus must bring severe warning to the church in Thyatira—"I have this against you" (v. 20). Prevalent for some time (v. 21a), and possibly well-known outside of Thyatira (v. 23, "then all the churches will know"), is a reprehensible false teaching and immoral practice which has been embraced by some within this church, whom Jesus still refers to as "my servants" (v. 20). Though there are also within this church those "who do not hold" (v. 24) to this false teaching and abominable manner, nevertheless they as a whole do (v. 20) "tolerate" (*aphiēmi*, "allow, permit"; the T.R. uses *eaō* with the same meaning) this wickedness in their midst.

This entire blight is attributable to one whom Jesus symbolically calls "Jezebel." Though this name is only referenced here in the New Testament, the original Jezebel is well known from the Old Testament as the cruel, immoral, and idolatrous wife of Israel's deplorable King Ahab (reign, c. 885 to 874 B.C.; cf. 1 Kings 16:29-30). This ancient queen, who originated from the coastal city of Sidon of the Phoenicians, continued in her foreign devotion to a great number of gods and goddesses, most notable among them Baal, the head fertility and agricultural god of the Canaanites. Upon marrying this foreign princess through political alliance, Ahab also embraced the false worship of Baal and brought it to the center of Israeli life (cf. 1 Kings 16:31-33; 18:18). Conversely, Jezebel rejected the God of Israel, so much so that in the second biblical reference to her she is found, "killing off the Lord's prophets" (1 Kings 18:4, 13). She also had employed the religious services of "four hundred and fifty prophets of Baal and the four hundred prophets of Asherah, who eat at Jezebel's table" (1 Kings 18:19).

The next development in the story of Jezebel follows the confrontation, ordered by the prophet Elijah, of the manifest power of Yahweh and the impotence of Baal at Mount Carmel. Humiliated and defeated, the four hundred and fifty prophets of Baal were then put to death at Elijah's word (1 Kings 18:40). Hearing this news, the queen vowed with rage to have Elijah put to death; "So Jezebel sent a messenger to Elijah to say, 'May the gods deal with me, be it ever so severely, if by this time tomorrow I do not make your life like that of one of them'" (1 Kings 19:2). Nevertheless, the Lord delivered Elijah, and he miraculously escaped the vengeance of Jezebel.

Again, the vileness of Jezebel is seen when she acts with a gross abuse of power, having the innocent Naboth put to death. This she did solely to gain his vineyard, a portion of his ancestral inheritance, in order to satisfy the greed of her husband (1 Kings 21:1-14). The final words attributed to Jezebel, here spoken to Ahab, read in 21:15, "Get up and take possession of the vineyard of Naboth the Jezreelite that he refused to sell you. He is no longer alive, but dead." At this Elijah is directed of the Lord to once again confront Ahab (21:19): "'This is what the Lord says: Have you not murdered a man and seized his property?' Then say to him, 'This is what the Lord says: In the place where dogs licked up Naboth's blood, dogs will lick up your blood—yes, yours!'" Concerning Ahab (Israel's most wicked king), a final word of disapproval is pronounced—"who sold himself to do evil in the eyes of the Lord, urged on by Jezebel his wife" (21:25). Concerning Jezebel, a final prophetic word of judgment was spoken as well—"Dogs will devour Jezebel by the wall of Jezreel" (21:23). Within approximately fourteen years, the prophet Elisha repeated this same verdict. Along with judgment upon "the whole house of Ahab" (2 Kings 9:8), we read, "As for Jezebel, dogs will devour her on the plot of ground at Jezreel, and no one will bury her'" (9:10). Her final end is contained in these words as she is thrown from a window at the order of the new King Jehu (9:33-37):

> So they threw her down, and some of her blood spattered the wall and the horses as they trampled her underfoot. Jehu went in and ate and drank. 'Take care of that cursed woman,' he said, 'and bury her, for she was a king's daughter.' But when they went out to bury her, they found nothing except her skull, her feet and her hands. They went back and told Jehu, who said, 'This is the word of the Lord that he spoke through his servant Elijah the Tishbite: On the plot of ground at Jezreel dogs will devour Jezebel's flesh. Jezebel's body will be like dung on the ground in the plot at Jezreel, so that no one will be able to say, 'This is Jezebel.'

We can now appreciate the strength of Christ's censure of the church in Thyatira, which harbored some who actively followed and some who irresponsibly "tolerated" their own "Jezebel." "That woman Jezebel" is no doubt a symbolic allusion to her ancient counterpart.[21] What we do know of Thyatira's "Jezebel" is that she has falsely claimed herself to be "a prophet" (here, the feminine *prophētis*), i.e., one who speaks forth a divine message. Assuming this place of authority, as deceptive as it is, she teaches a perverse doctrine, which (v. 20) "misleads" (*planaō*, "to deceive, even seduce") her followers "into sexual immorality" (*porneuō*, from *pornē*, "a prostitute") and "the eating of food sacrificed to idols" (*eidōlothytos*). Like the religiously motivated ancient Jezebel, her influence is both of a sexually deviant and idolatrous nature. In fact, she herself is charged with her own immorality (again *porneia* in verse 21).

It is well known within this first century culture of paganism and idolatry that craftsmen guilds, early labor unions as such, commonly adopted patron deities. In honor of these false gods and goddesses, meetings or festivities held by these guilds often took place within the associated pagan temples. Here the ancients participated in drunkenness and sexual orgies; here also food was served which first had been offered in sacrifice to the idols of these false deities. This, no doubt, presented a constant moral dilemma for Christian businessmen and women and craftsmen and women. To separate from these common practices or from the guilds themselves surely threatened their social acceptance and prosperity.

It is likely then that Thyatira's "Jezebel" taught as doctrine that for the sake of business there was no need for believers to separate from this idolatry and immorality. (Clearly, it was a far different matter for Paul to grant permission for believers to purchase meat in the local markets, which may possibly have been offered to idols, since there was no direct contact with this idolatry [cf. 1 Cor. 8 and 10:25-29]. Certainly, the "feast" to which Paul refers in 10:27 was not one held within the confines of a heathen temple [cf. vv. 20-21]).

Jesus, with patient mercy, had "given her time to repent [*metanoeō*]" (v. 21), i.e., "to change her mind"; but sadly, "she is unwilling" (*ou thelei metanoeō*), i.e., "she refused to repent." Therefore, her judgment is sealed, "I will cast her on a bed of suffering" (v. 22). Though the words "of suffering" are not included in the text, the word for "bed" (*klinē*) can refer to a bed or couch used to carry the sick (as in Matthew 9:2, 6). Implied is that her decadent bed of adultery will be turned to a bed of sickness and suffering.[22] The futuristic present active indicative is used for "I will cast," indicating the immediacy of this judgment. Added to Jezebel's judgment is that of "her children" (v. 23)—those who follow "her ways"—here described as "those who commit adultery [*moicheuō*] with her" (v. 22). As this word, more directly than the earlier *porneuō* (sexual immorality), indicates a violation of the marriage vow and oath, these have violated their spiritual marriage covenant with God Himself (cf. 2 Cor. 11:2-4).

Still merciful, Jesus must warn, "Unless they repent" He will cause them to "suffer intensely" (*megas thlipsis,* lit. "great tribulation"; cf. Rev. 7:14). He will indeed "strike" (*apokteinō,* lit. "kill") them "dead" (*thanatos*; i.e., "with death"; cf. Rev. 6:8; 20:6). The implication of this judgment is affliction, which will lead to death. As this judgment becomes known to "all the churches" (hence a reminder of the broad application of this message beyond this local church), all will see the ministry of Jesus, "who searches hearts and minds [*nephrous,* lit. 'kidneys'; here metaphorically, 'the innermost parts']." What is true of God the Father (Jer. 17:10; 20:12) and the Holy Spirit (Rom. 8:27; 1 Cor. 2:10) is here true of Christ. Consistent with many biblical warnings of coming judgment for those who reject the mercy and grace of God found in Jesus (cf. Ps. 62:12; Matt. 16:27; Rom. 2:6; Rev. 20:12), the Judge announces, "I will repay each of you according to your deeds" (v. 23b).

Finally, in correcting this church, Jesus speaks "to the rest of you in Thyatira." These are those "who do not hold to her teachings." In so doing they have resisted the demonic and deceptive invitation to "learn[ed] Satan's so-called secrets" (v. 24). "Secrets" is *bathos,* "deep things" (here used oppositely of 1 Corinthians 2:10). In this we see evidence that within the doctrine of "Jezebel" can be found some semblance of Gnostic teachings, now having gained a foothold not only within the Greek culture but, more sadly, within the visible church. To these who have stayed faithful, Christ directs the injunction, "I will not impose any other burden on you, except to hold on to what you have until I come" (cf. Acts 15:28-29). To the wicked, His Coming will bring judgment (2:16); to these faithful, His Coming will bring reward as He now goes on to declare.

Words of Blessing and Promise—2:26-29

As with each of the messages to these seven churches, Jesus concludes His words by addressing the faithful as "overcomers," that is, those who are in a constant place of victory (cf. 1 John 5:5). Here he sees not only the victor's continued faith but also his continued obedience. That he "does my will" (v. 26) literally reads that he continuously "attends" or "keeps" Christ's "works" (*erga*, "deeds" or "acts") (cf. Rev. 2:2, 5, 9, 13, 19; 3:8, 14:13). He has entered into the work of the Lord in the advance of His Gospel and of His Kingdom (cf. John 4:34; 9:4). And this he does "to the end" (*achri telous*) in the sense of "until the designated end." In light of the statements that follow, this "end" most likely has in view the culmination of Christ's Revelation upon the earth and the believer's part in maintaining his witness of the coming Christ (cf. Matt. 10:22; 24:13; Mark 13:13).

To overcomers, personally and corporately, Jesus promises "authority [*exousia*] over the nations [*ethnos*, 'nations' or 'people groups']" (v. 26). Here is introduced the truth of Christ's Millennial Reign in the Book of Revelation. He is the King of the Kingdom of God. While the rule of His Kingdom issues eternally from His throne, the realm of His Kingdom fills, both, believers' hearts (John 14:23; Col. 1:27; cf. Luke 17:21, "within you" in some versions) and the whole earth in righteousness and peace "for a thousand years" (Rev. 20:1-6; cf. 1:5 and 11:15).

Jesus had earlier given this same eschatological promise to His first disciples (Matt. 19:28; Luke 22:30). For believers in Thyatira, which throughout its history had known one invading army after another, this promise brought that future hope into their present reality. Jesus further (v. 27) brings promise, now quoting from the Messianic Second Psalm (v. 9), which tells of God's contention with the wickedness of His enemies and the ultimate victory of His Anointed One. In the same way the Father has given His Son authority to judge (John 5:22) and to "rule" (*poimainō*, lit. "shepherd") the nations "with an iron scepter"—*rhabdos siderous*, here either the shepherd's rod or the ruler's scepter, either way severe; cf. Rev. 12:5 and 19:15—so Jesus has given this authority to us (Rev. 3:21).

Finally, Jesus has also promised to give Himself—"the morning star"—to these overcomers (v. 28). As will be declared in the consummation of all things, Jesus Himself is "the bright Morning Star" (Rev. 22:16). In the natural world, "the morning star" is actually the planet Venus, the only "star" shining when all the other stars have faded from view. Now, as with each address to the churches, Jesus speaks by His Spirit beyond this local church to those who have ears to hear (v. 29).

Life Application

The modern city of Akhisar, home to about 107,000 residents, holds many similarities to its ancestral history as Thyatira. Ruins from the ancient past are present there but more limited than in such cities as Pergamum, Sardis, or Ephesus. Still today this urban area is a major trade center located at the intersection of several highways, which themselves lead to other great urban centers in western Turkey. Sprawling beyond this city center is the fertile Akhisar Plain, internationally known for its production of tobacco. As in the days of Thyatira, Akhisar city and district is also known for its agricultural production of cloth, wool, dye, olives, olive oil, grapes, and raisins.

It is to the church of Thyatira that Jesus chose to reveal Himself with the divine title "the Son of God" (2:18). Added to this claim is the revelation found in John's Gospel of Jesus as the "the Word" (Rev. 19:13), the Logos of God. From the absolute past—"in the beginning"—Jesus already and continuously "was the Word" (John 1:1). John goes on, "and the Word was with God," that is, He had always continued in personal, face to face communion with the Father, "and the Word was God," that is, He shares with the Father the very essence and nature of who God is (cf. Phil. 2:6-8; Heb. 1:1-3; Col. 1:15; 2:9).

This divine Son of God is the One who knows His Church best and judges His Church justly and thoroughly. He is the One who punishes rebellion (Rev. 2:20-25) and who rewards righteousness (2:26-29). The message He speaks to the church of Thyatira is a reminder to every church and every believer still today; the judgment this church received is an example to all. As Jesus spoke to that church, He speaks to all, (2:23) "Then all the churches will know that I am He who searches hearts and minds." The words of the Apostle Peter echo on, "For it is time for judgment to begin with God's household; and if it begins with us, what will the outcome be for those who do not obey the gospel of God?" (1 Peter 4:17).

Every local church and every believer should be on guard against those who think and act like Jezebel. While much has been written in recent years about "the Jezebel spirit," the Word of God still speaks the warning best. To be sure an attitude or spirit that is domineering and controlling with little or no regard for those who stand in his or her way is dangerous, inexcusable, and so opposite the heart of Jesus. Yet, Christ's greater issue with the "Jezebel" of Thyatira was her immoral and unrepentant lifestyle, which she wove into a false teaching that lured others into her trap. Sadly, the "Jezebels" of this world are most often challenged to spin their webs in local churches—sometimes successfully!

Christians beware! Immorality and a blatant disregard for holiness of heart have never been acceptable in the sight of God, regardless of how recognized, common place, and sophisticated it may become in any society. There is little difference in the eyes of God between the lewd pagan practices and idol worship of the first century and the sexual immorality and celebrated depravity of the 21st century. Jesus still calls to His Church, "Come out from them and be separate, says the Lord. Touch no unclean thing, and I will receive you" (2 Corinthians 6:17).

Chapter 2 Notes

1. "Early Bronze Age settlements apparently existed directly on the coast itself, while the settlement of the Hellenistic and Roman era lay further inland where ruins can be seen today. The city is situated in the Meander Valley in a plain south-east of the mouth of the Cayster River where it empties into the Mediterranean." Lance Jenott, "Ancient Ephesus," *Silk Road Seattle-Ephesus,* Walter Chapin Simpson Center for the Humanities at the University of Washington, 2004 <depts.washington.edu/silkroad/cities/turkey/ephesus/ephesus.html>.

2. "As a center of religious piety Ephesus was preeminent: the city itself developed from the earliest time around an ancient shrine of the earth goddess Artemis (Roman Diana) and became her chief place of worship." Jenott.

3. "*Ginōskō,* frequently suggests inception or progress in knowledge, while *oida* suggests fullness of knowledge." W. E. Vine, *An Expository Dictionary of New Testament Words* (Revell, 1966) 298.

4. Irenaeus (in his *Against Heresies*, Book 26, Chapter 26.3) states, "The Nicolaitans are the followers of that Nicolas who was one of the seven first ordained to the diaconate by the apostles. They lead lives of unrestrained indulgence. The character of these men is very plainly pointed out in the Apocalypse of John, [when they are repre-sented] as teaching that it is a matter of indifference to practice adultery, and to eat things sacrificed to idols." Alexander Roberts and James Donaldson, eds. "Irenaeus," *The Apostolic Fathers with Justin Martyr and Irenaeus, Vol. 1. The Anti-Nicene Fathers,* Edinburgh, 1867, reprint, (Grand Rapids: Eerdmans, 1973).

   Third Century theologian Hippolytus adds the following, "But Nicolaus has been a cause of the wide-spread combination of these wicked men. He, as one of the seven (that were chosen) for the diaconate, was appointed by the Apostles. (But Nicolaus) departed from correct doctrine, and was in the habit of inculcating indifference [sic] of both life and food. And when the disciples (of Nicolaus) continued to offer insult to the Holy Spirit, John reproved them in the Apocalypse as fornicators and eaters of things offered unto idols." F. Legge, trans. from the text of Cruice, "Hippolytus," *Philosophumena or, The Refutation of All Heresies,* Society for Promoting Christian Knowledge, (New York: Macmillan, 1921) vii. 36

5. John Walvoord writes, "This view considers the Nicolaitans as the forerunners of the clerical hierarchy superimposed upon the laity and robbing them of spiritual free-dom." John F. Walvoord, *The Revelation of Jesus Christ* (Chicago: Moody, 1966) 53.

6. Scholar Rick Renner, adds this insight, "Nicolas' deep roots in paganism may have produced in him a tolerance for occultism and paganism. Growing up in this

perverted spiritual environment may have caused him to view these belief systems as not so damaging or dangerous. This wrong perception would have resulted in a very liberal viewpoint that encouraged people to stay connected to the world. This is what numerous Bible scholars believe about the Nicolaitans." Rick Renner, *Sparkling Gems from the Greek* (Tulsa: Teach All Nations, 2003) 631-634.

Clement of Alexandria (in his *The Stromata*, Book 2, Chapter 20) speaks also of the vice of the Nicolaitans (though claiming their perversion of the original deacon's teaching), "But they, abandoning themselves to pleasure like goats, as if insulting the body, lead a life of self-indulgence; not knowing that the body is wasted, being by nature subject to dissolution; while their soul is buffed in the more of vice; following as they do the teaching of pleasure itself, not of the apostolic man." Philip Schaff, ed., "ANF02. Fathers of the Second Century: Hermas, Tatian, Athenagoras, Theophilus, and Clement of Alexandria (Entire)," *Christian Classics Ethereal Library*, 13 July 2005 <www.ccel.org/ccel/schaff/anf02.vi.iv.ii.xx.html>.

7. Tertullian (in his *Appendix. Against All Heresies*, Chapter 1) strongly adds, "A brother heretic emerged in Nicolaus. He was one of the seven deacons who were appointed in the Acts of the Apostles. He affirms that Darkness was seized with a concupiscence—and, indeed, a foul and obscene one—after Light: out of this permixture it is a shame to say what fetid and unclean (combinations arose). The rest (of his tenets), too, are obscene. For he tells of certain Aeons, sons of turpitude, and of conjunctions of execrable and obscene embraces and permixtures, and certain yet baser outcomes of these. He teaches that there were born, moreover, daemons, and gods, and spirits seven, and other things sufficiently sacrilegious. alike and foul, which we blush to recount, and at once pass them by. Enough it is for us that this heresy of the Nicolaitans has been condemned by the Apocalypse of the Lord with the weightiest authority attaching to a sentence, in saying, 'Because this thou holdest, thou hatest the doctrine of the Nicolaitans, which I too hate." Philip Schaff, ed., "ANF03. Latin Christianity: Its Founder, Tertullian," *Christian Classics Ethereal Library*, 1 June 2005 <www.ccel.org/ccel/schaff/anf03.v.xi.i.html?scrBook=Acts&scrCh=6&scrV=1#v.xi.i-p34.1>.

8. "Their lives were very busy but terribly barren." Stanley M. Horton, *The Ultimate Victory—An Exposition of the Book of Revelation* (Springfield, MO: Gospel Publishing House, 1991) 40.

9. "In typical Roman road construction, a mosaic of heavy paving blocks closely trimmed and fitted is laid over a bedding of gravel and sand. Often, sturdy curb stones limit the sides." Fikret Yegul, "Roads and Highways," *Roman Building Technology and Architecture*, University of California, Dec. 2017 <archserve.id.ucsb.edu/courses/arthistory/152k/roads.html>.

10. "The Theatre was used for large meetings of the entire city population (the *demos*), festivals like the annual procession of the city's goddess Artemis, and any other large gathering for which the Odeum was too small. (It is very likely that this Theatre was the site of the mob protest against St. Paul reported in Acts 19.) When Wood excavated the theatre he discovered a number of inscriptions lying about the stage relating to state embassies, religious festivals, city benefactors and Roman emperors." Lance Jenott, "Ancient Ephesus," Silk Road Seattle-Ephesus, Walter Chapin Simpson Center for the Humanities, 2004 <depts.washington.edu/silkroad/cities/turkey/ephesus/ephesus.html>.

11. William M. Ramsay, *Letters to the Seven Churches & Their Place in the Plan of the Apocalypse*. 2nd ed. (London: Hodder & Stoughton, 1906) 255.

12. "Their poverty in earthly possessions was due to persecution. Work and patronage in business may have been withheld from the Christians; again, mobs may have looted their homes, shops, and bazaars." R.C.H. Lenski, *An Interpretation of St. John's Revelation. Lenski's Commentary: NT* (Minneapolis: Fortress Press, 2008) 97.

13. "The Martyrdom of Saint Polycarp, Bishop of Smyrna, as Told in the Letter of the Church of Smyrna to the Church of Philomelium." Cyril Richardson, ed. and trans., "Early Christian Fathers," *Christian Classics Ethereal Library*, 1 June 2005 <www.ccel.org/ccel/richardson/fathers.vii.i.iii.html>.

14. Scholar Henry Alford cites various Scriptures, such as Genesis 24:55; Numbers 11:19; and Daniel 1:12 to support that, "The expression [ten days] is probably used to signify a short and limited time." Henry Alford, *The Greek New Testament—An Exegetical and Critical Commentary, Vol. IV* (Chicago: Moody, 1968) 567.

15. Interestingly the city of Smyrna in John's day was established on the slopes of Mount Pagus ("the hill"). At night, the lights of the columned buildings, which encircled the top of this acropolis glittered like a crown. This landmark was known as "the Crown of Smyrna" and the city itself at times was called "the crown city."

16. Verse 13 in the New King James Version reads, "I know your works, and where you dwell, where Satan's throne is." Here the Textus Receptus (Received Text) differs from those manuscripts associated with the Egyptian [or Alexandrian] text type, used in more modern versions.

17. As spoken of by ancient Greek geography and historian Strabo (d. A.D. 23) found in *The Geography of Strabo* 13.4.4. H. L Jones, ed., *The geography of Strabo* (New York: Harvard University Press, 1989).

18. Richard S. Ascough, *Lydia: Paul's Cosmopolitan Hostess* (Collegeville, MN: The Liturgical Press, 2009) 7.

19. There is much known about the Tyrian purple or royal purple dye derived from the mucous secretions of one or more species of predatory sea snails from the eastern Mediterranean. In ancient Rome, cloth of this color was highly valued and expensive. Colin Schultz, "In Ancient Rome, Purple Dye Was Made from Snails," *Smithsonian.com, Smithsonian Institution*, Oct. 10 2013 <www.smithsonian-mag.com/smart-news/in-ancient-rome-purple-dye-was-made-from-snails-1239931/>.

20. Christ's deity was also affirmed through the title "Son of God" when spoken by: the Father (Mark 1:11 and Mark 9:7); His disciples and followers (Matthew 14:33; 16:15-16; 27:43; John 1:49; 11:27); John Mark (Mark 1:1); Luke (Luke 3:38); Paul (Acts 9:20; Romans 1:4); Gabriel (Luke 1:35); a Roman centurion (Matthew 27:54; Mark 15:39); and even Satan and demons (Matthew 8:29; Mark 3:11; 5:7; Luke 4:3, 9, 41).

21. Limited early manuscripts (such as Codex Alexandrinus) read "*sou guné*," which would be translated "your wife" or "your woman." If this reading is correct, the implication is that this "Jezebel" was actually the wife of the "angel" (pastor or messenger) of this church or symbolically so, as Ahab was married to his wicked Jezebel. It is highly questionable that Jesus would have entrusted this letter to one knit together in covenant with such a spiritually dark "Jezebel." Therefore, nearly all, recent scholarship follows the manuscripts (such as Codex Sinaiticus) reading "that woman."

22. "It is as if Jesus says, 'You love an unclean bed. Here, I will give you one, and cast you into a sickbed.'" David Guzik, "Jesus Letters to the Churches," Blue Letter Bible, 2013 <http://www.blueletterbible.org/commentaries/guzik_david/>.

An Overview of the Messages to the Seven Churches of Asia

Church Location	Passage	Affirmation & Encouragement	Correction & Warning	Blessing & Promise	Identity of Jesus	Promise to the Victorious
Ephesus	2:1-7	2:1-3, 6	2:4-5	2:7	"holds the seven stars [...] walks among the seven golden lampstands"	"right to eat from the tree of life"
Smyrna	2:8-11	2:8-10a	None	2:10b-11	"the First and the Last"	"will not be hurt at all by the second death"
Pergamum	2:12-17	2:12-13	2:14-16	2:17	"has the sharp, double-edged sword"	"the hidden manna [...] a white stone with a new name"
Thyatira	2:18-29	2:18-19	2:20-25	2:26-29	"eyes like blazing fire [...] feet like burnished bronze"	"authority over the nations"
Sardis	3:1-6	None	3:1-3	3:4-6	"holds the seven spirits of God and the stars"	"dressed in white [...] acknowledge name before my Father"
Philadelphia	3:7-13	3:7-11	None	3:12-13	"holy and true [...] holds the key of David"	"a pillar in the temple of my God [...] my new name"
Laodicea	3:14-22	None	3:14-20	3:21-22	"the Amen, the faithful and true witness, the ruler of God's creation"	"right to sit with me on my throne"

— Photo by Thomas Keinath —

The Cave of the Apocalypse on Patmos, believed historically to have given shelter to the Apostle John

"I, John, your brother and companion in the suffering and kingdom and patient endurance that are ours in Jesus, was on the island of Patmos because of the word of God and the testimony of Jesus." (Revelation 1:9)

— Photo by Thomas Keinath —
The 25,000-seat Grand Theatre in ancient Ephesus

"You have persevered and have endured hardships for my name, and
have not grown weary." (Revelation 2:3)

* Photo used by Permission
The Agora (Marketplace) in ancient Smyrna (modern day Izmir, Turkey}

"I know your afflictions and your poverty—yet you are rich!"
(Revelation 2:9)

— Photo by Thomas Keinath —
The Sanctuary of Asclepius, the Greek god of medicine and healing,
in ancient Pergamum

"I know where you live—where Satan has his throne."
(Revelation 2:13a)

— Public Domain Photo —
The limited ruins of ancient Thyatira (modern day Akhisar, Turkey)

"To the one who is victorious and does my will to the end,
I will give authority over the nations—
that one 'will rule them with an iron scepter
and will dash them to pieces like pottery'—
just as I have received authority from my Father."
(Revelation 2:26-27)

— Photo by Thomas Keinath —
The Temple of Artemis in ancient Sardis

"Wake up! Strengthen what remains and is about to die,
for I have found your deeds unfinished in the sight of my God."
(Revelation 3:2)

— Public Domain Photo —

Two of several massive pillars from the seventh century A.D. Church of St. John
in ancient Philadelphia (modern day Alasehir, Turkey)

"The one who is victorious I will make a pillar
in the temple of my God." (Revelation 3:12a)

— Public Domain Photo —
The snow-white limestone cliffs of Hierapolis, near to Laodicea,
known in ancient and modern times for its relaxing hot springs

"So, because you are lukewarm—neither hot nor cold—
I am about to spit you out of my mouth." (Revelation 3:16)

CHAPTER 3

Revelation 3

Words from the One Who Knows Us Best—Part 2

Introduction to Revelation 3:1-22

Continuing into the third chapter of Revelation, we read Christ's messages to the remaining three of "the seven churches in the province of Asia" (1:4). Already addressed have been the churches in Ephesus, Smyrna, and Pergamum—which follow on a route south to north close to the Aegean Sea—and Thyatira, which is situated further inland. As explained in the Introduction to the prior chapter, Thyatira and the remaining three churches in Sardis, Philadelphia, and Laodicea complete the eastern flank of the inverted "u," which in fact followed an ancient Roman postal circuit.

We have also noted from 1:19 the three-part outline provided for this entire Revelation, "what you have seen, what is now and what will take place later." Following the first part of this book contained in John's vision of the glorious Risen Christ, these ongoing messages to the seven churches fill up the second part of The Apocalypse, "what is now." Further clarified is that the instruction and truths, which were so applicable to those particular local churches in John's day, are just as relevant to local churches and to the Church at large in our day—"what is now" lives on. In fact, each and every believer is called to read, hear, and obey the Master's voice: "Blessed is the one who reads aloud the words of this prophecy, and blessed are those who hear it and take to heart what is written in it" (1:3). And again, "He who has an ear, let him hear what the Spirit says to the churches" (2:7, 11, 17, 29; 3:6, 13, 22), an injunction accompanied each time by personal promise.

Of special note are the opening salutations and presentations of Jesus as the Author, "these are the words of [...]," which remind us of the context for all these messages. The Great High Priest walks "among the lampstands" (1:13), as it were inspecting and, when needed, correcting His Church. His pattern of three—words of affirmation and encouragement; words of correction and warning; and, words of blessing and promise—is abbreviated with these final three churches. For Sardis and Laodicea there is no opening praise, yet for the church in Philadelphia there is only praise.

The Message to the Church in Sardis—3:1-6

[1] "To the angel of the church in Sardis write: These are the words of him who holds the seven spirits of God and the seven stars. I know your deeds; you have a reputation of being alive, but you are dead. [2] Wake up! Strengthen what remains and is about to die, for I have found your deeds unfinished in the sight of my God. [3] Remember, therefore, what you have received and heard; hold it fast, and repent. But if you do not wake up, I will come like a thief, and you will not know at what time I will come to you. [4] Yet you have a few people in Sardis who have not soiled their clothes. They will walk with me, dressed in white, for they are worthy. [5] The one who is victorious will, like them, be dressed in white. I will never blot out the name of that person from the book of life, but will acknowledge that name before my Father and his angels. [6] Whoever has ears, let them hear what the Spirit says to the churches.

Biblical Insights

Background Information

With settlements dating as early as 1,300 B.C. during the height of the Hittite Empire, ancient Sardis had a diverse and complex cultural and political history, as had Thyatira, just thirty miles to her northwest. However, Sardis is best remembered as the capital of the Kingdom of Lydia, which continued to rule in Western Asia Minor (Anatolia) throughout the times of the biblical Neo-Assyrian (911-612 B.C.) and Neo-Babylonian (626-539 B.C.) Empires. Despite a brief occupation (652-619 B.C.) by the nomadic Cimmerians who invaded from the northeast, Sardis grew from kingdom to empire under the military might of the Lydian King Alyattes and his son Croesus, who together ruled from 619-546 B.C.

History tells that Croesus, Sardis' most famous king, under the prompting of a misinterpreted prediction from the Oracle (priestess) of Delphi, went into battle against King Cyrus II of Persia in 546 B.C. Losing tragically, Sardis and Lydia fell under Persian rule for the next two centuries. Later, in 334 B.C., the city and region were surrendered to the Macedonian King, Alexander the Great (356-323 B.C.). With his death and the expansion of the Greek Empire, Sardis became a capital and city-state under the rule of the Seleucid Dynasty (312-63 B.C.). Power again shifted in 189 B.C. to the Kingdom of Pergamum and eventually to the Roman Empire in 133 B.C.

Yet, through all these centuries of turmoil, Sardis remained a city of great influence, politically, culturally, and commercially. Two factors contributed to its significance. First, the city was situated along the expansive Hermus River (modern day Gediz River), flowing 250 miles from Mount Dindymus in central Phrygia (to its east) into the Gulf of Smyrna and the Aegean Sea (fifty-five miles to its west). Second, during the Persian Empire, by decree of King Darius I, the 1,500-mile Royal Road was built linking east-to-west commercial interests beginning in the Persian capital at Susa and ending at Sardis, then a Persian satrapy (or province) of the empire. Later under the Roman Empire, this road was extended to the Aegean Sea at Smyrna. Nearly three months were needed for people and goods to traverse this entire route. Additionally, Sardis was positioned at the crossroads of other major roads and trade routes.

It is no wonder then that Sardis and the region of Lydia was celebrated for its wealth and beauty. Of Lydian commerce, Greek historian Herodotus (484-425 B.C.) wrote, "They were the first men whom we know who coined and used gold and silver currency; and they were the first to sell by retail."[1] Through the work of metallurgists during the reign of King Croesus, gold and silver was refined with such success that Sardis was able to mint its own pure coins. Even in our day, wealth is expressed with the phrase, "rich as Croesus." But here is where truth overlaps with fable. Flowing through Sardis was the stream Pactolus, factually a source of gold sands or dust from nearby Mount Tmolus. But fable had it that this river became rich in gold when the mythical King Midas of Phrygia bathed in its headwaters to "rid himself of the 'golden touch.'"[2] In reality, Sardis was also well known, beyond its coinage, for the manufacturing of jewelry, fine textiles, and carpets.

With the wealth of Sardis also came its reputation for pleasure seeking, which in the days of Greek and Roman rule was indistinguishable from its worship of pagan gods and goddesses. Greatest amongst these deities was the goddess Cybele, known as the "Great Mother." To worship Cybele was to engage in unrestrained sexual immorality, and central to this "worship" was the temple built in her honor. Earlier, the Lydian King Croesus had paid for the building of the Temple of Artemis in Ephesus (c. 550 B.C.), known as one of the Seven Wonders of the Ancient World. In Sardis, however, a temple was built by the Hellenists beginning in 334 B.C. for the worship of Artemis, who was in that day closely associated with Cybele. This Temple remarkably measured more than twice the size of the Parthenon in Athens.

In the first century A.D., Sardis enjoyed a secure place as a leading city in the region of Lydia in the Roman province of Asia. Having sustained an unprecedented earthquake in A.D. 17, the devastated city was rebuilt with the significant aid of emperor Tiberius. In return, Sardis gave him cult status, erecting a statute in his honor in A.D. 43 with an inscription naming him the "founder of the city."[3] Perhaps in part, this favor with Rome allowed through many decades for a significant Jewish and Christian population to peacefully coexist with each other and within its Roman culture without the mention of persecution.

Words of Correction and Warning — 3:1-3
As with each of the seven letters, this message is sent through the "angel of the church." Again, the preferred view is that these "angels" or "messengers" are the human leaders commissioned to the seven churches (see note under 1:20). Yet, since no mention of Sardis is found in the Word of God apart from this letter, we cannot know this leader's

identity, though the church's founding may relate to the spread of the Gospel through Paul and his associates during his Third Missionary Journey some forty years earlier (Acts 19:10, "all the Jews and Greeks who lived in the province of Asia heard the word of the Lord"). But, here in this address is found much grace. Though Jesus brings no opening words of affirmation to the church in Sardis, He does still associate with their "lampstand" (1:13, 20), holding its leader—and representatively that local church—in His "right hand" (1:20).

Jesus then identifies Himself as the one "who holds the seven spirits of God and the seven stars." In 1:4 "the seven spirits" are witnessed "before his [the Father's] throne." This same scene is repeated with more detail in 4:5. In both cases (where see notes), it is clear in light of Ephesians 4:4 ("There is one body and one Spirit") that this "seven" refers to the "seven-fold" function of the ministry of the Spirit, the number signifying completeness (cf. Zech. 4:2, 6, 10). Yet here we read that it is the Son of God who "holds" (*echo*) these "seven spirits." Though there can be various nuances of meaning for this common verb, it seems clear in light of the fact that he also "holds [. . .] the seven stars" (1:16, 20) that Jesus continuously "possesses" the Holy Spirit. Here, perhaps in His ministry of inspecting the Church, He further "possesses" the leaders of His Church. This truth is again reinforced in 5:6 where we see that the Lamb "has [*echo*] seven eyes, which are the seven spirits of God sent out into all the earth." Jesus declared in His ministry on earth the full anointing of the Spirit of God upon Himself (Luke 4:18), and John adds that He had the Spirit "without limit" (John 3:34). In fact, Isaiah (11:2) saw the day of this seven-fold anointing upon the Messiah. Furthermore, the Holy Spirit is called "the Spirit of Christ" (Rom. 8:9; 1 Pet. 1:11) testifying to the co-substantial nature of the Trinity.

As in all seven letters, Jesus says, "I know" (*oida*), indicating His full and divine knowledge and perception. By His Spirit, He knows the real condition of every local church and of every individual heart, this contributing to the very nature of inspired apocalyptic literature, namely, to reveal the real behind the apparent. And here, as with the churches of Ephesus (2:2) and Thyatira (2:19), He openly sees their "deeds" (*erga*), namely, their works or activities. Yet, unlike the righteous actions of those earlier churches, in Sardis Jesus clearly finds their spiritual accomplishments "unfinished" (v. 2), i.e., their works were not found completed or fulfilled (*pleroo*) by true and active faith (cf. 3:15). Speaking to the corporate body, Jesus concludes that their outward show of good works has earned them no more than a "reputation of being alive." In fact, He finds them spiritually "dead."

Nevertheless, there is hope if they would only respond to Christ's urgent appeal. To begin, they must turn from their complacency to a state of spiritual watchfulness ("Wake up!"). With this they must "strengthen" ("make firm," even "re-establish") "what remains" of what they have known in Christ, lest even their last signs of life fade altogether. Church of Sardis, if only you would "remember" (as a life style; cf. 2:5) "what you have received and heard" (cf. 1 Thess. 2:13; Heb. 10:26) when the message of Christ first came to you. "Hold it fast"—keep, guard, and observe this life-giving truth (Rev. 1:3)—and "repent" (*metaneō*), i.e., change your minds about the preeminence of the word of Christ (Rev. 2:5, 16, 21; 3:19).

To ignore Christ's appeal to watchfulness and repentance would invite a sad alternative. Jesus Himself "will come like a thief" (cf. Rev. 16:15, where see note) emphasizing unexpected and sweeping judgment. Though most often associated with the eschatological Day of the Lord (Matt. 24:43; 1 Thess. 5:2, 4; 2 Pet. 3:10), this reference most likely speaks first of imminent judgment upon that contemporary local church (cf. 2:5). The ancient, surprise attacks on an overconfident Sardis at the hands of Cyrus II (in 546 B.C.) and Antiochus III (in 214 B.C.) may well be the historic metaphor for Christ's supernatural warning of the ruin of spiritual complacency.

Words of Blessing and Promise—3:4-6

Despite the corporate indictment against this church, Jesus does identify a faithful remnant in Sardis—"a few people"—lit. "a few names" (*onoma*). In great contrast to the compromised and shallow "reputation" (*onoma*) of the Church at large (3:1), these "few" have a favored and honored "name" with God. These individuals "have not soiled their clothes," i.e., they have not defiled (*molynō*; also Rev. 14:4) themselves with sin (cf. Rom. 13:14; Col. 3:12). Jesus may have a great irony in mind, for though the ancient Sardians were steeped in vile idolatry and immorality, they were nevertheless forbidden to approach their pagan deities dressed in soiled clothing.[4] How distinct is the remnant of Sardis who "walk with" Jesus in the sense of their godly conduct and close companionship (cf. Rom. 13:13; Gal. 5:16; Eph. 5:2; 1 John 1:7, etc.); these are "dressed in white" (Rev. 3:18; 7:9, 14; 19:8, 14), the garment of righteousness given to those counted "worthy" in Christ.

As with each of the messages to the seven churches, Jesus speaks blessings upon those who are victorious through faith in Him (1 John 5:4-5). Application beyond the original remnant of the righteous in Sardis is made with the words "like them," which may equally relate to those who would follow their example and to all who at any time are, through faith in Christ, found "dressed in white." To these all, Jesus promises to "never blot out the name of that person from the book of life" (cf. Exod. 32:32, 33; Deut. 29:20). God's Word speaks often of the inclusion of the names of His children in the "book of life" found in Heaven (Dan. 12:1; Luke 10:20; Phil. 4:3; Heb. 12:23). In Revelation, we further read of "the Lamb's book of life" (13:8; 21:27) in which the redeemed of the Lamb are included "from the creation of the world" (17:8). To not be included in the "book of life" means the judgment of eternal damnation (Rev. 20:12, 15). Again, in stark contrast to the compromised "name" (*onoma*, "reputation") of the many, true believers have a name that Jesus will "acknowledge" (*homologeō*, in the sense of "to openly declare") "before my Father and his angels" (Matt. 10:32; Luke 12:8).

Life Application

Once a major center of commercial, political, and religious power in the ancient world, Sardis exists today as no more than an archeological highpoint surrounding the small village of Sart. Her key ruins include: the Acropolis (the Upper City), of which little has survived centuries of weathering and earthquakes; the ancient and vast temple of Artemis; the Lower City, featuring an impressive Roman gymnasium and bathhouse, a Jewish synagogue, and many Byzantine shops; and, Bin Tepe (Turkish "Thousand Hills"), a vast cemetery of over 200 ancient burial mounds. Modern day tourists find a welcome in the larger city of Salihli just a short drive away.

History tells of the growth and influence of the Jewish population of Sardis for several hundred years before and long after John's day. Its synagogue, still visible, once drew many hundreds of worshipers to the very center of the Lower City. Along with the secure place held by the Jewish people, both secular history and the Bible indicate that Christians in the late first century A.D. also enjoyed a promising, if not favored, place in society. So, unlike the believers in Ephesus, Smyrna, Pergamum, and nearby Philadelphia, there is no mention that the Christians of Sardis had anything but a favorable "reputation" (3:1). Literally speaking, they had made a "name" for themselves; and why should the world be otherwise concerned with a church that Jesus called "dead"?

How is it that this church—or any church—can be birthed in holy fire in one generation only to be choked to death by religious smoke in the next! Church of Sardis, you have a "reputation of being alive." You look the part—busy, active, on top of your game. You pride yourself on your full calendar of events and social functions, outwardly thriving, inwardly dying—the wealth of the world over the treasures of Jesus—an appearance in the fast lane over a passion for His presence. You speak of a Jesus you no longer know. Quick! "Wake up! Strengthen what remains." Remember what once captured your hearts and minds; get a grip on what really matters when it's all said and done. And if you refuse…the only future that remains is swift and sudden judgment.

Yet Jesus has always had a people—"a few [...] who have not soiled their clothes"— untainted by the world. They remember that reputation is how others see them, image is how they see themselves, but character is how God sees them. Better still is integrity of heart, when reputation, image, and character come into agreement. Of these few, Jesus gladly affirms, "They will walk with me, dressed in white, for they are worthy"— despised by some on earth, loved by all in Heaven.

So, what does a living church really look like? Busy with well-run programs alone? Not really—it pays little to organize the lounge chairs of a sinking cruise ship! (In fact, some of the most well-organized sections of any city are its graveyards!) Having a good name in the community? For a while, perhaps, but Jesus warned, "Woe to you when everyone speaks well of you" (Luke 6:26). Surely it's in having our doctrines down! But true devotion to our beliefs should always lead us back to the foot of the cross and the doorway to the empty tomb in wonder. So, let those with an ear to hear, return, remember, and live large for Jesus.

The Message to the Church in Philadelphia—3:7-13

[7] "To the angel of the church in Philadelphia write: These are the words of him who is holy and true, who holds the key of David. What he opens no one can shut, and what he shuts no one can open. [8] I know your deeds. See, I have placed before you an open door that no one can shut. I know that you have little strength, yet you have kept my word and have not denied my name. [9] I will make those who are of the synagogue of Satan, who claim to be Jews though they are not, but are liars—I will make them come and fall down at your feet and acknowledge that I have loved you. [10] Since you have kept my command to endure patiently, I will also keep you from the hour of trial that is going to come on the whole world to test the inhabitants of the earth. [11] I am coming soon. Hold on to what you have, so that no one will take your crown. [12] The one who is victorious I will make a pillar in the temple of my God. Never again will they leave it. I will write on them the name of my God and the name of the city of my God, the new Jerusalem, which is coming down out of heaven from my God; and I will also write on them my new name. [13] Whoever has ears, let them hear what the Spirit says to the churches.

Biblical Insights

Background Information

As compared to the antiquity of the locales of the other six churches of Asia, Philadelphia was still relatively young as a city in John's day (though the ancient settlement of "Calletebus" did already exist in that area for hundreds of years). More recently, Macedonian soldiers had used the vicinity as a strategic outpost for the Kingdom of Pergamum. However, it was in 189 B.C. that the Pergamene King Eumenes II (221-160 B.C.) established the city, naming it "Philadelphos" (in Greek, "one who loves his brother") as a display of love for his own younger brother and successor Attalus II ("Philadelphus") (220-138 B.C.). When Attalus II's nephew and successor, Attalus III Philometer (c. 170-133 B.C.), lacked an heir, he then bestowed his kingdom—including the city of Philadelphia—to his Roman allies upon his death in 133 B.C. The Kingdom of Pergamum effectively came to an end, and the city of Philadelphia was added to the Roman province of Asia under the administration of Sardis its capital.

From its founding, Philadelphia was intended to be both a commercial hub and a center for Greco-Asian culture, spread through its Greek language and customs into the surrounding regions. Like Sardis just 27 miles to its northwest, the city was situated along the Persian, and later Roman, Royal Road, which connected it to Sardis and eventually to the Aegean Sea at Smyrna 75 miles to the west.

Philadelphia also lies near the Hermus and Meander Rivers; here a valley region rich in fertile soil allows it to excel in the cultivation and production of quality grapes and wine. No small wonder, then, that the chief deity of ancient Philadelphia was Dionysus (Roman, "Bacchus"), the god of wine to the Greeks. As a witness to their pagan devotion, ancient inscriptions have even been found referring to Dionysus's ability to receive confession of sin and to punish sin.[5] The city also earned the title "Little Athens" due to its many temples dedicated to the gods of Olympus and its public buildings, similar in architecture to Athens across the Aegean Sea.

Words of Affirmation and Encouragement — 3:7-11

The church of Philadelphia shares with the church of Smyrna the distinction of receiving nothing but praise from Christ. Once again, "the angel," or, here, minister of this local church at the time of John's writing remains unidentified. Beyond the foundational work of Paul and his associates (Acts 19:10), little is known historically of this first c. local congregation apart from these words of Christ. As Revelation continuously affirms the deity of Christ, Jesus shares with the Father in the attributes of His absolute holiness (4:8; 6:10; 15:4; 16:5) and in being "true," in the sense of genuine (3:14; 6:10; 15:3; 16:7; 19:2, 9, 11), in great contrast to the Satanic counterfeits yet to be foretold in this book.

Jesus further identifies Himself as the one "who holds the key of David," a declaration of royal authority and prerogative fulfilled in His Messiahship. In this book, replete with Old Testament references, affirmation is made of Christ's fulfillment of the Davidic Covenant (cf. 5:5; 22:16). Here and in the words that follow is a direct quotation from Isaiah 22:22. As "Eliakim son of Hilkiah," once had privileged authority as "administrator"—holding the master key, fastened on his shoulder—in Hezekiah's palace (2 Kings 18:18), so Jesus has governing authority in the household and plans of God (Isa. 9:6; Matt. 16:19), even as He earlier revealed His authority over "death and Hades" (1:18).

After Jesus asserts His authority to open doors His enemies cannot shut and shut doors His enemies cannot open, He then applies this power as favor toward His people—"See, I have placed before you an open door that no one can shut." We may find here a stark contrast with the planned mission of Philadelphia, namely to be a gateway, an open doorway, to the Eastern world for the spread of the Greek language and culture. But the Church has an inestimably greater purpose through an "open door" for the spread of the culture of Jesus (cf. 1 Cor. 16:9; 2 Cor. 2:12; Col. 4:3). The One who knows His Church best sees the faithful "deeds" (2:2, 19) of this embattled congregation. That they have "little strength" is far from criticism. Most likely they were small in number as compared to the prevailing pagan devotees of Philadelphia. Their strength was only "little" in quantity, not quality; and in their weakness, He was made strong (2 Cor. 12: 9-10). In obedience, they had "kept" (1:3; 12:17; 14:12; cf. 1 John 2:3), or attended to, Christ's Word, and in steadfastness and righteousness they had not "denied ['renounced' or 'forsaken'] my name."

Set against Christ's followers are those "who claim to be Jews though they are not" comprising "the synagogue of Satan" (just as in Smyrna; 2:9). They are false Jews (Rom. 2:28-29; Gal. 6:15)—even as there are false Christians who still persecute true Jews today. Just as the persecution of believers had come through hostile and blaspheming "slander" in Smyrna, here Christ calls their oppressors "liars" (*pseudomai*, "to speak falsely"; cf. 21:8; Matt. 5:11). Indeed, Jesus had met this strain before (John 8:44). Yet the tables will be turned! "I will make them come and fall down at your feet" (even as Job's "friends" and Joseph's brothers were brought to confessional humiliation). Since their lie had included a denial of the favor of God toward Christ-followers, Jesus will cause them to "acknowledge that I have loved you." (But look, the day will come when unbelieving Gentiles will bow before believing Jews—Isa. 45:14; 49:23.) Best is where faith in Christ unites true Christians and true Jews, the "one new man in place of the two, so making peace" (Eph. 2:14-16); here is the true "Israel of God" (Gal. 6:16).

In response to their persevering obedience to His command (cf. Mark 13:13—"But he who endures to the end shall be saved"), Jesus speaks a pivotal promise to His children. The message of reward is clear—because "you have kept [*tēreō*, in the sense of 'carefully attended to'] my command" (as in v. 8), "I will also keep [again *tēreō*, in the sense of 'carefully guard over'] you from the hour of trial [*peirasmos*; 'a trial,' 'adversity,' or 'affliction']." While their faithfulness is described as a past action, Christ's promise is described as a future hope. The words "that is going to come on the whole world to test [*peirazō*, 'to prove or try'] the inhabitants of the earth," gives clear and unquestioned focus upon the eschatological and global tribulation described in this Revelation (cf. Matt. 24:21). While Jesus has promised to carry believers victoriously through inevitable persecution for their faith (2:9-11), He has also promised to keep believers "from" (*ek*, 'out of') His coming judgment upon the "inhabitants of the earth" (6:10; 8:13; 11:10; 12:12; 13:8, 12, 14; 17:2, 8). How different will be the destinies of the earth-dwellers from those whose citizenship is in Heaven (Phil. 3:20).

The imminence of Christ's return is once again announced with the words "I am coming soon" (*tachy*; 'quickly,' 'without delay'). From the first (Rev. 1:1; where see note) to the last verses (22:7, 12, 20), this word comes as both bright promise to the believer and firm warning to the unbeliever. Again, we are reminded that, "the time is near [*eggys*; here, 'near in time']" (1:3; 22:10). With this in sight, "hold on to what you have" (2:25), namely, their faith, faithfulness, and every "open door." In doing this, "no one will take your crown," i.e., your *stephanos*, your victor's crown. As in the foot race, the crown goes to only one (1 Cor. 9:24), so be victorious to the end.

Words of Blessing and Promise—3:12-13

Christ's promise to these overcomers paints a picture of strength, permanence, and beauty. To a city well known for its frequent physical earthquakes, times of shaking would come spiritually as well. Yet in those times of testing, Jesus will establish His faithful as "pillars in the temple of my God." When all else falls around them, they will remain, standing strong upon the foundation of Christ (1 Cor. 3:11). Further, as this city was known for its many pagan temples, Jesus calls the assembly of His people, "the temple of my God" (cf. 2 Cor. 6:16; Eph. 2:21). Unlike the familiar pattern of fearful citizens fleeing to the open country during earthquakes, Christ followers will not be moved from their place in Him—"never again will they leave it."

Those who are victorious are also privileged to receive identifying, privileged, and secure names from Christ. To be inscribed with "the name of my God" (7:3; 9:4; 14:1; 22:4) speaks of the Father's claim upon us, as well as His authority working within us. "The name of the city of my God" speaks of citizenship above (21:2, 3, 19; 22:14; cf. Heb. 11:14-16). This is the "new Jerusalem" which is now God's dwelling place, and "which is coming down out of heaven from my God" with the establishment of the new Heavens and earth (Rev. 21:1-3). The practice of inscribing names of favored citizens upon the columns of the temples in ancient Philadelphia may be the historic metaphor here.[6] To bear "my new name" (2:17), speaks of the unique identity that comes to those who have a new covenant relationship with Christ through faith in His atoning work. As with each of the seven messages, Jesus calls to all who would wisely listen to the voice of His Spirit.

Life Application

Like John, the writer of this Revelation, Jesus does have "intimates," those whom He gladly holds close to His side. And truth be known, Jesus extends that invitation to all who choose to follow Him closely—"Draw near to God, and he will draw near to you" (James 4:8). This was the position of the church of Philadelphia, a congregation close to the heart of Jesus. In response to their faithfulness and steadfastness even under fire, the One who is "holy and true" speaks intimate favor and blessing over His very own. He is also the One who holds "the key of David," commissioned and in charge of the business of the Kingdom of His Father. To all who follow closely, Jesus has promised "an open door that no one can shut." Against the background of a city built for the purpose of spreading the Greek language and culture, the church of Philadelphia was commissioned and entrusted with the great opportunity to spread the language and culture of Jesus.

In centuries past, long before our modern harbors and instruments, ships waited off shore for the flood tide to rise before making it into port. An ancient Latin phrase was used to describe this scene—a ship was said to be "ob portu," against the port, waiting for the moment of the turning tide. We, too, who follow closely await the rising tide of the Spirit and the great open doors of "ob-portunity" Jesus sets before us.

Such was the man William Carey (1761-1834), at first a seemingly insignificant English cobbler. Yet while still a teen and young adult he taught himself Greek,

Hebrew, Latin, Italian, Dutch, and French, all while working on shoes. He had grasped the promise and potential of spiritual opportunity—He would not miss God's open door! First a schoolmaster, then a pastor, his vision to reach the unconverted only grew in intensity. At the age of 31, he along with his family embraced the call of God for the lost of India. For the next 41 years, his unprecedented ministry as missionary, translator, educator, and social reformer was legendary. In his work, he spoke and lived by the mottos every intimate follower of Jesus should take as his or her own: "Expect great things from God. Attempt great things for God"; and, "The future is as bright as the promises of God."

Along with Christ's open doors, come other promises to His "intimate" followers. He will have the final word of vindication toward His faithful; and He will fix them as "pillars" of strength in a world and in the visible church so easily shaken. While others run for cover, they will stand strong as the "temple" of God's spiritual house. And inscribed on each pillar is Christ's own name of identity and favor. Is it a coincidence that virtually all that remains of the ruins of the ancient church of Philadelphia are the four brick, massive pillars of a seventh century basilica? Sadly, however, there is no known Christian congregation in this modern city of Alasehir today.

Greatest of all promises to Christ's victorious followers is the word of His soon return—"I am coming soon." While the "whole world" will be tested by the wrath of God on its sin, we have the promise of God to be kept "from"—"out of"—"the hour of trial," echoing the words of Paul, "For God did not appoint us to suffer wrath but to receive salvation through our Lord Jesus Christ" (1 Thess. 5:9).

The Message to the Church in Laodicea—3:14-22

[14] "To the angel of the church in Laodicea write: These are the words of the Amen, the faithful and true witness, the ruler of God's creation. [15] I know your deeds, that you are neither cold nor hot. I wish you were either one or the other! [16] So, because you are lukewarm—neither hot nor cold—I am about to spit you out of my mouth. [17] You say, 'I am rich; I have acquired wealth and do not need a thing.' But you do not realize that you are wretched, pitiful, poor, blind and naked. [18] I counsel you to buy from me gold refined in the fire, so you can become rich; and white clothes to wear, so you can cover your shameful nakedness; and salve to put on your eyes, so you can see. [19] Those whom I love I rebuke and discipline. So be earnest and repent. [20] Here I am! I stand at the door and knock. If anyone hears my voice and opens the door, I will come in and eat with that person, and they with me.

[21] To the one who is victorious, I will give the right to sit with me on my throne, just as I was victorious and sat down with my Father on his throne. [22] Whoever has ears, let them hear what the Spirit says to the churches."

Biblical Insights

Background Information

Building upon the site of a town once known as Diospolis and later Rhoas, the Seleucid king Antiochus II Theos of Syria (c. 287-246 B.C.) founded Laodicea in the years 261-253 B.C., naming it in honor of his wife, Laodice.[7] Following the reign of the Seleucids and their expulsion from Asia Minor through the Treaty of Apamea Kibotos, the city came under the rule of the Kingdom of Pergamum in 188 B.C. Paralleling the history of Sardis and Philadelphia, Laodicea then came under full Roman control in 133 B.C. While under Seleucid and Pergamum rule, the city had been positioned at the junction of the Hellenistic regions known as Caria and Lydia. Once under Roman rule, through to New Testament times, Laodicea was situated within the Province of Asia.

Of the seven churches of Asia, the church in the city of Laodicea was located the furthest from the Aegean Sea, about 100 miles east of Ephesus and about 57 miles southeast of Philadelphia. Along with the nearby cities of Colosse and Hierapolis, "Laodicea on the Lycus," as it was known in ancient days, was situated in the Lycus River valley near to where the Lycus flows into the Maeander River. The city was also positioned along two major trade routes allowing it to prosper through two primary industries.

In this fertile land, large flocks of sheep grazed its pasture, providing soft, black wool. The harvesting and dying of this quality wool made Laodicea a great center for the manufacturing of textiles and clothing. In the first century A.D. the city was also host to a well-known school of medicine associated with the temple and worship of the Greek healing god Asklepios and the earlier Phrygian god of healing Men Karou. Following the medical theory of Herophilos (c. 330-c. 250 B.C.)—who popularized the use of compound mixtures to treat compound diseases—this school was famous for its production of an eye-salve made from a powdered form of a certain Phrygian stone mixed with oil.[8]

Along with the exports of textiles and eye-salve, Laodicea grew to be one of the wealthiest cities in the Greco-Roman world through its banking industry. Evidence of the self-sufficiency of its citizens was seen in its refusal to accept assistance from the Roman government when in A.D. 60 the city was devastated by a massive earthquake. Roman historian and senator Tacitus wrote, "One of the most famous cities of Asia, Laodicea, was in the same year overthrown by an earthquake and without any relief from us recovered itself by its own resources."[9]

The religious practices of Laodicea were also diverse during New Testament times. The worship of Zeus, known as "the father of the gods," had continued since its earliest history as the town of Diospolis, meaning "City of Zeus." The Phrygian goddess, Cybele, was also worshiped here. Further, coins minted in Laodicea tell of the worship of Asklepios, Apollo, and the Roman emperors. It is also well known that a large Jewish population inhabited the city and area. "According to Josephus,

Antiochus III (the Great) transported 2,000 Jewish families from Mesopotamia and Babylonia to the 'fortresses and most important places' of Phrygia and Lydia."[10] History also records that a large Christian church was present in Laodicea well into the fourth century.

Words of Correction and Warning—3:14-20

As with all seven churches of Asia, Jesus addresses this message to the "angel" of the church, which likely refers to the messenger or pastor of the church at the time of writing (see note under 1:16). We do know that Epaphras is acknowledged by Paul to have faithfully brought the Gospel message to Colossae (Colossians 1:6-7). Later in Colossians, Paul adds, "Epaphras, who is one of you" [...] "he is working hard for you and for those at Laodicea and Hierapolis" (4:12, 13). Paul's personal references which follow and his instruction that the content of his two letters be shared amongst these churches speak of the close connection of the churches and believers located in these three cities (4:14-17). Paul also states in Colossians 2:1 that he is "struggling for you and for those at Laodicea." Within this context he recognizes that their faith is being challenged through deceptive "fine-sounding arguments" (2:4), most likely a reference to insidious pre-gnostic heresy.

Jesus first presents Himself as "the Amen, the faithful and true witness." "Amen" is an expression of certainty transliterated from a Hebrew root word indicating "firmness" and "trustworthiness." When God the Father speaks His "Yes" of unwavering truth through His Son, we respond with our "Amen" of faith and trust (2 Cor. 1:20). (See also Isaiah 65:16 where God describes Himself with the name "amen"). Jesus many times spoke the words "truly [or 'verily'] I tell you" (*amēn legō hymin*) in His teachings, and He will end this Revelation with the certainty of His "Amen" again (22:20, 21). (See also Revelation 1:6, 7; 5:14; 7:12; and 19:4.)

Coupled with "the Amen," is the certainty found in the name "the faithful and true witness," further reinforcing the trustworthy and genuine nature of Christ's direct witness to the Revelation the Father has entrusted to Him for us (cf. John 1:9; 6:32; 15:1; 19:35). Jesus had already revealed himself as the "faithful witness" in Revelation 1:5, and He will yet be revealed from Heaven bearing the name "Faithful and True" (19:11). To this Jesus adds that He is, "the ruler of God's creation." "Ruler" here is *archē*, which as a noun indicates both a beginning and an active cause of something. Scripture declares that Jesus—who being God and having no beginning (John 1:1; 8:58)—was the instrument through whom the Father created all things (John 1:3, 10; 1 Cor. 8:6; Heb. 1:2). *"Arche"* also speaks of Christ's principal position as "ruler" above all creation, as indicated by Paul so powerfully in Ephesians 1:20-21 and Colossians 1:15-17.

It is with the Laodicean church as with each of the six prior churches; Jesus "knows" the real and complete spiritual condition of each congregation, and every prophetic detail flows from this knowledge. "Deeds," which in some of the churches spoke of good works or fruit, can here only speak of bad fruit. Sadly, this bad yield was indicative of a deeper issue, for Jesus has taught, "You will know them by their fruits" (Matt. 7:16, NASB) and again, "For out of the heart come evil thoughts, murders, adulteries, fornications, thefts, false witness, slanders" (Matt. 15:19, NASB). Jesus knew these Christians to be "neither cold nor hot" repeated as "neither hot nor cold" in verse 16 for emphasis. Rather, He has found them to be "lukewarm," which has revolted Him to the point of saying, "I am about to spit [lit. 'vomit'] you out of my mouth." Both "lukewarm" (*chliaros*) and "vomit" (*emeō*) are words found only here in the New Testament.

Commonly it is held that "hot" refers to spiritual fervor for Christ and "cold" refers to spiritual indifference, perhaps even indicating an unsaved state. If this is so, then Christ's strong preference found in the words "I wish you were either one or the other!" can only mean He would rather they be zealous enough to closely follow or "cold" enough to see their desperate need. How else could Jesus wish that they were "cold," especially when He is speaking to the local church at large?[11] It is more probable that Jesus is bringing an analogy drawn from the prominent water temperatures of two of Laodicea's closest neighboring cities. Approximately six miles to the northeast was Hierapolis, which was celebrated for its natural hot water springs and therapeutic thermal spas. Approximately ten miles to the southeast of Laodicea was Colossae, which was known to enjoy a refreshing cold and pure supply of water. In great contrast, Laodicea had no immediate fresh water supply, and so relied upon water brought in from a distance through a system of stone and clay pipes. Yet the lukewarm temperature and strong mineral content of the water upon arrival caused it to be distasteful if not nauseating.[12] And so Christ may well be saying that unlike the useful and refreshing waters known to their neighbors, their "lukewarm" condition has caused them to be of little use and spiritually repulsive.

Driving this spiritual ineptitude is the spiritual pride—to the point of self-deception—of these Laodicean Christians. Taking the lead from its self-confident, self-sufficient, and pride-filled host city, this church boasted, "I am rich; I have acquired wealth and do not need a thing." (How different from the humility of the believers in Smyrna! [Rev. 2:9].) What they "do not realize," what they fail to perceive correctly, is what Jesus sees so clearly. They are in His sight "wretched, pitiful, poor, blind and naked," so opposite of their prideful claim. While they had been blinded by their temporary and outward prosperity and apparent popularity (cf. 1 Cor. 4:8; 1 Tim. 6:9), they knew nothing of the spiritual riches promised to those who are "poor in spirit" (Matt. 5:3) and they knew nothing of "contentment" in Christ, with or without earthly goods (Phil. 4:11-12). And so, Jesus counsels His church (cf. Isa. 1:18; 9:6).

To a church and city that took great pride in its wealth as a great banking center, Jesus counsels them to "buy from me" (cf. Isa. 55:1; Eph. 3:8) "gold refined in the fire" (cf. 1 Pet. 1:7) "so you can become rich" (cf. Luke 16:11; 1 Tim. 6:18). To a church and city that thrived on its manufacturing of woolen and shiny black clothing, Jesus counsels them to "buy from me" [...] "white clothes to wear" (cf. Isa. 61:10; Rev. 19:8) "so you can cover your shameful nakedness" (cf. Gen. 2:25; 3:21). To a church and city, which boasted in its discovery and production of eye ointment, Jesus counsels them to "buy from me" [...] "salve to put on your eyes, so you can see" (cf. John 9:39-41; Psalm 13:3).

But Jesus is not through with this church. Though they have revolted his heart, He says, "I am about to [*mellō*; 'to intend to'] spit you out." He still holds the angel of this church in His right hand (Rev. 1:20) and he walks in their midst (1:13). And now He states His love for this church demonstrated in His rebuke and discipline. If "love" here as a verb was *agapaō*, we would see an emphasis on His constant, unconditional acceptance; rather, Jesus here expresses *phileō*, emphasizing His tender affection for his people. These He "rebukes" (*elegchō*) or convicts of sin (cf. John 16:8; Eph. 5:13) and continues to "discipline" (*paideuō*), which first applied to the instruction of children as in Hebrews 12:6, "because the Lord disciplines the one he loves, and he chastens everyone he accepts as his son." Their part then is to "be earnest" (*zēloō*), indicating zealous pursuit—so opposite of their current "lukewarmness"—"and repent" (*metanoeō*), "change your minds," as already seen in Revelation 2:5, 16, 22; 3:3 (cf. 9:20; 16:9, 11).

Jesus is waiting patiently for their response to His merciful invitation. "Here I am!" (*idou*) is better translated "Look!" With the words, "I stand at the door and knock," Jesus as the scorned lover of the soul assumes a place of humility and hopeful expectation that a wayward church will answer. How sad that He would not already be on the other side! "I stand," in the perfect tense means, "I have taken my stand"; yet, He continues to "knock" (present active). (We may see an allusion here to Song of Songs 5:2.) The openness of this call to this and any local church and more so toward every individual is captured in the phrase "If anyone hears my voice" (Rev. 22:17; cf. Matt. 11:28; 1 Tim. 2:4-6; 2 Pet. 3:9; etc.). He also now equates the words He has been speaking to His persistent knocking at the heart's door. We see here also the nature of Christ's election, conditioned upon obedient faith—"and opens the door" (cf. John 1:12; 3:15, 16, 36; 6:40; 11:25, 26; 20:31; Acts 10:43; Rom. 10:9, 13; 1 John 5:1; etc.). And this all by God's grace (cf. John 6:44; Eph. 2:8, 9; Titus 2:11; etc.)!

Jesus will always "come in" to the heart that repents and receives Him, and there He desires to remain (John 15:4-7). He further expresses His desire for restored fellowship with the words, "I will come in and eat with that person." "Eat" (*deipneō*) here needs a closer look for the word directly indicates the partaking and fellowship of the evening meal. Whereas the midday meal (*ariston*) was, as we would say, "a meal on the run," the evening meal (*deipnon*) was the main meal after the completion of the day's long work, which brought families and often friends together in extended fellowship.[13] Thus, Christ's desire to "eat" with us is a call to close and unbroken communion. Indeed, while we are the recipients of His mercy, forgiveness, and presence,

Jesus—with the words "and they with me" (cf. John 6:56)—also expresses His desire for our presence in right relationship with Him.

Words of Blessing and Promise—3:21-22

Though five of the seven churches of Asia had received Christ's strong correction and call to repentance, Jesus still walked in the midst of all seven and still spoke blessing over each. Faith that enters into the victory of Christ is a personal decision, so Jesus for the seventh time speaks a promise to the "one who is victorious." Amazingly, to the responsive heart in the most distant of the seven churches, Jesus offers the most intimate invitation.

Revelation declares that the Throne of Almighty God, the seat of His absolute glory and authority, is established at the center of the highest Heaven (4:2-6). It is here, after He had victoriously conquered over the grave, that Jesus took His place of full glory and authority at the Father's right hand (cf. Matt. 22:44; 26:64; Mark 16:19; Acts 2:33, 34; 5:31; Rom. 8:34; Eph. 1:20; Col. 3:1; Heb. 1:3, 13; 8:1; 10:12; 12:2; 1 Pet. 3:22). But it is also here that faith-filled and faithful overcomers are given a future place in Christ; "to sit with me on my throne" speaks of sharing in Christ's glory and authority in the closest of terms (cf. Matt. 19:28; 20:23; Luke 22:28-30; John 17:22, 24; 1 Cor. 6:2; 2 Tim. 2:12; Rev. 2:26, 27; 5:10; 20:6; 22:5). There we will also lead with Christ during His Millennial Reign and throughout eternity. Inasmuch as we by faith have citizenship in Heaven now, the Father has already "seated us with him in the heavenly realms in Christ Jesus" (Eph. 2:6).

As with each of the seven messages, the directive of Christ's words of encouragement, warning, and promise is made to all who will listen and receive—"whoever has ears"—certainly beyond the original recipients alone. The same Spirit who inspired this writing is still speaking His truth to hearts today (cf. John 16:13).

Life Application

For the seventh time, Jesus presents Himself to His Church as the One who knows us best. He knows when we are strong and He knows when we are weak. He knows when we need a word of comfort and He knows when we need a word of rebuke. He knows when we are moving forward in victory and He knows when we are lost in self-deception. And, as e Hewith the church in Laodicea, He knows whether the spiritual temperature of our hearts is "hot," "cold," or just "lukewarm."

Still visible today amongst the ancient ruins of Laodicea and its vicinity is an arched aqueduct along with an elaborate system of pipes of stone or clay and reservoirs. Without its own adequate source of water, the city was dependent upon water carried along these channels from its closest neighbors several miles away. To the southeast is Colossae, well known to this day for its refreshing cold water. To its northeast is Hierapolis (modern day Pamukkale), still renowned for its hot springs, thermal spas, and shimmering white terraces formed by its cascading, mineral-rich waters. It is most likely that Jesus has these preferred water temperatures in mind when He says, "you are neither cold nor hot." Sadly, the "deeds" ("works" or "fruit") of the Laodicean believers exemplified neither. If the marks of your Christian life were "cold" like the waters of Colossae, I would find you refreshing. If the evidence of your Christianity were "hot" like the waters of Hierapolis, I would find you so useful. "I wish you were either one or the other!" laments Christ Jesus. Instead, I have found you to be "lukewarm"—room temperature, tepid—pathetic and nauseating.

Listen again to "the faithful and true witness" crying out to those who conveniently speak His name on cue (with just enough of Jesus to be dangerous!). "I'd like you to stop pretending you don't hear my voice when I call." "I'd like you to stop your insensitive yawning when you're with Me, as if you've heard this all before." "And for goodness sake, I'd like you to stop dragging your wedding dress through the mud!"

Are there not "Laodicean Christians" still in the Church of our day?! On the outside, they look the part—but inside is no holy fire, no spiritual passion, no love for what Christ loves. On the outside, they are self-made, self-sufficient, "living large" like the world around them. On the outside, they boast, "we are rich; we have acquired wealth and do not need a thing." But on the inside Jesus finds them "wretched, pitiful, poor, blind and naked." Yet, on the outside of the "Laodicean heart" is Jesus, graciously standing, patiently knocking, still desiring to come in.

In 2003 I was honored to visit the West African nation of Angola. The city of Uige, close to the northern boundary with the Congo, evidenced the devastation of the forty years of civil war that had ravaged this country. As I completed a sixth day of teaching, I invited the hundred or so leaders who had walked in each day from across that city and the surrounding region to corporate prayer. Sitting on the floor of that communist theatre, they began to cry out to God for their beleaguered nation. The power of God was strong and His presence so refreshing when a young man began to speak under the anointing of the Holy Spirit. Though I was told by the missionary he knew no English, amongst the words he spoke in perfect English was this phrase again and again, "Jesus is here; Jesus is here!"

Jesus is here—close to all who call upon His name! As with all seven of these representative churches in Asia, though our "first love" may grow distant or our spiritual passion may be found "lukewarm," Jesus is here! Though our faith is under fire from enemies without or from compromise within the Church, Jesus is here! Standing near, knocking patiently, calling graciously, He unceasingly desires our communion.

Chapter 3 Notes

1. A D Godley, ed. and trans., "Herodotus, The Histories, Book 1, Chapter 94.1." (Harvard University Press. 1920), as contained in web site, *Perseus*, Department of the Classics, Tufts University, 11 Dec. 2017 <www.perseus.tufts.edu/hopper/text?do c=Perseus%3Atext%3A1999.01.0126%3Abook%3D1%3Achapter%3D94%3Asec tion%3D1>.

2. Dale Bargmann, "Sardis," *Seven Cities of Revelation*, 11 Dec. 2017 <www.wingsofea-glesct.com/REVELATION/Sardis.html>.

3. Fikret K Yegül, *The Bath-Gymnasium Complex at Sardis. Archaeological exploration of Sardis: reports* (New York: Harvard University Press, 1975).

4. William Barclay, *Letters to the Seven Churches* (Louisville, KY: John Knox Press, 2001) 77.

5. "Philadelphia, (Alaşehir-Turkey)" *Private Tour*, Ephesus Tours, 6 Oct. 2013 <www. ephesustoursguide.com/must-see-places-in-turkey/philadelphia-alasehir-turkey. html>.

6. "Philadelphia honored its illustrious sons by putting their names on the pillars of its temples, so that all who came to worship might see and remember." William Barclay, as quoted by David Guzik. David Guzik, "Study Guide for Revelation 3 by David Guzik," Blue Letter Bible, 2001 <www.blueletterbible.org/Comm/guzik_david/ StudyGuide2017-Rev/Rev-3.cfm?a=1170001>.

7. Izabela Sobota-Miszczak, "Laodicea on the Lycus," *Turkish Archaeological News*, ASLAN Izabela Sobota-Miszczak, 9 Mar. 2017 <turkisharchaeonews.net/site/ laodicea-lycus.

8. Otto F.A. Meinardus, *St. John of Patmos and the Seven Churches of the Apocalypse* (Athens, Greece: Lycabettus Press, 1974) 125.
   Also, "The word is doubtless an allusion to the Phrygian powder used by oculists in the famous medical school at Laodicea" W.E. Vine, *An Expository Dictionary of New Testament Words*, 17th Impression (Revell, 1966), Quoting Ramsay, *Cities and Bishoprics of Phrygia, Vol. I, 52*.

9. Alfred John Church and William Jackson Brodribb, transl., "The Annals by Tacitus, Book XIV," *The Internet Classics Archive*, 2009 <classics.mit.edu//Tacitus/annals.10. xiv.html>.

10. "Phrygia." *Jewish Virtual Library*, American-Israeli Cooperative Enterprise, 2017 <www.jewishvirtuallibrary.org/phrygia>.

[11.] David Guzik shares, "The thief on the cross was cold towards Jesus and clearly saw his need. The Apostle John was hot towards Jesus and enjoyed an intimate relationship of love. But Judas was lukewarm, following Jesus enough to be considered a disciple, but not giving his heart over to Jesus in fullness." David Guzik, "Study Guide for Revelation 3," *Blue Letter Bible*, 2001 <www.blueletterbible.org/Comm/archives/guzik_david/studyguide_rev/rev_3.cfm>.

[12.] "Water piped into Laodicea by aqueduct from the south was so concentrated with minerals that the Roman engineers designed vents, capped by removable stones, so the aqueduct pipes could periodically be cleared of deposits." John McRay, *Archaeology and the New Testament* (Grand Rapids, MI: Baker, 2008) 248.

Helpful information may also be found in Colin J. Hemer, *The Letters to the Seven Churches of Asia in Their Local Setting* (Grand Rapids, MI: Eerdmans, 2000) 188-189.

[13.] "It was the *deipnon* that Christ would share with the man who answered His knock, no hurried meal, but that where people lingered in fellowship. If a man will open the door, Jesus Christ will come in and linger long with him." William Barclay, *The Revelation of John, Vol. 1, The Daily Bible Study Series* (Louisville, KY: Westminster Press, 1978) 147–148.

CHAPTER 4

Revelation 4:1-11

The Sights and Sounds of Heaven

Introduction to Revelation 4:1-11

From the beginning of this Revelation, it is clear that the Triune God (1:4-5)—Father, Son, and Spirit—is absolutely sovereign and unquestionably transcendent within realms visible and invisible. Yet, just as clear is that our God is immanently close and intimately familiar with every detail of our human experience. Following Christ's very down to earth review of the condition of "the seven churches in the province of Asia," He once again engages John in a vision of Divine glory—with one major change. While John's earlier vision of the Risen Jesus took place within the environs of earth, a new vision now lifts John into the very highest heaven. Nevertheless, both ethereal visions came to John while he was "in the Spirit," the same Spirit who had just spoken so carefully to each church.

In Chapter 1, Jesus revealed Himself to John; in Chapters 2-3, Jesus revealed His Church to John. Moving into Chapter 4, Jesus calls John upward through "a door standing open in heaven" where He now reveals His Father to John, in all of His indescribable glory. At the center of the world, the absolute totality of all that is, both seen and unseen, is established the Throne Room of Almighty God. And surrounding His throne are visionary images of worshipers, some strangely familiar, some strangely otherworldly.

Here, as John is carried beyond "what you have seen" and "what is now" (1:19)—here, at the gateway of "what will take place later"—is one of the most beautiful descriptions of the throne room of God ever revealed to mortal flesh. Here, John encounters the unspeakable, indescribable sights and sounds of Heaven.

God's Throne is Established—4:1-2

[1] After this I looked, and there before me was a door standing open in heaven. And the voice I had first heard speaking to me like a trumpet said, "Come up here, and I will show you what must take place after this." [2] At once I was in the Spirit, and there before me was a throne in heaven with someone sitting on it.

Biblical Insights

A major transition in the Revelation John received is indicated with the phrase "after this" (*meta tauta*; or "after these things") contained at the beginning and ending of 4:1. The first "*meta tauta*" indicates a passing of time in John's experience; it is highly unlikely that John received this entire revelation in one continuous encounter. The second "*meta tauta*" has direct eschatological significance. Jesus used these words first in 1:19 when He outlined the unfolding vision John had begun to receive. There, "what you have seen" speaks of John's immediate revelation of the Resurrected Jesus in our Chapter 1. "What is now" is contained in Christ's seven messages to the seven churches of Asia (1:4), Chapters 2 and 3. "What will take place later [*meta tauta*]" speaks of the balance of the Revelation, which clearly to John implied future fulfillment. "*Meta taute*" will again be seen to indicate both John's experience and the unfolding drama in 7:1, 9; 9:12; 15:5; 18:1; 19:1; 20:3.

In a vision similar to that of Isaiah (6:1ff), Ezekiel (1:1), Stephen (Acts 7:55-56), and Paul (2 Cor. 12:2-7), John is privileged to view the glory of God in His throne room. At first John sees, apparently from an earthly perspective, "a door standing open in heaven." Referred to only here, this "door" or "entrance way" holds a message of access and welcome to John.[1] Along with this visual, John also hears the clear and distinct voice of Jesus, the same "voice I had first heard speaking to me like a trumpet" (1:10, 11, 17-19). This time the voice calls John to "Come up here," i.e., into the very Throne Room of God. Apparently, John's earlier vision of Jesus was viewed within the environment of earth; now he will view "what must take place after this" from the perspective of the third heavens.

Immediately, "at once," John is transported to Heaven. Here we must ponder as Paul did, "whether in the body or apart from the body, I do not know, but God knows" (2 Cor. 12:3). As in 1:10, John knew that he was "in the Spirit," in fact, four times in Revelation John was so moved and carried by the Holy Spirit (17:3 and 21:10). The English Standard Version aptly captures the awe of John and the establishment of God's throne in Heaven with the words of verse 2, "and behold, a throne stood in heaven, with one seated on the throne."

Life Application

Do you long for an "open heaven"? Such a blessing is the privilege of those who hunger to see more of Jesus. To be clear, the Bible does not promise to every believer a transport while still alive in the body on the level of John's vision into the very throne room of God. Truth be known, not many can claim an experience like Isaiah, Ezekiel, Paul, or John. But, if we mean by an "open heaven" a place where our vision is clear to see more of Jesus than we have ever seen before—a place where the glory of God eclipses earth's shadow land—then an "open heaven" is a promised reality for every longing heart.

Throughout the Bible and the ages of time, God has promised an "open heaven" in response to a righteous and obedient expectation for God's more. These are the ones who like John, "live by the Spirit" (Gal. 5:16) and are "led by the Spirit" (Rom. 8:14), and who may be found "in the Spirit" (Rev. 1:10). To these obedient comes the "open heaven" of greater blessing—"The Lord will open the heavens, the storehouse of his bounty, to send rain on your land in season and to bless all the work of your hands" (Deut. 28:12; also 28:1-11; Malachi 3:10 in response to obediently bringing the tithe in worship to the Lord; 2 Cor. 9:8-11). To these who are righteous comes the "open heaven" of greater glory—"Oh, that you would rend the heavens and come down, that the mountains would tremble before you!" (Isa. 64:1-5; cf. Isa. 45:8; 2 Cor. 3:18). To these expectants comes the "open heaven" of greater anointing—"Suddenly a sound like the blowing of a violent wind came from heaven and filled the whole house where they were sitting" (Acts 2:2; also 1:8; 2:1-4; 4:31).

Yes, visions and signs and wonders may also be expected from Heaven as a manifestation of the presence and authority of the Lord increasingly at work in and through us—"Very truly I tell you, you will see 'heaven open, and the angels of God ascending and descending on' the Son of Man" (John 1:51 [and 50]; cf. Gen. 28:12; 1 Kings 18:36-38; Acts 7:55-56; 10:11-16). And, though few have heard the audible voice of God from without, can we not all hear our Father's still voice from within? Can we not as "co-heirs with Christ" (Rom. 8:17; cf. John 14:12; 2 Cor. 1:21-22; 1 John 2:20, 27) hear our Father's words of favor and anointing under an "open heaven" just as Jesus did in answer to prayer (Luke 3:21-22)?

However, we cannot miss that the "open heaven" John experienced also brought a vision of judgment (cf. Isaiah 24:18; Rev. 19:11). If righteousness brings an "open heaven" of blessing, glory, and anointing, then unrighteousness will certainly bring an "open heaven" of judgment, even God's wrath upon the wicked. In fact, John encountered what every true child of God should recognize: His throne is established in Heaven and He will not be mocked.

The Sights of God's Throne Room—4:3-8a

³ And the one who sat there had the appearance of jasper and ruby. A rainbow that shone like an emerald encircled the throne. ⁴ Surrounding the throne were twenty-four other thrones, and seated on them were twenty-four elders. They were dressed in white and had crowns of gold on their heads. ⁵ From the throne came flashes of lightning, rumblings and peals of thunder. In front of the throne, seven lamps were blazing. These are the seven spirits of God. ⁶ Also in front of the throne there was what looked like a sea of glass, clear as crystal. In the center, around the throne, were four living creatures, and they were covered with eyes, in front and in back. ⁷ The first living creature was like a lion, the second was like an ox, the third had a face like a man, the fourth was like a flying eagle. ⁸ᵃ Each of the four living creatures had six wings and was covered with eyes all around, even under its wings.

Biblical Insights

What John is about to describe in otherworldly terms all has its source in "the one" ("he who sat"; NKJV, ESV; nom. sing. masc.) sitting upon the Throne of Heaven. The vagueness of this phrase only adds to its mystery and magnificence; in fact, God Himself is the source of the glory of Heaven and His throne the center of all that is perfect. To John the appearance of God resembled "jasper and ruby." Though "jasper" may refer to a precious stone of varying colors, its further use in Revelation 21:11, "like a jasper, clear as crystal" (also 21:18, 19) indicates a stone with crystal clear brilliance through which the glory of God radiates (21:23). "Ruby" (*sardinos*; NKJV, "sardius"; ESV, "carnelian"; see also 21:20) was most likely the blood-red stone we know as the ruby today. The glory of God appears to radiate from His throne with diamond-like brilliance with a crimson red tone, the color of mercy and redemption.

John also saw what Ezekiel (1:28) saw. A "rainbow" (*iris*; only here and 10:1 in the New Testament) "that shone like an emerald." Most likely a full circle, this rainbow is reminiscent of God's "everlasting covenant between God and all living creatures of every kind on the earth" (Gen. 9:16). The "emerald" (*smaragdinos*; cf. Rev. 21:19 and the Old Testament *bareqeth*, cf. Ezek. 28:13) is the familiar gem known for its light green color. In relationship to God, the rainbow that "encircled the throne" speaks of promise and the green hue speaks of eternal life and of His faithfulness. The imagery comes together in this: the Throne of God (cf. Ps. 47:7-8)—the central government of all that is seen and unseen—is wrapped in His covenant-keeping love (cf. Isa. 54:10).

With the Throne of God at the center of Heaven, all else is "surrounding the throne," the focus of worship and attention. John first sees "twenty-four other thrones," perhaps the same "thrones" Daniel saw in Daniel 7:9 (though these may relate to Rev. 20:4). Seated on these thrones "were twenty-four elders." In Old Testament Israel (continuing into Christ's day), "elders" (*zaqen*) were those men who by virtue of their age were respected representatives of the twelve tribes, entrusted with decision-making power (Exod. 3:16; Num. 11:16; Deut. 27:1). In the New Testament Church, the role of "elder" (*presbyteros*) transitioned from elder leaders in the church in Jerusalem (Acts 11:30; 15:2, 4, 6, 22, 23; 21:18) to appointed spiritual leaders within local churches (Acts 14:23; 1 Tim. 5:17, 19; Titus 1:5). It is clear that the terms "overseer" (*episkopos*) and "pastor" or "shepherd" (*poimēn*) are sometimes used interchangeably in the New Testament. (cf. Acts 20:17, 28; Titus 1:5-7; 1 Pet. 5:1, 2). Of these the writer of Hebrews (13:17) concludes, "they keep watch over you as those who must give an account."

While some commentators maintain that the "twenty-four elders" are angelic in nature, it is best to see them as representatives of God's people on earth in both the Old and New Covenants. This is supported inasmuch as they are "dressed in white"—already revealed to be the garments of believing overcomers (Rev. 3:4, 18; 7:9, 14; 19:6-8, 14 [cf. 17:14])—and, they "had crowns of gold on their heads" (cf. 4:10), that is, they wore the *stephanos* (once wilting wreaths, but here of enduring gold), the victory crowns already promised to Christ's faithful followers (Rev. 2:10; 3:11; cf. 1 Cor. 9:25; 2 Tim. 4:8; Jas. 1:12; 1 Pet. 5:4). While angels are said to wear white garments (Mark 16:5; John 20:12; Acts 1:10), they are never seen wearing crowns of any type. Furthermore, never in the Bible are angels addressed as "elders." In favor of the idea of the "twenty-four" as representatives of God's covenant people are the names of "the twelve tribes of Israel" and "the twelve apostles of the Lamb" written upon the gates (Rev. 21:12) and the foundations (21:14) of the New Jerusalem, the eternal dwelling place of God and of His people. It is also possible that the priestly duty of these "elders" (Rev. 5:8) is parallel to and in fulfillment of the twenty-four orders of priests spoken of in 1 Chronicles 24:4-18.

Jewish readers would quickly identify with the physical expressions of God's awe and power, "flashes of lightning, rumblings and peals of thunder" (Exod. 19:16; Ps. 18:13; 77:18) described as coming "from the throne" (v. 5; cf. Rev. 8:5; 11:19; 16:18). Ezekiel (Ezek. 1:4, 13) had a similar vision. In this context, however, these signs certainly anticipate coming judgment. Likewise, there is Old Testament basis for what John describes next: "In front of the throne, seven lamps were blazing. These are the seven spirits of God" (cf. 1:4, where see note). "The seven spirits of God" can only refer to the "seven-fold" manifested ministry of the Spirit of God "sent out into all the earth" (Rev. 5:6). By use of the completeness associated with the number "seven," we find this same idea in the anointing upon the coming Messiah in Isaiah 11:2 and, through Him, the empowering anointing of His Spirit in Zechariah 4:2, 6, 10. He again is seen as a "spirit of fire" in Isaiah 4:4, speaking of His holy judgment. Additionally, in the earthly Tabernacle there was positioned a seven-stemmed golden lampstand (Exod. 25:31-37). According to Hebrews 8:5 all that was found in the earthly sanctuary was "a copy and shadow of what is in heaven," a mere reflection of what John saw in its glorious fulfillment. Further, God's will, about to be worked out into the earth, is already settled in Heaven.

Reflecting the universe over which God presides in transcendence, John also sees "in front of the throne [...] what looked like a sea of glass, clear as crystal" (v. 6). "Crystal" (*krystallos*), from a root word meaning "ice," speaks of transparency. In the New Testament, this word is found only here and in 21:11, speaking of the glorious New Jerusalem, and 22:1, speaking of the crystal flowing river flowing from the throne in the New Jerusalem. Ezekiel (Ezek. 1:22) again had a similar vision, and David declares, "The Lord sits enthroned over the flood; the Lord is enthroned as King forever" (Ps. 29:10). Typology is seen again in the bronze laver in the first earthly tabernacle (Exod. 30:18-21) and in the vast basin positioned in Solomon's Temple just before the Holy Place. 2 Chronicles 4:2 states, "Then he cast a great round basin, 15 feet across from rim to rim, called the Sea. It was 7½ feet deep and about 45 feet in circumference" (NLT). Far from the bloody and troubled waters to come, this sea is crystal clear and perfectly calm.

Even more mysterious than the "twenty-four elders" are the "four living creatures" that stand "in the center, around the throne," i.e., immediately before and in a circle surrounding the throne, apparently closer to the throne than the "twenty-four elders." Derived from the verb *zaō* ("to live") and related to the noun *zōē* ("life") are these, *zoon*, best translated as "living creatures" (and very different from the first and second wild "beasts" [*thērion*] of 13:1, 11). These four *zoon* appear to relate most closely to the "four living creatures" seen by Ezekiel (1:5-25; 3:13), of which he later says, "and I realized that they were cherubim" (10:20; also 9:3; 10:1-22). Mentioned ninety-one times in the Old Testament (cf. Gen. 3:24; Exod. 25:18; Ps. 99:1; Isa. 37:16), these "cherubim" are the highest ranking of God's created angels (in fact, before his fall Lucifer himself had held this lofty station [Ezek. 28:14, 16]).

The "living creatures" John sees are "covered with eyes, in front and in back" (4:6, 8), a symbol of universal watchfulness, intelligence, alertness, and understanding (cf. Ezek. 1:18; Zech. 4:10). Each of the four has a different appearance, i.e., "like a lion," "like an ox," "like a man," and "like a flying eagle" (4:7; but contrast all four faces of each cherub in Ezekiel's vision [Ezek. 1:10]), which would imply that they represent all of creation before the Throne of God in worship and service.[2] Symbolically, it can be said that the "noblest, strongest, wisest, and swiftest in nature" submit to and witness to the will of Almighty God.[3] That each also has "six wings" represents their swiftness in serving God, here reminiscent of the "seraphim" (*saraphim*, "burning ones") seen by Isaiah (6:2, 6) before the throne (contrast Ezek. 1:6). The ministry of these "four living creatures" will include the releasing of God's fiery judgments into the earth (Rev. 6:1-, 3, 5, 6, 7; 15:7). Though angelic by nature, they stand apart in rank from the innumerable company of angels, which also stand before God's throne (5:11; 7:11).

Life Application

The first television set owned by my family was a black and white. I still remember picking it up from the store with my parents in the mid-60s. I even remember the very first show I watched in my own home. (Truth be known, that program is still one my favorites to watch today.) Maybe this is why some of my memories come back to me in gray tones. Man, was I excited when we caught up with the neighbors and "living color" TV came into my life a few years later!

On this side of Heaven so far away, we may be tempted to envision our Homeland in black and white. But John would tell us different—and he's been there! There is nothing at all dull, drab, or lackluster about Heaven! No, a better look at God's throne room gives new meaning to the words "Living Color." In fact, what John saw in the Spirit was so incredible that he needed to use the most beautiful colors on earth, the colors of precious jewels, to describe it. (We'll see that again towards the end of the Revelation!) God Himself "had the appearance of jasper and ruby"; with crystal-clear brilliance and blood-red glory we are forever reminded of the sacrificial love of God—a truth Heaven celebrates for eternity! And there encircling His throne is a full rainbow, glowing with an emerald green hue. Like the unbroken circle of a wedding ring, this rainbow promises the faithful covenant love of God for all eternity. Yes, the matter of God's grace and mercy has been settled in Heaven. From now and forever those who come to the Father through Jesus need never have an anxious thought, a question, or doubt. If God has already settled His love and favor in Heaven, then you and I need to let it be settled once and for all on earth.

In the months after John wrote the Revelation Jesus had entrusted to him, he wrote a far shorter work, the book we call First John. His vision of Heaven's throne room must have been in view when He referred to God as both "Light" and "Love." Many years before, another man with a heavenly vision, the Apostle Paul, wrote of the glorious One he had seen firsthand as well (2 Cor. 12:1-7a)—"who alone is immortal and who lives in unapproachable light" (1 Tim. 6:16). Perfect Light wrapped in Perfect Love! No wonder His throne is encircled in ceaseless praise!

The Sounds of God's Throne Room—4:8b-11

[8b] Day and night they never stop saying: "'Holy, holy, holy is the Lord God Almighty,' who was, and is, and is to come." [9] Whenever the living creatures give glory, honor and thanks to him who sits on the throne and who lives for ever and ever, [10] the twenty-four elders fall down before him who sits on the throne and worship him who lives for ever and ever. They lay their crowns before the throne and say: [11] "You are worthy, our Lord and God, to receive glory and honor and power, for you created all things, and by your will they were created and have their being."

Biblical Insights

Matched only by the glorious sights John saw in the Throne Room of God were the glorious sounds he heard there as well. Surrounding the throne, the four "living creatures" are not only ceaseless in their service and attentiveness, but also in their worship (Rev. 14:3; 19:4). "Day and night they never stop saying" is John's human perspective and witness, for there is no actual "night" in God's immediate presence (Rev. 21:25; 22:5). Before the throne they testify to the predominant attribute of God, i.e., His holiness, His absolute moral purity (cf. Exod. 15:11; Lev. 11:44, 45; 19:2; 20:26; 21:8; John 17:11; 1 Pet. 1:16). Created in His image, God's expectation, desire, and provision by grace is that each of His children also walk in His holiness (cf. Lev. 11:44; 19:2; 20:26; Deut. 23:14; 1 Pet. 1:15, 16) for "without holiness no one will see the Lord" (Hebrews 12:14). "Holy, holy, holy" is repeated for emphasis, but perhaps also in recognition of the triune nature of God (cf. the testimony of the seraphim in Isaiah 6:3).

Found many times throughout the Old Testament, the title "Lord God Almighty" is found in the New Testament only in the Book of Revelation (11:17; 15:3; 16:7; 19:6).

As "Almighty" (*pantokratōr*), He is ruler over all that is (cf. 2 Cor. 6:18; Rev. 1:8; 11:17; 15:3; 16:7, 14; 19:6, 15; 21:22). In further adoration of God in His fullness, additional phrases are written. God's eternality is described with the words "who was, and is, and is to come" (1:4, 8). His sovereignty is proclaimed in the words "who sits on the throne" (vv. 9, 10; cf. 3:21; 4:2; 5:13; 6:16; 7:10, 12:5; 22:1, 3). That He is Yahweh—the self-existent One ("the I Am that I Am," Exod. 3:14, 15)—is captured in the words "who lives for ever and ever" (vv. 9, 10; cf. 1:6; 5:13; 7:12; 10:6; 15:7).

The worship presented to God by the "living creatures" is further described as bringing "glory, honor and thanks" (cf. v. 11 and 7:12 where the full number of the angels lift such worship). "Glory" (*doxa*; cf. 1:6; 5:12, 13; 7:12; 11:17; 12:10; 15:8; 16:9; 19:1) is an all-encompassing word speaking of the worshipful recognition of God's excellence, preeminence, and splendor. The "honor" (*timē*) of God speaks of the inestimable value and preciousness of who He is. "Thanks" (*eucharistia*; also 7:12) is the gratitude of those whose lives are dependent upon His grace (cf. 2 Cor. 4:15; Phil. 4:6; Col. 2:7; 4:2). Though this highest dimension of worship is lifted continuously, John adds a further level. "Whenever" in addition to "they never stop saying" seems to indicate special times (though happening again and again)—perhaps as high points, waves, or crescendos—of praise and worship. A similar overflow of worship is seen again in 5:9, 12; 7:10, 12; 11:15-18; and 19:1-8.

In agreement with the worship of the living creatures—"whenever" those high waves of praise are lifted—the "twenty-four elders" "fall down before him" in humble acknowledgment of their utter dependence upon His grace, mercy and goodness. With this act of homage, they also "lay their crowns before the throne" (cf. v. 4, "crowns of gold"). The victory they have received has come only from the ultimate Victor. Though they themselves sit upon thrones of authority, the elders do not hesitate to proclaim the Source of that authority.

The worship of the "twenty-four elders" is verbalized as well. Declaring Christ's sovereignty, He is both "Lord" and "God" found singly and together many times in Revelation (1:8; 4:8, 11; 6:10; 11:4, 15, 17; 14:13; 15:3, 4; 16:7; 18:8; 19:6; 21:22; 22:5, 6; see also Thomas' declaration in John 20:28). He is also "worthy" (*axios*) according to the excellence of who He is and of what He has accomplished (cf. 5:9, 12, where of Jesus)—in stark contrast to the reprehensible emperor worship of John's day. [4] To "glory and honor" (v. 9) is added "power" (*dynamis*), God's complete and unlimited ability. That He "receives" these means that those created by Him recognize the absolute worthiness of His essence and attributes. We, the created, unreservedly acknowledge that He created "all things" (cf. Matt. 19:4; John 1:3; 1 Cor. 8:6; Eph. 3:9; Col. 1:16; Heb. 2:10; 11:3; Rev. 3:14; 10:6; 14:7) by his determined "will" (*thelēma*, which may also carry the idea of "desire" and "pleasure"), a truth so opposite the lie of a mindless, chance and accidental cause. Heaven's song triumphs over and silences the thankless and empty rhetoric of those on earth who deny their Maker (cf. Rom.

1:20-25). In fact, true worship includes the acknowledgment of our complete dependence upon Him for our very being.

Life Application

In January 1997, I received a frantic call that the Sight and Sound Theatre, a nationally renowned Christian entertainment center in Lancaster, Pennsylvania, was on fire. I drove the short distance from the church I was then pastoring to an open field where I watched, as though surreal, that $15 million building burn and collapse to the ground. In the investigation that followed, the uncontrolled inferno was traced to sparks from a welder's torch falling through tiny screw holes in the stage floor. As though rising from the ashes, a new and grander building was built in its place where hundreds of thousands through the years have continued to take in the amazing sights and sounds of fascinating Bible stories. Yet, even at its captivating best, this new and improved version is still only a temporary reflection of a far greater glory.

Far from our own space and time is the perfect source and true center of all that is really important—an eternal place where the most glorious sights and the most incomparable sounds will never pass away! "Living creatures" which reflect the created world and "twenty-four elders" who stand in for God's redeemed people together represent you and I before His throne. As they lift their ceaseless praise, we are called to lives of praise; as they fall before the Almighty in reverential fear, we are called to humility of heart and mind. Even now the sights and sounds of God's glory are reaching into the hearts of every man, woman, boy and girl who will say with the hosts of Heaven—"All the glory goes back to you!"

By God's will and design, you and I have been created for this. At a time before time, when all that was, was God Himself, He chose to create a world filled with beautiful sights and awesome sounds, a physical world that would reflect His own transcendent power and glory. And what a world it must have been—teeming with life, overflowing with bounty, everywhere the imprint of His creative beauty and design! And at the center of this vivid and verdant world filled with natural wonders, God chose to place His highest expression of creative power, you and me. Created "in the image of God," we are called to reflect Him and resemble Him, to need Him and to want Him, but most of all to worship Him. "On earth as it is in Heaven" there is nothing more important, more wonderful, more central to our very reason for being— for "You are worthy, our Lord and God, to receive glory and honor and power, for you created all things, and by your will they were created and have their being."

Chapter 4 Notes

1. The idea that John's transport to Heaven is directly symbolic of the Rapture of the Church is inconclusive at best. While the Rapture of the Church will be corporate and with permanence, John's experience was singular and for a defined and temporary purpose. Likewise, while the Rapture of the Church will align with the resurrection of the dead and living in Christ, John's conveyance took place while he remained in his earthly (non-glorified) body.

   The need to find a raptured Church before the presentation and opening of the six seals of Chapter 6 in order to maintain a pre-tribulation position is based on an incomplete understanding of the purpose of the seals. In fact, the raptured and resurrected Church *is* seen in Heaven (7:9-17) before the breaking of the seventh seal (8:1), which in itself opens the scroll and actuates the judgments contained in the scroll. Though God's people are not referred to as His "Church" between 3:22 and 22:16, who could deny that the Church is not described corporately in 7:9-17, 19:7-9, and 19:14 (cf. 17:14)? (See also below the summary statement under A Systematic Overview of the Theology of The Revelation—Eschatology: The Resurrection and Eternal Reward of the Righteous.)

2. Some commentators—as early as Victorinus of Pettau (A.D. 250-303; in his commentary under Revelation 4:7-10)—have found a direct correlation in metaphor between the four faces of the "living creatures" and the four Gospels. However, this view is subjective and without substantial biblical support. Philip Schaff, ed., Victorinus Commentary on the Apocalypse of the Blessed John, "ANF07. Fathers of the Third and Fourth Centuries: Lactantius, Venantius, Asterius, Victorinus, Dionysius, Apostolic Teaching and Constitutions, Homily," *Christian Classics Ethereal Library*, 1 June 2005 <www.ccel.org/ccel/schaff/anf07.vi.ii.iv.html>.

3. William Barclay, *Letters to the Seven Churches* (Louisville, KY: John Knox Press, 2001) 173.

4. Stanley Horton comments, "The entrance of the Roman emperors in triumphal procession was greeted with the words: 'Worthy are thou!' And the title 'Lord and God' was introduced by Domitian into the cult of emperor worship. The prayer of the elders is a contrast to and a protest against the worship of the emperor and the exaltation of any human being, man or woman." Stanley M. Horton, *The Ultimate Victory—An Exposition of the Book of Revelation* (Springfield, MO: Gospel Publishing House, 1991) 81.

Revelation 5:1-14

The Lamb and the Scroll of Redemption

Introduction to Revelation 5:1-14

John's enthralling vision of the glory of God and the fascinating entities that surround His throne now continues into Chapter 5 and beyond. His attention is immediately drawn to a mysterious scroll in the hands of God the Father. Unique to this vision alone is the concealing of the contents of this mysterious scroll with "seven seals." The breaking of these seven and the content of the scroll itself will in God's timing prove to unfold His culminating and eternal will for humanity, both redeemed and lost, and for the created world. Further, the identity and significance of this scroll does in fact hold the key to a proper understanding of what Jesus had promised "will take place later."

At the heart of this passage is the worthiness of Jesus alone to receive and to open this scroll. In strong contrast to the inability of all other beings, human or angelic, to break its seals and to look within, Jesus is proclaimed magnificently worthy by virtue of his own redemptive work. He alone as God's "Lion" and God's "Lamb" has the authority and the ability to release the will of the Father into the earth and to restore the forfeited inheritance into the possession of the righteous.

With His reception of the scroll, a crescendo of worship is presented before the Lamb. Each of the beings John had just described—the "twenty-four elders" and the "four living creatures"—now, along with countless angels, release their songs in two waves of glorious and demonstrative praise. Still a third hymn of eternal celebration and honor rises ubiquitously from across the created world. To Him alone belongs all glory and praise!

The Seven-Sealed Scroll and the Lion Who Is Worthy—5:1-5

[1]Then I saw in the right hand of him who sat on the throne a scroll with writing on both sides and sealed with seven seals. [2] And I saw a mighty angel proclaiming in a loud voice, "Who is worthy to break the seals and open the scroll?" [3] But no one in heaven or on earth or under the earth could open the scroll or even look inside it. [4] I

wept and wept because no one was found who was worthy to open the scroll or look inside. [5] Then one of the elders said to me, "Do not weep! See, the Lion of the tribe of Judah, the Root of David, has triumphed. He is able to open the scroll and its seven seals."

Biblical Insights

With the conjunction "then" (*kai*; or "and"), in contrast to *meta tauta* in 4:1, the glorious vision begun in Chapter 4 continues uninterrupted into Chapter 5. John once again reveals God with the mysterious "him who sat on the throne" (4:2, 3, 9; 5:7; cf. Ps. 45:6; 47:8; 103:19; Isa. 6:1; Dan. 7:9), the center and focus of all activity and worship in Heaven (4:4-6). In the Father's "right hand" speaks of His own absolute authority and majesty and of the recipient's privilege and blessing (cf. Gen. 48:18; Exod. 15:6; Deut. 33:2; Ps. 16:11; 110:1; Eccles. 10:2; Isa. 48:13; Matt. 25:34, Mark 16:19; Acts 5:31; Eph. 1:20; Col. 3:1; etc.).[1]

John's focus now comes to "a scroll" (*biblion*, "a small book"; here, a "bookroll") that holds crucial significance for the judgments it contains soon to be released upon the earth. Although evidence exists of first century A.D. use of bound wax-covered wooden tablets and other early prototypes, the codex or familiar "book" of stacked and bound pages only gradually replaced the scroll over the next several hundred years.[2] John's ongoing description almost certainly indicates a rolled scroll, the common writing format for nearly two thousand years.[3] Uniquely, this scroll contained writing "on both sides," or more literally, "within and on the back" (ESV). Due to the difficulty of writing on the reverse side of papyrus (where the reeds ran vertically), ancient scrolls used publicly were generally written on one side (where the reeds ran horizontally), while scrolls written on both sides—called an "opisthograph"—were generally reserved for private use.[4] Pertaining to this all-important writing, "on both sides" may indicate that the judgments contained within and without are full and complete (cf. Ezekiel 2:9-10).

Further, this scroll is "sealed with seven seals." A "seal" here refers to the mark or impression left in wax or clay and placed upon a document or other object, indicating authority, authenticity, honor, security, and/or ownership. Such a "seal" was made through the imprint of a signet ring (cf. Gen. 41:42; Num. 31:50; Jer. 22:24; Hag. 2:23) also called a "seal," which was worn and used by an authority or witness. The use of various types of seals is well documented and evidenced within the ancient world of both Judaism and its many surrounding and influencing cultures.[5] Throughout the Bible, references to the use of seals are both literal (cf. Num. 31:50; 1 Kings 21:8; Neh. 9:38; Esther 3:12; 8:8, 10; Dan. 6:17; Jer. 32:44; Matt. 27:66) and figurative (cf. Song of Sol. 8:6; Isa. 29:11-12; Dan. 9:24; 12:4; John 3:33; 6:27; Rom. 4:11; 1 Cor. 9:2; 2 Tim. 2:19; Rev. 10:4; 20:3; 22:10).

Knowing the nature of seals to both authenticate and to withhold disclosure of a scroll's content until the proper time, we find initial evidence to the identity of this seven-sealed scroll in the words spoken by Gabriel to Daniel (12:4, 9)—"But you, Daniel, roll up and seal the words of the scroll until the time of the end" [...] "Go your way, Daniel, because the words are rolled up and sealed until the time of the end." The eschatological nature of both scrolls quite certainly connects the scrolls as one and the same. If this is true, then we also see a direct connection to what Gabriel calls, "the Book of Truth" in Daniel 10:21. However, before any further technical identification of the seven-sealed scroll can be made—whether in the form of a last will or of a title deed or of some other—we must follow John's discovery of the vital connection between this scroll and the biblical theme of redemption, which now culminates in the Revelation.

Thus, John's vision falls next upon a strong, "mighty angel" (cf. 10:1; 18:21). If not Gabriel, so often God's messenger in the Bible (cf. Dan. 8:16; 9:21), this angel has a similar ministry. He is heard "proclaiming" (*kēryssō*; as a herald, most often used of preaching in the Bible) his message with urgency and authority "in a loud voice" (cf. 14:7, 9, 15). A question reverberates through the Throne Room of God, "Who is worthy to break the seals and open the scroll?" Far more than a matter of willingness (of which we hear of none other), such worthiness must come with personal aptitude and ability (v. 3, "could," *dunamis*), yet "no one in heaven or on the earth or under the earth" (cf. Phil. 2:10; implying all humans, living or departed, and all angels, holy or unholy) was found worthy. That John "wept and wept" with much distress and pain indicates the cosmic importance of the contents of this scroll and perhaps also the realization of his own utter inability.

John's anguish is interrupted and relieved by two commands from "one of the elders" (of the "twenty-four" in 4:4; 7:13)—"Do not weep!" and "See" (*idou*; a demonstrative call to observe, used many times in Revelation). There is one whose victory has positioned him "to open the scroll and its seven seals"; there is one who has emphatically "triumphed" (*nikaō*; "conquer" or "overcome"; cf. 3:21; 17:14) over the kingdom of darkness (Col. 2:15) and over death (2 Tim. 1:10). He is declared "the Lion of the tribe of Judah" in fulfillment of the prophetic words of Jacob over his fourth son Judah (Gen. 49:8-10). He is also "the Root of David" in fulfillment of the prophetic words of Isaiah (Isa. 11), which saw the glory and ubiquitous reach of the coming Messiah's rule. Both titles speak of the certain fulfillment of the Davidic Covenant in Christ. Only Jesus in His specific ministry as the sacrifice Lamb (5:6) "is able"; only Jesus holds the authority and victory needed to take the scroll "from the right hand of him who sat on the throne" (5:7), "to break the seals and open the scroll" (5:2, 5), and to "look inside" (5:4). In pursuit of the full identity and significance of the seven-sealed scroll, we must not disregard Christ's worthiness and His sacrificial work as will be strengthened ahead in verses 9 and 12.

Life Application

Neither the destiny of this world nor the details of your personal tomorrow are in the hands of a weak and passive God. No! Securely in the right hand of our Father in Heaven—His hand of authority and favor—is everything important to living confidently within His promises over us. Seated upon His throne, our God stands in defiance of Satan's false claim to ownership and control of the future of this world. Welcomed before His throne are those who come honestly submitted to His will; and there we find forgiveness, healing, and empowerment.

"Seven seals"—a complete number—witness to the authenticity of this scroll, as the perfect will of God. Sealed "until the time comes for God to restore everything" (Acts 3:21), John is now witness to God's detailed plan for the release of His inheritance in Christ to all who overcome by faith in Him. Inside this scroll is the Father's expressed will to reclaim, redeem, and recover this lost world; and inside this scroll is the Father's perfect plan to establish His Kingdom in righteousness and His children within His glory.

It is no small wonder then that John was for a moment moved with deep pain at the thought that no one was worthy to open the scroll and release its promised plan. Is mankind's fate hopelessly shut up within that book? Perhaps, just for that moment, John represented every doubt, every fear, every anguished "Why?" we have all at some time carried to the Throne of God. But the sound of a roar will soon silence every question! We've all said it, or at least thought it, "Look *what* the world has come to!" But this mighty Revelation announces, "Look *Who* has come to this world!"

Late in the summer of 1997, following a restless night in our very open and unprotected campsite (that is, apart from the spears of the Maasai warriors standing guard), I faced the new day with great anticipation of the adventure my ministry colleague, Jackson, had promised me on my birthday. As the sun rose on Kenya and we shared breakfast around an open fire, our ministry team set out for our "off day" safari in the Maasai Mara. The excitement kicked in quickly when our van driver stopped within safe distance of a lioness resting from her satisfying kill and morning meal. With every bend in the road came another thrill as we viewed an incredible menagerie of God's creative genius. But standing out amongst it all was our high noon—"up close and personal"—visit with a pride of lions resting in the blazing sun (too contented to pay attention to us).

For good reason, the lion is called "king of the beasts." A male lion's size alone is intimidating, weighing as much as 600 pounds; from nose to end of tail, most males grow to about 9 feet long and 3 ½ feet tall at the shoulder. As Solomon said, lions are known for their strength—"a lion, mighty among beasts, who retreats before nothing" (Prov. 30:30)—and for their courage—"the wicked man flees though no one pursues, but the righteous are as bold as a lion" (Prov. 28:1). But above all, lions are known for their commanding roar, which can be heard from five miles away: "The lion has roared—who will not fear? The Sovereign LORD has spoken—who can but prophesy?" (Amos 3:8); "He [the Lord] shall roar like a lion ..." (Hosea 11:10).

"Do not weep! See, the Lion of the Tribe of Judah, the Root of David, has triumphed." This is the same Jesus whose "roar" caused winds and waves to obey. This is Jesus whose "roar" sent demons screaming to their judgment; this is Jesus whose "roar" of two brief words sent a small army backwards to the ground. And, with His all-wise and powerful roar, He answers back to every doubt and fear you could ever know. "Have I gone too far, for too long to be forgiven?" "Can I ever break loose from these fears, these doubts, these chains?" "Will I ever know peace in my mind and peace in my heart?" Listen to the Lion King roar with power over your marriage and children, your home and finances, your every need in spirit, soul, and body! Listen as He roars to take back your tomorrow and to restore your full inheritance! What He will do throughout this world in the Last Days, He will do in you today!

The Lamb Who Was Slain Takes the Scroll—5:6-7

[6] Then I saw a Lamb, looking as if it had been slain, standing at the center of the throne, encircled by the four living creatures and the elders. The Lamb had seven horns and seven eyes, which are the seven spirits of God sent out into all the earth. [7] He went and took the scroll from the right hand of him who sat on the throne.

Biblical Insights

John no doubt expected to see a "lion" (used of Jesus, only here); instead, he saw a "Lamb" (*arnion*; found 28 times in Revelation and in John 21:15). (Another word for "lamb," *amnos*, emphasizes the nature of Christ's sacrificial work in John 1:29, 36; Acts 8:32 and 1 Peter 1:19, while *arnion* seems to exclusively point to the majesty and power accompanying His sacrificial work.)[6] Jesus appeared with the marks of his suffering still upon him, "Looking as if it had been slain." Yet, this Lamb was alive (Rev. 1:18) and "standing" (as opposed to the helpless posture of a dead, slain animal) "at the center [*mesos*; 'the midst' or 'between'] of the throne." As in 4:6 (also 7:17), the picture is of the Lamb before the throne (as compared to His current position "at the right hand of the Majesty in heaven," Heb. 1:3; cf. Heb. 8:1; 10:12; 12:2; Rev. 3:21) "encircled by the four living creatures and the elders" (4:4, 6).

Uniquely here, John sees that the Lamb "had seven horns"—speaking of his perfect and full royal authority in executing the will of the Father (cf. 1 Sam. 2:10). The Lamb also appears with "seven eyes"—speaking of His perfect and full understanding in executing the will of the Father. These eyes John relates to the "seven spirits of God sent out into all the earth," symbolically, the seven-fold ministry of the one Spirit of God (already introduced in 1:4; 3:1; and 4:5) sent from the presence of the Father and the Son (cf. John 16:7).

The Lamb's Reception of the Inheritance

That which no other human or angel had right or ability to do, the living Lamb did with recognized and welcomed authority (cf. Matt. 28:18). "He went" ("He came," NASB; or, from the context, "He stepped forward" NLT) and "took the scroll" (*eilēphen*; lit. "has taken").[7] In having taken the scroll "from the right hand of him who sat on the throne" (v. 1), the Son of God took into His possession the culmination of the Father's plan for the "restoration of all things about which God spoke by the mouth of His holy prophets from ancient time" (Acts 3:21, NASB). Without question, the prophet Daniel foresaw this same event (7:13-14):

> In my vision at night I looked, and there before me was one like a son of man, coming with the clouds of heaven. He approached the Ancient of Days and was led into his presence. He was given authority, glory and sovereign power; all nations and peoples of every language worshiped him. His dominion is an everlasting dominion that will not pass away, and his kingdom is one that will never be destroyed.

As concerns the Lamb, Jesus the Son of God, we now understand that the seven-sealed scroll relates to the presentation from God the Father of an everlasting kingdom encompassing global "authority, glory and sovereign power." We have also seen that this scroll contains eschatological truths as concerns Israel and the nations, prophesies that "are rolled up and sealed until the time of the end" (Daniel 12:9). With this understanding, we are now ready to move toward a more complete appreciation of the content, significance, and form of the scroll as we link the idea of Christ's inheritance—and we as His co-heirs—with the biblical theme of redemption culminated in the Revelation (5:9, "For You were slain, and have redeemed us to God by Your blood out of every tribe and tongue and people and nation"; NKJV).

Jesus—Our Kinsman-Redeemer

In light of the fact that the Book of Revelation contains more references to the Old Testament than any other New Testament book, we see parallel if not allusion in these verses to the law of the Kinsman-Redeemer. Grounded in the Pentateuch, provision was made for the purchasing back of people and property during situations of hardship and poverty. In ancient Israel where an individual was unable to pay a debt, the creditor could have the debtor sold as a slave to cover that debt (Matt. 18:23-27). Additionally, a poor man in debt could choose to indenture himself to his creditor (Lev. 25:39-40, 47; Deut. 15:12; 24:14-15). Such a man could remain a "hired worker" for up to six years until the seventh year, the Year of Jubilee (Exod. 21:2; Lev. 25:39-41; Deut. 15:1-2, 9-11, 18). Where property had been sold under duress, such property could legally be repurchased within the first year according to the provisions memorialized in a scroll. In both of these cases, God provided that a male relative acting as a "Kinsman-Redeemer" (Hebrew, *go'-el*; from verb *ga¢al*) could intervene and come to the rescue of his relative. This rescuer, of necessity, must be a blood relative, demonstrating willingness and resources to meet the need. In the redemption from indentured work, Leviticus 25:47-49 reads:

> If a stranger or sojourner with you becomes rich, and your brother beside him becomes poor and sells himself to the stranger or sojourner with you or to a member of the stranger's clan, then after he is sold he may be redeemed. One of his brothers may redeem him, or his uncle or his cousin may redeem him, or a close relative from his clan may redeem him. Or if he grows rich he may redeem himself. (ESV)

In the redemption from loss of property, Leviticus 25:25 states: "If your brother becomes poor and sells part of his property, then his nearest redeemer shall come and redeem what his brother has sold" (ESV) (cf. Jer. 32:6-9; Ruth 2:20; 3:1-4).

In the Old Testament, the Lord God Himself is many times also called the "Goel," the "Redeemer" of Israel (cf. Exod. 6:6; 15:13; Ps. 103:4; 106:10; 107:2; Isaiah 41:14; 43:1, 14; 44:6, 22, 23, 24; 47:4; 48:17, 20; 49:7, 26; 54:5, 8; 59:20; Jer. 31:11; 50:34; Hos. 13:14; etc.). The theme of redemption carries on and finds its ultimate and eternal fulfillment in the New Testament through the New Covenant established in the blood of Jesus. "Redemption" is now captured in the word *apolytrōsis* (cf. Luke 21:28; Rom. 3:24; 8:23; 1 Cor. 1:30; Eph. 1:7, 14; etc.), which literally speaks of a "release" or "deliverance" through the payment of a "ransom" (*lutron*) (cf. Matt. 20:28; Mark 10:45). New Covenant theology of redemption also includes the idea of forgiveness and justification, as the payment of the ransom completely atones for the sins of the past and purchases back to God those who receive His salvation. The parallel to Old Testament Kinsman-Redeemer law, then, is found in that: Jesus is our blood relative (Gal. 4:4, 5; Heb. 2:11-17); Jesus has established His unquestioned ability and resources (1 Cor. 6:20; Heb. 2:18; 1 Pet. 1:18, 19); and, Jesus has demonstrated His incomparable willingness to set us free (Matt. 20:28; John 10:15-18; Heb. 4:14-16; 1 John 3:16).

The Scroll of Redemption

When we know as John did that the seven-sealed scroll is received and opened by the only One who was ready, willing, and able to rescue us from our sin and sin's consequences—our true Kinsman-Redeemer—we begin to realize that the greatest significance of this mystery is as a Scroll of Redemption.[8] In receiving the scroll, it is Jesus who reclaims and restores our forfeited inheritance.

Essential to the scroll, now in the hands of Jesus, is our understanding of the "now and still yet" dynamics associated with our redemption both personally and as concerns God's creation once entrusted to humanity. First, we know that by faith we are *already* personally redeemed (*apolytrōsis*) from our sin, salvation and sanctification being grounded in the finished work of Christ and in our position in Him—Romans 3:24; 1 Corinthians 1:30; Ephesians 1:7; Colossians 1:14; Hebrews 9:15. Yet, we also hear the Word of God promising the *full, future* realization of that redemption in the following passages where *apolytrōsis* is also emphasized:

- Luke 21:28—"When these things begin to take place, stand up and lift up your heads, because your redemption is drawing near."
- Romans 8:23—"Not only so, but we ourselves, who have the firstfruits of the Spirit, groan inwardly as we wait eagerly for our adoption to sonship, the redemption of our bodies."
- Ephesians 1:14—"[...] who is a deposit guaranteeing our inheritance until the redemption of those who are God's possession—to the praise of his glory."
- Ephesians 4:30—"And do not grieve the Holy Spirit of God, with whom you were sealed for the day of redemption."

Certainly it is people—first and foremost—for whom Jesus died and in whom he has restored freedom and authority (Rev. 5:9—"you purchased for God ['redeemed us to God by Your blood'; NKJV] persons from every tribe and language and people and nation"; also 1:5; 14:3, 4; cf. Mark 10:45; 2 Cor. 5:17-21). Nevertheless, there is yet a secondary and vital consequence of humanity's redemption found in the emancipation and restoration of the creation to its intended purpose as once entrusted to us. Paul writes, "that the creation itself will be liberated from its bondage to decay and brought into the freedom and glory of the children of God" (Romans 8:21; cf. Isa. 11:9; Ezek. 47:9; Hab. 2:14; Acts 3:21; Rom. 8:19-23). As concerns the natural world in response to the Revelation of Christ, we do see creation recognizing and joining in the worship of the Lamb for His redemptive work (5:13). Further, we see God's interest in bringing vengeance upon those "who destroy the earth" (11:18) and "corrupt the earth" (19:2). Finally, we see God's replacement of the present heaven and earth with "a new heaven and a new earth" (21:1).

Early in the Bible we learn that God had entrusted all of creation to humanity (Gen. 1:26-30; cf. 1 Cor. 3:22; Heb. 2:6-8). Yet, through humanity's rebellion and fall, the creation—then ruined and corrupted—"was subjected to frustration, not by its own choice, but by the will of the one who subjected it, in hope" (Romans 8:20; cf. Gen. 3:17-18). Satan came deceptively as an intruder and thief to steal away the spiritual and natural heritage of the Lord; and so, empowered by humanity's disobedience, the inheritance was forfeited. Since that day the usurper has falsely assumed right and ownership of what was once in the hands of an innocent humanity. Indeed, to this present day Satan continues to have a practical reach and control—albeit by deception (Luke

4:6)—of the earth and the heavens. Jesus called him, "the prince of this world" (John 12:31; 14:30; 16:11) and Paul called him both "the god of this world" (2 Corinthians 4:4, ESV; cf. Eph. 6:12) and "the prince of the power of the air" (Ephesians 2:2, NASB). He even now, "prowls around like a roaring lion looking for someone to devour (1 Pet. 5:8); to this day, he is "deceiving the nations" (Rev. 20:3).

In response to Satan's false claim over the earth, God's Word again declares a "now and still yet" fulfillment of declared truth. As God eternally and sovereignly rules from His throne, He *now* truthfully possesses the deed to His own created world—"The earth is the Lord's, and everything in it, the world, and all who live in it" (Psalm 24:1; cf. Gen. 14:19, 22; Exod. 9:29; 19:5; 1 Chron. 29:14; Job 41:11; Ps. 50:10-12; 89:11; 104:24; Hag. 2:8; 1 Cor. 10:26). Furthermore, even *now* the Bible declares that the glory and knowledge of God fills the earth—"the whole earth is full of his glory" (Isaiah 6:3; cf. Num. 14:21; Ps. 19:1; 72:19). Yet, the same Bible declares that a *future realization* of the restoration of creation to the glory of God still remains. There is a sense in which the global and pervasive glory and knowledge of God still awaits the return and future reign of the Lord extending to all of creation; and in that day, His Kingdom will fill the earth, physically as well as spiritually—"For the earth will be filled with the knowledge of the glory of the LORD as the waters cover the sea" (Habakkuk 2:14; cf. Isa. 11:6-9; 65:25; Eph. 1:10; 2 Thess. 2:8; Rev. 5:10; 19:11-15).

Thus, in the Lamb's reception of the seven-sealed scroll, we find full and final assurance that what is *now* in the possession of God will be *then* realized personally and throughout creation in the Revelation of our Kinsman-Redeemer. Here Paul declares, "For God was pleased to have all his fullness dwell in him, and through him to reconcile to himself all things, whether things on earth or things in heaven, by making peace through his blood, shed on the cross" (Colossians 1:19-20). The forfeited inheritance once lost through sin—both spiritually and naturally, and personally and in creation—will be restored through God's wisdom and power. As "co-heirs with Christ" (Rom. 8:17; cf. Ps. 2:8; Matt. 5:5; 19:28; Rev. 21:7) we have a reserved inheritance that "can never perish, spoil or fade. This inheritance is kept in heaven for you, who through faith are shielded by God's power until the coming of the salvation that is ready to be revealed in the last time" (1 Peter 1:4-5).

With this understanding we are now able to address with confidence the technical form in which the seven-sealed Scroll of Redemption is presented from the Father to the Son. (Of note, there is no other reference to "seven seals" found in the Bible outside of the Book of Revelation.) Amongst the many and varied opinions offered for the form of this scroll, only two have strong merit.

The Seven-Sealed Scroll as a Last Will and Testament
It is well documented through primary sources that first century A.D. Roman law required certain forms of a last will and testament to be sealed seven times by seven

witnesses.[9] Typically, after a testator wrote or had written for him his testament, he presented it to seven qualified male witnesses. Upon witnessing the testator's signature, these seven added their signatures and finally affixed their seals placed into a wax dollop placed upon the knots of the cords or strings, which together held the scroll closed and secure.[10] Here, we see the clear parallel to the seven-sealed scroll in the hands of Jesus.

This position is further strengthened in that it is common to wills and testament law that the testator must die in order to actuate the promised inheritance. In fact, the Scriptures declare the Son, who is one with the Father, to be the Creator and Testator—"[...] and there is but one Lord, Jesus Christ, through whom all things came and through whom we live" (1 Corinthians 8:6). It is through Jesus "all things were made; without him nothing was made that has been made" (John 1:3). Again, "He is before all things, and in him all things hold together" (Colossians 1:17) as He is found "sustaining all things by his powerful word" (Hebrews 1:3). And here the Word gives further commentary—"In the case of a will, it is necessary to prove the death of the one who made it, because a will is in force only when somebody has died; it never takes effect while the one who made it is living" (Hebrews 9:16-17). Again, we see correspondence in John's emphasis upon the sacrificial death of Jesus (Rev. 1:6, 9), who alone has authority to open the scroll and release its contents.

Now it is also common to wills and testament law that only a rightful heir may receive the promised inheritance. Once more, the Word speaks boldly of Christ as the rightful "Heir" of all the promises of the Father (Matt. 21:38; Heb. 1:2) and of us found in Him as "co-heirs" (Rom. 8:17; Gal. 3:29; 4:7; Titus 3:7; Heb. 1:14; 6:17; 1 Pet. 1:4-5).

With the reception of the Scroll of Redemption, we find in the will of the Father through the Son—established in Heaven and released into the created world—the vindication and upholding of His own honor against Satan who has deceptively laid claim and brought ruin to what has always rightly belonged to the Creator. Following the idea of a final testament, with the opening and actuating of God's will: the false claimant is exposed and destroyed; the testator is vindicated of this cosmic fraud; those who have forfeited their inheritance are forgiven and redeemed to God; and, all things once lost and ruined are restored to the rightful Heir as His Kingdom fills the earth.

We need also to consider the language found in Revelation 11:15, 18; 19:15; and 20:3-6, which directly corresponds to the day of the Messiah's appointment seen by David in Psalm 2:6-9:

> I have installed my king on Zion, my holy mountain. I will proclaim the LORD's decree: He said to me, 'You are my son; today I have become your father. Ask me, and I will make the nations your inheritance, the ends of the earth your possession. You will break them with a rod of iron; you will dash them to pieces like pottery.

In full accord with the position of a last will and testament, we find both David and John praising the fulfillment of the will of God, the anointing upon the promised Heir, the gathering to Him of those who follow on in His inheritance, and the destruction of all those who oppose His true rule and reign.

To those who find a failure in this position to accommodate the prominence of the judgments contained in the scroll, we need only emphasize again the need within the will of God to utterly expose and destroy the murderer and father of lies and all those nations and people who align themselves within the kingdom of darkness against the rule and realm of the True Heir (cf. 2 Thess. 2:8-12).[11]

The Seven-Sealed Scroll as a Title Deed

Another common view of the identity of this Scroll of Redemption is as a title deed to the earth and all creation. Here we find that an inheritance has been forfeited through the moral poverty of its first heirs. In accordance with the ancient law of the Kinsman-redeemer, the purchase price has been made through the sacrifice of a close, blood relative. Though there has been a delay in time between the purchase and possession, the Redeemer has now come to claim possession of the inheritance and restore its richness to his co-heirs. And with His coming, His judgment wrath comes to dispossess those who falsely claim and control what rightly belongs to God and to the people of His Kingdom.[12]

Perhaps the strongest biblical basis for this position is in its parallel with the lesson taught to Israel through Jeremiah pertaining to the redemption of their land. In approximately 590 B.C., the Lord spoke to his servant indicating the imminent overthrow of Judah and Jerusalem at the hands of the Babylonian King Nebuchadnezzar (Jer. 32:3-5, 24, 26-36; 33:4-5) and God's merciful plan to subsequently restore the nation to its homeland and to right standing with Him (Jer. 29:10-14; 32:15, 37-44; 33:6-11). Because of the sordid disobedience and idolatry of the nation, God had determined a timetable of "seventy years" for Judah's punishment at the hands of a corrupt nation—"This whole country will become a desolate wasteland, and these nations will serve the king of Babylon seventy years" (Jeremiah 25:11; cf. Dan. 9:2). But again, after seventy years Judah would be, and was, restored to their land—"This is what the Lord says: 'When seventy years are completed for Babylon, I will come to you and fulfill my good promise to bring you back to this place'" (Jeremiah 29:10).

As often the case with the biblical prophets, the Lord used a natural occurrence to teach his people a spiritual lesson about his mercy, wisdom, and authority. Jeremiah was instructed to enter into a purchase agreement at the request of a close relative who would invoke the law of the kinsman-redeemer as recorded in Jeremiah 32:6b-8:

The Word of the Lord came to me: Hanamel son of Shallum your uncle is going to come to you and say, 'Buy my field at Anathoth, because as nearest relative it is your right and duty to buy it.' Then, just as the LORD had said, my cousin Hanamel came to me in the courtyard of the guard and said, 'Buy my field at Anathoth in the territory of Benjamin. Since it is your right to redeem it and possess it, buy it for yourself.' I knew that this was the word of the Lord.

We then have insight into the details of an ancient transaction involving a title deed in the words, which follow in Jeremiah 32:9-14 (emphasis added):

[...] so I bought the field at Anathoth from my cousin Hanamel and weighed out for him seventeen shekels of silver. I **signed and sealed the deed**, had it witnessed, and weighed out the silver on the scales. I took **the deed of purchase—the sealed copy** containing the terms and conditions, as well as the unsealed copy—and I gave this deed to Baruch son of Neriah, the son of Mahseiah, in the presence of my cousin Hanamel and of the witnesses who had signed the deed and of all the Jews sitting in the courtyard of the guard. In their presence, I gave Baruch these instructions: 'This is what the LORD Almighty, the God of Israel, says: Take these documents, **both the sealed and unsealed copies of the deed of purchase**, and put them in a clay jar so they will last a long time.'

The lesson to be received by Judah from Jeremiah's actions was clear; the Lord in His mercy would restore to them their inheritance once forfeited through their sin. Jeremiah 32:15; 42-44 states:

For this is what the LORD Almighty, the God of Israel, says: Houses, fields and vineyards **will again be bought in this land**. [...] This is what the LORD says: As I have brought all this great calamity on this people, so I will give them all the prosperity I have promised them. **Once more fields will be bought in this land** of which you say, 'It is a desolate waste, without people or animals, for it has been given into the hands of the Babylonians.' Fields will be bought for silver, and **deeds will be signed, sealed and witnessed** in the territory of Benjamin, in the villages around Jerusalem, in the towns of Judah and in the towns of the hill country, of the western foothills and of the Negev, because I will restore their fortunes, declares the LORD.

Several parallels are evident between Jeremiah's experience of redeeming the forfeited inheritance of Judah in that day and God's larger promise to redeem, regain, and restore the created world held in ruin due to the sins of humanity.[13]

- The land once given by God as an inheritance (Jer. 32:22) was lost because of the rebellion of those who had first received it (32:23); i.e., the inheritance had been forfeited (cf. Lam. 5:2).
- The land to be purchased back was still in the hands of the enemy at the time of purchase, hence the redemption held a "now and still yet" dynamic.
- Though Jeremiah had paid the redemption price, a period of time necessarily passed before he could take actual possession of the land since he, himself, was imprisoned by a rebellious king at the time of his purchase (Jer. 32:2-3) and because the land to be purchased was still in the possession of Babylon (32:24, 28).
- After a period of time determined by God, the land redeemed by contract and price would be restored to its rightful owners; the once forfeited inheritance would be restored (32:15, 37, 41).
- In the end, severe judgment would come upon that evil nation that had dared to steal away and inhabit the land once given as an inheritance to His very own people (25:12-14; and see the extensive judgment of Babylon in Jeremiah Chapters 50-51). God recognizes the wickedness of their hearts as well as their wicked actions and releases His wrath upon them.
- Due to what the Lord knew about the duration of time between promise and possession, He instructed the sealed document to be kept in a secure place till the time of the regaining and restoration of the inheritance (32:14—"This is what the Lord Almighty, the God of Israel, says: Take these documents, both the sealed and unsealed copies of the deed of purchase, and put them in a clay jar so they will last a long time.")

Thus, the comparison between God's message through Jeremiah and His revelation to John is abundantly clear. The themes of a forfeited inheritance, a Kinsman-Redeemer, a "now and still yet" dynamic, the sealing of the document, and the judgment of the usurper stand in both cases. As a forfeited inheritance, some commentators view the title deed more as a mortgage deed or even as a judgment lien.[14] Yet, two challenges have been raised to this position.

While there is much evidence that the seals of witnesses were used according to first century A.D. Roman law for various legal processes, specific evidence pertaining to title deeds, and more so to seven seals, is lacking. The same is true of ancient Jewish law. In the case of Jeremiah's purchased and verified title deed (Jer. 32:6-15), only the single seal of Jeremiah is placed on the document (v. 10), while other witnesses only "subscribed" their names (v. 12). The common claim that ancient Roman or Jewish law or practice required seven seals for a title deed to be authenticated is without historical evidence.[15] Nevertheless, it is still possible that God's choice of "seven seals" *symbolically* indicates the completeness and thoroughness of the terms in which the forfeited inheritance must be redeemed.[16]

A second challenge to this position is theological in nature. If indeed the scroll is the title deed to the earth—deceptively stolen by Satan and forfeited to him by humanity—then how is it that John now sees the scroll in the hand of the Father; should it not be in the usurpers hand?[17] In answer, we need only to be reminded that God has always been in possession of His inheritance for His people. Though Adam and Eve, and we in agreement with them in our fall (Romans 5:12), forfeited and abdicated the dominion of the earth to Satan *functionally*—and though Jesus did call Satan "the prince of this world" (John 12:31) and Paul likewise, "the god of this world" (2 Corinthians 4:4, ESV)—is not Satan's claim of legal ownership, in fact, a strategic lie! And was not Satan's appeal to Jesus: "I will give you all their ['the king-doms'] authority and splendor; it has been given to me, and I can give it to anyone I want to" (Luke 4:6) also a false claim!

Furthermore, has not the Spirit of God declared assertively, "The earth is the Lord's, and everything in it, the world, and all who live in it" (Psalm 24:1)! And is not the final thwarting of this deception of the nations one of the chief accomplishments of Jesus as He reigns, and we with Him, for one thousand years upon the earth (Revelation 20:3-4)! Indeed, Satan's deceptive and permitted control over the earth does not equate to legal ownership required by a sealed title deed. Though the posses-sion of the inheritance rests upon the redemptive work of Jesus and His apprehension of the scroll at the end of time, the fact remains that God the Father has never truly lost the scroll!

Summary Conclusion

From the evidence provided both scripturally and historically, it becomes clear that both views of the scroll—as last will and testament and as title deed—are compatible with Revelation's message of Christ's redemption of the forfeited inheritance. In fact, it is not a stretch to see both as compatible with each other. Can not the Godhead's final will for humanity and creation, secured through the blood of Christ, be actu-ated by the parallel fulfillment of the restoration of the title deed into the hands of Christ, the "Heir," and we as "co-heirs" with Him? Thus, the major portion of God's eschatological will is the restoration to humanity and the celebration before His throne of His once forfeited inheritance.

Life Application

All of eternity, all of human history, and all that concerns your destiny turn on John's words, "Then I saw a Lamb." Expecting to "see" a triumphant Lion, he rather "saw" a sacrificed Lamb. And what wisdom is hidden within this mysterious revelation! To overcome your enemy, wouldn't you move with bitter revenge; wouldn't you pounce without mercy on your prey? Yet absent a show of treacherous domination, this Lion roars with passionate humility and love! And what kind of Lamb is this…weak and pathetic? Not on your life! In His obedience is His unrivaled authority—in His sacrifice His absolute victory!

God's "will" from the start was declared that we should "rule over the fish of the sea and the birds of the air, over the livestock, over all the earth, and over all the creatures that move along the ground." Instead, what a tragic mess our sin has made of the promised inheritance! God's "will" has announced, "...no good thing will He withhold from those whose walk is blameless" (Psalm 84:11). Instead, our sin has earned the chilling review, "You say, 'I am rich; I have acquired wealth and do not need a thing.' But you do not realize that you are wretched, pitiful, poor, blind and naked" (Revelation 3:17). All that our Creator ever willed for us was promise and blessing; yet, all that our self-will ever claimed in return was a forfeited inheritance. Until Jesus took the scroll!

"Where would I be without Jesus!" With arms held high to Heaven, often with heavy tears running down his face, "Brother Phil" spoke out boldly in times of worship, unashamed of His Redeemer, Sunday after Sunday. He knew *where* he once had been: lost, vile, and angry. He knew *what* he once had been: an alcoholic and abusive, hard-hearted husband and father. But the Lion pursued him in the midst of his pain, the Lion Who had heard the cries of his saved, yet hurting, wife. At the leading of the Spirit, my uncle (at that time also my pastor) shared words of life. With obedience and the passion of Heaven, he spoke as God spoke through him. The Lion roared—the Lamb took the scroll—and Satan was defeated! Fifty years later I too speak those words in unreserved worship—the shameless confession of every rescued life—"Where would I be without Jesus!"

The Worship of the Lamb—5:8-14

[8] And when he had taken it, the four living creatures and the twenty-four elders fell down before the Lamb. Each one had a harp and they were holding golden bowls full of incense, which are the prayers of God's people. [9] And they sang a new song, saying: "You are worthy to take the scroll and to open its seals, because you were slain, and with your blood you purchased for God persons from every tribe and language and people and nation. [10] You have made them to be a kingdom and priests to serve our God, and they will reign on the earth." [11] Then I looked and heard the voice of many angels, numbering thousands upon thousands, and ten thousand times ten thousand. They encircled the throne and the living creatures and the elders. [12] In a loud voice they were saying: "Worthy is the Lamb, who was slain, to receive power and wealth and wisdom and strength and honor and glory and praise!" [13] Then I heard every creature in heaven and on earth and under the earth and on the sea, and all that is in them, saying: "To him who sits on the throne and to the Lamb be praise and honor and glory and power, for ever and ever!" [14] The four living creatures said, "Amen," and the elders fell down and worshiped.

Biblical Insights

With the Lamb's reception of the scroll from the right hand of the Father (v. 7), a symphony of adoration and praise is directed not only to God, the Father, i.e., "him who sits on the throne" (4:9), but now specifically to Jesus. Here again is a clear declaration of His deity, especially in light of the instruction of the angel to John in 22:9, "Worship God!" Once again, the "four living creatures" first seen in 4:6-9—there identified as a special ranking of angels (cf. Ezekiel 1:5-25; 3:13; 10:20, "cherubim") who represent the created world before God's throne—are viewed in their worship of the Lamb. Also seen again (4:4, 10) are the "twenty-four elders," representatives of God's people on earth in both the Old and New Covenants. Together, these unique beings "fell down before the Lamb" (1:17; 4:10; 5:14; 7:11) humbly prostrate in His presence. In context, "each one" indicate the elders. These all held a "harp" (*kithara*, hence our "guitar"; also 14:2; 15:2), the ten-stringed plectrum-strummed lyre well known in John's day (Vine). The elders also held wide and shallow "golden bowls" (*phialē*). These were "full of incense, which are the prayers of God's people" evoking the image of the priestly fire pan or censer filled with incense in the Old Testament (cf. Lev. 16:12; Num. 16:17, 18; also Ps. 141:2). As in 8:3-4 the prayers of believers, here represented by the elders, are lifted in agreement with God for His judgment upon this sinful world.

The worship brought by the elders now focuses upon the redemptive work of the Lamb. The song they sing is called "a new song" (also 14:3) so often referenced in the Old Testament (cf. Ps. 33:3; 40:3; 96:1; 98:1; 144:9; 149:1) where the Psalmist seems to indicate the newness of a refreshed soul in worship. Isaiah 42:10, however, is in response to God's promise of the "new things" (42:9) which anticipate a new covenant with God's people. The theme of newness in Revelation, such as a "new name" (2:17; 3:12); the "new Jerusalem" (3:12; 21:2); the "new heaven and a new earth" (21:1); and "all things new" (21:5) all point to God's redemptive work fulfilled in and through Christ.

Christ's proclaimed worthiness to "take the scroll and to open its seals" (5:2, 5, 7) is now directly attributed to His sacrifice and atoning work of redemption on the cross. "You were slain" (*sphazō*)—as in 5:6, 12 and 13:8—carries the strength of a "violent slaughter" (cf. 1 John 3:12; Rev. 6:9; 18:24). "With your blood" speaks of the presentation of Christ's blood as the ransom or "purchase" price of many "for God." Jesus spoke of His own life as a "ransom [*lytron*] for many" in Matthew 20:28 and Mark 10:45. Then Paul in 1 Timothy 2:6 (there, *antilytron*) and the writer of Hebrews in 9:15 (there, *apolytrōsis*) use related words, all of which indicate the price of the redemption of a slave or of the release of a captive (cf. 1 Cor. 6:20; 7:23; Gal. 3:13). Together, these words are built upon the verb *lyō*, "to loose or release" as found in Revelation 1:5, "[...] and has freed us from our sins by his blood." The breadth of Christ's redemptive work is then seen in the vast multitude of people purchased for

God "from every tribe and language and people and nation" (cf. Rev. 7:9; 19:1, 6), clearly a prophetic message since this far exceeded the extent of the Gospel in John's immediate day.

Important to the further identity of the "twenty-four elders" are the distinct textual differences reflected in the reading of portions of verses 9 and 10 in varying versions and in the two primary families of manuscripts upon which they are based. The Egyptian or Alexandrian text is reflected in the wording of verses 9 and 10 in such versions as (emphasis added):

- NIV (v. 9) "you purchased for God persons"; (v. 10) "You have made **them** to be [...] **they** will reign"
- NASB (v. 9) "and purchased for God"; (v. 10) "You have made **them** *to be* [...] and **they** will reign upon the earth."
- ESV (v. 9) "you ransomed people for God"; (v. 10) "you have made **them** [...] and **they** shall reign"
- NLT (v. 9) "has ransomed people for God"; (v. 10) "you have caused **them** to become [...] And they will reign"

The Byzantine or Majority text is reflected in the wording of verses 9 and 10 in such versions as:

- AKJV (v. 9) "hast redeemed **us** to God"; (v. 10) "hast made **us** unto our God [...] and **we** shall reign"
- NKJV (v. 9) "redeemed **us** to God by Your blood"; (v. 10) "And have made **us** [...] And **we** shall reign"
- WYC (v. 9) "boughtest **us** to God in thy blood"; (v. 10) "madest **us** a kingdom, and priests to our God; and **we** shall reign on earth."

The superiority of one or the other text type is long debated and beyond the scope of this work, both being held by true conservative scholars. However, if the best reading here follows the Alexandrian text, then there is strong reason to view the "twenty-four elders" as angelic in nature. Conversely, if the Majority text reads best here, then the "twenty-four elders" are representative of God's people (see note under 4:4, which comments on the title "elders" and the *stephanos* victory crowns and white garments they wear). Yet, there is more to be considered here. If the Alexandrian text *is* the better reading, it is not out of the question that the "elders" may—even as angels—be representing God's people on earth as they speak objectivity on behalf of us and in the third person. Further, it is also possible that the third person is used simply because in context the "four living creatures" may also be joining in this hymn of praise.

What is certain is that the redeemed from all the earth are commissioned by God "to be a kingdom and priests to serve our God" (v. 10a). (See this theme also in 1:6 and 20:6.) Rather than being served by a priesthood as were the Old Testament saints, we, the redeemed according to the New Covenant, are now ourselves a priesthood fulfilled in our immediate access before the Father through Christ, where we bring worship and intercession. Peter is clear in proclaiming the present reality of our dual calling as "a holy priesthood" and "royal priesthood" (1 Pet. 2:5, 9).

Jesus also promised that we would be brought into His authority as we share in His Kingdom rule over the earth (v. 10b)—"and they will reign on the earth." Even as there is a "now and still yet" dynamic to the full redemption plan (see notes under 5:6-7), the same is true of our reign with Christ. We now share in Christ's authority as He has "seated us with him in the heavenly realms in Christ Jesus" (Eph. 2:6; Rev. 1:6), yet we will also reign with Him in the future realm of His Kingdom upon the earth. While textual evidence varies in 5:10 between the future tense "they will reign" and the present tense "they reign," Revelation 1:6 and 20:4 validate both applications. The preposition *epi* ("on") accompanying *tēs gēs* ("the earth") in the genitive case is properly translated "on" or "upon." Many New Testament passages, such as Matthew 5:5 and 19:28; Luke 22:29; 1 Corinthians 4:8 and 6:2; 2 Timothy 2:12; and, Revelation 20:6, join with the elders' song in proclaiming that the redeemed will reign with Christ "on the earth" during His future Millennial Reign.

Adding to this glorious scene, John then sees and hears "the voice of many angels." "Ten thousand" is the translation of *myrias* (the English "myriad"); "ten thousand times ten thousand" (ESV, "myriads of myriads") or "one hundred million" was the largest number used in the ancient Greek language. However, *myrias* also was commonly used to mean an unlimited number. Certainly, John is indicating a host of angels beyond number, just as Daniel reported as well (Dan. 7:10). These countless angels "encircled the throne and the living creatures and the elders" indicating a pattern of concentric circles of worshipers radiating from the Throne of God.

John had earlier learned that worship before the Throne of God is constant (4:8, "Day and night they never stop saying [...]"); now He discovers that worship in Heaven only builds with crescendo. While the elders sing their glorious "new song," the innumerable angels, followed then by all creation, proclaim the worthiness of the Lamb. In contrast to singing (*adō*, "singing praise to God"; Eph. 5:19; Col. 3:16) in the Revelation—found only in 5:9; 14:3; and 15:3—the angels in 5:12 and all creation in 5:13 are heard "saying" (*legō*, general word for "speaking") the praises of God the Father and the Son.

"In a loud voice" (cf. 5:2; 12:10; 14:7) the angels bring a seven-fold declaration of the worthiness of Jesus as the sacrificed Lamb (cf. 5:9). In His possession and through His completed mission are:

- "power" (*dynamis*, "inherent ability"; cf. Mark 13:26; Acts 10:38)
- "wealth" (*ploutos*; "riches, abundance"; cf. Eph. 1:7, 18; 2:7; 3:8, 16)

- "wisdom" (*sophia*; of Christ's "transcendent knowledge"; cf. Matt. 13:54; Rom. 11:13; 1 Cor. 1:24, 30)
- "strength" (*ischys*; "mighty power"; cf. Eph. 1:19; 6:10)
- "honor" (*timē*; "valued honor and esteem"; cf. 1 Tim. 1:17; Heb. 2:9; 3:3; 1 Pet. 2:7)
- "glory" (*doxa*; of Christ's "majesty and splendor"; Matt. 25:31; John 1:14)
- "praise" (*eulogia*; "a good word of blessing"; cf. Eph. 1:3).

In these attributes the angels praise the absolute victory of the Lamb. He has prevailed to regain and restore the once forfeited inheritance to every believer and to secure the bright destiny of all creation.

Added to the angels' proclamation is the praise of (v. 13a) "every creature" (*ktisma*, with an emphasis on God's creative act as in 1 Tim. 4:4 and James 1:18). Reflecting the complete nature of the restored inheritance in Christ (see Summary Conclusion under 5:7), the scope of creation's praise extends to "in heaven and on earth and under the earth and on the sea, and all that is in them" which encompasses all humanity—those still physically alive and those as departed spirits—and every rank of holy angels (cf. Phil. 2:10, 11; Col. 1:20). This four-fold reference to the created world may speak poetically of the completeness of creation, such as with "the four corners of the earth" and "the four winds of the earth" (7:1); the four directions, "east and west and north and south" (Luke 13:29); and, as represented in the "four living creatures" (see notes under 4:6-8).

The praise of all creation is now directed toward the Father, "him who sits on the throne" (v. 13b; cf. 4:2, 9) and toward the Son "the Lamb" (cf. 5:7). Added to those divine qualities lauded in the praise of the angels, i.e., "praise and honor and glory" is now added "power," here *kratos* (cf. Eph. 1:19; 1 Tim. 6:16; 1 Pet. 5:11), meaning "manifested power or dominion" and this "for ever and ever!" Again, we are reminded of Daniel's vision and prophecy of the Messiah's everlasting bestowal of authority and dominion from the Ancient of Days in Daniel 7:13-14. As Revelation is preeminently a book of worship from beginning to end, the fulfillment of Heaven's worship is reflected again in the antiphonal "Amen" (i.e., "so let it be"; cf. Rev. 1:6, 7; 7:12; 19:4) of the "four living creatures" and the continued obeisance and worship of the "elders."

Life Application

Worship is the language of Heaven. Earlier, John saw that the praise of cherubim and elders before God's throne is ceaseless, "day and night they never stop" (4:8). Yet, John's worship-filled experience continues to grow in awe as the presentation and exaltation of the Lamb unfolds before him. With Jesus' reception of the scroll and His reclaiming of the lost inheritance, a crescendo of praise—waves and waves of boundless adoration—is released through the halls of Heaven.

At the height of this glorious encounter, John hears a song resounding with one unwavering focus and one unending theme. The song of Heaven is a "new song," free and victorious, rising from the hearts of the redeemed and only the redeemed. The focus of Heaven is Christ alone, the worthy One. All eyes are on Jesus whose completed mission has restored us to our Father, revived our hope, and restored our dignity and authority in Him. And the anthem of Heaven—never ending and always empowering—is the blood of the Lamb, declared by the Father, shed by the Son, witnessed by the Spirit.

For John, before the Triune God, Heaven's celebration was an all-embracing, "total worship" experience. Every part of the created world was swept in—every believer of all the ages; every angel of which there is no number; and every living creature that has ever drawn life from God. In the words of King David at the conclusion of his many songs, "Let everything that has breath praise the Lord. Praise the Lord" (Psalm 150:6). Look and listen with John as that great assembly brings their all-encompassing expression, their "total worship," before God's throne. See them kneel and fall and pray; hear them sing and shout and play.

You and I, too, have been created for this and nothing can mean more! Before you are a man or a woman, you are a worshipper of God. Before you are a husband or wife, child or parent, leader or follower, your highest call is as an instrument of worship. "Total worship" that invests your entire being from the inside out—"total worship" that engages your thoughts and desires, your emotions and your passion. "Total worship" that joins with the assembly of Heaven and blesses the heart of God.

Chapter 5 Notes

1. "The right side of things is recognized in many ways as better than the left […] The right side, or right limb, of a person receives special prominence; the place of honor is at his right." Joseph Jacobs and Judah David Eisenstein, "Right and Left," *JewishEncyclopedia.com*, The Kopelman Foundation, 2011 <www.jewishencyclopedia.com/articles/12757-right-and-left>.

2. "The transition from the roll to the codex took place gradually over roughly three hundred years, from the first or second through fourth or fifth centuries CE." Jeremy Norman, "The Transition from the Roll to the Codex: Technological and Cultural Implications," *History of Information.com*, Jeremy Norman & Co., Inc., 2017 <www.historyofinformation.com/narrative/roll-to-codex.php>.

3. "From the beginnings of Greek written literature until deep into the Roman era, a 'book' was fashioned by taking a premanufactured papyrus roll, writing out the text, attaching additional fresh rolls as the length of text required, and, when finished, cutting off the blank remainder. Needed were the papyrus rolls, ink, pen sponge, glue, and knife… Books on papyrus in the form of rolls ('bookrolls') were the norm from the beginnings through the early Roman era." William A. Johnson, "The Ancient Book," ed. Roger S. Bagnall *The Oxford Handbook of Papyrology* (Oxford University Press, 2011) 256.

4. Edward Maunde Thompson, *An Introduction to Greek and Latin Paleography* (Oxford: Clarendon, 1912) 49-50. As quoted in *The Expositors Bible Commentary, Vol. 12, Hebrews through Revelation*, 465.

5. "The seal was employed from the beginning of the historical era as a method of identifying property, as protection against theft, to mark the clay stoppers of oil and wine jars or the strip with which packaged goods were bound, and for other uses. […] They were normally used for signing documents, however, though generally the signature of witnesses alone was sufficient." "Encyclopedia Judaica: Seal, Seals," *Jewish Virtual Library*, American-Israeli Cooperative Enterprise, 2017 <www.jewishvirtuallibrary.org/seal-seals>.

   Of great interest is this statement describing records contemporaneous to John's writing. Here a codex prototype of bronze tablets is used and sealed; yet reading the bronze inner "pages" does not require the breaking of the seals affixed on the outer front "page": "Many of these [i.e., copies of military discharges] have been found consisting of two bronze tablets bound together to form four pages, of which the inner pages contain the certified copy and the name of the soldier concerned. One outer page carries the names and the seals of seven Roman citizens who served as witnesses; the other [outer] page has another copy of the material found on the inside.

This was done as a matter of convenience, so that the seals closing the two tablets need not be broken wherever the document was consulted." Clyde Pharr, ed., *Ancient Roman Statutes: A Translation with Introduction, Commentary, Glossary, and Index* (Austin: University of Texas Press, 1961).

6. W. E. Vine, *An Expository Dictionary of New Testament Words* (Revell, 1966) 307.

7. A.T. Robertson points out the difference in tenses between "he came" (ἦλθεν; *ēlthen*; aorist active indicative) and "he has taken" (εἴληφεν; *eilēphen*; perfect active indicative) to bring a "vivid dramatic picture of the actual scene." Archibald Thomas Robertson *Word Pictures in the New Testament. VI* (Nashville: Broadman, 1933) 335.

8. "[I]t is my understanding that the primary, fundamental, chief reference and significance of this book has to do with the redemption of God's created universe and everything in it. That book is a book of redemption." W.A. Criswell, *Expository Sermons on Revelation* (Grand Rapids, MI: Zondervan, 1966) 56.

9. A prime authority on the subject of ancient seals and stamps in the Graeco-Roman world, Katelijn Vandorpe writes the following: "Much is known about the seals on Roman wills, not because they are preserved, unfortunately, but because the testator himself (53) and the six or seven witnesses (σφραγισταί) describe their seals at end of the will, sometimes even quite precisely [...] When the will had to be opened, a majority (57) of the witnesses (three of the five, four of the six or seven) had to be present (58). Witnesses were allowed, however, to send a friend or a representative (ϝφίλος (59)) if they could not be present personally. The witnesses or their representatives had to recognize (γνωρίζω (60) , ἐπιγιγνώσκω (61)) the seal or establish that the seal was "healthy" (ὑγιής (62)), i.e., unbroken (διαρρήγνυμι (63)). Then the will was opened and read. Under a copy of the will, the witnesses present had to subscribe that they recognized their seals." Katelijn Vandorpe, "Roman wills," *Seals and Stamps from Graeco-Roman and Byzantine Egypt*, 2010 <www.trismegistos.org/seals/overview_3b.html>.

10. George Long, M.A., Fellow of Trinity College writes the following in an article entitled "Testamentum": "A passage in a Novel of Theodosius II. (A.D. 439, De Testamentis) states the old practice as to the signature of the witnesses. 'In ancient times a testator showed (offerebat) his written testament to the witnesses, and asked them to bear testimony that the will had so been shown to them (oblatarum tabularum perhibere testimonium)' [...] The Novel enacted what we may presume to have been the old usage, that the testator might produce his will sealed, or tied up, or only closed, and offer it to seven witnesses, Roman citizens and puberes, for their sealing and adscription, provided at the same time he declared the instrument to be his will and signed it in their presence, and then the witnesses affixed their seals and signatures at the same time also."

Further commenting on the Praetorian Testament form of will (as compared to the Civil), which began during the Roman Republic and lasted long into the Roman Empire (beginning 27 B.C.), George Long adds the following: "This socalled Praetorian Testament existed in the Republican period, and for a long time after [...] It required seven male witnesses of competent age and legal capacity, and the act must be done in the presence of all, at the same place, and at the same time, that is, it must be continuous. The testator might declare his last will orally (sine scriptis) before seven witnesses, and this was a good will. If it was a written will, the testator acknowledged it before the witnesses as his last will, and put his name to it, and the witnesses then subscribed their names and affixed their seals." William Smith, ed., *Smith's Dictionary of Greek and Roman Antiquities* (Boston: Little, Brown, and Co., 1875) 11131118.

[11.] In disagreement with the view of a last will and testament, George Eldon Ladd posits the following: "This view is attractive, but it faces a major difficulty; namely, that the seals as well as the trumpets do not have to do with the Christian's inheritance but with the plagues of judgment which God will pour out upon a rebellious civilization." George Eldon Ladd, *A Commentary on the Revelation of John* (Grand Rapids, MI: Eerdmans, 1972) 80.

[12.] Theologian J. A. Seiss writes, "Everything testifies that it was a high, holy, and blessed investiture. But, alas, its original possessor sinned, and it passed out of his hands to the disinheritance of all his seed. The sealed book, the title-deeds of it forfeiture and mortgage, are in the hands of God, and strangers and intruders have overrun and debased it." J.A. Seiss, *The Apocalypse—Lectures on the Book of Revelation* (Grand Rapids, MI: Zondervan, 1966) 112.

W. A. Criswell adds, "An interloper, an intruder, an alien, an enemy, has taken it, and that book of redemption awaits a *goel*, a kinsman-redeemer, a worthy, qualified and legal kinsman to buy it back and to restore it to its rightful owners. When that book of redemption is taken by one who is worthy, and those seals are opened, then that interloper, that intruder, that alien, that enemy is to be cast out; and finally, the whole purchased possession is to be redeemed, and sin, hell, death, and Satan are to be cast into the lake of fire, forever destroyed. The judgment of God creates for us a new heaven and a new earth and gives us back the inheritance that we lost in Adam. Such is the meaning of the seven-sealed book that lies upon the hand of God. It is the symbol of a forfeited and lost inheritance." Criswell 66-67.

[13.] Here, we cannot miss the broader application of Jeremiah's redemptive actions. In the end, God would establish his people in the land and His righteousness in their hearts all in fulfillment of the work and accomplishments of the coming Messiah.

14. Professional business man, Robert V. Fullertion, CPA, brings an interesting perspective to this approach, viewing the seven-sealed title deed as actually a court ordered "judgment lien" that must be satisfied: "The scene in Revelation 5 is in fact a court session being called to order by the strong angel before the Righteous Judge in which man (possibly represented by the weeping John) is subject to sentence. John wept because he knew that man's fate was sealed in that scroll. Then, steps forward, the only Person worthy to take the scroll of judgement from the right hand of the Righteous Judge; the Lamb who was slain and who righteous sacrifice paid the debt on behalf of man" [...] "A person subject to a judgment lien is subject to lawful judgement and forfeiture and is often forced to declare bankruptcy (seek protection of the court)." Robert V. Fullerton, *God's Strategic Plan* (Life Purpose Books, 2014).

15. This author's careful search through scores of commentaries and historic documents revealed no primary sources to verify the claim of a seven-sealed title deed.

    Interestingly, "In 1960 twenty-three tied deeds without seals were found in the Cave of Letters near the Dead Sea. (Yadin, *Bar-Kokhba,* 228–231)." Robert C. Lewis, "Title Deed to the Earth," *Quicknotes.org,* Aug. 2010 <biblequicknotes.com/files/present/rev4-5.pdf>.

16. "'Seven seals' are upon this book, indicative of the completeness of those bonds of forfeit which have all this while debarred Adam's seed from their proper inheritance. [...] so those seals unbroken, set forth the completeness of the alienation, and the thoroughness of the incumbrances (sic) which are upon the estate, until that competent Goel has performed his work." Seiss 112.

    In support of the view of a title deed, Seiss continues (p. 112): "This book was '*written within and on the back.*' This again tends to identify it with these books of forfeited inheritances. Within were the specifications of the forfeiture; without were the names and attestations of the witnesses; for this is the manner in which these documents were attested." Here, Seisss cites Hebraists John Weemse on the Judicial Law of Moses, Chapter 30: "For the manner of writing the contract, he who was to buy the ground wrote two instruments; the one to be sealed with his own signet, the other he showed unclosed to the witnesses, that they might subscribe and bear witness of that which was written. *This, the witness did subscribe* UPON THE BACK *of the inclosed* (sic) *instrument.*" Seiss 112.

17. Writes David Guzik, "If God has to get the title deed back, when did God ever 'lose' the title deed to planet earth? In fact, God holds this scroll – it isn't lost." David Guzik, "Study Guide for Revelation Chapter 5," *Blue Letter Bible,* 2001 <http://web.ccbce.com/multimedia/BLB/Comm/david_guzik/sg/Rev_5.html>.

CHAPTER 6

Revelation 6:1-17

The Opening of Six of the Seven Seals

Introduction to Revelation 6:1-17

Immediately following the incomparable declaration of the worthiness of the Lamb and the glorious worship that fills the Throne Room of God, John is ushered into a much different turn of events. Though the contrast could not be greater, this unfolding vision is in keeping with the earlier instruction of Jesus, "Write, therefore, what you have seen, what is now and what will take place later" (1:19; cf. 4:1). Within the scroll, now firmly in the possession of the Lamb, is God's plan for the redemption of the forfeited inheritance. Within the scroll, sealed with seven seals, is the will of the Father through the Son to restore all that sin had stolen away. Within the Scroll of Redemption, filled with unparalleled judgment and events, is the future destiny of mankind and all creation.

Seven seals, the physical evidence of the presence of seven witnesses, have withheld the contents of the scroll until the appointed time—as the angel had said long before, "Go your way, Daniel, because the words are rolled up and sealed until the time of the end" (Daniel 12:9). Seven seals affixed along the outer edge of the scroll await the actions of the Testator, now raised from the dead. One by one the Lamb breaks open the seals; together they announce, before the throne and the assembly that looks on, the coming wrath of God and the dreadful events awaiting a world lost in sin.

Six of the seven seals are now being opened, the seventh remaining for a time, holding the scroll closed until two great multitudes are called unto God's service and into God's presence. And with each of these six opened seals, we along with angels and elders are given a glimpse into the coming Tribulation upon the earth.

The First Four Seals are Opened—6:1-8

[1] I watched as the Lamb opened the first of the seven seals. Then I heard one of the four living creatures say in a voice like thunder, "Come!" [2] I looked, and there before me was a white horse! Its rider held a bow, and he was given a crown, and he rode out as a conqueror bent on conquest.

[3] When the Lamb opened the second seal, I heard the second living creature say, "Come!" [4] Then another horse came out, a fiery red one. Its rider was given power to

take peace from the earth and to make people kill each other. To him was given a large sword. [5] When the Lamb opened the third seal, I heard the third living creature say, "Come!" I looked, and there before me was a black horse! Its rider was holding a pair of scales in his hand. [6] Then I heard what sounded like a voice among the four living creatures, saying, "Two pounds of wheat for a day's wages, and six pounds of barley for a day's wages, and do not damage the oil and the wine!" [7] When the Lamb opened the fourth seal, I heard the voice of the fourth living creature say, "Come!" [8] I looked, and there before me was a pale horse! Its rider was named Death, and Hades was following close behind him. They were given power over a fourth of the earth to kill by sword, famine and plague, and by the wild beasts of the earth.

Biblical Insights

Though the outlook abruptly shifts from glorious to harrowing, the vision that began with John's call to the Throne Room of God (4:1) now continues from Chapters 4 and 5 into Chapter 6. Within that setting John "watched as the Lamb opened the first of the seven seals." Through the offering of His own lifeblood (5:9), Jesus alone holds the authority "to open the scroll and its seven seals" (5:5). As was studied in Chapter 5, the book in Christ's possession is God's Scroll of Redemption, and the presence of the seven authenticating seals identifies the scroll, according to ancient customs, as a last will and testament—perhaps also serving as a title deed to the creation that has always truly remained in the hands of its Creator (Psalm 24:1). In either case, the proceeding events will sovereignly establish the Lamb's restoration of the once-forfeited inheritance back to Himself as both Testator and Heir and to those who follow Him as co-heirs.

Beginning with the first seal, the Lamb sequentially breaks each of the seven from their position along the outside edge of the rolled scroll. The opposing view, i.e., that the seven seals were hidden sequentially within the scroll and that the breaking of these seven bring the actual occurrence of judgment and events before and distinct from the trumpets and the bowls, has several real problems. To begin, though often claimed by Bible teachers (yet without primary citations), the practice of placing seals within the interior of ancient scrolls has little to no historic evidence. It is also important to note that the act of breaking the seventh seal comes without mention of any judgment in itself. As will be seen in 8:1, with this event comes only "silence in heaven for about half an hour"—in great contrast to the earlier crescendo of praise—and the positioning of seven angels whose trumpets sound with great details of God's wrath. Thus, the unique significance of the seventh seal is evident only if it has been placed with the other six along the exterior of the scroll; with its breaking, the scroll is freely opened and the detailed judgments within are released. Finally, it must be pointed out that when John "saw" the scroll, he saw seven seals, an impossibility if the seals were actually distributed within the scroll.[1]

Maintaining that the seven seals served both to authenticate and to secure the document from premature entry, it is proper to see the first six seals as bringing to its readers and observers a broad description, overview, or panorama of the content of the book.[2] The phrase "when he opened" consistently announces each of the six seals (6:1, 3, 5, 7, 9, 12; but note the change to "whenever" [*hotan* rather than *hote* in the UBS text, etc.] with the seventh seal in 8:1). Note that the descriptions accompanying these six are more generalized in detail than the descriptions of the "trumpet" and "bowl" judgments to follow. It is also very unlikely that the judgments and events described with each of the six are meant to be isolated and mutually exclusive in their impact; again they seem more general and broad.[3] Finally, as will be seen below, the detailed description of the sixth seal indicates total, cataclysmic and irreversible destruction of the earth and heavens (6:14, "The heavens receded like a scroll being rolled up, and every mountain and island was removed from its place"), hardly the picture often associated with the earlier portion of the Tribulation if the seals stand apart in their timing from the "trumpets" and "bowls."

With Christ's breaking of the first seal, John hears the thunderous voice of "one of the four living creatures," which were introduced in 4:6 as high ranking angelic cherubim (cf. Ezekiel 1:5-25; 3:13; 10:20). "Covered with eyes" (4:6, 8) and having "six wings" (4:8), each "living creature" is prepared to serve the God of Creation with great watchfulness and understanding along with swiftness, as they are messengers of His judgment. Clearly, the judgments they bring are at the sovereign command of God.

Since John had earlier identified each of the "living creatures" as "the first," "the second," "the third," and "the fourth"—and each with a unique appearance (4:7)—it is likely that the "living creature" that responds to the breaking of the first seal is the one described there as "the first," which was "like a lion." Perhaps his voice, "like thunder," sounded as a roar when it spoke the powerful command to "Come!" Here and in the parallel call of each of the "four living creatures" (6:3, 5, 7) a textual variant exists. If the Textus Receptus is correct, then the reading "Come and see" is a call to John, to which he responds (6:2) "and I looked." If the Egyptian text is correct, omitting "and see," then the call is most likely to the horsemen themselves. This is preferred, for it is unlikely that John, already riveted by the vision needed to be called out to "come."

Appearing now before John is "a white horse" with a rider seated upon it. Like this, each of the first four seals will reveal a uniquely colored horse and a particular rider bringing devastation into the earth, often referred to as the "Four Horsemen of the Apocalypse." Some teachers associate this first "rider" with Jesus, who is clearly seen in Revelation 19:11-16 riding on "a white horse" from Heaven at His public and visible Revelation. However, a white horse—the typical mount of an ancient conqueror—is where the similarity begins and ends. Clearly, Jesus is not, at the same time, both the one who holds the scroll and breaks its seals and the rider who is called by the "living creature" onto the scene. We also find the following contrasts between this unnamed rider of Chapter 6 and King Jesus, the Rider in Chapter 19:

- This rider is seen riding at the introduction of the events within the scroll—Jesus is seen riding at the very end of those events.
- This rider "held a bow" (but no arrow, perhaps symbolic of only partial conquest)—yet, from Jesus' mouth comes "a sharp sword with which to strike down the nations" (further, "He will rule them with an iron scepter.")
- This rider "was given a crown"—on Jesus' head "are many crowns."
- This rider's crown is a *stephanos*, the wreath of victory, which quickly wilts away—Jesus wears many diadems (*diadēma*) of enduring royalty and authority.
- This rider "rode out as a conqueror bent on conquest" and is then followed by violence, famine, plagues, and death throughout the earth—Jesus comes to bring a quick end to rebellion and to inaugurate peace throughout the earth.
- This rider is accompanied by three other riders, all of whom bring death and destruction—Jesus is seen riding with "the armies of heaven […] dressed in fine linen, white and clean."
- This rider's horse is contrasted with three other horses of different colors—those who ride with Jesus all follow Him on "white horses."
- This rider is nameless—but Jesus carries the names "Faithful and True," "the Word of God," and "KING OF KINGS AND LORD OF LORDS."

The rider on the white horse of Chapter 6 is on one hand representative of the world's lust for acquisition and rule by force; he is "bent on conquest" (in the spirit of ancient Nimrod of Babylon; Gen. 10:8-12). Yet, he is also an individual person who militarily and politically leads the final expression of human-based government in rebellion against God and His holy people (13:7). This first "rider" is none other than the one Daniel called "the prince that shall come" (9:26), Paul called, "the man of lawlessness […] the man doomed to destruction" (2 Thess. 2:3), and John called both "the Antichrist" (1 John 4:3) and "the Beast" (Rev. 13:1). John further identifies him as the final world dictator (13:7, 17) and an unquestioned military conqueror (13:4, "who can wage war against it?"). As the beast "coming out of the sea" (13:1), he is clearly commissioned by Satan—"The dragon gave the beast his power and his throne and great authority" (13:2).

As Jesus the Lamb "opened the second seal," John now hears the voice of "the second living creature" (cf. 4:7). With his command to "Come!" another horse comes riding, this time a fiery red one" no doubt representative of violence and bloodshed (cf. 12:3). It, too, has a rider who "was given power to take peace from the earth and to make people kill each other." The phrase "was given power" (*edothē*) comes from the root verb *didōmi*, meaning "to give or grant" (no word for "power" is included here). The same word is used again in v. 4, "was given [*edothē*] a large sword"; in v. 2, "was given [*edothē*] a crown"; and in v. 8, "were given [*edothē*] power." Though this granting of power and authority is seen many times throughout the Revelation, there are instances where this empowering is directly from God (7:2; 8:2; 9:1, 3, 5; 12:14) and times where the empowerment explicitly comes from Satan (13:2, "The dragon gave the beast his power"; 13:4, "the dragon because he had given authority to the beast"; v. 5, "The beast was given a mouth to utter proud words and blasphemies"; v. 7, "It was given power to wage war against God's holy people").

In determining the source of this often-lethal empowerment, we must look at the context and we must remember that while God sovereignly rules and overrules in the affairs of men, He remains righteous and "cannot be tempted by evil, nor does he tempt anyone" (James 1:13; cf. Deut. 32:4). While He clearly does employ the bent of evil men to bring chastening and judgment (cf. Isa. 10:5; Hab. 1:5-11), He Himself is not the instrument of that evil. Thus, in v. 4 it is men "dragged away by their own evil desire and enticed (James 1:14) who "make people kill each other"; and, in v. 8, it is the work of darkness—"Death" and "Hades"—who "kill by sword, famine and plague, and by the wild beasts of the earth." In a very real sense, it must be seen that the judgments described with the opening of the first four seals come as God sovereignly turns humanity and the earth over to its own demise; these are the eventual and inevitable consequences of a world in unrepentant rebellion against its Creator.

The theological approach of the preterist (from Latin, *praeter*, meaning "past"), namely that these events were all fulfilled within the first century A.D., does not fit John's statement here. "Its rider was given power to take peace from the earth and to make people kill each other" (v. 4; cf. 1 Thess. 5:3) can hardly be said during this period known for the *Pax Romana* ("Roman Peace"; lasting c. 27 B.C. – A.D. 180). While Rome's rule came with an "an iron fist," it did successfully secure international peace in John's day and beyond (cf. Acts 24:2). The power to "kill" in v. 4 (*sphazō*) speaks of violent murder and slaying. The "large sword" (*machaira megas*) is usually the word for a large knife or small sword often used for violence and dissensions, not the broad, "double-edged sword" (*rhomphaia*) that proceeds from the mouth of Jesus (Rev. 1:16; 2:12, 16; 19:15, 21), that is, the Word of God (but see also *rhomphaia* in 6:8). It will become clear throughout this Revelation that no ultimate, final, and lasting peace will come to this earth until Jesus, the Prince of Peace, establishes the realm of His Kingdom in the earth (cf. Isa. 9:6, 7; Zech. 9:10; Col. 1:20).

Following as with the first two events, the Lamb "opened the third seal" and the command to "Come!" sounded from "the third living creature" (4:7). Before John now appears "a black horse" that evidently speaks of a spirit of mourning which follows in the wake of hunger and famine, which in themselves are often prevalent in the wake of widespread violence, the aftermath of power-hungry conquest. (A comparison may be made to the black "horses" of Zechariah 6:2, 6 to the extent that they are seen "going out from standing in the presence of the Lord.") In this rider's hand, strangely enough is a "balance" or "pair of scales" used for measuring (*zygos*; everywhere else in the New Testament used of a "yoke"). What follows explains the mystery.

Coming from amongst the "four living creatures," perhaps in their role as nature's representatives before the throne (see under 4:7), came a voice of lament for this natural tragedy (even as "the whole creation has been groaning" in Romans 8:22). "Two pounds" is a translation of one *choinix*, for us a dry measure of less than one quart, about one day's ration for one man; "six pounds" translates three times this amount. Though all four commodities were common staple foods throughout the Mediterranean region (cf. Deut. 7:13; Joel 2:19; Hag. 1:11), barley was still considered the food of the poor while wheat, oil, and wine would be considered an extra amenity, if not a luxury, during time of famine. "A day's wages" is the translation of *dēnarion*; a denarius was the first century Roman silver coin, which represented a common laborer's wages for one day (cf. Matt. 20:2, 9). The situation foresees an inflation rate of at least 1,200 percent based on the economy of that day. "Do not damage the oil and the wine!" is most likely a statement about the wealthy. While the rich man may still demand the amenities of life, his common neighbor would have to make a choice between using his full day's wages to buy one portion of wheat or three portions of barley for himself and his family with nothing left over.[4] Thus, we understand the mystery of the "balance" in the hand of the third rider.

As the Lamb now opens the fourth seal, the last of the four horses and riders is now summoned at the command of "the fourth living creature" (4:7) to "Come!" Again, each seal speaks broadly with prophetic insight as to the effects of the judgments and events contained within the scroll. Following the same pattern, John now sees before him "a pale horse." The color *chlōros* in this context would be ashen or yellowish pale (though used of "green" in 8:7 and 9:4); here it is immediately associated with the rider named "Death" (*thanatos*). That "Hades was following close behind him" is understandable, though it is unclear whether on the same or another horse, or walking. "*Hadēs*" (corresponding to the Old Testament "Sheol") is variously translated as "hell," "the grave," or as here, "Hades," the place of the disembodied souls of the unsaved (since Christ's ascension, and of all persons before). In the Old Testament we see these two in tandem using poetic parallelism (cf. Psalm 49:14; 89:48; Isa. 28:15, 18; Hosea 13:14). In Revelation, we see the two together here and in 1:18 and 20:13, 14, where Jesus is seen in victory and authority over both.

Both "Death" and "Hades" are given "power" (*exousia*, "authority") "over a fourth of the earth," a major intensification of the devastation brought by the three riders going before them. Never before has the human population seen such loss of life on an international level. These two will use four instruments to work their trade (cf. Jer. 15:2-3; Ezek. 14:21): they will "kill by sword" (here, the broader and longer *rhomphaia*, used as a battle weapon of widespread destruction); by "famine" (*limos*, or "hunger") well beyond the scarcity of the third rider; by "plague" (again *thanatos*, i.e., "death," but here a distinct type of sweeping death); and, by "the wild beasts of the earth" (*thērion*, wild animal; far from *zōon* used of the "four living creatures," this word is also used for the two satanically driven "Beasts" of Rev. 13). No doubt, war, famine, and noxious plague—bringing catastrophic casualties and death—will invite the ravages of hungry wild animals drawn out of their natural surroundings.

Life Application

While teaching at a Midwestern college, I walked alongside a professor friend of mine as we transitioned between classrooms. What put us on the subject, I don't remember, but his somber words still trouble me. "Tom, it's unthinkable what human beings have been known to do to each other down through history. The horrors of human torture and violence are beneath even what is found in the animal kingdom." Coming from a teacher of history, the reality of what he said was sobering, to say the least.

Humanity—though created with so much promise—has been poisoned by sin; our depravity has become our own undoing. The symptoms come in many strains— hate, violence, abuse, racism, greed, lust, deceit, and on—but the common source of it all is sin against God and man, plain and simple. In Jesus, we know that the curse of sin and death is destroyed and the curse upon the earth is beneath our feet. In Jesus, we overcome the world and rise above its ruin. But tragically, in a future world where Jesus is renounced, where depravity rules, and where the "salt and light" of the Church is removed, sin will reach its ugly climax.

With the breaking of the first four seals, a world gone wild is released, as God's hand of protection has been lifted. At first John sees what some will call their "knight in shining armor." Leading the parade of the four horsemen is one "bent on conquest." Looking the part of the "savior of the world" his true colors will soon be seen. It's true what's been said, "Power corrupts and absolute power corrupts absolutely" (Lord Acton; 1834–1902). Riding close on his heels are the worst of human tragedies— unprecedented violence and war, famine, hunger, disease, and the unleashing of fierce animals now with a taste for human blood. While none of these are foreign to human experience, their global impact and growing intensity is. These four seals—these predictions of things to come—are just the start. But in all of this, we know now what John knew then. Jesus stands in full control; the destiny of the world is in His hands; and, the enemy of our soul is beneath His feet.

The Fifth Seal is Opened—6:9-11

[9] When he opened the fifth seal, I saw under the altar the souls of those who had been slain because of the word of God and the testimony they had maintained.[10] They called out in a loud voice, "How long, Sovereign Lord, holy and true, until you judge the inhabitants of the earth and avenge our blood?" [11] Then each of them was given a white robe, and they were told to wait a little longer, until the full number of their fellow servants, their brothers and sisters, were killed just as they had been.

Biblical Insights

In great contrast to the thunderous call of the "four living creatures" and the unspeakable desolation of the four horsemen, is the scene that unfolds with the Lamb's opening of the fifth seal. For this moment John's focus is drawn away from the chaos and destruction caused by sin and toward those who have been severely persecuted unto death for their devotion to Christ.

John "saw under the altar the souls of those who had been slain." There are two possibilities in identifying this altar in Heaven, one the antitype of the Old Testament altar of incense and the other the antitype of the Old Testament altar of burnt sacrifice. The writer of Hebrews speaks of the earthly Temple as only "a copy and shadow of what is in heaven" (Heb. 8:5); so, now in the Book of Revelation we find the clearest view and teaching about the light that casts that shadow, "God's temple in heaven" (11:19; cf. Ps. 18:6; 29:9; Micah 1:2). In this "temple" John witnesses the Throne of God—where the Father and the Son are seated in glorious authority, "the altar" (6:9; 8:3, 5; 9:13; 14:18; 16:7), and "the ark of his covenant" (11:19). And, John will come to know that once the "new Jerusalem" descends from Heaven, there is no further mention of a detailed heavenly "temple" as before, for now "the Lord God Almighty and the Lamb are its temple" (21:2).

Without question, there is in heaven the antitype, that is, the perfect completion of the "altar of incense." The earthly type or "shadow" is described in detail in Exodus 30:1-10. On this physical altar, incense was burned each day during the morning and evening sacrifices as a symbol of the prayer of God's people rising before Him (cf. Ps. 141:2; Luke 1:10). In Revelation 8:3 we see an angel standing at the heavenly altar holding a golden censer; "He was given much incense to offer, with the prayers of all God's people, on the golden altar in front of the throne." This passage goes on to show the direct involvement of the prayers of God's people in the impending judgments upon the wicked (8:4-5). This same altar is referenced again in 9:13, and in the absence of any change in description, we may assume the same in 14:18 and 16:7. If this is the altar in 6:9, then the prayers of the martyrs ascend from beneath this altar like incense.

A second possibility for the altar of 6:9, under which are "the souls of those who had been slain," is the antitype of the "altar of burnt offering." In the Old Testament tabernacle and temple (cf. Exod. 27:1-8; 40:29; Lev. 4:25, 30, 34; 1 Chron. 21:26; 2 Chron. 29:18), this was a place of bloodletting and sacrifice. We do read in Leviticus 4:7 that the blood of animal sacrifices was poured by the priest at the base of the altar, here a possible connection with the souls "under the altar" (Rev. 6:9). While no redemptive work is ever to be found in either the animal sacrifices of the Old Covenant (Heb. 10:4) or through the blood of the righteous (1 Tim. 2:5-6), there is much said in the Scriptures about identifying with Christ in His sufferings and sacrificial death. Paul speaks of "participating in his sufferings, becoming like him in his death" (Phil. 3:10) and "being poured out like a drink offering" (2 Tim. 4:6; and Phil. 2:17).

Support for this view over the prior may come from Isaiah's visionary experience and reference to the "altar" from which a seraph had lifted a live coal then touched to Isaiah's mouth (Isa. 6:6). Identity with an atoning work—"this has touched your lips; your guilt is taken away and your sin atoned for" (6:7)—aligns more so with the altar of burnt offering than the altar of incense. If the altar of Revelation 6:9 is indeed the antitype of the "altar of burnt offering," this would acceptably constitute a second "altar" in the heavenly "Temple," under which John sees the souls of the martyrs speaking of the sacrifice of their blood for the cause of Christ.

John notes that these faithful had been "slain," here *sphazō*, the same word used consistently for the sacrifice of Christ in 5:6, 9, 12; 13:8, speaking of a violent slaughter. Their sacrifice came "because of the word of God and the testimony they had maintained" even as John himself was presently suffering on Patmos "because of the word of God and the testimony of Jesus" (1:9). The violent death of God's righteous people will again be referenced several times in the Revelation, such as in 18:24, "the blood of prophets and of God's holy people, of all who have been slaughtered on the earth." As was true through many centuries, martyrdom will be a constant reality for those who accept Christ during the Tribulation (cf. Rev. 12:11; 13:7, 15; 14:13; 16:6; 17:6).

Now it is important that John calls these under the heavenly altar "souls" (*psychē*). He will use this same term in 20:4 at the time of the resurrection of their bodies, where he notes, "they came to life." Contrary to the false teaching of the "soul sleep" of the intermediate state of the dead, (that is, before their resurrection), these souls are conscious, active, and in the immediate presence of God in His throne room. John will affix the time of the bodily resurrection of Tribulation martyrs—"They had not worshiped the beast or his image [...]"—as being after the Revelation of Jesus and before the commencement of his thousand-year reign of Christ (20:4).

We must now make a comparison between the "souls" under the altar in 6:9 and the multitude in 7:9; these saints too are "wearing white robes" and are associated with "the great tribulation" (7:14). However, a clear contrast is seen between these two groups beginning with the fact that the saints of 7:9 comprise an innumerable number "standing before the throne and in front of the Lamb"; they are not found under the altar. Twice more we will find the redeemed clothed in "fine linen, bright [or 'white,' v. 14] and clean"—once as a bride (19:7-8) and once as an army (19:14; cf. 17:14). It would seem then that those dressed in white as a great multitude (7:9) "standing before the throne" and "holding palm branches in their hands" are the same as "his bride [who] has made herself ready" (19:7) and "the armies of heaven [...] riding on white horses," battling and defeating the physical kings and armies of the earth. Given their activities and clear contrast with the "souls" of 6:9—who are resurrected only after the Revelation of Jesus at the end of the Tribulation (20:4)—it stands to reason that the multitude (7:9), the bride (19:7-8), and the army (19:14) are those who have already been gathered to the Lord at the Rapture of the Church (2 Thess. 2:2; 1 Thess.

4:13-17; Rev. 3:10) and who have already experienced their resurrection (1 Cor. 15:51-52), i.e., their "white robes" constitute their eternal glorified bodies. Supporting this further is the bodily resurrection (11:11) and ascension into heaven (11:12) of the "two witnesses" (11:3) well before the Revelation of Jesus.

If this is true, then what can it mean that each of the martyed souls of 6:9 "was given a white robe" well before their resurrection foretold in Revelation 20:4? Some have seen these robes as symbolic of purity, justification, or blessedness.[5] While these attributes certainly attend, there is a further reality here. We can easily deduce that the "souls of those who had been slain" (6:9) are only those who have died during the coming great tribulation; inasmuch as they comprise the fifth seal, they relate directly to the events and timeframe contained within the scroll. Additionally, "they were told to wait a little longer, until the full number of their fellow servants, their brothers and sisters, were killed just as they had been" (6:11; also 14:3). Therefore, those John sees presently under the altar (6:9) along with the "full number" yet to be killed are all Tribulation martyrs. These together are identified as those, "Who had been beheaded because of their testimony about Jesus and because of the word of God. They had not worshiped the beast or its image and had not received its mark on their foreheads or their hands" (20:4). Since it is only at that time—after Christ's Revelation (19:11-16; cf. 1:7)—that they receive their glorified bodies, it stands to reason as many scholars teach that the "white robes" of 6:11 are actually temporary, provisional garments, i.e., the coverings of the intermediate state between physical death and bodily resurrection.[6]

John also hears the solemn cry, "in a loud voice," of these martyred "souls." "How long" may have in view not only the specific years of persecution during the events of the tribulation; it may also include an affinity with the countless millions of God's saints who have died in the millennia of time spanning Old Testament and New. This view is certainly implied in 16:6, "for they have shed the blood of your holy people and your prophets" and in 18:24, "In her was found the blood of prophets and of God's holy people, of all who have been slaughtered on the earth" (also 18:20).

This martyr's cry is lifted up with an acknowledgment of absolute trust in the authority and character of God. "Sovereign Lord" translates the title *despotēs* ("master"; one with absolute authority) often used of God the Father and the Son (cf. Acts 4:24; 2 Tim. 2:21; 2 Pet. 2:1; Jude 1:4). We may find in the description "under the altar" a statement of closeness to and protection by God. "How long [...] until you judge the inhabitant of the earth" is a reference beyond their immediate persecutors to all of the wicked and unrepentant of all ages, this phrase being used in this way many times (3:10; 8:13; 11:10; 13:8, 14; 17:8). "Judge" here is *krinō*, which in this context and in 11:18; 19:11; 20:12-13 speaks of final condemnation and punishment at God's hand alone. "Avenge" here is *ekdikeō*, which speaks of vindication based upon the justice of the Lord (cf. Rom. 12:19). The answer to their prayer will come with the Revelation of Jesus at the end of the tribulation. We read in 2 Thessalonians 1:6-8, "God is just: He will pay back trouble to those who trouble you and give relief to you who are troubled, and to us as well. This will happen when the Lord Jesus is revealed from heaven in blazing fire with his powerful angels. He will punish those who do not know God and do not obey the gospel of our Lord Jesus" (cf. Rev. 19:2, 11-15).

Life Application

"How do they do it?" I have many times asked that question, wondering how the many millions throughout the centuries and the countless thousands each year in our lifetime stay true to Jesus even in the face of unthinkable torture and execution. We must start with the knowledge that there is a price to be paid for faithfulness to Christ; as Paul and Barnabas declared, "We must go through many hardships to enter the kingdom of God" (Acts 14:22). Paul said it again; "everyone who wants to live a godly life in Christ Jesus will be persecuted" (2 Timothy 3:12). Peter added his counsel too, "do not be surprised at the painful trial you are suffering" (1 Peter 4:12). In this very Revelation, Jesus warns, "I tell you, the devil will put some of you in prison to test you, and you will suffer persecution for ten days. Be faithful, even to the point of death, and I will give you life as your victor's crown" (Revelation 2:10).

Yet, the question remains, "How do the faithful do it?" And the word of God is not silent. Those who stay faithful even to death count it an honor to suffer for the name of Jesus (Acts 5:41). Those who stay faithful believe that if you live in honor you will die in honor. There is no comparison between the last breaths of Steven (Acts 6:15) and of Herod (12:23). Those who stay faithful know that death has no sting to the believer (1 Corinthians 15:55). Those who stay faithful even to death remember that they are "Persecuted, but not abandoned; struck down, but not destroyed [...]" (2 Corinthians 4:9). Those who stay faithful to Jesus hold to His Word, "If God is for us, who can be against us? [...] Who shall separate us from the love of Christ? Shall trouble or hardship or persecution or famine or nakedness or danger or sword? As it is written: 'For your sake we face death all day long; we are considered as sheep to be slaughtered.' No, in all these things we are more than conquerors through him who loved us" (Romans 8:31b, 35-37). Those who stay faithful even to death hold on to their faith (period)!

For these who are faithful, whether in John's day, our day, or in the coming day of unthinkable tribulation, there is a place near to the Throne of God. "Robes of righteousness" we have worn here will be met with "white robes" of honor there. For, of these it still is said, "the world was not worthy of them" (Hebrews 11:38).

The Sixth Seal is Opened—6:12-17

[12] I watched as he opened the sixth seal. There was a great earthquake. The sun turned black like sackcloth made of goat hair, the whole moon turned blood red,[13] and the

stars in the sky fell to earth, as figs drop from a fig tree when shaken by a strong wind. [14] The heavens receded like a scroll being rolled up, and every mountain and island was removed from its place. [15] Then the kings of the earth, the princes, the generals, the rich, the mighty, and everyone else, both slave and free, hid in caves and among the rocks of the mountains. [16] They called to the mountains and the rocks, "Fall on us and hide us from the face of him who sits on the throne and from the wrath of the Lamb! [17] For the great day of their wrath has come, and who can withstand it?"

Biblical Insights

Immediately upon watching Jesus open the sixth seal, John witnesses a release of unprecedented judgment falling upon the earth and the skies above. The language that follows speaks of cataclysmic devastation of the natural world, aligning only with the movement toward the end of the Tribulation period. This timing is supported well by the view explained above (see under 5:6-7), namely, that the opening of these six seals serve as a general overview of the scroll's content within, as it were a preface to the book, and the breaking of the seventh results in the actual opening and releasing of its judgments and events. As seen earlier, the seals together were meant to authenticate and secure the book until the proper time for its opening by the Lamb. Now, in comparison to the first four seals and the four horsemen that followed, we see in the sixth seal a great intensification and final outpouring of God's judgment. It also becomes clear that the horsemen relate more so to the chaos and consequences of a world gone mad with sin—as though God had altogether removed His protective hand of mercy—while the events of the sixth seal now witness the direct infusion of the wrath of the Father and the Son. Nevertheless, all takes place within the will of God.

At first John observes "a great earthquake." We will see "earthquakes" (the word *seismos* can refer to any level of shaking) again in 8:5; 11:13, 19; 16:18. However, it is this last "severe earthquake" (16:18), one of the seventh "bowl" events, that aligns best with the earthquake of 6:12. Certainly this is what Isaiah sees as he writes of this day of judgment (24:19), "The earth is broken up, the earth is split asunder, the earth is violently shaken." Yet, Zechariah speaks of one additional earthquake to follow, one localized to the east of Jerusalem, at the time Jesus in His Revelation stands upon the Mount of Olives (Zech. 14:4). A shaking of the earth is often recorded as evidence of God's presence (cf. Exod. 19:18; 1 Sam. 14:15; 1 Kings 19:11; Matt. 27:51; 28:2; Acts 16:26). There is no reason not to read the earthquake of the sixth seal as a literal event.

John's attention is now turned to the heavens, and we must wonder if he is transported to an earthly perspective or if he continues to view this from heaven's perspective. The darkness that results from the obscuring of the light of the sun, as John now sees, had physically happened before through divine intervention in Egypt (cf. Exod. 10:22; and see Ezek. 32:7-8) and again as Jesus breathed His last on the cross (Luke 23:44). Joel had prophesied the same (Joel 2:10; 3:15) and had foreseen this same "last days" event "before the coming of the great and dreadful day of the Lord" (2:31; cf. Acts 2:20). Isaiah too saw the darkening of the sun in the day of the Lord's judgment (13:10), as did Zephaniah (1:14-15). Greatest of all, Jesus saw that day just before His Revelation when "the sun will be darkened, and the moon will not give its light; the stars will fall from the sky, and the heavenly bodies will be shaken" (Matt. 24:29). Yet it is John alone who describes this abject darkness as "black like sackcloth made of goat hair." The analogy is clear.[7]

As with Joel's prophecy and with Peter's quotation referenced above, the darkness of the sun is also accompanied by another celestial event, "the whole moon turned blood red." With no other reference in the Bible than these three, this occurrence is reserved for this "last days" event. Though "the blood moon" is a relatively common astronomical phenomenon, these additional signs have not yet correlated with them.

What is described next has caused some students of the Bible to question the literal intention of John's words here. Yet, as with the prior descriptions, we can expect real meaning even if the language John uses is somewhat poetic. Though *astēr* is the consistent Greek word for "star" in the New Testament, it is believed by etymologists to be related to the verb *stōnnyō*, meaning to spread, implying what is seen spread across the heavens. It is likely that John uses this word freely for what he sees spreading out across the heavens. Now, while physical stars exist in a wide range of sizes, any collision with a star would certainly annihilate the planet or at least its population instantly. In this case, it is likely that John sees what we would understand as a widespread meteor shower, yet now on an apocalyptic level. (And who even today does not speak of "shooting" or "fallen stars" when what is meant are meteors or comets?)

The Bible does indicate many astronomical anomalies related to the "last days" before the return of the Lord such as in Isaiah 13:10, 13; 34:4; Jeremiah 4:23, 28; Joel 2:10, 30, 31; Haggai 2:6; and most importantly with the words of Jesus in Matthew 24:29 (par. Mark 13:24-25). We should also recognize John's common allusions to and wording drawn from the Old Testament and from the Lord Himself, as is next seen in his metaphor, "as figs drop from a fig tree when shaken by a strong wind." "Fig" here is *olynthos*, the unripe, green, winter fig. These would easily fall from the tree in a brisk wind (cf. Mark 13:28).

Just as catastrophic is what John sees next, "The heavens receded like a scroll being rolled up, and every mountain and island was removed from its place." Certainly John has the words of Isaiah 34:4 in mind, "and the sky rolled up like a scroll; all the starry host will fall like withered leaves from the vine, like shriveled figs from the fig tree." We see similar language again in Hebrews 1:12 as a quotation of Psalm 102:27, "You will roll them up like a robe; like a garment they will be changed" (see also Heb. 12:26 quoting Hag. 2:6). While Old Testament allusions appear to align more so with John's words in

Revelation 21:1 concerning the establishment of "a new heaven and a new earth, for the first heaven and the first earth had passed away" (cf. 20:11), John may be borrowing from this language to describe what he sees at the height of the destruction during the Tribulation, just before the rejuvenating of the earth and the Millennial reign of Christ (cf. Romans 8:19-21). In accordance with the "great earthquake," it follows that John saw that, "every mountain and island was removed from its place" (v. 14; cf. Isa. 54:10). That there is a measure of the poetic here is possible since John will next see men fleeing to these same mountains for safety. Again, here is a clear statement of catastrophic, planetary, and cosmic chaos and destruction described with prophetic statements from an earthly perspective.

John now describes the human element during this time of great devastation. He refers to "seven"—again a number of completion—classifications of men from a human, not a divine perspective, "kings," "princes," "generals," "rich," "mighty," "slave," and "free" (cf. 19:18). The terms are meant to include all of humanity, "everyone else." These all "hid in caves and among the rocks of the mountains." Those who take a purely allegorical approach to Revelation have interpreted the cataclysmic language of the preceding verses to speak of the overthrow of governments in the first century and throughout history. But when has history recorded such an international reaction on this level, a global panic, to any shift in government? Jesus spoke of the days before His return as "days of distress unequaled from the beginning, when God created the world, until now—and never to be equaled again" (Mark 13:19; par. Matt. 24:21). Shall we question Jesus as well?!

There will be no more atheist or agnostic in this day just before the Revelation of Christ. The colloquial phrase "acts of God" will take on new meaning. As Jesus warned, "Men's hearts failing them for fear, and for looking after those things which are coming on the earth: for the powers of heaven shall be shaken" (Luke 21:26). All classes of humans will call "to the mountains and the rocks"; those who would not pray to God who lives, now call out to the inanimate for protection! (cf. Isa. 2:10, 18-21). "Fall on us and hide us from the face of him who sits on the throne," is drawn from the prophecy of Hosea 10:8, which Jesus also quoted in Luke 23:30. We remember the earlier words of John in Revelation 1:7, "and all the peoples of the earth will mourn because of him."

"Wrath" is now used for the first time in the Revelation. We will find in the opening of the scroll, that this is the overwhelming theme of God's dealings with a rebellious world. Wrath is the most consistently used term in Revelation to describe this coming tribulation, the translation of the word *orgē* ("anger, wrath, indignation" [Thayer]) in 6:16, 17; 11:18; 14:10; 16:19; 19:15) and *thymos* ("anger forthwith boiling up and soon subsiding again" [Thayer]) in 14:19; 15:1, 7; 16:1. Both words come together in 14:10, 16:19, and 19:15 to describe the "fury" of God's passion-driven and holy "wrath," which is also often pictured through the metaphor of grapes thrown into a winepress, the wine then being "poured full strength in the cup of his wrath" (14:10,

15-19; 16:19; 18:6; 19:15). The clear reason for God's wrath is directly related to humanity's continued wickedness; "they cursed the name of God, who had control over these plagues, but they refused to repent and glorify him" (16:9, 11; 9:20, 21; 21:8).

There is also then a recognition by earth's inhabitants that this wrath comes both from God the Father, i.e., "him who sits on the throne," and from God the Son, "the wrath of the Lamb!" (v. 16). Again, "the great day of their wrath has come" (v. 17; cf. Zeph. 1:15, 18; 2:3; Rom. 2:5). Jesus, the meek Lamb, is now angry at sin and rebellion, and as one with the Father shares in His divine justice! He directly opens each seal, and at the will of the Father releases its judgments.

Beginning with the first seal and intensifying through the sixth seal, is the unprecedented period of time known variously in the Scriptures as:

- "The tribulation" (*thlipsis*; speaking of "the pressing in of distress and affliction"; variously translated as "trouble," "distress," "anguish")—Daniel 12:1; Matthew 24:29; Mark 13:19, 24
- "The great tribulation" (*megas thlipsis*; lit. "the tribulation, the great one"; variously translated as "great distress," "greater anguish"—Matthew 24:21; Revelation 7:14 (but note 2:22)
- "The time of Jacob's trouble" (KJV, NIV); "a time of trouble for my people Israel" (NLT)—Jeremiah 30:7
- "The hour of trial" (NKJV, NIV); "the great time of testing" (NLT); here *peirasmos*, meaning "a trial, adversity, or affliction"—Revelation 3:10 (here *peirazō*, meaning "to prove or try")

During this tribulation, four primary developments and intentions are clear:

- The chastening of Israel by God, resulting in a national revival—"the time of Jacob's trouble" (Jeremiah 30:4-7)—see also Zechariah 12:10; Romans 11:25-31; Revelation 1:7
- The outpouring of God's wrath upon this world's sinful system, corporately & individually—seen throughout Revelation Chapters 6-18
- The final expression of Satan's rebellion through the Times of the Gentiles led by the Beast and those who follow him—Luke 21:24; Revelation 13:7-8, 16-18; 17:8-14
- The avenging of the blood of God's children—Revelation 6:9-10; 16:6; 17:6; 18:24; 19:2

Many students of the Bible believe that this period of Tribulation aligns with the "seventieth week" of Daniels prophecy (Dan. 9:24-27). While the timeframe of seven years is not found in the Revelation, several references to half of this time is referenced—"a time, times, and an half," Rev. 12:14 (cf. Daniel 7:25; 12:7); "a thousand two hundred and ninety days," Rev. 11:3; 12:6 (cf. Daniel 12:11); and, "forty-two months," Rev. 11:2; 13:5.

All of this is what John calls "the great day of their wrath." Not to be viewed as a 24-hour day, this "great day" is the beginning of "the day of the Lord" (2 Thess. 2:2; cf. 1 Cor. 1:8; 2 Cor. 1:14; Phil. 1:10), which sees God's severe judgment upon unrighteousness and the establishment of the realm of His righteousness Kingdom upon the earth. Paul speaks of this same period as "the day of redemption" (Eph. 4:30) and "the day of wrath" (Rom. 2:5). We also see close correlation in time and detail between the six seals and the description of eschatological events spoken by Jesus in the Olivet Discourse of Matthew 24. Again, much of John's phraseology is drawn from the prophets of old and from Jesus, and in this ageless agreement we are assured of the oversight, authority, power, and wisdom of God in the affairs of men.

Finally, John hears the admission of a judged humanity—"and who can withstand it?" As Malachi (3:2) had prophesied, "who can withstand the day of His coming?" (cf. Nah. 1:6). The answer is, "No one." As Paul declared in Romans 1:18, "The wrath of God is being revealed from heaven against all the godlessness and wickedness of people, who suppress the truth by their wickedness"; and again in 2:16, "This will take place on the day when God judges people's secrets through Jesus Christ, as my gospel declares." In that day only the righteous will stand in the presence of God, kept "from [*ek*, 'out of,' 'away from'] the hour of trial that is going to come on the whole world to test the inhabitants of the earth" (Rev. 3:10). These are the ones to whom Paul declared, "For God did not appoint us to suffer wrath but to receive salvation through our Lord Jesus Christ" (1 Thess. 5:9).

Life Application

Still in my early twenties, I must admit to having mixed emotions when my senior pastor asked me to participate in a debate with a seasoned minister on a well-known radio station. My apprehension came in having virtually no time to prepare and in being clueless on what to expect. My excitement came because, well, I've always liked a good challenge! So, here we sat, the middle aged, veteran cleric and the very young, rookie youth pastor. Yikes! Our moderator had chosen questions based on the common social issues of modern life in America. If my memory isn't too biased, I think I held my own and expressed myself reasonably well. But, it was the final question and our very divergent answers that stand out to me like it was yesterday. When asked to grade the moral climate of America and what we felt God thought of it all, to say we parted ways is an understatement. My debate opponent made it clear that my view was outdated and, in his word, "pessimistic." I do hope the smile I felt on the inside wasn't showing when I was given the last thirty seconds of the show to respond. My words fell something like this, "It's true that I believe the destiny of people who reject a personal relationship with

God through Jesus is not bright, but I find a very optimistic future promised to those who turn to God for forgiveness and mercy." Thirty-four years later, I say the same.

A day of wrath is coming on a level this world has never seen before. God's Word will come to pass and His judgment will be poured upon a rebellious, unrepentant world; He means what He says, and says what He means. A pessimistic destiny belongs only to those whom John will hear, "refused to repent of what they had done" (16:11). God's words through Jeremiah still hold true:

> Have you not brought this on yourselves by forsaking the Lord your God when he led you in the way? [...] Your wickedness will punish you; your backsliding will rebuke you. Consider then and realize how evil and bitter it is for you when you forsake the Lord your God and have no awe of me, declares the Lord, the Lord Almighty. (Jeremiah 2:17, 19)

Yet a very bright future awaits those who have given their lives to Jesus, whose sins have been forgiven, whose hearts are made pure in the blood of the Lamb. Pardoned and kept from the coming wrath, our destiny too is contained in the Scroll of Redemption; and no outlook could be more optimistic!

Chapter 6 Notes

1. "Robert van Kampen owns one of the world's most extensive private collections of biblical manuscripts, with many dating back to the second century. He writes in his book, 'The Sign,' [The Sign—of Christ's Coming and the End of the Age. Crossway, 2000] that of the many scrolls in his possession not one has a seal on the inside. When sealed, the scrolls are all done so from the outside. When one seal is present, it was usually placed there by the author of the scroll. When more than one seal is present it indicates a series or set of conditions that must be met before the scroll can actually be opened. He also cites that the Shrine of the Book located on the grounds of the Israel Museum in Jerusalem has many scrolls that have multiple seals placed on them, yet not one scroll has a seal on the inside. "Scroll," *Philologos.org*, Philologos. org, 3 Oct. 1998 <philologos.org/bpr/files/s006.htm>.

2. Eldon Ladd calls the breaking of the seven seals to be "preliminary and preparatory to the actual opening of the scroll" (p. 80) […] "The breaking of the seven seals is preliminary to the actual opening of the book and the events of the end time. It pictures forces that will be operative throughout history by which the redemptive and judicial purposes of God will be forwarded" (p. 96). George Eldon Ladd, *A Commentary on the Revelation of John* (Grand Rapids, MI: Eerdmans, 1972) 80, 96.

    Quoting E.W. Bullinger (Commentary on Revelation), David Guzik adds, "The first six seals are a 'Summary of the judgments distributed over the whole book; a brief summary of what will occur in "the day of the Lord," up the time of His actual Apocalypse or Unveiling in Chapter 19.'" David Guzik, "Study Guide for Revelation Chapter 6," *Blue Letter Bible*, 2001 <http://web.ccbce.com/multimedia/BLB/Comm/david_guzik/sg/Rev_6.html>.

3. "[…] it seems unlikely that conquest will occur for a while, then war for a while, then famine for a while, then death for a while." Stanley M. Horton, *The Ultimate Victory* (Springfield, MO: Gospel Publishing House, 1991) 95-96.

4. Walvoord explains this best: "To put it in ordinary language, the situation would be such that one would have to spend a day's wages for a loaf of bread with no money left to buy anything else. The symbolism therefore indicates a time of famine when life will be reduced to the barest necessities; for famine is almost always the aftermath of war." John Walvoord, *The Revelation of Jesus Christ* (Moody Press: Chicago, 1966) 129.

5. Hence, commentator Robert Mounce speaks of the robes as "symbols of blessedness and purity." Robert H. Mounce, *The Book of Revelation. The New International Commentary on the New Testament* (Grand Rapids, MI: Eerdmans, 1977) 160.

6. John Walvoord speaks to this point: "The fact that they are given robes would almost demand that they have a body of some kind. A robe could not hang upon an immaterial soul or spirit. It is not the kind of body that Christians now have, that is, the body of earth; nor is it the resurrection body of flesh and bones of which Christ spoke of after His own resurrection. It is a temporary body suited for their presence in heaven but replaced in turn by their everlasting resurrection body given at the time of Christ's return." Walvoord 134-5.

7. Horton finds possible explanation for the physical darkness as a result of seismic activity; "It could be that the various parts of the crust will all break loose and bring about this 'great earthquake,' which would break out multitudes of volcanoes, sending dust, gas and ash to obscure the sun and the moon." Horton 105.

CHAPTER 7

Revelation 7:1-17

The Two Great Multitudes

Introduction to Revelation 7:1-17

Incredibly, through the inspired authorship of the Holy Spirit, we continue in the same Revelation given by Jesus to His servant. Along with John we have received a glorious vision of the resurrected Jesus, the Great High Priest who walks amongst His Church (Chapter 1). He alone perfectly encourages, corrects, and blesses those He knows so well (Chapters 2 and 3). We too have been lifted into the Third Heaven, the very Throne Room of God, where countless angels worship and where humanity and nature find their Source (Chapter 4). With John, we have watched as the Lion of Judah—appearing as a sacrificed Lamb—received the seven-sealed scroll from the Ancient of Days (Chapter 5). *Within* this mysterious book is contained God's final and complete will and testament for His Creation. *Without* we have watched the breaking of the first six of seven seals (Chapter 6); and with each we have gained a panoramic view toward the distressing events of "what will take place later" (1:19).

With these awe-inspiring encounters as our backdrop, John, and we with him, are now presented a pivotal, twofold vision. At first a remnant out of Israel is identified on earth—"144,000" in all—sealed as the "servants of our God." In great contrast, a second victorious congregation appears in Heaven, and these without number. Having left the tribulation of the earth behind, these are the multitude of "white-robed" worshipers "from every nation, tribe, people and language." Sheltered by God's presence and shepherded by His love, they worship and serve before His throne "day and night."

Vital to a proper understanding of God's appointment with Israel and the Church is the fact that both are viewed in their destiny *before* the breaking of the seventh seal and the opening of the Scroll of Redemption. By the mercies of God—*before* God releases judgment in the earth—we, in such a beautiful way, now encounter with John both the victorious plan of God and the unending love of God.

The 144,000 Sealed Servants—7:1-8

[1]After this I saw four angels standing at the four corners of the earth, holding back the four winds of the earth to prevent any wind from blowing on the land or on the sea or

on any tree. [2] Then I saw another angel coming up from the east, having the seal of the living God. He called out in a loud voice to the four angels who had been given power to harm the land and the sea: [3] "Do not harm the land or the sea or the trees until we put a seal on the foreheads of the servants of our God." [4] Then I heard the number of those who were sealed: 144,000 from all the tribes of Israel. [5] From the tribe of Judah 12,000 were sealed, from the tribe of Reuben 12,000, from the tribe of Gad 12,000, [6] from the tribe of Asher 12,000, from the tribe of Naphtali 12,000, from the tribe of Manasseh 12,000, [7] from the tribe of Simeon 12,000, from the tribe of Levi 12,000, from the tribe of Issachar 12,000, [8] from the tribe of Zebulun 12,000, from the tribe of Joseph 12,000, from the tribe of Benjamin 12,000.

Biblical Insights

Once again John indicates the next phase of the unfolding Revelation with the words "after this" (*meta tauta*) (see note under 4:1; cf. 1:19; 7:1, 9; 9:12; 15:5; 18:1; 19:1; 20:3). Clearly John's vantage point was still from Heaven when he "saw four angels." Since these otherwise unidentified beings "had been given power to harm the land and the sea" (v. 2) at the proper time, they may be the same as the four angels who bring judgment in 9:14-15. That these angels were "standing at the four corners of the earth" is figurative language for the four points of the compass, no less anti-intellectual than the scientist who speaks of "the rising of the sun." In fact, well before the ancient Greeks erroneously taught that the world was flat and supported by the Titan god Atlas—amongst many other ancient cosmological myths—God's true Word proclaimed that "He suspends the earth over nothing" (Job 26:7) and that "He sits enthroned above the circle of the earth" and "stretches out the heavens like a canopy" (Isa. 40:22).

As with the proverbial "calm before the storm" these four angels are empowered to "hold back" or restrain "the four winds of the earth [i.e., from the primary directions of north, south, east, and west] to prevent any wind from blowing" (compare the metaphor in 6:13) "until" the proper time. Reference to "the land," "sea," or "any tree(s)" in verses 1, 2, and 3 may represent the entirety of the natural earth down to a single tree.

Throughout the Book of Revelation, angels are commissioned by God to carry out the details of His judgment upon the wicked (see section The Role and Activities of God's Holy Angels under Angelology in the Theological Overview). Here, "another angel" is seen "coming up from the east." The relevance of "the east" is associated several times in Scripture with Christ's Return (cf. Ezek. 8:16; 11:23; 43:2; 47:1; Zech. 14:4; Matt. 24:27). This angel carries "the seal of the living God," which, accompanied by the prior four angels, he will place "on the foreheads of the servants of our God." As with the seals placed on the Scroll of Redemption in Chapters 5 and 6, ancient seals gave assurance of ownership and authenticity. As God's seal placed upon

His servants, this divine mark now speaks of His personal care and protection, i.e., from His own wrath. (See the clear and strong parallel of the protection of the godly in time of God's wrath in Ezekiel 9:3-6.) Placed "on the forehead," the seal (by metaphor) will also conspicuously speak of the nobility of God's favor. (In fact, in Revelation 14:1 and 22:4 it is the very name of the Lamb and of the Father that has been placed as a seal on the foreheads of His servants.) This unique remnant will be distinguished and protected during God's judgment upon the wicked even as was Noah (Matt. 24:38) and Lot (Luke 17:29) and their families. Further, these "servants" (*doulos*, a bond-servant; cf. Matt. 20:27; 24:46; 25:21; Rom. 1:1; 2 Cor. 4:5, etc.) are those who are freely and responsibly bound to God, ready and willing to fulfill His will. Now, all of this takes place at the authoritative "loud voice" (cf. 5:2; 14:7, 9, 15, 18; 19:17) of an angel of the Lord.

John next "heard the number of those who were sealed"—"144,000"—which is clearly explained to be "12,000" times each of the twelve tribes of Israel. Understanding that numbers typically have symbolic meaning in apocalyptic literature (as has already been seen with the use of "seven" throughout the Revelation), we might also expect special significance to "twelve" in this passage. In consideration of just a few of the 187 references to the number "twelve" in the Bible, a clear pattern develops. For example, in the Old Testament we find twelve tribes of Israel represented by twelve precious stones in the high priest's breastplate (Exod. 39:14). Joshua also chose twelve men, one from each tribe, who carried twelve stones out of the Jordan to build "a memorial to the people of Israel forever" (Joshua 4:2-7). The earlier Testament also contains twelve historical books and twelve Minor Prophets. In addition to the twelve original disciples in the New Testament, we find in the Book of Revelation the New Jerusalem with "twelve gates, and with twelve angels at the gates" (21:12). Additionally, "The wall of the city had twelve foundations, and on them were the names of the twelve apostles of the Lamb" (21:14). Its dimensions are a cubed "12,000 stadia" and its surrounding wall "144 cubits thick" (21:16-17). Likewise, twelve precious stones decorate the foundations of the city's walls (21:18-20) and "The twelve gates were twelve pearls, each gate made of a single pearl" (21:21).

According to biblical use then, we can assert that the number "twelve" speaks broadly of completion and fulfillment within the administration of God's redemption plan. While in all of the above cases the number "twelve" is to be taken literally, it is still possible that—within the context of apocalyptic genre—the "twelve" of Revelation 7:4-8 is a symbolic representation of either the first fruit of a great national revival of Israel or of the full number of Jews who will be saved throughout the Tribulation.

These "144,000" are "from all the tribes of Israel." The idea that "Israel" is here spiritualized to refer to the Church at large has no credibility. On several accounts, John makes a clear distinction, if not purposeful contrast, between this remnant and the congregation that follows in 7:9-17. The first group is numbered and limited while the second "no one could count." The first is "from all the tribes of Israel" while the second is "from every nation, tribe, people and language." Likewise, the first remains for a time on the earth while the second is already "standing before the throne and before the Lamb." Finally, the first is purposefully "sealed" for protection and service while the second, of whom no sealing is mentioned, have finished their earthly service. It should also be clear that the Church is never spoken of as being divided in anyway whatsoever; on the contrary, in the context of unity, "there is one body" (Ephesians 4:4); and, "There is neither Jew nor Gentile, neither slave nor free, nor is there male and female, for you are all one in Christ Jesus" (Galatians 3:28). In Christ, all former divisions are no more! Furthermore, never is the Church identified as the "tribes" or "sons" of Israel.[1]

The twelve "tribes," from which "12,000" each are "sealed," are listed as: "Judah," "Reuben," "Gad," "Asher," "Naphtali," "Manasseh," "Simeon," "Levi," "Issachar," "Zebulun," "Joseph," and "Benjamin." Conspicuously missing from this list is the tribe of Dan (contrast with 1 Chronicles 2:2). It is highly possible that the tribe's abandonment of their God-given inheritance, as well as their long-standing idolatry, are the major reasons for Dan's exclusion. From the time that Joshua allotted territories to each tribe (c. 1,400 B.C.), Dan never fully took possession of their inheritance (Josh. 19:40-48). Though the track of land they received by promise was relatively small, its fertile land and Mediterranean coastline brought ample provision. Nevertheless, in apathy and in fear of the Philistines to their south, Dan forsook God's blessing, choosing rather to conquer the secluded and peaceful agricultural city of Laish (later "Dan") in the northernmost part of Israel. Judges 18 also tells the story of the start and perpetuation of idolatry amongst the Danites: (vv. 30-31) "And the people of Dan set up the carved image for themselves [...] So they set up Micah's carved image that he made, as long as the house of God was at Shiloh." In this way Dan was the first tribe to practice widespread idolatry, even leading the nation into this abomination.[2] Years later (c. 930-920 B.C.), at the start of the divided kingdom, the idolatrous King Jeroboam built one of two altars for the northern kingdom in the city of Dan, where false, man-made worship included a golden calf (1 Kings 12:28-30).[3]

Interesting as well is the absence of the name Ephraim, the brother of Manasseh (Gen. 48:1, 5, 13) who is mentioned. Since "Manasseh" and "Joseph" are both included in the "144,000," it is strongly possible that the name "Joseph" is used representatively of Ephraim the younger brother, who at his father Israel's directive received the greater blessing in Genesis 48:17-20. On the other hand, Ephraim just as with Dan was noted in the Old Testament for its idolatry (Hosea 4:17, "Ephraim is joined to idols; leave him alone!").

Along with the absence of Dan and the substitution of "Joseph" for Ephraim, the twelve tribes are completed with the inclusion of "Levi" in this list. Although priestly Levi was never given their own territory as an inheritance (cf. Numbers

2:33)—inasmuch as they were called to represent the nation as a whole before God at the tabernacle—their inclusion in the "144,000" may be a strong statement of Christ's priesthood alone in the New Covenant relationship between Israel and God (cf. Jer. 31:31-34; Ezek. 36:24-28). Finally, it is altogether possible that—whether a literal or symbolic indicator of either the first fruit of a revived Israel or the full number of Jews who are saved during the "time of trouble for Jacob" (Jer. 30:7; also Dan. 12:1-2; Isa. 45:17; Rom. 11:25-27)—the sealing of the "144,000" speaks not only of God's personal care and protection but also of the salvific work of the Spirit of God. Paul's words then apply here:

> Ephesians 1:13-14—And you also were included in Christ when you heard the message of truth, the gospel of your salvation. When you believed, you were marked in him with a seal, the promised Holy Spirit, who is a deposit guaranteeing our inheritance until the redemption of those who are God's possession—to the praise of his glory.

> Romans 11:11-12—Again I ask: Did they stumble so as to fall beyond recovery? Not at all! Rather, because of their transgression, salvation has come to the Gentiles to make Israel envious. But if their transgression means riches for the world, and their loss means riches for the Gentiles, how much greater riches will their full inclusion bring!

But there is more! For how can it be said that these who are sealed are "servants of our God"? Does not this sealing also speak of Israel's vital calling on earth as "a light for the Gentiles" in ultimate fulfillment of the words of Isaiah 49:6, "I will also make you a light for the Gentiles, that my salvation may reach to the ends of the earth" (cf. Acts 13:47).

Life Application

Church, do not ignore Israel! The God of Abraham, Isaac, and Jacob has a Last Days appointment with this nation, its people, and its land. He will not break that appointment, nor will He be late!

While still no more than a large, extended family, the children of Israel received the word of the Lord as His chosen people. Joseph, now "in charge of the whole land of Egypt" (Gen. 41:43), acknowledged the favor of God in preserving the family of Jacob from starvation in the wilderness. With forgiveness in his heart, he comforted his brothers, "You intended to harm me, but God intended it for good to accomplish what is now being done, the saving of many lives" (Gen. 50:20). Decades later, while on his deathbed, Joseph once again reminded his family of God's appointment with their fledgling nation. "I am about to die. But God will surely come to your aid ['to appoint, to attend, to visit'] and take you up out of this land to the land he promised on oath to Abraham, Isaac, and Jacob" (Gen. 50:24).

Again and again throughout the centuries, the nation of Israel has wavered between their faithfulness to God and their affair with this world. Yet, for over 3,700 years since Joseph's day, God has never failed to keep His appointment with His chosen people. When their hearts have turned toward Him, He has "visited" the nation with protection and blessing. When their hearts have turned away, He has often "visited" them with corrective judgment. Sometimes with joy—sometimes with a broken heart—God has always kept His appointment with the children of Israel.

Then with a view long down the road, Ezekiel was told to speak to a valley of dry bones, "the whole house of Israel" under the judgment of God (Ezek. 37:11). When all seemed as dead as dead could be, God spoke of the day of His timely visitation once again.

> Ezekiel 37:12b–14—This is what the Sovereign Lord says: My people, I am going to open your graves and bring you up from them; I will bring you back to the land of Israel. Then you, my people, will know that I am the Lord, when I open your graves and bring you up from them. I will put my Spirit in you and you will live, and I will settle you in your own land. Then you will know that I the Lord have spoken, and I have done it, declares the Lord.

In fulfillment of God's irrevocable call, and for the first time in the history of humanity, a nation considered "dead" on all accounts was resurrected "in a moment"! "Who has ever heard of such things? Who has ever seen things like this? Can a country be born in a day or a nation be brought forth in a moment?" (Isa. 66:8). The appointment made by God was kept, and not a minute too soon. On May 14, 1948 in Tel Aviv (in what is now known as Independence Hall) an official statement—the *Declaration by the Israel Ministry of Foreign Affairs*—was read with the endorsement of the United Nations General Assembly. The first and last sentences read as follows:

> The Land of Israel was the birthplace of the Jewish people. Here their spiritual, religious and political identity was shaped. Here they first attained to statehood, created cultural values of national and universal significance and gave to the world the eternal Book of Books. [...] PLACING OUR TRUST IN THE 'ROCK OF ISRAEL', WE AFFIX OUR SIGNATURES TO THIS PROCLAMATION AT THIS SESSION OF THE PROVISIONAL COUNCIL OF STATE, ON THE SOIL OF THE HOMELAND, [...]

Church, pray for Israel because God is about to visit her again! The plan to restore her to the Promised Land has been fulfilled, but the reality of her spiritual resurrection still lies ahead! As the prophets of old foretold, "a time of trouble for Jacob" is coming and "How awful that day will be!" (Jer. 30:7). In that day, "all the nations of the earth [will be] gathered against her" (Zech. 12:3) and outwardly all will seem lost. But God will keep His appointment! "The Lord will [...] cleanse the bloodstains from Jerusalem by a spirit of judgment and a spirit of fire" (Isa. 4:4). In the end, when the dust of Last Days judgment has settled, a great nation—a "light to the Gentiles" (Isa. 49:6), revived and holy—will rise from the ashes! The appointment will be kept, "And I will pour out on the house of David and the inhabitants of Jerusalem a spirit of grace and supplication. They will look on me, the one they have pierced, and they will mourn for him as one mourns for an only child and grieve bitterly for him as one grieves for a firstborn son" (Zech. 12:10).

And so, John saw that revived, resurrected nation in the sealing of the "144,000." Even before God's wrath had begun to fall upon the wicked with the breaking of the seventh seal—even before God's discipline had come to draw out His chosen people— even before the Scroll of Redemption had rolled open before the citizens of Heaven— God sealed the remnant of His people as "servants of our God" (Rev. 7:3), distinguished, protected...called. Church, do not ignore the nation of Israel!

The Countless Worshipers—7:9-17

[9] After this I looked, and there before me was a great multitude that no one could count, from every nation, tribe, people and language, standing before the throne and before the Lamb. They were wearing white robes and were holding palm branches in their hands. [10] And they cried out in a loud voice:

"Salvation belongs to our God, who sits on the throne, and to the Lamb." [11] All the angels were standing around the throne and around the elders and the four living creatures. They fell down on their faces before the throne and worshiped God, [12] saying: "Amen! Praise and glory and wisdom and thanks and honor and power and strength be to our God for ever and ever. Amen!" [13] Then one of the elders asked me, "These in white robes—who are they, and where did they come from?" [14] I answered, "Sir, you know." And he said, "These are they who have come out of the great tribulation; they have washed their robes and made them white in the blood of the Lamb. [15] Therefore, "they are before the throne of God and serve him day and night in his temple; and he who sits on the throne will shelter them with his presence. [16] 'Never again will they hunger; never again will they thirst. The sun will not beat down on them,' nor any scorching heat. [17] For the Lamb at the center of the throne will be their shepherd; 'he will lead them to springs of living water.' 'And God will wipe away every tear from their eyes.'"

Biblical Insights

With the words "after this" (*meta tauta*), John's attention is now drawn away from the earth to a further vision in Heaven. Here we must remember the breathtaking presence of God unveiled in Chapters 4 and 5. But to this glorious sight—and for the first time seen in Heaven—we with John are introduced to the definitive culmination of grace, the corporate people of God washed in the blood of the Lamb. Standing just before him, John saw "a great multitude that no one could count" in contrast to the purposefully numbered "144,000" of the prior vision upon the earth.[4] While being inclusive of the Jewish nation, the scope of this congregation reaches beyond, for this inestimable multitude has come "from every nation, tribe, people and language." Here is the reward of Christ's sacrificial work on the cross, "and with your blood you purchased for God persons from every tribe and language and people and nation" (5:9); and, here is the harvest that follows the proclamation of the eternal gospel, "to every nation, tribe, language and people" (14:6).

John saw this multitude "standing before the throne and before the Lamb," an affirmation of unconditional acceptance and nearness to the Father in and through Christ alone (cf. Psalm 1:5; 24:3; Rom. 5:1). To be clear, this "standing" in grace and acceptance is the diametric opposite of the "standing" of the wicked before the "great white throne" judgment at the end of time (Rev. 20:11-12).

That these saints of God are "wearing white robes" requires careful attention. We have already heard Jesus speak of the "white clothes" of the overcomer with a clear reference to righteousness (Rev. 3:4, 5, 18; and see 19:8, 14). We have also seen the "white" garments worn by the "twenty-four elders" in 4:4. But how shall we relate this "great multitude" with the "souls" John saw "under the altar" who were each "given a white robe" to wear (6:9-11)?

As is explained more fully in the Summary Statement under The Resurrection and Eternal Reward of the Righteous (Eschatology; Theological Overview), we will find that the resurrection of the martyred Tribulation saints takes place after the Second Coming of Christ (19:11-16) and before the commencement of His Millennial reign. Revelation 20:4 reads, "And I saw the souls of those who had been beheaded because of their testimony about Jesus and because of the word of God. They had not worshiped the beast or its image and had not received its mark on their foreheads or their hands. They came to life and reigned with Christ a thousand years." There can be no question that the "souls of those who had been beheaded" of 20:4 are the same as those "souls of those who had been slain" of 6:9, now inclusive of the completed number of these martyrs (6:11). Since they only "came to life" in 20:4—a clear statement of bodily resurrection (cf. 2:8)—we must then conclude that the "white robes" of 6:11 are actually a temporary covering as opposed to their permanent resurrected bodies, given after Christ's glorious Revelation. (This may be included in the hope Paul expresses for all believers in 2 Corinthians 5:3, "[...] because when we are clothed, we will not be found naked.")

Yet, there is a clear contrast between the "souls" of 6:9 and the multitude of 7:9. While the first group is found only "under the altar" (see note under 6:9 for this significance), the second is an innumerable number "standing before the throne and in front of the Lamb." Twice more we find the redeemed clothed in "fine linen, bright [or 'white,' v. 14] and clean"—once as a bride (19:7, 8) and once as an army (19:14; cf. 17:14). It would seem then that those dressed in white as a great multitude (7:9) "standing before the throne" and "holding palm branches in their hands" (a sign of victorious praise and celebration) are the same as "his bride [who] has made herself ready" (19:7) and "the armies of heaven [...] riding on white horses," battling and defeating the physical kings and armies of the earth. Given their activities and clear contrast with the "souls" of 6:9—who are resurrected only after the Revelation of Jesus at the end of the Tribulation (20:4)—it stands to reason that the "great multitude," "the bride," and "the army" are one and the same, the raptured Church having already experienced their resurrection *before* 20:4 (cf. 1 Thess. 4:13-18). Supporting this further is the bodily resurrection (11:11) and ascension into heaven (11:12) of the "two witnesses" (11:3) well before the Revelation of Jesus. The "white robes" of the multitude, then, are the same as their resurrected bodies, which reflect the righteousness of Jesus.

With the "loud voice" of passionate praise and thanksgiving (cf. Luke 17:15; Rev. 5:12), the multitude expresses their worship. As was seen in Chapter 4, the Throne of God is the focal point of Heaven and of all creation. In keeping with the eternal anthem—"To him who loves us and has freed us from our sins by his blood" (1:5)—these saints of God freely confess, "Salvation belongs to our God," i.e., to the Father through the sacrificial, atoning work of the Son, who alone is the Source of such amazing grace and love. In a similar picture to the scene of 5:9-14, the myriad of angels in Heaven also adds their "loud voice" of zealous worship. Though they "were standing around the throne and around the elders and the four living creatures," it is best to see that the host of angels is not the closest to the throne (cf. 5:11). Peter tells that holy angels "long to look into these things" (1 Pet. 1:12). While they objectively worship God for His great salvation, they themselves do not fully know the freedom and nearness of the redeemed to the heart of their Father. Yet, Jesus says "there is rejoicing in the presence of the angels of God over one sinner who repents" (Luke 15:10). How much greater is their rejoicing now in the presence of this innumerable congregation of the redeemed!

In abject humility, the angels "fell down on their faces" (cf. 4:10; 5:8, 14; 11:16; 19:4). As they affirm ("Amen!") the worship of the redeemed, they also lift their own seven-fold cry of adoration, which is nearly identical to the praise lifted before the Lamb by the angels in 5:12 (where see notes). Now "thanksgiving" (*eucharistia*; cf. 2 Cor. 4:15; Col. 2:7) has replaced "wealth" (*ploutos*). That each of these qualities finds its ultimate and complete fulfillment in the Almighty God is indicated with the use of the definite article "the" before each attribute (as also in 4:11 and 5:13). With these the angels again add their "Amen!" as a statement of certainty and assurance.

One of the "twenty-four elders" now asks a two-fold question of John—"These in white robes—who are they, and where did they come from?" If, as was maintained earlier under Revelation 4:4, these "elders" are representatives of God's people on earth in both the Old and New Covenants, then it is not unreasonable that one of them would ask this objective question on behalf of the whole. Perhaps John should have known in light of 3:5, but he instead defers to the elder, "Sir, you know."

In answer to "who" "these" are, the second portion of the elder's answer speaks more directly. "These," comprising the innumerable and worldwide "multitude," are "they [who] have washed their robes and made them white in the blood of the Lamb." This statement in itself—along with the proceeding promise of the eternal comfort and restoration of God's shepherding presence—is the language of the Overcomers in Christ, which cannot be limited to one segment of God's people alone. Rather, the elder's answer is applicable to the entirety of the body of Christ, the Church—the full people of God New Testament and Old Testament (cf. Heb. 11:39-40).

The elder's words, "These are they who have come out of the great tribulation" are more directly in response to his question, "and where did they come from?" Central to the identity of this multitude is the phrase "come out of the great tribulation." To begin, "come" is here a present participle, which indicates a continuous "coming." While the implication grammatically is clear, the application, i.e., the timing of this "coming" is wide ranging (as reflected in the different translation of this verb from version to version, e.g., KJV, "came"; NKJV and NIV, "come"; ESV, "coming"; the NLT avoids the word altogether). The words "out of" are one word, *ek*, best interpreted as "out from" (as already seen in 3:10).

But, what or when is "the great tribulation"? The word "tribulation" (*thlipsis*), which speaks of "pressure" or a "pressing in upon," is found many times in the New Testament. Jesus used the word broadly when He, for instance, said, "In this world you will have trouble [*thlipsis*]" (John 16:33), and "When trouble [*thlipsis*] or persecution comes because of the word, they quickly fall away" (Mark 4:17). Paul used the word to speak more so of persecutions, "We must go through many hardships [*thlipsis*] to enter the kingdom of God" (Acts 14:22). But this current "tribulation" is said to be "great" (*mega*), which can mean great in intensity or in duration. Jesus used these words together, *mega thlipsis,* in Matthew 24:21, "For then there will be great distress, unequaled from the beginning of the world until now—and never to be equaled again." Yet, not every use of this description applies eschatologically. Jesus has already stated in Revelation 2:22 of Jezebel, "[...] and I will make those who commit adultery with her suffer intensely [*mega thlipsis*]." Surprisingly, only twice—in Matthew 24:21 and Revelation 7:14—do we read of "great tribulation" (*mega thlipsis*) in the context of the Last Days' timing of God's wrath.

Many students of Revelation hold firmly that this multitude refers exclusively to the martyred Tribulation saints due to the definite article "the" (tēs) used twice here.

The literal reading is emphatically "the tribulation, the great one." While this is compelling—and certainly in the context of Revelation John must indicate a great, growing intensity of Last Days persecution—there is nothing in this phraseology that removes altogether a connection to the suffering and martyrdom of believers throughout the ages. In fact, how could John not have in mind those first century believers who were martyred by the tens of thousands? (In fact, John's first audience was a severely persecuted church, tortured, torn, burned for their faith—Revelation 1:9.) Did not the Bible foretell the martyrdom of countless millions who have died for their faith throughout the centuries (cf. Rev. 2:10, 13)? While those continuously "coming out of the great tribulation" will certainly include Tribulation saints (cf. 6:9-11; 13:15; 17:6— which implies that many Jews and Gentiles will receive the Gospel and turn to the Lord during that time [cf. Matt. 24:14; Rev. 11:3-7])—it cannot preclude the suffering Church at large throughout the ages. Did not Paul say, "In fact, everyone who wants to live a godly life in Christ Jesus will be persecuted" (2 Tim. 3:12)? Furthermore, John does not specifically state that all within the "great multitude" were martyred (here the NLT is in error), only that they continuously are coming out of intense persecution and suffering.

We must remember again that the "great multitude" of Revelation 7:9-17, described as a gathering of the redeemed from throughout the earth, is found in Heaven *after* six "seals" have been opened and *before* the seventh "seal" is opened. Thus, following a panoramic foretelling of what is contained in the Scroll of Redemption (Chapter 6), the Church is seen before God's throne. It is only after this visionary event that the seventh seal is broken (8:1), the scroll is opened (5:4), and the unprecedented wrath of God is released (6:17). In consideration of this all, it is best to view the "great multitude" as the raptured Church, "caught up" [*harpazō*, "snatched away powerfully"; Latin, *raptus*] to the Bridegroom (1 Thess. 4:16-17); "gathered to him" (2 Thess. 2:1); "changed," resurrected, "in a flash, in the twinkling of an eye" (1 Cor. 15:52; also Rom. 8:23). Together, this is in keeping with the promise to the redeemed of the Lord: "For God did not appoint us to suffer wrath but to receive salvation through our Lord Jesus Christ" (1 Thess. 5:9); and again, "I will also keep you from the hour of trial that is going to come on the whole world to test the inhabitants of the earth" (Rev. 3:10). It is for this reason that Paul could write to Titus (2:13), "[...] while we wait for the blessed hope—the appearing of the glory of our great God and Savior, Jesus Christ" ... not signs ... not wrath ... no, we look and long for His appearing alone (2 Tim. 4:8).

Because this "great multitude" wears the "white robes" of Christ's righteousness and His sacrificial cleansing (cf. Rom. 3:25; 5:9; Rev. 1:5), now reflected in their glorified bodies, John hears the elder further explain their place of acceptance and welcome "before the throne of God" (as in v. 9). Their part is to "serve him day and night in his temple," i.e., in "God's temple in heaven" (11:19), and this in ultimate and eternal fulfillment as "a chosen people, a royal priesthood" (1 Pet. 2:9; Rev. 20:6; 22:3). Once in our resurrected bodies, we will join with the angels and the "four living creatures" in tireless worship and service to God "day and night" (cf. 4:8).

But it is God's part that receives the greater attention. He "who sits on the throne" of His majesty and authority (cf. 3:21; 4:2, 9, 10; 5:13; 6:16; 12:5; 22:1, 3) "will shelter [skēnoō, lit. 'spread his tent over'] them with his presence" (cf. 1 Thess. 2:19; Jude 1:24). In this promise of protection and communion is the fulfillment of God's original plan and restored hope for humanity in right relationship with Him, i.e., He so desires to intimately dwell with us and we with Him (Rev. 21:3—"God's dwelling place [skēnē] is now among the people, and he will dwell [skēnoō] with them."). With language reminiscent of Isaiah 49:10, the elder continues to tell of God's glorious provisions, which shelter the redeemed from the suffering of "hunger," "thirst," and "scorching heat," all of which represents (actually and metaphorically) the trouble believers face at any time while under persecution (cf. 2 Cor. 11:23-27; Heb. 11:35-38; Rev. 13:17). Far removed from earth's hardships and from persecution's atrocities— now in the presence of the Father and the Son—the redeemed find only comfort, restoration, and refreshment. In the infinite wisdom and mercy of God, the One called "the Lamb" will now also be the "shepherd" (cf. Psalm 23:1; Isa. 40:11; Zech. 9:16; John 10:11-14), especially in His role of leading His sheep "to springs of living water," no doubt eternal life provided through Jesus (cf. Ps. 36:8; 46:4; Jer. 2:13; John 4:10-14; 7:38; 22:1). Finally, "God will wipe away every tear from their eyes" (cf. 21:4), certainly the tears of the sorrows of earth—and even those of human unfaithfulness (Rev. 3:18), now forgiven and forgotten (cf. Isa. 25:8).

Life Application

There are images deeply impressed in my memory that could never be erased, such as the thousands of beautiful faces as far as the eye could see along the outskirts of Mathare Valley in Nairobi, Kenya. Despite the blazing heat and the unthinkable poverty of the Valley's population of 180,000, no less than 25,000 had gathered that morning under adjoining tents and structures to hear the Word of God with an insatiable hunger. And could they sing! I saw and heard much the same several days later in Mombasa along the eastern coastline—countless thousands of men, women, boys, and girls who had already greeted the morning with united shouts of "Jesus is Lord over Mombasa"!

Then there were the hundreds in Sumbe, Angola, who pressed in tightly around the altar to seek the face of God and the moving of His Spirit upon their lives. In fact, there were so many that hungered for God's presence that the pastor had to call upon the men first, then the women, and then the children, each in their turn to pack in around the entire front of the church. Again, the sight of countless thousands in India, dressed in colorful garments surpassed only by the presence of Jesus that radiated from their beautiful faces. They sang and prayed and listened to the Word of God for hours on end with such a passion for their Lord! And the same can be told of mass gatherings of the redeemed in the Philippines and in South Korea and in Fiji and in Latin America and in the Caribbean, all of them with one desire for more of Jesus!

Yet, all of these images together only begin to compare with what John must have seen. "Standing before the throne and before the Lamb [. . .] was a great multitude that no one could count, from every nation, tribe, people and language," a mosaic of skin tones, yet all dressed in white, a reflection of the glory and holiness of the God who has called them to Himself. They will come from across the planet, from vastly different cultures, speaking vastly different languages, having vastly different backgrounds and stories to tell. But this one thing—this eternally all-important thing—unites them before the Throne of their Creator—"They have washed their robes and made them white in the blood of the Lamb." In the words of the song writer, "Some through the waters, some through the flood; Some through the fire, but all through the blood!"[5]

Chapter 7 Notes

1. Stanley Horton notes in light of this list, "The New Testament does recognize Jews as the Twelve Tribes (Luke 22:30; Acts 26:7; James 1:1). Stanley M. Horton, *The Ultimate Victory* (Springfield, MO: Gospel Publishing House, 1991) 112.

   Similarly, John Walvoord sees here "a refutation of the idea that the tribes of Israel are lost, as well as the theory that the lost tribes are perpetuated in the English-speaking people of the world." John Walvoord, *The Revelation of Jesus Christ* (Moody Press: Chicago, 1966) 143.

2. Both Irenaeus (A.D. 130-202) and Hippolytus of Rome (A.D. c. 170-c. 236) went as far as arguing that the Antichrist would rise out of the tribe of Dan. Irenaeus in his *Against Heresies*, Book V, Chapter 30.2 writes, "And Jeremiah does not merely point out his sudden coming, but he even indicates the tribe from which he shall come, where he says, 'We shall hear the voice of his swift horses from Dan; the whole earth shall be moved by the voice of the neighing of his galloping horses: he shall also come and devour the earth, and the fulness (sic) thereof, the city also, and they that dwell therein.' This, too, is the reason that this tribe is not reckoned in the Apocalypse along with those which are saved." "Against Heresies." Philip Schaff, ed., "ANF01. The Apostolic Fathers with Justin Martyr and Irenaeus," *Christian Classics Ethereal Library*, 13 July 2005 <www.ccel.org/ccel/schaff/anf01.ix.vii.xxxi.html>.

   Hippolytus adds, in his *"Treatise on Christ and Antichrist,"* Part II, Section 14, "Thus did the Scriptures preach before-time of this lion and lion's whelp. And in like manner also we find it written regarding Antichrist. For Moses speaks thus: 'Dan is a lion's whelp, and he shall leap from Bashan.' But that no one may err by supposing that this is said of the Saviour, let him attend carefully to the matter. 'Dan,' he says, 'is a lion's whelp;" and in naming the tribe of Dan, he declared clearly the tribe from which Antichrist is destined to spring. For as Christ springs from the tribe of Judah, so Antichrist is to spring from the tribe of Dan [...]" "Treatise on Christ and Antichrist." Schaff, "ANF05. Fathers of the Third Century: Hippolytus, Cyprian, Caius, Novatian, Appendix," *Christian Classics Ethereal Library*, 1 June 2005 <www.ccel.org/ccel/schaff/anf05.iii.iv.ii.i.html>.

3. How interesting then that the tribe of Dan is listed first in the allotted inheritance of land in the Millennial Kingdom on earth—see Ezekiel 47:21-48:2. Here too is fulfillment of God's promise that through national repentance and turning to Christ, "All Israel will be saved" (Romans 11:26). Here too is the mercy and grace of God!

4. F.F. Bruce notes that, "The Christian Clement of Rome and the pagan Tacitus both describe the victims of Nero's persecution as 'a great multitude'; how much greater,

then, must be the full complement of Christian martyrs!" F.F. Bruce, ed., *The International Bible Commentary* (Grand Rapids: Zondervan, 1986) 1609.

5. Lyrics drawn from hymn *God Leads Us Along*; words and music by G.A. Young; public domain.

SECTION 3

A Theological Overview of the Book of Revelation

with Textual Concordance and Summary Statements

Theological Overview

Theology Proper—The Study of God
- The Essence of God (Descriptive of Who He Is; Inclusive of the Trinity)
- The Attributes and Appearance of God (Descriptive of What He is Like; Inclusive of the Trinity)
- The Worship and Praise of God (Inclusive of the Trinity)
- The Distinctive Names of God the Father
- The Distinctive Roles and Activities of the Father
- The Unity and Trinity of the Godhead

Bibliology—The Study of the Bible
- The Inspired, Written Word of God

Christology—The Study of Jesus Christ, the Son of God
- The Distinctive Names and Descriptive Titles of the Son
- The Deity of Jesus Christ Seen in His Essence (Descriptive of Who He Is)
- The Deity of Jesus Christ Seen in His Attributes and Appearance (Descriptive of What He is Like)
- The Deity of Jesus Christ Seen in His Role and Activities
- The Humanity of Jesus Christ Seen in His Essence, Attributes, and Role
- The Finished Work of Jesus
- The Current and Eternal Work of Jesus

Pneumatology—The Study of the Spirit of God
- The Essence (Descriptive of Who He Is) and the Attributes and Appearance (Descriptive of What He Is Like) of the Spirit of God
- The Role and Activities of the Spirit of God

Angelology—The Study of Angels (Holy and Fallen)
Including the Study of Satan (Satanology) and of Demons (Demonology)
- The Essence, Appearance, and Attributes of God's Holy Angels
- The Role and Activities of God's Holy Angels
- The Names, Essence, Attributes, Appearance, Role, and Activities of Satan (Satanology)
- The Essence, Attributes, Appearance, Role, Activities, and Judgment of Unholy, Fallen Angels (Demonology)

Anthropology—The Study of Humanity
- The Creation of Humanity, of the World, and of the Earth as Our Habitation
- The Essence, Attributes, and Appearance of Human Beings
- The Activities of Human Beings, Including Their Continuous Wickedness
- Spiritual and Physical Death, the Consequence of Unrepentant Wickedness
- The Effect of Humanity's Sin Upon the Natural/Physical Earth and World
- God's Ultimate Will for Redeemed Humanity Expressed

Hamartiology—The Study of Sin
* Humanity's Personal Sin and Rebellion
* Humanity's Corporate Sin and Rebellion—The Rise and Fall of the Three-Fold "Babylon" World System
* God's Call to Repentance & God's Judgment upon the Unrepentant

Soteriology–The Study of Salvation
* Salvation Provided Graciously Through the Atoning Work of Christ Alone
* Salvation Received Personally Through Repentance from Sin and Faith in Christ
* The Blessings and Privileges of Salvation

Israelology—The Study of Israel
* General References to the Nation of Israel, Jerusalem, the Jewish People, and the Temple
* The New Jerusalem and the "Temple" in Heaven

Ecclesiology—The Study of the Church
* The Constituents and Character of the True Church—the Redeemed of All Ages
* The Activities and Experiences of the True Church—the Redeemed of All Ages
* God's Promises to the True Church—the Redeemed of All Ages
* The Identity and Judgment of the Unrepentant and False Church and Its False Leaders and Teachers

Eschatology—The Study of the Last Days
* The Revelation of Christ in His Second Coming
* The Gathering of the Church To Christ and Into Heaven
* The Great Tribulation—The Wrath of God in Judgment Upon the Unrepentant
* Persecution and Martyrdom of Tribulation Saints and of the Jewish People
* Spiritual Warfare Led by Satan in the Last Days and His Final Demise and Judgment
* The Appearance and Nefarious Work of the First and Second Beasts and Their Final Demise and Judgment
* The Resurrection and Final Judgment of Unrepentant Humanity, Including the Lake of Fire
* The Resurrection and Eternal Reward of the Righteous
* The Millennial Reign of Christ and the Eternal Kingdom of God
* Heaven (Where God's Throne Is), The New Heavens and Earth, and The New Jerusalem

Theology Proper—The Study of God

The Essence of God
(Descriptive of Who He Is; Inclusive of the Trinity)

1:4—"from him who is, and who was, and who is to come" (also 1:8; 4:8; 11:17; 16:5)

1:8a—"I am the Alpha and the Omega" (also 21:6; 22:13)

1:8b—"the Lord God" (also 4:8, 11; 6:10; 11:4, 8, 15, 17; 14:13; 15:3, 4; 16:7; 17:14; 18:8; 19:6, 16; 21:22; 22:5, 6, 20, 21)

1:17—"Do not be afraid. I am the First and the Last" (also 2:8; 22:13)

3:21—"and sat down with my Father on his throne" (also 4:2, 9, 10; 5:13; 6:16; 7:10, 15; 12:5; 22:1, 3)

4:3—"A rainbow that shone like an emerald encircled the throne"

4:9—"and who lives for ever and ever" (also 1:6; 4:10; 5:13; 7:12; 10:6; 15:7)

4:11—"You are worthy, our Lord and God" (also 5:2, 9, 12)

6:10—"How long, Sovereign Lord"

7:2—"having the seal of the living God" (also 1:18)

7:15—"they are before the throne of God" (also 7:9, 11; 14:3, 5 [KJV]; 20:12)

10:7—"the mystery of God"

11:1—"the temple of God" (also 3:12; 7:15; 11:19; 15:8)

11:4—"they stand before the Lord of the earth"

11:11—"the breath of life from God"

11:13—"the God of heaven" (3:12; 4:2; 11:13, 19; 16:11; 21:2, 10)

12:10—"and the kingdom of our God" (also 11:15)

12:17—"those who keep God's commands" (also 14:12)

15:8—"from the glory of God" (also 1:6; 5:12, 13; 7:12; 15:8; 19:1; 21:11, 23)

Summary Statement: From the beginning to the conclusion of the Revelation, emphasis is placed upon the timeless nature of God. His eternality—together with His sovereignty and transcendence over the affairs of humanity and the natural and supernatural worlds—is offered to His followers as comfort and encouragement. He is indisputably the "Lord" (*kyrios*) of Heaven and earth. He is also the immanent God; though seated upon His throne in majestic glory above, He is near to and intensely interested and involved in the lives of His children. God's living nature is demonstrated in the Son's victory over death.

▶ See also under Christology: The Deity of Jesus Christ Seen in His Essence

The Attributes and Appearance of God
(Descriptive of What He is Like; Inclusive of the Trinity)

1:5—"To him who loves us and has freed us from our sins by his blood" (also 3:19; 20:9)

1:6—"to him be glory and power" (also 4:11; 5:12, 13; 7:12; 11:17; 12:10; 15:8; 16:9; 19:1)

1:8—"the Almighty" (also 4:8; 11:17; 15:3; 16:7, 14; 18:8; 19:6, 15; 21:22)

2:2—"I know" (also 2:9, 13, 19; 3:1, 8 [2x], 15)

3:19—"Those whom I love I rebuke and discipline" (also 1:5)

4:3—"And the one who sat there had the appearance of jasper and ruby"

4:5—"From the throne came flashes of lightning, rumblings and peals of thunder"

4:8—"Holy, holy, holy is the Lord God Almighty" (also 3:7; 6:10; 15:4; 16:5)

5:12—"to receive power and wealth and wisdom and strength and honor and glory and praise!" (also 7:12; 15:8)

6:10—"holy and true" (also 3:7, 14; 6:10; 15:3; 16:7; 19:2, 9, 11)

7:10—"Salvation belongs to our God" (also 12:10; 19:1)

14:7—"Fear God and give him glory" (also 15:4, 19:5)

14:9—"God's fury, which has been poured full strength into the cup of his wrath" (also 14:19; 15:1, 7; 16:1; 19:15)

15:3a—"Great and marvelous are your deeds"

15:3b—"Just and true are your ways" (also 16:5, 7; 19:2, 11)

15:4—"For you alone are holy. All nations will come and worship before you, for your righteous acts have been revealed"

19:9—"These are the true words of God" (also 21:5; 22:6)

Summary Statement: That God is declared to be omnipotent (all-powerful), omniscient (all-knowing), and omnipresence (present everywhere) calls every person and all of creation to attention. Governing all that He speaks and accomplishes is His holiness and righteousness, expressed in His justice and truth. Because of His love and mercy, He is also the God of salvation. His appearance is magnificent and resplendent, and His presence demands holy fear. God's divine attributes in themselves call the peoples of the earth, angelic beings, and creation itself to worship before His throne.

> ▶ See also under Christology: The Deity of Jesus Christ Seen in His Attributes and Appearance (Descriptive of What He is Like)

The Worship and Praise of God (Inclusive of the Trinity)

1:6—"to him be glory and power for ever and ever! Amen" (also 4:11; 5:12, 13; 7:12; 11:17; 12:10; 15:8; 19:1)

4:8—"'Holy, holy, holy is the Lord God Almighty,' who was, and is, and is to come" (also 3:7; 6:10; 15:4; 16:5)

4:9—"the living creatures give glory, honor and thanks to him who sits on the throne" (also 4:6, 8; 5:6, 8, 11, 14; 7:11; 14:3; 19:4)

4:10a—"the twenty-four elders fall down before him who sits on the throne and worship him who lives for ever and ever" (also 4:4; 5:8; 11:16; 19:4)

4:10b—"They lay their crowns before the throne" (also 4:4)

4:11—"You are worthy, [...] for you created all things and by your will they were created and have their being" (also 10:6; 14:7)

5:9—"And they sang a new song, saying: 'You are worthy to take the scroll and to open its seals, [...]'" (also 14:3)

5:11—"Then I looked and heard the voice of many angels, numbering thousands upon thousands, and ten thousand times ten thousand. They encircled the throne [...]" (also 7:11)

5:12—"In a loud voice they were saying: "Worthy is the Lamb, who was slain, to receive power and wealth and wisdom and strength and honor and glory and praise!" (also 1:6; 7:12)

5:13—"Then I heard every creature in heaven and on earth and under the earth and on the sea, and all that is in them, saying: 'To him who sits on the throne and to the Lamb be praise and honor and glory and power, for ever and ever!'" (also 1:6; 5:12)

7:9—"They were wearing white robes and were holding palm branches in their hands"

7:10—"And they cried out in a loud voice: 'Salvation belongs to our God, who sits on the throne, and to the Lamb" (also 12:10; 19:1)

7:11—"They fell down on their faces before the throne and worshiped God" (also 5:8, 14; 19:4)

7:12—"saying: 'Amen! Praise and glory and wisdom and thanks and honor and power and strength be to our God for ever and ever. Amen!'" (also 5:12)

11:13—"and the survivors were terrified and gave glory to the God of heaven"

11:17—"[...] saying: 'We give thanks to you, Lord God Almighty, the One who is and who was, because you have taken your great power and have begun to reign"

11:18—"your people who revere your name, both great and small"

14:2—"And I heard a sound from heaven like the roar of rushing waters and like a loud peal of thunder. The sound I heard was like that of harpists playing their harps" (also 15:2; 19:6)

14:3a—"And they sang a new song before the throne and before the four living creatures and the elders" (also 5:9)

14:3b—"No one could learn the song except the 144,000 who had been redeemed from the earth"

14:7—"Fear God and give him glory, because the hour of his judgment has come" (also 15:4; 19:5)

15:3a—"and sang the song of God's servant Moses and of the Lamb: [...]"

15:3b—"Great and marvelous are your deeds, Lord God Almighty"

15:3c—"Just and true are your ways, King of the nations" (also 15:4; 21:26)

19:1—"After this I heard what sounded like the roar of a great multitude in heaven shouting: 'Hallelujah! Salvation and glory and power belong to our God [...]'" (also 19:3, 4, 6)

19:5—"Praise our God, all you his servants" (also 22:3)

19:6—"Then I heard what sounded like a great multitude, like the roar of rushing waters and like loud peals of thunder, shouting: 'Hallelujah! For our Lord God Almighty reigns [...]'" (also 14:2)

19:7—"Let us rejoice and be glad and give him glory!" (also 18:20)

19:10—"Worship God!" (also 22:9)

Summary Statement: Revelation is preeminently a book of worship from beginning to end. Worship is commanded and freely given in recognition of God's wondrous nature, attributes, and accomplishments. Four "living creatures" represent all creation in bringing worship to God. Twenty-four "elders" represent the people of God under the Old and New Covenants in bringing a "new song" of worship to God. And with reverential fear and ecstatic joy, an innumerable gathering from the nations worship God their Savior who has delivered and rescued them. In Heaven, worship will be expressed outwardly and openly, with singing and "harps."

The Distinctive Names of God the Father

The name "God" used singularly, as well as with personal pronouns (i.e., "my God," "our God," "his God," or "their God") and possessive pronouns (God's) occurs ninety-one times.

1:6—"Father" (also 2:27 [28 NLT]; 3:5, 21; 14:1)

1:8a—"I am the Alpha and the Omega" (also 21:6; cf. 22:13, where of Jesus)

1:8b—"the Lord God" (also 4:8, 11; 6:10; 11:4, 15, 17; 14:13; 15:3, 4; 16:7; 18:8; 19:6; 21:22; 22:5, 6)

1:8c—"the Almighty" (also 4:8; 11:17; 15:3; 16:7, 14; 19:6, 15; 21:22)

1:18—"I am the Living One" (also 11:17; 16:5)

5:13—"To him who sits on the throne" (also 1:4; 3:21; 4:2, 9, 10; 5:1, 7, 13; 6:16; 7:10, 15; 12:5; 19:4; 20:11; 21:5)

6:10—"Sovereign Lord"

11:4—"the Lord of the earth"

11:13—"the God of heaven" (also 16:11)

11:17—"the One who is and who was" (also 16:5)

15:3—"King of the nations" (KJV "King of saints")

16:5—"O Holy One" (also 4:8; 6:10; 15:4)

21:6—"the Beginning and the End" (cf. 22:13, where of Jesus)

22:6—"the God who inspires the prophets"

Summary Statement: The One who is above all and fills all is prolifically called "God." Distinct reference is made to the person of the "Father" within the godhead, while His many other names testify to His glorious essence and attributes including His eternality, self-existence, holiness, sovereignty, and omnipotence.

▶ See also under Christology: The Distinctive Names and Descriptive Titles of the Son

The Distinctive Roles and Activities of the Father

1:1—"The revelation from Jesus Christ, which God gave him"

2:27—"just as I have received authority from my Father" (also 5:6, 7)

3:12—"the new Jerusalem, which is coming down out of heaven from my God" (also 21:2)

4:2—"and there before me was a throne in heaven with someone sitting on it" (also 1:4; 3:21; 4:3, 9, 10; 5:1, 7, 13; 6:16; 7:10, 15; 12:5; 19:4; 21:5)

4:11—"for you created all things, and by your will they were created and have their being" (also 3:14; 10:6; 14:7)

5:1—"Then I saw in the right hand of him who sat on the throne a scroll" (also 5:7)

6:9—"because of the word of God" (also 1:2, 9; 6:9; 20:4)

6:10—"until you judge the inhabitants of the earth and avenge our blood" (also 11:18; 14:7; 16:5, 7; 19:2; 20:12)

7:2—"having the seal of the living God [...]" (also 7:3; 9:4; 14:1; 22:4)

7:15—"and he who sits on the throne will shelter them with his presence" (also 21:3)

7:17—"And God will wipe away every tear from their eyes" (also 21:4)

8:2—"seven angels who stand before God, and seven trumpets were given to them" (also 7:2; 8:3; 9:4, 5; 10:7, 8; 15:1; 16:1)

10:7—"the mystery of God will be accomplished, just as he announced to his servants the prophets" (also 1:20; 10:4)

11:11—"But after the three and a half days the breath of life from God entered them"

11:17—"because you have taken your great power and have begun to reign" (also 19:6)

11:18—"your wrath has come. The time has come for judging the dead" (also 20:12)

12:6—"a place prepared for her by God"

12:10—"Now have come the salvation and the power and the kingdom of our God" (also 7:12)

14:9—"God's fury, which has been poured full strength into the cup of his wrath" (also 16:1, 19; 19:15)

14:13—"Then I heard a voice from heaven say, 'Write this [...]'" (also 18:4)

15:2—"They held harps given them by God"

15:3—"Great and marvelous are your deeds, Lord God Almighty"

15:8—"And the temple was filled with smoke from the glory of God and from his power" (also 7:15; 11:19; 15:5)

16:9—"God, who had control over these plagues"

16:17—"a loud voice from the throne, saying, 'It is done!'"

17:17—"For God has put it into their hearts to accomplish his purpose [...] until God's words are fulfilled"

18:5—"for her sins are piled up to heaven, and God has remembered her crimes"

18:8—"for mighty is the Lord God who judges her" (also 18:20)

19:2—"He has condemned the great prostitute [...] He has avenged on her the blood of his servants"

19:17—"Come, gather together for the great supper of God, so that you may eat the flesh [...]"

20:11—"Then I saw a great white throne and him who was seated on it" (also 14:7)

21:2—"the new Jerusalem, coming down out of heaven from God, prepared as a bride beautifully dressed for her husband" (also 3:12; 21:10, 11)

21:3a—"God's dwelling place is now among the people, and he will dwell with them" (also 7:15)

21:3b—"They will be his people, and God himself will be with them and be their God" (also 21:7)

21:5—"He who was seated on the throne said, 'I am making everything new!'"

21:6—"To the thirsty I will give water without cost from the spring of the water of life"

21:22—"because the Lord God Almighty and the Lamb are its temple"

22:5—"for the Lord God will give them light"

22:6—"The Lord, the God who inspires the prophets"

22:6—"sent his angel to show his servants the things that must soon take place"

22:18—"God will add to that person the plagues described in this scroll"

22:19—"God will take away from that person any share in the tree of life"

Summary Statement: God alone is Creator of all things, Who through time and eternity controls the destiny of man, nature, and the unseen realm. He ceaselessly rules and overrules from His throne in Heaven; there is no power or agency higher. He brings present and endless blessing upon the righteous and the repentant and present and endless destruction upon the wicked and unrepentant. His authority is delegated to his holy angels and to his righteous followers. Jesus Himself acknowledges that God the Father had entrusted this very Revelation and the redemption of the world to Him.

▶ See also under Christology: The Deity of Jesus Christ Seen in His Role and Activities
▶ See also under Pneumatology: The Role and Activities of the Spirit of God

The Unity and Trinity of the Godhead

1:1—"The revelation from Jesus Christ, which God gave him"

1:2—"the word of God and the testimony of Jesus Christ"

1:4-5—"to you from him who is, and who was, and who is to come, and from the seven spirits before his throne, and from Jesus Christ" (also 1:8; 3:1; 11:17)

1:6—"his God and Father" (also 14:1)

1:8—"'I am the Alpha and the Omega,' says the Lord God" (also 22:13)

2:27—"just as I have received authority from my Father" (also 1:6; 5:7; 14:1)

3:1—"These are the words of him who holds the seven spirits of God and the seven stars" (also 1:4)

3:5-6—"I [...] will acknowledge that name before my Father and his angels. Whoever has ears, let them hear what the Spirit says to the churches" (also 1:4-5)

3:12—"I will write on them the name of my God and the name of the city of my God, the new Jerusalem, which is coming down out of heaven from my God" (also 1:6)

3:21—"[...] I will give the right to sit with me on my throne, just as I was victorious and sat down with my Father on his throne" (also 2:27)

5:6—"The Lamb had seven horns and seven eyes, which are the seven spirits of God" (also 3:1)

5:7—"He went and took the scroll from the right hand of him who sat on the throne" (also 2:27)

5:9—"and with your blood you purchased for God" (also 14:4)

5:13—"To him who sits on the throne and to the Lamb" (also 6:16; 7:9, 10; 21:22, 23)

6:16—"hide us from the face of him who sits on the throne and from the wrath of the Lamb!" (also 11:18)

7:17—"For the Lamb at the center of the throne will be their shepherd; 'he will lead them to springs of living water.' 'And God will wipe away every tear from their eyes'" (also 21:4)

11:15—"the kingdom of our Lord and of his Messiah" (also 12:10)

12:5—"And her child was snatched up to God and to his throne"

14:1—"Then I looked, and there before me was the Lamb, [...] and with him 144,000 who had his name and his Father's name written on their foreheads" (also 1:6; 2:27)

14:4—"They were purchased from among mankind and offered as firstfruits to God and the Lamb" (also 5:9)

19:10—"Worship God! For it is the Spirit of prophecy who bears testimony to Jesus'"

20:6—"but they will be priests of God and of Christ and will reign with him" (also 5:10)

21:22—"the Lord God Almighty and the Lamb are its temple"

21:23—"for the glory of God gives it light, and the Lamb is its lamp"

22:1—"from the throne of God and of the Lamb" (also 5:13; 22:3)

Summary Statement: All three persons of the Trinity: Father, Son, and Holy Spirit are clearly and frequently referenced. Yet, their distinct, personal identity is one of function and role; they minister in full cooperation. The Father has entrusted kingdom authority, the Atonement, the care of God's people, and this very Revelation to the Son. For His faithfulness, Jesus is seated in honor with the Father. Just as the "seven-fold" Spirit of God proceeds from the Father's throne, He is also directed by the Son in bringing Christ's messages to the churches. In the Revelation are positive statements affirming—and nothing negating—that the persons of the Trinity are consubstantial, co-equal, and co-existent. Both the Father and the Son receive worship—which is clearly reserved for deity (cf. 22:9), and both identify themselves as the living and eternal "Alpha and Omega" (cf. 1:8 with 22:13). The people of God relate to the Father and the Son in humble worship and service equally.

- ▶ See also under Christology: The Deity of Jesus Christ Seen in His Essence (Descriptive of Who He Is)
- ▶ See also under Pneumatology: The Essence (Descriptive of Who He Is) and the Attributes and Appearance (Descriptive of What He Is Like) of the Spirit of God

Bibliology—The Study of the Bible

The Inspired, Written Word of God

1:2—"who testifies to everything he saw—that is, the word of God and the testimony of Jesus Christ" (also 1:9; 6:9; 12:11, 17; 19:10; 20:4; 22:16)

1:3a—"Blessed is the one who reads aloud the words of this prophecy" (also 19:10; 22:7, 10, 18, 19)

1:3b—"and blessed are those who hear it and take to heart what is written in it" (also 22:7, 9)

1:11—"Write on a scroll what you see and send it to the seven churches" (also 1:4, 19; 2:1, 8, 12, 18; 3:1, 7, 14; 14:13; 19:9; 21:5; 22:16)

1:16—"and coming out of his mouth was a sharp, double-edged sword" (also 2:12; 19:15, 21)

1:19—"Write, therefore, what you have seen, what is now and what will take place later" (also 1:2)

2:1—"These are the words of him who holds the seven stars" (also 2:8, 12, 18; 3:1, 7, 14)

6:9—"the souls of those who had been slain because of the word of God and the testimony they had maintained" (also 1:2, 9; 12:11, 17; 19:10; 20:4; 22:16)

10:10—"I took the little scroll from the angel's hand and ate it. It tasted as sweet as honey in my mouth, but when I had eaten it, my stomach turned sour" (also 10:2, 8-9)

10:11—"Then I was told, 'You must prophesy again about many peoples, nations, languages and kings'"

19:9—"These are the true words of God" (also 1:2, 9; 2:18; 6:9; 20:4)

21:5b—"Then he said, 'Write this down, for these words are trustworthy and true'" (also 1:3)

22:7—"Blessed is the one who keeps the words of the prophecy written in this scroll" (also 1:3; 22:9)

22:10—"Do not seal up the words of the prophecy of this scroll" (also 10:4)

22:18a—"I warn everyone who hears the words of the prophecy of this scroll"

22:18b—"If anyone adds anything to them, God will add to that person the plagues described in this scroll"

22:19—"And if anyone takes words away from this scroll of prophecy [...] which are described in this scroll"

Summary Statement: The inspiration of Revelation is certain since it is presented as the word(s) "of God" (genitive case of possession). First spoken directly by God the Father (and also by the Son [2:1, etc.]), these words were written down at His command, carrying the "truthfulness" of God's own character. John equates what he "saw" by revelation with the "word of God and the testimony of Jesus Christ" (1:2; 19:10), which is here specifically addressed to those righteous and unrighteous in the churches. This written word is also equated with "prophecy," the anointed forth-telling and foretelling of God's will. The relevance and nearness of fulfillment of this prophecy and testimony is such that these words are not to be "sealed up" but rather, with little exception (10:4), they are to be made open. The Spirit acknowledges that great persecution has and will come, to the end of time, to those who stay true to His Word. Yet, eternal blessing is pronounced to those who read and obey the Word of God. For the righteous, the testimony they embrace through God's Word is their victory. Conversely, a curse is promised to those who "add to" or "take[s] from" these written words.

Well over 400 allusions to Old Testament verses and motifs contained in the Revelation (cf. 10:7)—along with a theology and vocabulary consistent with the balance of the New Testament—reinforce the continuity and divine nature of the Bible through to its closing words. In similar fashion to the prophetic ministry of Old Testament and New Testament prophets (cf. 10:7; 11:18; 16:6; 18:20, 24; 22:6, 9), unlike the inscripturated, written prophetic words known in the canon of Scripture, some prophetic words, such as of the "two witnesses" of Revelation 11:3-12, remain unrecorded. Warning is also given concerning "false prophets" who do not speak for God at all (cf. 2:20; 16:13; 19:20; 20:10).

Christology—The Study of Jesus Christ, the Son of God

The Distinctive Names and Descriptive Titles of the Son

1:1—"Jesus" (also 1:2, 5, 9; 12:17; 14:12; 17:6; 19:10; 20:4; 22:16, 20)

1:1—"Christ" (also 20:4, 6)

1:5a—"the faithful witness" (also 3:7, 14; 19:11)

1:5b—"the firstborn from the dead" (also 1:18; 2:8)

1:5c—"the ruler of the kings of the earth" (also 11:15; 19:15)

1:13—"like a son of man" (also 14:14)

1:17—"I am the First and the Last" (also 2:8; 22:13)

1:18—"I am the Living One" (also 2:8)

2:12—"him who has the sharp, double-edged sword" (also 1:16; 19:15, 21)

2:18—"the Son of God" (cf. 2:27; 3:5, 21, where "my father" and 14:1, "his father")

3:14a—"the Amen" (also 22:20, 21)

3:14b—"the faithful and true witness" (also 1:5; 3:7, 14; 19:11)

3:14c—"the ruler of God's creation"

5:5a—"See, the Lion of the tribe of Judah" (also 10:3)

5:5b—"the Root of David" (also 22:16)

5:6—"Then I saw a Lamb" (also 5:8, 12, 13; 6:1, 3, 5, 7, 16; 7:9, 10, 14, 17; 12:11; 13:8; 14:1, 4, 10; 15:3; 17:14; 19:7, 9; 21:9, 14, 22, 23; 22:1, 3)

11:15—"and of his Messiah" (also 12:10; same as "Christ" in 1:1; 20:4, 6)

11:17a—"Lord God Almighty" (where indistinguishable from the Father; also 4:8; 15:3 [cf. 1:5]; 16:7; 19:6; 21:22)

11:17b—"the One who is and who was" (also 1:4, 8)

12:4—"her child" (12:5)

12:5—"a son, a male child" (also 12:13)

17:14—"he is Lord of lords and King of kings" (also 19:16)

19:11—"whose rider is called Faithful and True" (also 3:7, 14)

19:13—"and his name is the Word of God"

19:19—"the rider on the horse"

22:13—"I am the Alpha and the Omega, the First and the Last, the Beginning and the End" (also 1:17; 2:8)

22:16—"I, Jesus [...] I am the Root and the Offspring of David, and the bright Morning Star" (also 5:5)

22:20—"the Lord Jesus" (also 22:21)

Summary Statement: No less than thirty names and descriptive titles are used to refer to Jesus in the Revelation. The very Jesus who decades before had drawn John's heart close to His, now appears to His servant in unspeakable glory and power. Most prominent is the title "Lamb" (used 28 times), which directly relates to His sacrificial work on the cross (11:8). His given name, "Jesus," is next in prominence with 11 references. Gloriously and victoriously, when Jesus is presented as the Lion of the Tribe of Judah before the Throne of the Father, He appears as the slain Lamb of God. The hallmarks of both advents of Jesus in humility and in triumph are captured in the many names of Jesus, as are both His humanity and His divinity. His very name is "the Word of God" (19:13). As with the names of the Father, the names of the Son testify directly to His divine nature and attributes including His eternality, sovereignty, omnipotence, faithfulness, and truthfulness.

The Deity of Jesus Christ Seen in His Essence (Descriptive of Who He Is)

1:5—"and the ruler of the kings of the earth" (also 15:3)

1:17—"I am the First and the Last" (also 2:8; 22:13)

1:18a—"I am the Living One; I was dead, and now look, I am alive for ever and ever!" (also 2:8)

1:18b—"And I hold the keys of death and Hades" (also 20:14)

2:18—"These are the words of the Son of God"

2:27—"just as I have received authority from my Father" (also 5:6-7)

3:14—"the ruler of God's creation"

3:21—"I was victorious and sat down with my Father on his throne" (also 22:1, 3)

5:12—"to receive power and wealth and wisdom and strength and honor and glory and praise!'" (also 5:7-14; 7:9-12)

11:17a—"Lord God Almighty, the One who is and who was" (where indistinguishable from the Father; also 4:8; 15:3 [cf. 1:5]; 16:7; 19:6; 21:22)

11:17b—"because you have taken your great power and have begun to reign"

12:10—"and the authority of his Messiah"

17:14—"he is Lord of lords and King of kings" (also 19:16)

19:12—"and on his head are many crowns" (also 14:14)

22:1—"flowing from the throne of God and of the Lamb" (also 22:3)

22:4—"They will see his face, and his name will be on their foreheads" (also 7:3; 14:1)

22:13a—"I am the Alpha and the Omega" (cf. 1:8 and 21:6, where of the Father)

22:13b—"the first and the last, the beginning and the end" (also 1:17; 2:8; 21:6, where of the Father)

Summary Statement: It is most important to see Christ's clear claim to hold the same eternal nature as the Father, both persons within the godhead identifying as "the Alpha and the Omega" (cf. 22:13 with 1:8) and "the beginning and the end" (cf. 22:13 with 21:6). Both are also seen as sovereign over creation (3:14) and over the nations (1:5), Jesus holding absolute power and authority, delegated from the Father. Christ's deity is also asserted in the detailed description of His worship as He sits with the Father upon His throne in Heaven (5:7-14; 7:9-12), accompanied by the directive to "Worship God!" alone (19:10). Note also the singular pronouns "his" and "him" in 22:3 and 4, when clearly speaking of both the Father and the Lamb seated together.

- ▶ See also under Theology Proper: The Essence of God (Descriptive of Who He Is; Inclusive of the Trinity)
- ▶ See also under Theology Proper: The Worship and Praise of God (Inclusive of the Trinity)
- ▶ See also under Theology Proper: The Unity and Trinity of the Godhead

The Deity of Jesus Christ Seen in His Attributes and Appearance (Descriptive of What He is Like)

1:10—"and I heard behind me a loud voice like a trumpet" (also 4:1)

1:13—"dressed in a robe reaching down to his feet and with a golden sash around his chest" (also 19:13)

1:14a—"The hair on his head was white like wool, as white as snow"

1:14b—"and his eyes were like blazing fire" (also 2:18; 19:12)

1:15a—"His feet were like bronze glowing in a furnace" (also 2:18)

1:15b—"and his voice was like the sound of rushing waters" (also 3:20)

1:16a—"and coming out of his mouth was a sharp, double-edged sword" (also 2:12, 16; 19:15, 21)

1:16b—"His face was like the sun shining in all its brilliance"

1:17—"When I saw him, I fell at his feet as though dead"

2:2—"I know" (also 2:9, 13, 19; 3:1, 8 [2x], 15)

2:23—"I am he who searches hearts and minds"

3:7—"These are the words of him who is holy and true" (cf. 6:10, where of the Father)

3:14a—"These are the words of the Amen" (also 22:20, 21)

3:14b—"the faithful and true witness" (also 1:5; 3:7, 14; 19:11)

5:6—"The Lamb had seven horns and seven eyes, which are the seven spirits of God sent out into all the earth" (also 3:1)

5:12—"to receive power and wealth and wisdom and strength and honor and glory and praise!'"

5:13—"to the Lamb be praise and honor and glory and power, for ever and ever!"

11:17—"because you have taken your great power and have begun to reign" (also 11:15; 19:15; 20:4, 6)

14:14—"one like a son of man with a crown of gold on his head" (also 19:12)

19:11a—"whose rider is called Faithful and True" (also 3:7, 14)

19:11b—"With justice he judges and wages war" (also 17:14)

19:12a—"His eyes are like blazing fire, and on his head are many crowns" (also 1:14; 2:18; 19:12)

19:12b—"He has a name written on him that no one knows but he himself" (also 15:4)

22:21—"The grace of the Lord Jesus be with God's people. Amen" (also 1:4)

Summary Statement: Christ's appearance to John in his first vision is not that of a mere human being. His resplendent glory causes John to fall "at his feet as though dead" (1:17). John sees Him again in such majesty as He—crowned with many crowns—leads the army of Heaven in supernatural, all-encompassing victory (19:11-20). He who walks amongst His churches is the omniscient one who "searches" and "knows" hearts and minds. His justice and judgment are perfect, displayed in His eyes of "blazing fire." He, whose hair is "white as snow" and whose feet are like "glowing bronze" is called "holy." He is several times described with the divine attributes of "Faithful" and "True," confirmed in His name "the Amen." His worshippers ascribe to Him the "power" and "strength" of the omnipotent One who reigns from His throne. His voice is the voice of God. His divine omnipresence is seen in His identity with "the seven spirits of God sent out into all the earth" (5:6; cf. 3:1). Even His name, known to no one else, carries divine mystery (19:12). With John's closing words, Jesus is pronounced gracious.

    ▶ See also under Theology Proper: The Attributes and Appearance of God (Descriptive of What He is Like; Inclusive of the Trinity)

The Deity of Jesus Christ Seen in His Role and Activities

1:5a—"the faithful witness, the firstborn from the dead, and the ruler of the kings of the earth" (also 1:17; 2:8; 19:11)

1:5b—"To him who loves us and has freed us from our sins by his blood" (also 5:9; 7:14; 12:11)

1:7—"Look, he is coming with the clouds" (also 2:25; 3:3)

1:10—"and I heard behind me a loud voice like a trumpet" (also 4:1)

1:13—"and among the lampstands was someone like a son of man" (also 2:1)

1:16—"and coming out of his mouth was a sharp, double-edged sword" (also 2:12, 16; 19:15, 21)

1:18—"And I hold the keys of death and Hades" (also 20:13, 14)

1:20—"The mystery of the seven stars that you saw in my right hand" (also 2:1; 3:1)

2:1a—"These are the words of him who […]" (also 2:8, 12, 18; 3:1, 7, 14)

2:1b—"him who holds the seven stars in his right hand and walks among the seven golden lampstands" (also 1:20)

2:2—"I know" (also 2:9; 2:13; 2:19; 3:1; 3:8 [2x]; 3:15)

2:4—"Yet I hold this against you" (also 2:14; 2:20)

2:5—"I will come to you and remove your lampstand from its place" (also 1:13; 2:1)

2:7—"I will give the right to eat from the tree of life" (also 22:2, 19)

2:10—"I will give you life as your victor's crown" (also 3:11)

2:16—"I will soon come to you and will fight against them with the sword of my mouth" (also 19:15, 21)

2:17a—"To the one who is victorious, I will give some of the hidden manna"

2:17b—"I will also give that person a white stone with a new name written on it" (also 3:12; 22:4)

2:21—"I have given her time to repent of her immorality, but she is unwilling"

2:22—"So I will cast her on a bed of suffering, and I will make those who commit adultery with her suffer intensely, unless they repent of her ways" (also 2:23)

2:23—"I am he who searches hearts and minds, and I will repay each of you according to your deeds" (also 20:12, 13)

2:26—"I will give authority over the nations" (also 19:15; 20:4, 6)

2:27—"just as I have received authority from my Father" (also 5:6, 7)

2:28—"I will also give that one the morning star" (also 22:16)

3:1—"him who holds the seven spirits of God and the seven stars" (also 1:20; 2:1; 5:6)

3:2—"I have found your deeds unfinished in the sight of my God" (also 2:23)

3:3—"I will come like a thief, and you will not know at what time I will come to you" (also 16:15)

3:5a—"I will never blot out the name of that person from the book of life" (also 20:15)

3:5b—"but will acknowledge that name before my Father and his angels" (also 14:1)

3:7a—"These are the words of him […] who holds the key of David" (also 5:5; 22:16)

3:7b—"What he opens no one can shut, and what he shuts no one can open" (also 3:8)

3:11—"I am coming soon" (also 22:7, 12, 20)

3:12—"The one who is victorious I will make a pillar in the temple of my God"

3:14—"These are the words of the Amen, the faithful and true witness, the ruler of God's creation" (also 1:5; 19:11)

3:16—"I am about to spit you out of my mouth"

3:18—"I counsel you"

3:19—"Those whom I love I rebuke and discipline"

3:20—"Here I am! I stand at the door and knock. If anyone hears my voice and opens the door, I will come in and eat with that person, and they with me"

3:21—"To the one who is victorious, I will give the right to sit with me on my throne" (also 20:4, 6)

5:2—"Who is worthy to break the seals and open the scroll?" (also 5:5, 9)

5:5—"See, the Lion of the tribe of Judah, the Root of David, has triumphed" (also 3:7; 22:16)

5:6a—"standing at the center of the throne, encircled by the four living creatures and the elders" (also 7:17)

5:6b—"The Lamb had seven horns and seven eyes, which are the seven spirits of God sent out into all the earth" (also 3:1)

5:7—"He went and took the scroll from the right hand of him who sat on the throne" (also 5:9)

5:9a—"You are worthy to take the scroll and to open its seals" (also 6:1, 3, 5, 7, 9, 12; 8:1)

5:9b—"because you were slain, and with your blood you purchased for God persons from every tribe and language and people and nation" (also 1:5; 7:9, 14; 12:11)

6:1—"I watched as the Lamb opened the first of the seven seals" (also 6:3, 5, 7, 9, 12; 8:1)

6:16—"and from the wrath of the Lamb" (also 6:17; 11:18)

7:17—"For the Lamb at the center of the throne will be their shepherd; 'he will lead them to springs of living water'" (also 21:6; 22:1, 17)

11:3—"And I will appoint my two witnesses"

11:15—"and he will reign for ever and ever" (also 11:17; 19:15; 20:4, 6)

12:5—"a male child, who 'will rule all the nations with an iron scepter'" (also 19:15)

14:1—"the Lamb, standing on Mount Zion, and with him 144,000"

14:10—"They will be tormented with burning sulfur in the presence of the holy angels and of the Lamb"

14:14—"and seated on the cloud was one like a son of man with a crown of gold on his head and a sharp sickle in his hand" (also 19:15)

14:15—"Take your sickle and reap, because the time to reap has come" (also 14:16)

19:8—"Fine linen, bright and clean, was given her to wear" (also 7:14)

19:11—"With justice he judges and wages war" (also 17:14)

19:13—"and his name is the Word of God" (also 1:2, 9; 20:4)

19:15a—"Coming out of his mouth is a sharp sword with which to strike down the nations" (also 2:16; 11:18; 19:21)

19:15b—"He will rule them with an iron scepter" (also 12:5)

19:15c—"He treads the winepress of the fury of the wrath of God Almighty" (also 11:18; 14:14-16)

19:21—"The rest were killed with the sword coming out of the mouth of the rider" (also 2:16; 19:15)

20:4—"They came to life and reigned with Christ a thousand years" (also 20:6)

21:23—"for the glory of God gives it light, and the Lamb is its lamp" (also 21:24)

22:12—"My reward is with me, and I will give to each person according to what they have done" (also 20:12, 13)

22:18—"I warn everyone who hears the words of the prophecy of this scroll" (also 22:19)

22:20—"Yes, I am coming soon." Amen. Come, Lord Jesus" (also 1:17; 3:11; 22:7, 12)

Summary Statement: Jesus is the Lamb of God, who through His own blood has the authority to set His followers free from their sin and to clothe them in His own pure righteousness. These He has "purchased for God" out of all the peoples of the earth (5:9). As He is the "firstborn from the dead" (1:5), they too live through Him. Jesus is also revealed as the Great High Priest, walking amongst the lampstands—representative of the visible Church on earth—inspecting it according to His own righteousness and holding its leaders in His hands. He alone "knows" and "searches hearts and minds" (2:23), having the authority to reward and commend those who are righteous and to reject and condemn those who are unrighteous. Revealing His deity, Jesus "holds [in the sense of possessing] the seven spirits of God" (3:1), "sent out into all the earth" (5:6). Identified through seven magnificent titles, Jesus counsels the heart, calls to repentance, warns, and rebukes. He, in fact, has the authority to "remove" a lampstand (symbolic then of a rebellious local church) "from its place" (2:5).

Because of His great sacrifice, Jesus has received the Father's charge and authority to fulfill judgment in the earth. As time draws to a close, He will enter into and directly carry out "the wrath of God Almighty" (19:15). He is coming with a double-edged sword of judgment in His mouth and a sickle of judgment in His hand. He is coming in the clouds with glory and triumph to resurrect and reward the righteous and to judge the unrighteous with eternal punishment. He who already is "the ruler of God's creation" (3:14) will then at His appearing rule the nations "with an iron scepter" (12:5; 19:15), and those who He empowers will rule with Him (2:26; 3:21). The Lamb's reign, which begins over the earth, will continue from the Holy City forever. John saw Him there, illuminating Heaven with His glory. As He is now, Jesus will forever be at the center of Heaven's activities and Heaven's worship.

The Humanity of Jesus Christ Seen in His Essence, Attributes, and Role

1:5a—"and from Jesus Christ, the faithful witness, the firstborn from the dead" (also 1:18; 2:8)

1:5b—"To him who loves us and has freed us from our sins by his blood" (also 5:9; 7:14; 12:11)

1:13—"and among the lampstands was someone like a son of man" (also 14:14)

1:18—"I was dead, and now look, I am alive for ever and ever!" (also 1:5; 2:8)

2:8—"him who is the First and the Last, who died and came to life again" (also 1:5, 18)

5:6—"Then I saw a Lamb, looking as if it had been slain" (also 5:9, 12)

5:9—"you were slain, and with your blood you purchased for God" (also 5:6, 12)

5:12—"Worthy is the Lamb, who was slain" (also 5:6, 9)

11:8—"where also their Lord was crucified"

12:4—"her child the moment he was born" (also 12:2, 5)

12:5—"a son, a male child" (also 12:13)

13:8—"the Lamb who was slain from the creation of the world" (also 5:6, 9, 12)

19:13—"He is dressed in a robe dipped in blood" (also 1:5; 5:9; 7:14; 12:11)

22:16—"I am the Root and the Offspring of David" (also 5:5)

Summary Statement: While Christ's deity is revealed in His eternal nature as the Alpha and Omega, His humanity is revealed in that He gave His life for His followers. Jesus was born a human to die as a human, and in His substitutionary death to conquer the grave as "the firstborn from the dead" (1:5). Even in the eternal framework of Heaven, John sees Jesus as "a Lamb, looking as if it had been slain" (5:6). Though His crucifixion and death took place in space and time, the plan and consequence of His sacrifice is ubiquitous and timeless in Heaven. Twice John sees Jesus in appearance "like a son of man" (1:13; 14:14; cf. Dan. 7:13). His humanness is also seen in that he was born as a male child in the lineage of King David.

The Finished Work of Jesus

1:5a—"and from Jesus Christ, who is the faithful witness, the firstborn from the dead" (also 1:18; 2:8)

1:5b—"To him who loves us and has freed us from our sins by his blood" (also 5:9; 7:14; 12:11)

1:6—"and has made us to be a kingdom and priests to serve his God and Father" (also 5:10)

1:18a—"I was dead, and now look, I am alive for ever and ever!" (also 1:5; 2:8)

1:18b—"And I hold the keys of death and Hades" (also 3:7; 20:13, 14)

2:8—"who died and came to life again" (also 1:5, 18)

3:7—"These are the words of him [...] who holds the key of David" (also 1:18; 5:5; 22:16)

5:5—"See, the Lion of the tribe of Judah, the Root of David, has triumphed" (also 3:7; 22:16)

5:6—"Then I saw a Lamb, looking as if it had been slain, standing at the center of the throne" (also 5:9, 12; 12:5)

5:9—"because you were slain, and with your blood you purchased for God persons from every tribe and language and people and nation" (also 1:5; 5:6, 12; 7:9, 14)

7:14—"they have washed their robes and made them white in the blood of the Lamb" (also 1:5; 5:9; 12:11)

11:8—"where also their Lord was crucified"

12:4—"her child the moment he was born" (also 12:2, 5, 13)

12:5—"And her child was snatched up to God and to his throne" (also 5:6)

12:11—"They triumphed over him by the blood of the Lamb" (also 1:5; 5:9; 7:14)

13:8—"the Lamb who was slain from the creation of the world" (also 5:6, 9, 12)

19:13—"He is dressed in a robe dipped in blood" (also 1:5; 5:6, 9, 12; 7:14; 12:11)

Summary Statement: The full scope of the finished work of Jesus is celebrated in the Revelation: His birth, His life, His death, His Resurrection, and His Ascension to His throne in glory. Though eternally efficacious, Christ's sacrifice was accomplished once in time through the shedding of His blood at His crucifixion. Forever, the inhabitants of Heaven bear witness that Jesus, the Lamb, is the Redeemer of humanity, who obediently laid down His life. His blood has made us both righteous and victorious. The finished work of His First Coming now gives way to the finished work of His Second Coming. Because He alone has purchased us for God with His own lifeblood, He has also qualified to finish the work of redemption, i.e., the eradication of sin and sin's curse from the created universe. Heaven also celebrates Christ's resurrection and His ultimate victory over the grave expressed in His proclamation, "And I hold the keys of death and Hades" (1:18).

▶ See also under Soteriology: Salvation Provided Graciously Through the Atoning Work of Christ Alone

The Current and Eternal Work of Jesus

1:5—"and the ruler of the kings of the earth" (also 11:15; 19:15; 20:4, 6)

1:7—"Look, he is coming with the clouds" (also 3:11; 22:7, 12, 20)

1:13—"and among the lampstands was someone like a son of man" (also 2:1)

1:20—"The mystery of the seven stars that you saw in my right hand" (also 2:1; 3:1)

2:2—"I know" (also 2:9; 2:13; 2:19; 3:1; 3:8 [2x]; 3:15)

2:5—"I will come to you and remove your lampstand from its place" (also 1:13; 2:1)

2:7—"I will give the right to eat from the tree of life" (also 22:2, 19)

2:10—"I will give you life as your victor's crown"

2:16—"I will soon come to you and will fight against them with the sword of my mouth" (also 19:15, 21)

2:17a—"To the one who is victorious, I will give some of the hidden manna"

2:17b—"I will also give that person a white stone with a new name written on it" (also 3:12; 22:4)

2:21—"I have given her time to repent of her immorality, but she is unwilling"

2:22—"So I will cast her on a bed of suffering, and I will make those who commit adultery with her suffer intensely, unless they repent of her ways" (also 2:23)

2:23—"Then all the churches will know that I am he who searches hearts and minds, and I will repay each of you according to your deeds" (also 20:12, 13)

2:26—"I will give authority over the nations" (also 19:15)

2:28—"I will also give that one the morning star" (also 22:16)

3:1—"him who holds the seven spirits of God and the seven stars" (also 1:20; 2:1; 5:6)

3:3—"I will come like a thief, and you will not know at what time I will come to you" (also 16:15)

3:5—"but will acknowledge that name before my Father and his angels"

3:7—"What he opens no one can shut, and what he shuts no one can open" (also 3:8)

3:11—"I am coming soon" (also 1:7; 22:7, 12, 20)

3:12—"The one who is victorious I will make a pillar in the temple of my God"

3:14—"These are the words of the Amen, the faithful and true witness, the ruler of God's creation" (also 19:11)

3:16—"I am about to spit you out of my mouth"

3:18—"I counsel you"

3:19—"Those whom I love I rebuke and discipline"

3:20—"Here I am! I stand at the door and knock. If anyone hears my voice and opens the door, I will come in and eat with that person, and they with me"

3:21—"To the one who is victorious, I will give the right to sit with me on my throne"

5:2—"Who is worthy to break the seals and open the scroll?" (also 5:5, 7, 9)

5:6a—"Then I saw a Lamb [...] standing at the center of the throne" (also 7:17)

5:6b—"The Lamb had seven horns and seven eyes, which are the seven spirits of God sent out into all the earth" (also 3:1)

5:7—"He went and took the scroll from the right hand of him who sat on the throne"

6:1—"I watched as the Lamb opened the first of the seven seals" (also 6:3, 5, 7, 9, 12; 8:1)

6:16—"and from the wrath of the Lamb!" (also 6:17; 11:18)

7:17—"For the Lamb at the center of the throne will be their shepherd; 'he will lead them to springs of living water'" (also 21:6; 22:17)

11:3—"And I will appoint my two witnesses"

11:15—"and he will reign for ever and ever" (also 11:17; 19:4, 6)

11:17—"because you have taken your great power and have begun to reign" (also 11:15)

12:5—"a male child, who 'will rule all the nations with an iron scepter'" (also 19:15)

14:1—"the Lamb, standing on Mount Zion, and with him 144,000"

14:10—"They will be tormented with burning sulfur in the presence of the holy angels and of the Lamb" (also 20:14)

14:14—"and seated on the cloud was one like a son of man with a crown of gold on his head and a sharp sickle in his hand" (also 19:12)

14:15—"Take your sickle and reap, because the time to reap has come" (also 14:16)

16:15—"Look, I come like a thief!" (also 3:3)

19:8—"Fine linen, bright and clean, was given her to wear" (also 7:14)

19:11a—"and there before me was a white horse, whose rider is called Faithful and True" (also 1:5; 3:14)

19:11b—"With justice he judges and wages war" (also 17:14)

19:15a—"Coming out of his mouth is a sharp sword with which to strike down the nations" (also 11:18; 19:21)

19:15b—"He will rule them with an iron scepter" (also 12:5)

19:15c—"He treads the winepress of the fury of the wrath of God Almighty" (also 14:14-16)

19:21—"The rest were killed with the sword coming out of the mouth of the rider" (also 2:16; 19:15)

20:4—"They came to life and reigned with Christ a thousand years" (also 20:6)

21:23—"for the glory of God gives it light, and the Lamb is its lamp"

22:12—"My reward is with me, and I will give to each person according to what they have done" (also 20:12, 13)

22:20—"Amen. Come, Lord Jesus" (also 1:17; 2:25; 3:11; 22:7, 12)

Summary Statement: In addition to Christ's finished work fulfilled in His First Advent, Jesus continues from His throne of glory to fulfill both current and eternal ministry. Presently—as from the perspective of space and time—Jesus is exercising rule over God's creation and the nations as well as headship over His own Church and its leaders. Intimating His great high priesthood, John sees Jesus inspecting His Church, represented by seven "lampstands." With divine omniscience, He "knows" completely and fully the condition and issues of the hearts and minds of His people, both individually and corporately. Even now He is actively commending, counseling, disciplining, and rewarding the righteous and obedient within the Church, with present and eternal blessings. Likewise, He is even now searching out, reproving, warning, and (where unrepentance remains) condemning those who are unrighteous and disobedient in the visible church and in the world.

John also saw the time when Jesus, as the sacrificed Lamb, will join with the Father in releasing divine wrath upon unrepentant humanity. In a move that will fix the final destiny of this present evil world, Jesus will approach the Throne of the Father to receive a scroll filled with unspeakable judgments. Demonstrating His active lead, it is the Lamb who will personally break open each of the seven seals of the scroll, which till then conceal each element of the coming wrath. With the fulfillment of these great judgments in the earth, Jesus is seen holding a sickle, an omen of the harvest of damnation He is coming to reap from the earth. All of this judgment will culminate as Jesus unexpectedly and victoriously comes in the clouds at His Revelation, riding as the conquering King, waging war against all ungodliness.

With this cleansing of the earth of rebellion and the binding of Satan in a bottomless pit, Jesus will rule over the earth for one thousand years, and the righteous with Him. Yet, this measured reign will only open the way to His eternal reign from His glorious throne, from which He illuminates Heaven, brings healing to the nations, and ministers spiritual refreshment to His righteous followers forever.

- ▶ See also under Eschatology: The Revelation of Christ in His Second "Coming"
- ▶ See also under Eschatology: The Millennial Reign of Christ and the Eternal Kingdom of God

Pneumatology—The Study of the Spirit of God

The Essence (Descriptive of Who He Is) and the Attributes and Appearance (Descriptive of What He Is Like) of the Spirit of God

1:4—"and from the seven spirits before his throne" (also 3:1; 4:5; 5:6)

1:10—"On the Lord's Day I was in the Spirit" (also 4:2; 17:3; 21:10)

2:7—"let them hear what the Spirit says to the churches" (also 2:11; 2:17; 2:29; 3:6; 3:13; 3:22)

3:1—"the seven spirits of God" (also 1:4; 4:5; 5:6)

4:5—"In front of the throne, seven lamps were blazing. These are the seven spirits of God" (also 1:4; 3:1; 5:6)

5:6—"The Lamb had seven horns and seven eyes, which are the seven spirits of God sent out into all the earth" (also 1:4; 3:1; 4:5)

21:10—"And he carried me away in the Spirit" (also 1:10; 4:2; 17:3)

Summary Statement: In the Book of Revelation there are much fewer references to the Spirit of God than to the Father and the Son. That He is alive and personal, as opposed to being an inanimate force, is seen in that He actively speaks to the Church. His divine nature—being co-equal within the Godhead—is seen in that He is "before" and "in front of the throne" of God and that He is called "the seven spirits of God" ("seven" being a statement of completeness). He is likewise co-substantial within the Godhead, which is captured in the phrase, "The Lamb had seven horns and seven eyes, which are the seven spirits of God" (5:6). Further, a connection to Yahweh of the Old Testament is made in a comparison of 4:5 and 5:6 with Zechariah 4:10, "These seven [lamps] are the eyes of the LORD, which range through the whole earth" (ESV). Here also is seen the omnipresence and omniscience of the Spirit. While the Spirit transcends human experience, John also knew His immanent, pervading presence as he states four times that he was found "in the Spirit" (1:10; 4:2; 17:3; 21:10).

The Role and Activities of the Spirit of God

1:10—"On the Lord's Day I was in the Spirit" (also 4:2; 17:3; 21:10)

2:7—"let them hear what the Spirit says to the churches" (also 2:11; 2:17; 2:29; 3:6, 13, 22)

4:5—"In front of the throne, seven lamps were blazing. These are the seven spirits of God" (also 1:4; 3:1; 5:6)

5:6—"which are the seven spirits of God sent out into all the earth" (also 1:4; 3:1; 4:5)

11:4—"They are 'the two olive trees' and the two lampstands"

11:11—"But after the three and a half days the breath [*pneuma*, or "spirit"] of life from God entered them"

14:13—"'Yes,' says the Spirit, 'they will rest from their labor, for their deeds will follow them'"

19:10—"Worship God! For it is the Spirit of prophecy who bears testimony to Jesus'"

22:17—"The Spirit and the bride say, 'Come!'"

Summary Statement: John personally witnessed and experienced the active ministry of the Holy Spirit as He is sent out from the Throne of God in Heaven "into all the earth" (5:6). The description of the Spirit with the words "seven lamps were blazing" (4:5) is a likely allusion to the seven-stemmed golden lampstand of the earthly tabernacle (Exod. 37:23), suggesting that the earthly type is a mere reflection of the perfect prototype eternally in Heaven (cf. Heb. 8:5). Upon the earth the Spirit speaks authoritatively, commending, encouraging, and rebuking those in the visible Church. Above all, He, "the Spirit of prophecy" (19:10) testifies of Jesus and stirs a desire in the heart of the Church for His return. The description of the "two witnesses" of Chapter 11 as "the two olive trees" and "the two lampstands" is strikingly similar to the description of the two anointed servants of God who draw upon the Spirit's inexhaustible anointing in Zechariah 4:11-14. John sees them performing wonders and miracles through the Spirit's anointing and being raised up through the Spirit's resurrection power.

▶ See also under Theology Proper: The Worship and Praise of God (Inclusive of the Trinity)

▶ See also under Theology Proper: The Unity and Trinity of the Godhead

242 CONQUEST & GLORY

Angelology—The Study of Angels (Holy and Fallen)

Including the Study of Satan (Satanology) and of Demons (Demonology)

The Essence, Appearance, and Attributes of God's Holy Angels

4:6—"In the center, around the throne, were four living creatures, and they were covered with eyes, in front and in back" (also 4:7-9; 5:6, 8, 11, 14; 6:1, 3, 5-7; 7:11; 15:7; 19:4)

4:7—"The first living creature was like a lion, the second was like an ox, the third had a face like a man, the fourth was like a flying eagle"

4:8—"Each of the four living creatures had six wings and was covered with eyes all around, even under its wings"

5:2—"And I saw a mighty angel proclaiming in a loud voice" (also 18:2)

5:11—"Then I looked and heard the voice of many angels, numbering thousands upon thousands, and ten thousand times ten thousand"

7:1—"After this I saw four angels standing at the four corners of the earth"

7:2a—"Then I saw another angel coming up from the east, having the seal of the living God"

7:2b—"He called out in a loud voice to the four angels who had been given power to harm the land and the sea"

10:1a—"Then I saw another mighty angel coming down from heaven" (also 18:1)

10:1b—"He was robed in a cloud, with a rainbow above his head; his face was like the sun, and his legs were like fiery pillars"

10:2—"He planted his right foot on the sea and his left foot on the land"

10:3—"and he gave a loud shout like the roar of a lion. When he shouted, the voices of the seven thunders spoke"

10:8—"Go, take the scroll that lies open in the hand of the angel who is standing on the sea and on the land"

14:6—"Then I saw another angel flying in midair"

14:10—"They will be tormented with burning sulfur in the presence of the holy angels"

15:1—"seven angels with the seven last plagues" (also 15:6)

15:6—"They were dressed in clean, shining linen and wore golden sashes around their chests"

18:1a—"After this I saw another angel coming down from heaven" (also 10:1)

18:1b—"He had great authority, and the earth was illuminated by his splendor"

18:21—"Then a mighty angel picked up a boulder the size of a large millstone and threw it into the sea"

19:10—"At this I fell at his feet to worship him. But he said to me, 'Don't do that! I am a fellow servant with you" (also 22:9)

19:14—"The armies of heaven were following him" (also 19:19)

Summary Statement: As John is lifted into Heaven, he provides a detailed description of four "living creatures" (*zōon*), positioned "around" the throne (4:6). Ezekiel (Ezek. 1:5-25; 3:13) brought a similar description of four "living creatures," and "realized that they were cherubim" (10:20). Mentioned ninety-one times in the Old Testament, these "cherubim" are the highest ranking of God's created angels. The "living creatures" John sees are "covered with eyes, in front and in back" (Rev. 4:6, 8), a symbol of universal watchfulness, intelligence, and understanding. Each of the four has a different appearance, i.e., "like a lion," "like an ox," "like a man," and "like a flying eagle" (4:7), which implies that they represent all of creation before the Throne of God in worship and service. That each also has "six wings" represents their swiftness in fulfilling God's will, here reminiscent of the seraphs Isaiah (6:2) saw before the throne. Though angelic by nature, the "living creatures" stand apart in ranking from the innumerable company of angels, which also stand before God's throne (5:11).

In addition to the myriad of angels John saw in Heaven, certain "mighty" (cf. 5:2; 10:1; 18:21) angels are authorized to carry out work on earth. They operate above spatial limitations, even "flying," implying that they are spirit beings. John also describes certain angels as shining with the glory of Heaven and "dressed in clean, shining linen" (15:6), implying holiness. While they serve God faithfully, they themselves are not to be worshiped (19:10; 22:9).

Of note is that John's frequent use of "another" when referencing angels is through the word *allos* and never *heteros* (which would indicate "another of a different kind"). Though the "mighty angel" of Chapter 10 certainly stands in the authority of Jesus, he could not be said to be Jesus since he is "another [*allos*] mighty angel," that is, another of the same kind as the others. Though "angel" (*aggelos*) may also simply indicate a "messenger," the term is never used in Scripture to describe the Son of God. Finally, it is likely that "the angels of the seven churches" (1:20) are human messengers.

The Role and Activities of God's Holy Angels

1:1—"He made it known by sending his angel to his servant John"

4:8—"Day and night they never stop saying: 'Holy, holy, holy is the Lord God Almighty,' who was, and is, and is to come" (also 4:6, 7)

4:9—"Whenever the living creatures give glory, honor and thanks to him who sits on the throne"

5:2—"And I saw a mighty angel proclaiming in a loud voice, 'Who is worthy to break the seals and open the scroll?'"

5:6—"encircled by the four living creatures"

5:8—"the four living creatures and the twenty-four elders fell down before the Lamb" (also 7:11)

5:11a—"Then I looked and heard the voice of many angels" (also 4:8; 5:2)

5:11b—"They encircled the throne and the living creatures and the elders" (also 7:11)

5:14—"The four living creatures said, 'Amen'"

6:1—"Then I heard one of the four living creatures say in a voice like thunder, 'Come!'" (also 6:3, 5, 7)

6:6—"Then I heard what sounded like a voice among the four living creatures"

7:1a—"After this I saw four angels standing at the four corners of the earth"

7:1b—"holding back the four winds of the earth to prevent any wind from blowing on the land or on the sea or on any tree"

7:2a—"Then I saw another angel coming up from the east, having the seal of the living God"

7:2b—"He called out in a loud voice to the four angels who had been given power to harm the land and the sea"

7:3—"until we put a seal on the foreheads of the servants of our God"

8:2—"And I saw the seven angels who stand before God, and seven trumpets were given to them" (also 8:6-8, 10, 12; 9:1, 13; 11:15)

8:3a—"Another angel, who had a golden censer, came and stood at the altar"

8:3b—"He was given much incense to offer, with the prayers of all God's people, on the golden altar in front of the throne" (also 8:4)

8:5—"Then the angel took the censer, filled it with fire from the altar, and hurled it on the earth"

8:7—"The first angel sounded his trumpet, and there came hail and fire mixed with blood, and it was hurled down on the earth"

8:8—"The second angel sounded his trumpet, and something like a huge mountain, all ablaze, was thrown into the sea"

8:10—"The third angel sounded his trumpet, and a great star, blazing like a torch, fell from the sky on a third of the rivers and on the springs of water"

8:12—"The fourth angel sounded his trumpet, and a third of the sun was struck, a third of the moon, and a third of the stars, so that a third of them turned dark"

8:13—"Woe! Woe! Woe to the inhabitants of the earth, because of the trumpet blasts about to be sounded by the other three angels!"

9:1a—"The fifth angel sounded his trumpet, and I saw a star that had fallen from the sky to the earth"

9:1b—"The star was given the key to the shaft of the Abyss"

9:13—"The sixth angel sounded his trumpet, and I heard a voice coming from the four horns of the golden altar that is before God"

9:14—"It said to the sixth angel who had the trumpet, 'Release the four angels who are bound at the great river Euphrates.'"

9:15—"And the four angels who had been kept ready for this very hour and day and month and year were released to kill a third of mankind"

10:1—"Then I saw another mighty angel coming down from heaven [...]" (also 10:2, 3, 8; 18:1)

10:2a—"He was holding a little scroll, which lay open in his hand"

10:2b—"He planted his right foot on the sea and his left foot on the land"

10:3—"and he gave a loud shout like the roar of a lion. When he shouted, the voices of the seven thunders spoke"

10:5—"Then the angel I had seen standing on the sea and on the land raised his right hand to heaven"

10:6—"And he swore [...] and said, 'There will be no more delay!'"

10:7—"But in the days when the seventh angel is about to sound his trumpet, the mystery of God will be accomplished"

10:8—"Go, take the scroll that lies open in the hand of the angel who is standing on the sea and on the land"

10:9—"So I went to the angel and asked him to give me the little scroll"

10:10—"I took the little scroll from the angel's hand and ate it"

11:15—"The seventh angel sounded his trumpet, and there were loud voices in heaven"

12:7—"Michael and his angels fought against the dragon"

14:6—"Then I saw another angel flying in midair, and he had the eternal gospel to proclaim to those who live on the earth"

14:7—"He said in a loud voice, 'Fear God and give him glory'"

14:8—"A second angel followed and said, 'Fallen! Fallen is Babylon the Great'"

14:9—"A third angel followed them and said in a loud voice: 'If anyone worships the beast and its image and receives its mark on their forehead or on their hand [...]'"

14:10—"They will be tormented with burning sulfur in the presence of the holy angels"

14:15—"Then another angel came out of the temple and called in a loud voice"

14:18a—"Still another angel, who had charge of the fire, came from the altar and called in a loud voice to him who had the sharp sickle"

14:18b—"Take your sharp sickle and gather the clusters of grapes from the earth's vine, because its grapes are ripe"

14:19—"The angel swung his sickle on the earth, gathered its grapes and threw them into the great winepress of God's wrath"

15:6—"Out of the temple came the seven angels with the seven plagues" (also 15:1, 7)

15:7—"Then one of the four living creatures gave to the seven angels seven golden bowls"

16:1—"saying to the seven angels, 'Go, pour out the seven bowls of God's wrath'" (also 16:2-4, 8, 10, 12, 17)

16:2—"The first angel went and poured out his bowl on the land"

16:3—"The second angel poured out his bowl on the sea"

16:4—"The third angel poured out his bowl on the rivers and springs of water, and they became blood"

16:5—"Then I heard the angel in charge of the waters say"

16:8—"The fourth angel poured out his bowl on the sun"

16:10—"The fifth angel poured out his bowl on the throne of the beast"

16:12—"The sixth angel poured out his bowl on the great river Euphrates"

16:17—"The seventh angel poured out his bowl into the air"

17:1—"One of the seven angels who had the seven bowls came and said to me, 'Come, I will show you'" (also 21:9)

17:3—"Then the angel carried me away in the Spirit"

17:7—"Then the angel said to me: "Why are you astonished?" (also 17:15)

18:1—"He had great authority, and the earth was illuminated by his splendor"

18:2—"With a mighty voice he shouted"

18:21—"Then a mighty angel picked up a boulder the size of a large millstone and threw it into the sea"

19:9—"Then the angel said to me, 'Write this […]'"

19:10—"I am a fellow servant with you" (also 22:8, 9)

19:14—"The armies of heaven were following him" (also 19:19)

19:17—"And I saw an angel standing in the sun, who cried in a loud voice"

20:1—"And I saw an angel coming down out of heaven, having the key to the Abyss and holding in his hand a great chain"

20:3a—"He threw him into the Abyss, and locked and sealed it over him"

21:3b—"And I heard a loud voice from the throne saying, 'Look!'"

21:12—"and with twelve angels at the gates"

21:15—"The angel who talked with me had a measuring rod of gold"

21:17—"The angel measured the wall using human measurement"

22:6—"The angel said to me, 'These words are trustworthy and true […]'"

22:6—"The Lord, the God who inspires the prophets, sent his angel"

22:10—"Then he told me, 'Do not seal up the words of the prophecy of this scroll'"

22:16—"I, Jesus, have sent my angel to give you this testimony for the churches"

Summary Statement: Positioned around God's throne are "four living creatures" (perhaps "cherubim" angels; cf. Ezekiel 10:20), which bring ceaseless adoration. By their description, they may represent all of creation before God. Encircling these "living creatures" and the throne are a great number of less-descript angels who also lift their voices and bow in worship. Angels, too, are positioned at the twelve gates of the New Jerusalem. As messengers, angels also bring loud, authoritative proclamation and warning in Heaven and in earth of God's coming wrath, of the destruction of the world's rebellious system, and of the final harvest and damnation of the wicked. At one point, John sees an angel engaging the prayers of God's people in bringing about this judgment (8:3-5). Yet, John also sees an angel engaged in proclaiming the Gospel in the earth (14:6). The angels of God communicate and cooperate with each other in their ministry to God and man, including to John personally and to Christ's Church.

From the first verse to the last chapter, John speaks of angels as servants under assignment, standing in God's absolute authority. Some powerful angels are sent from the presence of the

Father and Son directly into the earth to administer God's wrath against the ungodly, while also sealing God's people from the effects of judgment. Seven other angels standing before God are assigned to sound seven "trumpets" of judgment (8:6). With the blast of each trumpet, horrific events will take place in the physical earth and skies above. In one instance alone, four angels are released to bring death to one third of humanity (9:15). Finally, seven additional angels are assigned to complete God's wrath in the earth through the seven last and most intense plagues, which are poured out as "bowls" filled with judgment into every dimension of the physical earth (16:1).

John also sees that angels are directly engaged in spiritual warfare. As an archangel, Michael leads holy angels in battle against the Dragon, Satan. The army which John later sees coming down from Heaven (19:14, 19) must include God's angels when compared with 2 Thessalonians 1:7. An angel from God is also given authority to bind Satan in the Abyss, and the wicked are seen as suffering eternal judgment in the presence of God's holy angels.

The Names, Essence, Attributes, Appearance, Role, and Activities of Satan (Satanology)

2:9—"but are a synagogue of Satan" (also 3:9)

2:13a—"I know where you live—where Satan has his throne"

2:13b—"who was put to death in your city—where Satan lives"

2:24—"and have not learned Satan's so-called deep secrets"

9:11—"They had as king over them the angel of the Abyss, whose name in Hebrew is Abaddon and in Greek is Apollyon (that is, Destroyer)"

12:3—"Then another sign appeared in heaven: an enormous red dragon with seven heads and ten horns and seven crowns on its heads" (also 12:4, 7, 9, 16, 17; 13:1, 2, 4, 11; 16:13; 20:2)

12:4a—"Its tail swept a third of the stars out of the sky and flung them to the earth"

12:4b—"The dragon stood in front of the woman who was about to give birth, so that it might devour her child the moment he was born" (also 12:13)

12:7—"Michael and his angels fought against the dragon, and the dragon and his angels fought back"

12:8—"But he was not strong enough"

12:9a—"The great dragon was hurled down—that ancient serpent called the devil, or Satan, who leads the whole world astray" (also 12:3)

12:9b—"He was hurled to the earth, and his angels with him" (also 12:7)

12:10—"For the accuser of our brothers and sisters, who accuses them before our God day and night"

12:12a—"But woe to the earth and the sea, because the devil has gone down to you!" (also 12:9)

12:12b—"He is filled with fury, because he knows that his time is short"

12:13—"When the dragon saw that he had been hurled to the earth, he pursued the woman who had given birth to the male child" (also 12:4, 17)

12:14—"out of the serpent's reach" (also 12:15)

12:15—"Then from his mouth the serpent spewed water like a river, to overtake the woman and sweep her away with the torrent" (also 12:16)

12:16—"swallowing the river that the dragon had spewed out of his mouth"

12:17—"Then the dragon was enraged at the woman and went off to wage war against the rest of her offspring" (also 12:4, 13)

13:1—"The dragon stood on the shore of the sea" (also 12:3)

13:2—"The dragon gave the beast his power and his throne and great authority"

13:4—"People worshiped the dragon because he had given authority to the beast"

13:6—"It opened its mouth to blaspheme God, and to slander his name and his dwelling place and those who live in heaven"

13:7—"It was given power to wage war against God's holy people and to conquer them"

13:11—"It had two horns like a lamb, but it spoke like a dragon" (also 12:3; 13:1)

16:10—"the throne of the beast, and its kingdom was plunged into darkness"

16:13—"they came out of the mouth of the dragon" (also 12:3; 13:1)

20:2—"He seized the dragon, that ancient serpent, who is the devil, or Satan, and bound him for a thousand years" (also 12:3; 13:1)

20:3a—"to keep him from deceiving the nations anymore until the thousand years were ended" (also 20:8)

20:3b—"After that, he must be set free for a short time"

20:7—"When the thousand years are over, Satan will be released from his prison" (also 20:3)

20:8—"and will go out to deceive the nations in the four corners of the earth—Gog and Magog—and to gather them for battle" (also 20:3, 10)

20:10a—"And the devil, who deceived them, was thrown into the lake of burning sulfur" (also 19:20)

20:10b—"They will be tormented day and night for ever and ever"

Summary Statement: The names and descriptions of Satan are numerous in the Revelation, including: "the angel of the Abyss," "Abaddon," "Apollyon," "Destroyer," "the great dragon," "the ancient serpent," "the devil," "Satan," and "the accuser." Without question he is identified as a living, personal, and very active created angel (9:11). In contrast to the holy angels led by Michael, Satan is seen ruling and directing fallen angels in his nefarious activity, which includes blaspheming and slandering God, Heaven, and those who dwell in Heaven.

From "heaven" (12:3; which can only be "the heavenlies" or "high places" of Ephesians 6:12), Satan directs his activities in the earth (cf. Eph. 2:2, "the prince of the power of the air"). He deceives the nations and "leads the whole world astray" in rebellion against God (Rev. 12:9). As the accuser, he is relentless in his lies and slander not only against God, but against God's people. He also opposes, hates, and persecutes both Israel—"the woman" (see under Israelology), especially in her role of bringing forth "her child" Jesus (12:4, 13)—and the Church (13:7). As an evil angelic being, he is also associated with false religious practice, in part through "so-called deep secrets" (2:24). Satan also receives false worship (13:4).

At a time, which appears to align with the midway point of the Tribulation on earth, Satan suffers defeat at the hands of Michael and his angels. He and his angels are cast to the earth initiating a time of Satan's increased, furious activity in the earth. A clear parallel and connection is made with the coming "beast" of Chapter 13 through his appearance with "seven heads and ten horns and seven crowns on its heads" (12:3; cf. 13:1; 17:3, 7, 9). The dragon then directs and empowers the beast (13:2, 4) and the false prophet (13:11). Though Satan is relentless in his attacks, he is not ultimately successful. He loses the battle in the heavens against Michael and his angels, he fails to destroy Israel and the Church, and, at the end of the Tribulation and following Christ's glorious revelation, Satan will be "bound for a thousand years" and later freed "for a short time" (20:3). Finally, he is delivered into eternal damnation in the "lake of burning sulfur" (20:10).

▶ See also under Eschatology: Spiritual Warfare Led by Satan in the Last Days and His Final Demise and Judgment

▶ See also under Eschatology: The Final Judgment of Satan, the Antichrist, the False Prophet, and the Babylon World System

The Essence, Attributes, Appearance, Role, Activities, and Judgment of Unholy, Fallen Angels (Demonology)

12:4—"Its tail swept a third of the stars out of the sky and flung them to the earth"

12:7—"and the dragon and his angels fought back"

12:8—"But he was not strong enough, and they lost their place in heaven"

12:9—"He was hurled to the earth, and his angels with him"

16:13—"Then I saw three impure spirits that looked like frogs"

16:14a—"They are demonic spirits that perform signs"

16:14b—"and they go out to the kings of the whole world, to gather them for the battle"

16:16—"Then they gathered the kings together"

18:2—"She has become a dwelling for demons and a haunt for every impure spirit"

Summary Statement: Limited reference to fallen angels is made primarily in Revelation 12. It is likely that the ancient rebellion of Satan, "the dragon," and his eviction from Heaven (cf. Isa. 14:12-15 and Ezek. 28:15-16) is described in Revelation 12:4, "Its tail swept a third of the stars out of the sky and flung them to the earth." These unholy, fallen angels belong to Satan, who also directs their evil activities, which includes the gathering of world rulers against the Kingdom of God. However, like Satan, they are not ultimately victorious, for they too are cast out of "heaven" and they too ultimately come to the same eternal judgment (20:10). What is strongly implied in the New Testament—that fallen angels are the same as demons—can only be assumed in the Revelation. What is clear is that these spirit beings are "impure" (16:13, 14; 18:2).

Anthropology—The Study of Humanity

The Creation of Humanity, of the World, and of the Earth as Our Habitation

3:10—"on the whole world to test the inhabitants of the earth" (also 6:10; 8:13; 11:10; 13:8, 12, 14; 16:18; 17:2, 8)

4:11—"for you created all things, and by your will they were created and have their being"
5:3—"But no one in heaven or on earth or under the earth" (also 5:13)

7:9—"a great multitude that no one could count, from every nation, tribe, people and language, standing before the throne and before the Lamb" (also 14:6)

10:6—"who created the heavens and all that is in them, the earth and all that is in it, and the sea and all that is in it"

11:9—"from every people, tribe, language and nation" (also 14:6)

11:15—"The kingdom of the world" (also 16:10; 17:12)

11:18—"The nations were angry" (also 18:23; 19:15; 20:3, 8)

14:7—"Worship him who made the heavens, the earth, the sea and the springs of water"

16:12—"the kings from the East" (also 16:16)

17:8—"from the creation of the world"

20:8—"the nations in the four corners of the earth—Gog and Magog" (also 7:1; 20:9)

20:11—"The earth and the heavens fled from his presence, and there was no place for them"

21:1—"for the first heaven and the first earth had passed away, and there was no longer any sea"

Summary Statement: The existence of humanity is clearly the work of God's creative will and power; through Him alone we have our being. God has also "created all things" (4:11; 14:7), including the world and the earth. Nine times humans are referred to as "the inhabitants of the earth" (16:18). It is clear that the earth (*gē*) itself has great significance in God's end-time strategy, being referenced 67 times. In fulfillment of God's plan, the "first heaven and earth" will "pass away" (or "perish") and be replaced by "a new heaven and new earth" (21:1). While on the earth humanity is identified and distinguished according to "nation, tribe, language and people" (11:9; 14:6). (Of note, John also uses these four descriptives of God's people seen gathered before His throne [7:9].) Human life then is described as being found "in heaven or on earth or under the earth [the abode of the dead]" (5:3, 13). A stark contrast is seen between human civilization on earth—organized as nations and cities and led by unrighteous "kings"—and the Heavenly city, the New Jerusalem, which has only one glorious King.

The Essence, Attributes, and Appearance of Human Beings

1:1—"to show his servants [...] to his servant John" (also 10:7; 15:3; 19:10; 22:9)

1:9—"your brother and companion in the suffering and kingdom and patient endurance"

1:17—"When I saw him, I fell at his feet as though dead"

3:17—"You say, 'I am rich; I have acquired wealth and do not need a thing.' But you do not realize that you are wretched, pitiful, poor, blind and naked"

4:7—"The first living creature [...] the third had a face like a man"

6:9—"I saw under the altar the souls of those who had been slain" (also 12:11; 20:4)

6:15—"Then the kings of the earth, the princes, the generals, the rich, the mighty, and everyone else, both slave and free" (also 17:2, 18; 18:3, 9; 19:18, 19)

7:9—"a great multitude that no one could count, from every nation, tribe, people and language"

9:7—"The locusts [...] On their heads they wore something like crowns of gold, and their faces resembled human faces" (also 9:8)

9:8—"Their hair was like women's hair" (also 9:7)

10:11—"[...] many peoples, nations, languages and kings" (also 17:15)

13:1a—"And I saw a beast coming out of the sea" (also 11:7; 13:2-5, 8, 12, 14, 17, 18; 14:9, 11; 15:2; 16:2, 10, 13; 17:3, 7, 8, 11-13, 16, 17, 19; 19:19, 20; 20:4, 10)

13:1b—"It had ten horns and seven heads, with ten crowns on its horns, and on each head a blasphemous name"

13:11—"Then I saw a second beast, coming out of the earth. It had two horns like a lamb, but it spoke like a dragon" (also 13:12, 14, 15; 16:13; 19:20; 20:10)

13:18—"Let the person who has insight calculate the number of the beast, for it is the number of a man. That number is 666"

17:1—"the great prostitute, who sits by many waters'" (also 17:15, 16; 19:2)

17:9—"This calls for a mind with wisdom"

17:10—"They are also seven kings. Five have fallen, one is, the other has not yet come; but when he does come, he must remain for only a little while"

17:11—"The beast who once was, and now is not, is an eighth king" (also 19:19)

17:12—"The ten horns you saw are ten kings who have not yet received a kingdom, but who for one hour will receive authority as kings along with the beast" (also 13:1)

17:15—"The waters you saw, where the prostitute sits, are peoples, multitudes, nations and languages"

17:18—"the great city that rules over the kings of the earth" (also 18:10)

18:10—"'Woe! Woe to you, great city, you mighty city of Babylon! [...]'" (also 14:8; 17:18; 18:18, 19)

18:13—"and human beings sold as slaves"

18:23—"By your magic spell all the nations were led astray" (also 11:18; 19:15; 20:3, 8)

19:18—"so that you may eat the flesh of kings, generals, and the mighty, of horses and their riders, and the flesh of all people, free and slave, great and small" (also 6:15; 17:2, 18; 18:3, 9; 19:19)

19:19—"Then I saw the beast and the kings of the earth and their armies"

20:4a—"And I saw the souls of those who had been beheaded"

20:4b—"They came to life" (also 11:11)

20:8—"In number they are like the sand on the seashore"

20:12—"And I saw the dead, great and small"

21:8—"But the cowardly, the unbelieving, the vile, the murderers, the sexually immoral, those who practice magic arts, the idolaters and all liars"

21:17—"The angel measured the wall using human measurement"

Summary Statement: Human life consists of both a physical nature—which after death will be resurrected—and an immaterial nature contained in the words *psuchē* (12:11; 16:3; 18:13; 20:4; translated "soul," "life," and "being") and *zōē* (translated "life"). God's view of humanity is determined by the status of our relationship with Him, regardless of our station in life. The righteous, known here as "companions," "brothers," and "servants," are blessed and rewarded by God for eternity. On the contrary, the wicked from every stratum of society are described with such terms as "cowardly," "vile," "sexually immoral," "idolatrous," and "lying" (21:8). Even those in the visible church, who remain self-deceived by sin, are described as "wretched, pitiful, poor, blind and naked" (3:17).

Interestingly, the prevalence of both the rebellious and the righteous out of the earth are described in vast terms. Wickedness and opposition has spread widely throughout the earth, globally comprising "the kingdom of the world" (also 16:10; 17:12). Yet God's people are also found in great numbers throughout the nations. While the wicked are described, "like the sand on the seashore" (20:8), the righteous before the Throne of God appear as "a great multitude that no one could count" (7:9).

Anthropomorphisms are used to describe greatly opposing entities, such as: one of the "four living creatures" (4:7); the "locusts" from the Abyss (9:2-8); and, "the great prostitute" (17:1). The symbolic, even mysterious application of numbers (common to Revelation) is used to describe the beast, which has "the number of a man. That number is 666" (13:18).

The Activities of Human Beings, Including Their Continuous Wickedness

1:9—"your brother and companion in the suffering and kingdom and patient endurance"

1:17—"When I saw him, I fell at his feet as though dead" (also 1:12)

2:2—"I know your deeds, your hard work and your perseverance" (also 2:3, 19; 14:13)

2:5—"Consider how far you have fallen!"

2:10—"and you will suffer persecution for ten days. Be faithful, even to the point of death"

2:14—"There are some among you who hold to the teaching of Balaam, who taught Balak to entice the Israelites to sin so that they ate food sacrificed to idols and committed sexual immorality" (also 2:20)

2:15—"Likewise, you also have those who hold to the teaching of the Nicolaitans" (also 2:6)

2:20—"You tolerate that woman Jezebel [...] By her teaching she misleads my servants into sexual immorality and the eating of food sacrificed to idols" (also 2:14)

3:1—"you have a reputation of being alive, but you are dead"

3:4—"They will walk with me, dressed in white, for they are worthy" (also 3:5; 7:9, 14; 22:14)

3:8—"yet you have kept my word and have not denied my name"

3:16—"So, because you are lukewarm—neither hot nor cold—I am about to spit you out of my mouth" (also 3:15)

3:17—"You say, 'I am rich; I have acquired wealth and do not need a thing.' But you do not realize that you are wretched, pitiful, poor, blind and naked"

5:4—"I wept and wept because no one was found who was worthy to open the scroll or look inside"

5:10—"You have made them to be a kingdom and priests to serve our God, and they will reign on the earth" (1:6; 20:4, 6)

6:2—"Its rider held a bow, and he was given a crown, and he rode out as a conqueror bent on conquest"

6:4—"Its rider was given power to take peace from the earth and to make people kill each other"

6:15—"Then the kings of the earth, the princes, the generals, the rich, the mighty, and everyone else, both slave and free, hid in caves and among the rocks of the mountains" (also 6:16)

7:9a—"a great multitude that no one could count, from every nation, tribe, people and language, standing before the throne and before the Lamb" (also 7:15; 15:4)

7:9b—"They were wearing white robes and were holding palm branches in their hands" (also 3:4; 7:14; 22:14)

7:10—"And they cried out in a loud voice: 'Salvation belongs to our God, [...]'" (also 19:6)

9:20a—"The rest of mankind who were not killed by these plagues still did not repent of the work of their hands" (also 9:21; 16:9, 11)

9:20b—"they did not stop worshiping demons, and idols of gold, silver, bronze, stone and wood—idols that cannot see or hear or walk" (also 21:8)

9:21—"Nor did they repent of their murders, their magic arts, their sexual immorality or their thefts" (also 16:9)

10:11—"You must prophesy again about many peoples, nations, languages and kings"

11:5—"If anyone tries to harm them, fire comes from their mouths and devours their enemies"

11:6—"They have power to shut up the heavens so that it will not rain [...] and they have power to turn the waters into blood and to strike the earth with every kind of plague as often as they want"

11:9—"from every people, tribe, language and nation will gaze on their bodies and refuse them burial"

11:10—"The inhabitants of the earth will gloat over them and will celebrate by sending each other gifts"

11:18—"and for destroying those who destroy the earth"

12:9—"Satan, who leads the whole world astray"

13:3—"The whole world was filled with wonder and followed the beast" (also 13:4, 7, 8, 12, 14)

13:4—"People worshiped the dragon because he had given authority to the beast, and they also worshiped the beast [...]" (also 13:3, 8, 12; 14:9, 11)

13:11—"Then I saw a second beast [...] but it spoke like a dragon" (also 13:12, 14, 15; 16:13)

13:14—"It ordered them to set up an image in honor of the beast [...]" (also 14:9, 11)

13:16—"It also forced all people, great and small, rich and poor, free and slave, to receive a mark on their right hands or on their foreheads" (also 13:17; 14:9, 11; 16:2)

14:3—"And they sang a new song before the throne and before the four living creatures and the elders"

14:4a—"These are those who did not defile themselves with women, for they remained virgins"

14:4b—"They follow the Lamb wherever he goes"

14:5—"No lie was found in their mouths; they are blameless"

14:8—"'Babylon the Great,' which made all the nations drink the maddening wine of her adulteries" (also 17:2; 18:3, 9, 10; 19:2)

14:11—"There will be no rest day or night for those who worship the beast and its image, or for anyone who receives the mark of its name" (also 13:16, 17; 16:2)

14:12—"the people of God who keep his commands and remain faithful to Jesus"

15:2—"those who had been victorious over the beast [...] They held harps given them by God"

15:3—"and sang the song of God's servant Moses and of the Lamb"

15:4—"All nations will come and worship before you" (also 7:9)

16:6—"for they have shed the blood of your holy people and your prophets" (also 17:6; 18:24)

16:9—"and they cursed the name of God [...] but they refused to repent and glorify him" (also 9:21; 16:11, 21)

17:2a—"With her the kings of the earth committed adultery" (also 18:3, 9, 10)

17:2b—"and the inhabitants of the earth were intoxicated with the wine of her adulteries" (also 14:8; 18:3; 19:2)

17:12—"The ten horns you saw are ten kings who have not yet received a kingdom, but who for one hour will receive authority as kings along with the beast" (also 13:1; 17:13)

17:14—"They will wage war against the Lamb, but the Lamb will triumph over them" (also 19:19)

18:3—"the merchants of the earth grew rich from her excessive luxuries" (also 18:11, 15, 17, 19, 23)

18:10—"Terrified at her torment, they will stand far off and cry: 'Woe! Woe to you, great city, you mighty city of Babylon!'" (also 18:11, 15, 16, 18, 19)

18:13—"and human beings sold as slaves"

18:17—"Every sea captain, and all who travel by ship, the sailors, and all who earn their living from the sea, will stand far off" (also 18:19)

18:22a—"The music of harpists and musicians, pipers and trumpeters"

18:22b—"No worker of any trade will ever be found in you again. The sound of a millstone will never be heard in you again"

18:23a—"The voice of bridegroom and bride will never be heard in you again"

18:23b—"By your magic spell all the nations were led astray" (also 11:18; 19:15; 20:3, 8)

18:24—"In her was found the blood of prophets and of God's holy people, of all who have been slaughtered on the earth"

19:19—"Then I saw the beast and the kings of the earth and their armies gathered together to wage war against the rider on the horse and his army" (also 17:14)

20:9—"They marched across the breadth of the earth" (also 20:8)

20:13—"and each person was judged according to what they had done"

21:8—"But the cowardly, the unbelieving, the vile, the murderers, the sexually immoral, those who practice magic arts, the idolaters and all liars" (also 17:2; 21:27; 22:15)

21:24—"The nations will walk by its light, and the kings of the earth will bring their splendor into it" (also 21:26; 22:14)

22:11a—"Let the one who does wrong continue to do wrong; let the vile person continue to be vile"

22:11b—"let the one who does right continue to do right; and let the holy person continue to be holy"

22:18—"If anyone adds anything to them" (also 22:19)

22:19—"And if anyone takes words away from this scroll of prophecy" (also 22:18)

Summary Statement: The activities of humanity are divided along lines of faith, obedience, and loyalty to God on one hand and unbelief, disobedience, and self-determination on the other. Believers are those who walk with God and reflect His holiness and righteousness, staying true and faithful to His name. These who "follow the Lamb" willingly endure suffering for His sake, even to the point of death. Their highest activity as "priests" (1:6; 5:10) unto God is to bring worship before His throne with a "new song" (14:3). The promise that "they will reign on the earth" (1:6; 5:10) is fulfilled in the thousand-year reign of Christ (20:4, 6). Nevertheless, the exposure and rebuke of sin—even in the visible church—comes early in Revelation, inclusive of "sexual immorality and the eating of food sacrificed to idols" (2:20) and self-deceptive, spiritual "lukewarmness" (3:15-17).

Outside the Church the pervasive wickedness of humanity throughout the earth and through every stratum of society is diverse, inclusive of sexual immorality, murder, human slavery, idolatry, greed, lying deceit, the worship of demons and witchcraft, blasphemy against the God of Heaven, and the persecution of God's people. Those who refuse to repent, encompassing "all the nations" (18:23), God calls "vile" and "impure."

Organized wickedness and rebellion will specifically be driven under the leadership of a blasphemous and dictatorial "beast," a deceptive "second beast," and a ubiquitous "great prostitute." Another looming image of humanity's pride, self-confidence, and distain for righteousness is found in the great city of "Babylon." Each of these evil entities appears to have a localized or personalized fulfillment as well as a global and corporate expression and significance. Together they control and direct human self-will politically, economically, and spiritually.

▶ See also under Ecclesiology: The Character, Activity, and Experience of the True Church—the Redeemed of All Ages

▶ See also under Hamartiology: Humanity's Personal Sin and Rebellion

▶ See also under Hamartiology: Humanity's Corporate Sin and Rebellion—The Rise and Fall of the Three-Fold "Babylon" World System

Spiritual and Physical Death, the Consequence of Unrepentant Wickedness

2:11—"The one who is victorious will not be hurt at all by the second death" (also 20:6, 14; 21:8)

2:23—"And I will kill her children with death"

6:4—"Its rider was given power to take peace from the earth and to make people kill each other. To him was given a large sword."

6:8a—"I looked, and there before me was a pale horse! Its rider was named Death, and Hades was following close behind him"

6:8b—"They were given power over a fourth of the earth to kill by sword, famine and plague, and by the wild beasts of the earth"

6:17—"For the great day of their wrath has come, and who can withstand it?"

9:4—"They were told not to harm the grass of the earth or any plant or tree, but only those people who did not have the seal of God on their foreheads"

9:6—"During those days people will seek death but will not find it; they will long to die, but death will elude them" (also 6:16)

9:15—"And the four angels [...] were released to kill a third of mankind" (also 9:18)

9:18—"A third of mankind was killed by the three plagues of fire, smoke and sulfur" (also 9:15, 20)

11:13—"Seven thousand people were killed in the earthquake"

14:11—"There will be no rest day or night for those who worship the beast and its image, or for anyone who receives the mark of its name" (also 13:16, 17; 16:2)

14:15—"the time to reap has come, for the harvest of the earth is ripe" (also 14:16, 18, 19)

14:20—"They were trampled in the winepress outside the city, and blood flowed out of the press, rising as high as the horses' bridles for a distance of 1,600 stadia"

16:2—"ugly, festering sores broke out on the people who had the mark of the beast and worshiped its image" (also 13:16, 17; 14:11)

16:19—"and the cities of the nations collapsed"

16:21—"From the sky huge hailstones, each weighing about a hundred pounds, fell on people"

17:14—"They will wage war against the Lamb, but the Lamb will triumph over them"

19:21—"The rest were killed [...] and all the birds gorged themselves on their flesh"

20:12—"And I saw the dead, great and small, standing before the throne"

20:13—"The sea gave up the dead that were in it, and death and Hades gave up the dead that were in them"

20:14—"Then death and Hades were thrown into the lake of fire. The lake of fire is the second death" (also 20:6; 21:8)

20:15—"Anyone whose name was not found written in the book of life was thrown into the lake of fire"

21:27—"Nothing impure will ever enter it, nor will anyone who does what is shameful or deceitful"

22:15—"Outside are the dogs, those who practice magic arts, the sexually immoral, the murderers, the idolaters and everyone who loves and practices falsehood" (also 17:2; 21:8)

Summary Statement: With the opening of the scroll of God's final judgments, widespread death at the hands of humans, animals, and natural disasters is released upon the wicked. "Death" and "Hades" are personified and empowered to kill "over a fourth of the earth" (6:8). Later, "a third of mankind" (of those still alive) is killed "by the three plagues of fire, smoke and sulfur" (9:15, 18). The outpouring of God's wrath in the earth upon those who remain in unrepentant wickedness will bring suffering and horrors such that human beings "will long to die, but death will elude them" (9:6; cf. 6:16). Yet, physical death will be followed by spiritual death for those "who worship the beast and its image" (14:11), aligning with the Dragon who wages war against the Lamb. These will stand before the "great white throne and him who was seated on it," where they will be "judged according to what they had done" (20:11, 13). Absent of a right relationship with God, they will be "thrown into the lake of fire" (20:15), which is the "second death" (20:6, 14; 21:8).

> ▶ See also under Eschatology: The Tribulation—The Wrath of God in Judgment Upon the Unrepentant
> ▶ See also under Eschatology: The Resurrection and Final Judgment of Unrepentant Humanity, Including the Lake of Fire

The Effect of Humanity's Sin Upon the Natural/Physical Earth and World

6:6—"Two pounds of wheat for a day's wages, and six pounds of barley for a day's wages, and do not damage the oil and the wine!"

6:8—"They were given power over a fourth of the earth to kill by sword, famine and plague, and by the wild beasts of the earth" (also 11:6)

6:12—"There was a great earthquake. The sun turned black like sackcloth made of goat hair, the whole moon turned blood red" (also 8:12; 16:18)

6:13—"and the stars in the sky fell to earth, as figs drop from a fig tree when shaken by a strong wind" (also 8:10)

6:14—"The heavens receded like a scroll being rolled up, and every mountain and island was removed from its place" (also 16:20; 20:11)

8:7a—"there came hail and fire mixed with blood, and it was hurled down on the earth" (also 11:19)

8:7b—"A third of the earth was burned up, a third of the trees were burned up, and all the green grass was burned up" (also 9:18, 20)

8:8a—"and something like a huge mountain, all ablaze, was thrown into the sea"

8:8b—"A third of the sea turned into blood" (also 11:6; 16:3)

8:9—"a third of the living creatures in the sea died"

8:10—"and a great star, blazing like a torch, fell from the sky on a third of the rivers and on the springs of water" (also 6:13; 9:1)

8:11—"the name of the star is Wormwood. A third of the waters turned bitter"

8:12a—"a third of the sun was struck, a third of the moon, and a third of the stars, so that a third of them turned dark" (also 6:12; 9:2)

8:12b—"A third of the day was without light, and also a third of the night"

9:1—"and I saw a star that had fallen from the sky to the earth" (also 6:13; 8:10)

9:2a—"When he opened the Abyss, smoke rose from it like the smoke from a gigantic furnace"

9:2b—"The sun and sky were darkened by the smoke from the Abyss" (also 6:12; 8:12)

9:3—"And out of the smoke locusts came down on the earth and were given power like that of scorpions of the earth"

9:4—"They were told not to harm the grass of the earth or any plant or tree"

9:18—"A third of mankind was killed by the three plagues of fire, smoke and sulfur" (also 8:7; 9:20; 16:8)

10:3—"When he shouted, the voices of the seven thunders spoke" (also 10:4)

11:6a—"They have power to shut up the heavens so that it will not rain"

11:6b—"and they have power to turn the waters into blood and to strike the earth with every kind of plague" (also 6:8; 8:8)

11:13—"At that very hour there was a severe earthquake and a tenth of the city collapsed. Seven thousand people were killed in the earthquake" (also 16:18)

11:18—"and for destroying those who destroy the earth"

11:19—"And there came flashes of lightning, rumblings, peals of thunder, an earthquake and a severe hailstorm" (also 8:7)

12:12—"But woe to the earth and the sea, because the devil has gone down to you!"

12:16—"But the earth helped the woman by opening its mouth and swallowing the river that the dragon had spewed out of his mouth"

16:1—"Go, pour out the seven bowls of God's wrath on the earth"

16:3—"The second angel poured out his bowl on the sea, and it turned into blood like that of a dead person, and every living thing in the sea died" (also 8:8)

16:4—"The third angel poured out his bowl on the rivers and springs of water, and they became blood" (also 8:8)

16:8—"The fourth angel poured out his bowl on the sun, and the sun was allowed to scorch people with fire" (also 8:7; 9:18, 20)

16:9—"They were seared by the intense heat"

16:12—"the great river Euphrates, and its water was dried up"

16:18a—"Then there came flashes of lightning, rumblings, peals of thunder and a severe earthquake"

16:18b—"No earthquake like it has ever occurred since mankind has been on earth, so tremendous was the quake" (also 6:12)

16:19—"The great city split into three parts, and the cities of the nations collapsed"

16:20—"Every island fled away and the mountains could not be found" (also 6:14)

16:21—"From the sky huge hailstones, each weighing about a hundred pounds, fell on people"

18:21—"Then a mighty angel picked up a boulder the size of a large millstone and threw it into the sea"

20:11—"The earth and the heavens fled from his presence, and there was no place for them" (also 6:14)

21:1a—"Then I saw 'a new heaven and a new earth,' for the first heaven and the first earth had passed away"

21:1b—"and there was no longer any sea"

Summary Statement: During the Tribulation—as a direct result of humanity's unrepentant wickedness—global and universal devastation will take place in the earth and the heavens above. This physical destruction will range from interruption of rain and natural light to plagues, famine, and earthquakes to the removal of "every mountain and island [. . .] from its place" (6:14). Ultimate destruction will be sustained when "the stars in the sky [fall] fell to earth" (6:13) and "the heavens [recede] receded like a scroll being rolled up" (6:14).

Supernatural elements to these calamities are seen in such phenomena as "hail and fire mixed with blood" (8:7) and the opening of the Abyss (9:2), and in such statements as: "the voices of the seven thunders spoke" (10:3); "the earth helped the woman by opening its mouth and swallowing the river" (12:16); and, "woe to the earth and the sea, because the devil has gone down to you!" (12:12). It is clear that God is sovereign over all of the events that are to take place within the Tribulation. In some cases, such as with the calamities generally described in the opening of the first four "seals" (Rev. 6:1-8), destruction may come primarily for more natural reasons, i.e., as the direct consequences and aftermath of humanity's depraved actions. But even here, such ruin comes within the sovereign will of God in bringing judgment upon the wickedness of humanity. More certain are that all of the events of the "trumpet" and "bowl" judgments come at the direct decree of God. (This is not to be confused with passages that clearly foretell the particular death and mayhem, which will come at the hands of Satan and his agents, e.g., Rev. 13:15.) Ultimately, the present earth and heavens will completely pass away and be replaced by "a new heaven and a new earth" (21:1).

▶ See also under Eschatology: The Tribulation—The Wrath of God in Judgment Upon the Unrepentant

God's Ultimate Will for Redeemed Humanity Expressed

1:5—"To him who loves us and has freed us from our sins by his blood" (also 5:9)

1:6—"and has made us to be a kingdom and priests to serve his God and Father (also 5:10; 20:6)

2:7—"To the one who is victorious, I will give the right to eat from the tree of life, which is in the paradise of God" (also 22:14)

2:11—"The one who is victorious will not be hurt at all by the second death" (also 20:6)

2:26—"I will give authority over the nations" (also 2:27; 20:6; 22:5)

3:5a—"The one who is victorious will, like them, be dressed in white" (also 7:9; 19:8)

3:5b—"I will never blot out the name of that person from the book of life, but will acknowledge that name before my Father and his angels" (also 3:12)

3:12—"I will write on them the name of my God and the name of the city of my God, the new Jerusalem" (also 14:1; 22:4)

3:21—"I will give the right to sit with me on my throne"

5:10—"and they will reign on the earth" (also 20:4, 6; 22:5)

7:9—"After this I looked, and there before me was a great multitude that no one could count, from every nation, tribe, people and language" (also 5:9; 15:4)

7:16—"Never again will they hunger; never again will they thirst"

7:17a—"For the Lamb at the center of the throne will be their shepherd"

7:17b—"he will lead them to springs of living water" (also 21:6; 22:17)

14:3—"And they sang a new song before the throne [...]" (also 5:9)

14:13—"Blessed are the dead who die in the Lord from now on"

21:3a—"Look! God's dwelling place is now among the people, and he will dwell with them" (also 7:15)

21:3b—"They will be his people, and God himself will be with them and be their God" (21:7; 22:4)

21:4—"'He will wipe every tear from their eyes. There will be no more death' or mourning or crying or pain, for the old order of things has passed away" (also 7:17)

21:24—"The nations will walk by its light, and the kings of the earth will bring their splendor into it" (also 21:26; 22:5, 14)

22:3—"No longer will there be any curse"

22:21—"The grace of the Lord Jesus be with God's people. Amen"

Summary Statement: Though the majority of the human population will remain rebellious and unrepentant until the time of Christ's Revelation, God remains eternally loving and gracious to those who follow Him. Through the sacrificial and redeeming work of Jesus, God has separated to Himself a remnant, which will worship and serve Him as "a kingdom and priests" (1:6) [...] "from every nation, tribe, people and language" (7:9). Ultimately, "They will be his people, and God Himself will be with them and be their God" (21:3). Those who follow the Lamb are given full acceptance and identity in Him; great victory and great authority with

Him; deliverance from the curse and the "second death"; and, a place of healing, protection, blessing, and provision before His throne for eternity.

- ▶ See also under Soteriology: The Blessings and Privileges of Redemption
- ▶ See also under Ecclesiology: God's Promises to the True Church—the Redeemed of All Ages
- ▶ See also under Eschatology: The Resurrection and Eternal Reward of the Righteous

Hamartiology—The Study of Sin

Humanity's Personal Sin and Rebellion

2:5—"Consider how far you have fallen!"

2:14—"There are some among you who hold to the teaching of Balaam, who taught Balak to entice the Israelites to sin so that they ate food sacrificed to idols and committed sexual immorality" (also 2:20)

2:15—"Likewise, you also have those who hold to the teaching of the Nicolaitans" (also 2:6)

3:1—"you have a reputation of being alive, but you are dead"

3:16—"So, because you are lukewarm—neither hot nor cold—I am about to spit you out of my mouth" (also 3:15)

3:17—"You say, 'I am rich; I have acquired wealth and do not need a thing.' But you do not realize that you are wretched, pitiful, poor, blind and naked" (also 16:15)

9:4—"but only those people who did not have the seal of God on their foreheads"

9:20a—"The rest of mankind who were not killed by these plagues still did not repent of the work of their hands" (also 9:21; 16:9, 11)

9:20b—"they did not stop worshiping demons, and idols of gold, silver, bronze, stone and wood—idols that cannot see or hear or walk"

9:21—"Nor did they repent of their murders, their magic arts, their sexual immorality or their thefts"

11:18—"and for destroying those who destroy the earth"

12:9—"Satan, who leads the whole world astray"

13:3—"The whole world was filled with wonder and followed the beast" (also 13:4, 7, 8, 12, 14)

13:16—"It also forced all people, great and small, rich and poor, free and slave, to receive a mark on their right hands or on their foreheads" (also 13:17; 14:11; 16:2)

13:17—"so that they could not buy or sell unless they had the mark, which is the name of the beast or the number of its name" (also 13:16; 14:11; 16:2)

14:8—"'Babylon the Great,' which made all the nations drink the maddening wine of her adulteries" (also 17:2; 18:3; 21:8; 22:15)

14:11—"There will be no rest day or night for those who worship the beast and its image, or for anyone who receives the mark of its name" (also 13:16, 17; 16:2)

16:9a—"they cursed the name of God" (also 16:11, 21)

16:9b—"they refused to repent and glorify him" (also 9:20, 21; 16:11)

16:11—"and cursed the God of heaven" (also 16:9, 21)

17:8—"The inhabitants of the earth whose names have not been written in the book of life"

17:14—"They will wage war against the Lamb, but the Lamb will triumph over them"

18:24—"In her was found the blood of prophets and of God's holy people, of all who have been slaughtered on the earth"

20:9—"They marched across the breadth of the earth" (also 20:8)

20:12—"The dead were judged according to what they had done" (also 20:13)

21:8—"But the cowardly, the unbelieving, the vile, the murderers, the sexually immoral, those who practice magic arts, the idolaters and all liars" (also 17:2; 21:27; 22:15)

21:27—"Nothing impure will ever enter it, nor will anyone who does what is shameful or deceitful"

22:11—"Let the one who does wrong continue to do wrong; let the vile person continue to be vile"

22:15—"Outside are the dogs, those who practice magic arts, the sexually immoral, the murderers, the idolaters and everyone who loves and practices falsehood" (also 17:2; 21:8)

22:18—"If anyone adds anything to them" (also 22:19)

22:19—"And if anyone takes words away from this scroll of prophecy" (also 22:18)

Summary Statement: A major portion of Revelation is given to the exposure and punishment of personal sin. Humanity's rebellion is widespread, seen in such phrases as, "the whole world" (13:3), "all the nations" (14:8), and "the inhabitants of the earth" (17:8). Identified as sinful in the sight of God is idolatry, sexual immorality, deceitfulness, lying, murder, the practice of magic arts, the cursing of God, and unbelief. Even amongst the visible church are those who hold to false teachings, which promote and practice sin. While sin issues from self-deception, God sees the true condition of the heart and calls it vile, impure, cowardly, and shameful. Those who live this way, God calls spiritually "dead" (3:1). Behind such widespread rebellion is "Satan, who leads the whole world astray" (12:9). Though subjected to the wrath of God during the Tribulation, humanity as a whole—apart from those numbered as God's people—will remain unrepentant.

▶ See also under Anthropology: The Activities of Human Beings, Including Their Continuous Wickedness

Humanity's Corporate Sin and Rebellion—The Rise and Fall of the Three-Fold "Babylon" World System

14:8—"'Fallen! Fallen is Babylon the Great,' which made all the nations drink the maddening wine of her adulteries" (also 16:19; 17:2, 4; 18:2, 3, 9; 19:2)

16:19—"God remembered Babylon the Great" (also 14:8; 17:6; 18:8; 19:2)

17:1—"I will show you the punishment of the great prostitute, who sits by many waters" (also 17:15)

17:2—"With her the kings of the earth committed adultery, and the inhabitants of the earth were intoxicated with the wine of her adulteries" (also 14:8; 17:4; 18:3, 9; 19:2)

17:3—"There I saw a woman sitting on a scarlet beast that was covered with blasphemous names and had seven heads and ten horns" (also 17:7, 9, 16)

17:4a—"The woman was dressed in purple and scarlet, and was glittering with gold, precious stones and pearls" (also 18:16)

17:4b—"She held a golden cup in her hand, filled with abominable things and the filth of her adulteries" (also 14:8; 17:2; 18:3, 9; 19:2)

17:5—"The name written on her forehead was a mystery: babylon the great the mother of prostitutes and of the abominations of the earth" (also 14:8; 16:19; 17:1, 7)

17:6—"I saw that the woman was drunk with the blood of God's holy people, the blood of those who bore testimony to Jesus" (also 6:10; 18:24; 19:2)

17:7—"the mystery of the woman and of the beast she rides" (also 17:3, 9, 16)

17:9—"The seven heads are seven hills on which the woman sits" (also 17:3, 7)

17:15—"The waters you saw, where the prostitute sits, are peoples, multitudes, nations and languages" (also 17:1)

17:16a—"The beast and the ten horns you saw will hate the prostitute" (also 17:3, 7)

17:16b—"They will bring her to ruin and leave her naked; they will eat her flesh and burn her with fire"

17:18—"The woman you saw is the great city that rules over the kings of the earth" (also 18:10)

18:2—"She has become a dwelling for demons and a haunt for every impure spirit, a haunt for every unclean bird, a haunt for every unclean and detestable animal"

18:3a—"The kings of the earth committed adultery with her" (also 14:8; 17:2, 4, 18; 19:2)

18:3b—"and the merchants of the earth grew rich from her excessive luxuries" (also 18:9, 11-15, 17, 19, 23)

18:4—"so that you will not share in her sins, so that you will not receive any of her plagues" (also 18:5, 8)

18:6—"Give back to her as she has given; pay her back double for what she has done. Pour her a double portion from her own cup" (also 18:7)

18:7a—"Give her as much torment and grief as the glory and luxury she gave herself" (also 17:4; 18:14)

18:7b—"In her heart she boasts, 'I sit enthroned as queen. I am not a widow; I will never mourn'"

18:8a—"Therefore in one day her plagues will overtake her: death, mourning and famine" (also 18:4)

18:8b—"She will be consumed by fire, for mighty is the Lord God who judges her" (also 18:9, 20)

18:9—"When the kings of the earth who committed adultery with her and shared her luxury see the smoke of her burning, they will weep and mourn over her" (also 14:8; 17:2, 4; 18:3, 7, 11, 15; 19:2)

18:10—"Terrified at her torment, they will stand far off and cry: 'Woe! Woe to you, great city, you mighty city of Babylon! In one hour your doom has come!'" (also 14:8; 16:19; 17:5; 18:9, 15, 16, 18, 19)

18:14—"They will say, 'The fruit you longed for is gone from you. All your luxury and splendor have vanished, never to be recovered'"

18:17—"In one hour such great wealth has been brought to ruin!" (also 18:10, 21-23)

18:18—"When they see the smoke of her burning, they will exclaim, 'Was there ever a city like this great city?'" (also 17:18; 18:8, 9, 10, 19; 19:3)

18:19—"'Woe! Woe to you, great city, where all who had ships on the sea became rich through her wealth! In one hour she has been brought to ruin!'" (also 18:3, 10, 17, 18)

18:20—"For God has judged her with the judgment she imposed on you" (also 14:8; 16:19; 17:6; 18:6, 7; 19:2)

18:21a—"Then a mighty angel picked up a boulder the size of a large millstone and threw it into the sea"

18:21b—"With such violence the great city of Babylon will be thrown down, never to be found again" (14:8; 16:19; 18:10, 17-19, 22, 23)

18:23—"Your merchants were the world's important people. By your magic spell all the nations were led astray" (also 18:3, 9, 11-15, 17, 19)

18:24—"In her was found the blood of prophets and of God's holy people, of all who have been slaughtered on the earth" (also 6:10; 17:6; 19:2)

19:2a—"He has condemned the great prostitute who corrupted the earth by her adulteries" (also 14:8; 17:2, 4; 18:3, 9)

19:2b—"He has avenged on her the blood of his servants" (also 16:6; 17:6; 18:20, 24)

19:3—"And again they shouted: 'Hallelujah! The smoke from her goes up for ever and ever'" (also 14:8; 16:19; 18:9, 18)

Summary Statement: Leading the world in corporate rebellion against God is a complex entity called "Babylon." Her widespread corruption and influence is seen in such statements as: "which made all the nations drink" (14:8); "who sits by many waters" (17:1); "the inhabitants of the earth were intoxicated with the wine of her adulteries" (17:2); "the mother of prostitutes and of the abominations of the earth" (17:5); and, "the waters you saw, where the prostitute sits, are peoples, multitudes, nations and languages" (17:15). The first four references to Babylon speak of "Babylon the Great," personifying this affluent, self-consumed, and mysterious entity with female characteristics as "her" (14:8; 16:19), "the Mother" (17:5), and "she" (18:2). Here "she" is seen leading the world as a spiritual prostitute in "abominable things and the filth of her adulteries" (17:4). "She" is also known for her strong persecution of "God's holy people" (17:6) and for her own corrupt spirituality found in the description "a dwelling for demons and a haunt for every impure spirit" (18:2) and in the warning to God's children, "'Come out of her, my people,' so that you will not share in her sins" (18:4).

Interestingly, this woman who appears to have religious connotation and influence is directly supported by and related for a time to "a scarlet beast" (17:3, 7, 9), no doubt "the beast" of Chapter 13, who inflicts unquestioned governmental control over the inhabitants of the earth. A further association between the beast and the woman is seen in the seven heads of the beast on which the woman sits (17:3, 7; cf. 12:3; 13:1)—"The seven heads are seven hills on which the woman sits. They are also seven kings [...]" (17:9-10). While associated, these two entities are still distinct, even to the point of animosity and the ultimate destruction of the woman at the hands of the beast and his ten horns (cf. 17:3, 7, 16).

Along with religious and governmental elements, Babylon is likewise viewed as having a ubiquitous and absolute commercial reach throughout the earth as a "great" and "mighty" city

(18:10). "Babylon the Great the mother of prostitutes" (17:5) is also identified as "the great city that rules over the kings of the earth" (17:18; cf. 17:2; 18:3, 18, 19). Through the commercial, mercantile, and economic stronghold of Babylon the city (18:23), the world is steeped in "excessive luxuries" (18:3) and "adultery" (18:9).

All three aspects of Babylon—religious, governmental, and commercial—are given to corporate wickedness and opposition to the Lamb (17:14) and to His people (17:6; 18:24; 19:2). Yet, God has destined all three to condemnation at the height of their rebellion (14:8; 16:19; 18:2, 8, 19-21; 19:2, 3).

▶ See also under Eschatology: The Appearance and Nefarious Work of the First and Second Beasts and Their Final Demise and Judgment

God's Call to Repentance & God's Judgment upon the Unrepentant

2:5—"Repent and do the things you did at first. If you do not repent, I will come to you and remove your lampstand from its place"

2:16—"Repent therefore!"

2:21—"I have given her time to repent of her immorality, but she is unwilling" (also 2:22)

3:3—"Remember, therefore, what you have received and heard; hold it fast, and repent"

3:18—"I counsel you to buy from me gold refined in the fire, so you can become rich; and white clothes to wear, so you can cover your shameful nakedness; and salve to put on your eyes, so you can see"

3:19—"So be earnest and repent" (also 2:16)

9:20—"The rest of mankind who were not killed by these plagues still did not repent of the work of their hands" (also 9:21; 16:9, 11)

18:4—"'Come out of her, my people,' so that you will not share in her sins, so that you will not receive any of her plagues"

Summary Statement: Within the messages to "the seven churches in the province of Asia" (1:4), are found numerous gracious calls from Christ to "repent." While imperative in nature, these appeals also come with a plea for spiritual reason (e.g., "Consider how far you have fallen!" [2:5]; "I counsel you" [3:18]), acknowledging that the hearer is capable of the choice of obedience (e.g., "but she is unwilling" [2:21]). To disobey the call to repentance comes with ultimate spiritual consequences. Though the call to repentance is not overtly announced to those outside the Church, both the need and call to repent and the capability of repentance is inferred. Even while suffering God's wrath upon sin, "the rest of mankind [. . .] still did not repent" (9:20).

▶ See also under Ecclesiology: The Identity and Judgment of the Unrepentant and False church and Its False Leaders and Teachers

▶ See also under Eschatology: The Resurrection and Final Judgment of Unrepentant Humanity, Including the Lake of Fire

Soteriology–The Study of Salvation

Salvation Provided Graciously Through the Atoning Work of Christ Alone

1:4—"Grace and peace to you from him who is, and who was, and who is to come" (also 22:21)

1:5a—"and from Jesus Christ, who is the faithful witness, the firstborn from the dead" (also 1:18)

1:5b—"To him who loves us and has freed us from our sins by his blood" (also 5:9; 7:14; 12:11; 19:13)

1:18a—"I was dead, and now look, I am alive for ever and ever!" (also 1:5; 2:8)

1:18b—"And I hold the keys of death and Hades" (also 20:13, 14)

3:20a—"Here I am! I stand at the door and knock"

3:20b—"If anyone hears my voice and opens the door, I will come in and eat with that person, and they with me"

5:6—"Then I saw a Lamb, looking as if it had been slain" (also 5:12; 13:8)

5:9—"because you were slain, and with your blood you purchased for God persons from every tribe and language and people and nation" (also 1:5; 5:6; 7:9, 14; 12:11; 14:4; 19:13)

7:10—"Salvation belongs to our God, who sits on the throne, and to the Lamb'" (also 19:1)

7:14—"they have washed their robes and made them white in the blood of the Lamb" (also 1:5; 3:5; 5:6, 9; 7:9, 13; 12:11; 19:8, 13)

11:8—"where also their Lord was crucified"

12:10—"Now have come the salvation and the power and the kingdom of our God"

12:11—"They triumphed over him by the blood of the Lamb and by the word of their testimony" (also 1:5; 5:6, 9; 7:14; 19:13)

13:8—"the Lamb who was slain from the creation of the world" (also 5:6; 17:8)

14:3—"the 144,000 who had been redeemed from the earth"

14:4—"They were purchased from among mankind and offered as firstfruits to God and the Lamb" (also 5:9)

14:6—"and he had the eternal gospel to proclaim to those who live on the earth—to every nation, tribe, language and people" (also 5:9; 7:9)

19:8—"[…] 'Fine linen, bright and clean, was given her to wear.' (Fine linen stands for the righteous acts of God's holy people.)" (also 19:7)

19:13—"He is dressed in a robe dipped in blood, and his name is the Word of God" (also 1:5; 5:9; 7:14; 12:11)

22:1—"flowing from the throne of God and of the Lamb" (also 5:6)

Summary Statement: Salvation is the provision of God's loving grace, pronounced by both the Father and the Son at the very beginning and ending of the Revelation. Those who are saved are set free from their sins and brought into right, holy relationship with God. As "his bride" (19:7), those who are saved are given "fine linen, bright and clean" (19:8) to wear. All salvation is the direct result of Christ's atoning sacrifice in shedding His blood in His crucifixion as the Lamb of God, a finished work recognized by God the Father and the residents of Heaven for eternity (5:6; 13:8). Further, the power and authority of Jesus to save and the effectiveness and totality of His sacrifice is sealed and declared through His resurrection power over the grave. Such complete salvation is also declared in His final victory over the kingdom of darkness through the pouring out of His wrath upon sin and in His Revelation (12:10). The proclamation of the Good News of salvation has been sent from Heaven "to those who live on the earth—to every nation, tribe, language and people" (14:6; cf. 5:9; 7:9). The "anyone" of 3:20 correlates with Christ's unlimited atonement, provided only by grace and received only by faith.

▶ See also under Christology: The Finished Work of Jesus

Salvation Received Personally Through Repentance from Sin and Faith in Christ

2:5—"Consider how far you have fallen! Repent and do the things you did at first" (also 2:16; 3:3, 19)

2:10—"Be faithful, even to the point of death, and I will give you life as your victor's crown" (also 14:12)

2:13—"You did not renounce your faith in me"

2:19—"I know your deeds, your love and faith, your service and perseverance"

3:11—"Hold on to what you have, so that no one will take your crown" (also 2:10)

3:20—"If anyone hears my voice and opens the door, I will come in and eat with that person, and they with me"

12:11—"They triumphed over him by the blood of the Lamb and by the word of their testimony" (also 1:2, 9; 6:9; 11:7; 12:17; 17:6; 19:10; 20:4)

12:17—"those who keep God's commands and hold fast their testimony about Jesus" (also 14:12)

14:4—"They follow the Lamb wherever he goes"

14:12—"This calls for patient endurance on the part of the people of God who keep his commands and remain faithful to Jesus" (also 2:10; 12:17)

19:7—"and his bride has made herself ready" (also 21:2, 9; 22:17)

Summary Statement: In response to God's grace, God requires personal repentance from sin, faith in Christ, and faithfulness to Christ in order for salvation to be received. Jesus invites this response of faith in the words, "if anyone hears my voice and opens the door" (3:20). John expresses the same in the words, "and his bride has made herself ready" (19:7). The believer's faith-filled "testimony" (12:11) of salvation through the blood of the Lamb brings victory over the kingdom of darkness. True believers, then, are those who "follow the Lamb wherever he goes" (14:4) and those who "keep God's commands and hold fast their testimony about Jesus" (12:17; 14:12).

▶ See also under Hamartiology: God's Call to Repentance & God's Judgment upon the Unrepentant

▶ See also under Ecclesiology: The Character, Activity, and Experience of the True Church—the Redeemed of All Ages

The Blessings and Privileges of Salvation

1:6—"and has made us to be a kingdom and priests to serve his God and Father" (also 5:10)

2:7—"To the one who is victorious, I will give the right to eat from the tree of life, which is in the paradise of God" (also 22:2, 14, 19)

2:10—"Be faithful, even to the point of death, and I will give you life as your victor's crown" (also 2:7; 3:5; 13:8; 17:8; 20:4, 5, 12, 15; 21:6, 27; 22:1, 2, 14, 17, 19)

2:11—"The one who is victorious will not be hurt at all by the second death" (also 20:6)

2:17—"I will also give that person a white stone with a new name written on it, known only to the one who receives it" (also 3:12)

3:4—"They will walk with me, dressed in white, for they are worthy" (also 3:5, 18; 4:4; 6:11; 7:9, 13, 14; 19:14)

3:5—"I will never blot out the name of that person from the book of life, but will acknowledge that name before my Father and his angels" (also 2:10; 13:8; 17:8; 20:12, 15; 21:27)

3:12—"and I will also write on them my new name" (also 2:17)

3:18a—"I counsel you to buy from me gold refined in the fire, so you can become rich"

3:18b—"and white clothes to wear, so you can cover your shameful nakedness" (also 3:4; 4:4; 6:11; 7:9, 13, 14; 19:14)

3:18c—"and salve to put on your eyes, so you can see"

3:20—"If anyone hears my voice and opens the door, I will come in and eat with that person, and they with me"

3:21—"To the one who is victorious, I will give the right to sit with me on my throne, just as I was victorious and sat down with my Father on his throne"

4:4—"They were dressed in white and had crowns of gold on their heads" (also 3:4, 18; 6:11; 7:9, 13, 14; 19:8, 14)

5:9—"And they sang a new song" (also 14:3)

7:9—"They were wearing white robes and were holding palm branches in their hands" (also 7:13,14)

13:8—"all whose names have not been written in the Lamb's book of life" (also 3:5; 17:8; 20:12, 15; 21:27)

14:3a—"And they sang a new song before the throne and before the four living creatures and the elders"

14:3b—"No one could learn the song except the 144,000 who had been redeemed from the earth"

14:4—"They were purchased from among mankind and offered as firstfruits to God and the Lamb"

19:7—"For the wedding of the Lamb has come, and his bride has made herself ready" (also 21:9)

19:8—"Fine linen, bright and clean, was given her to wear" (also 19:14)

21:3a—"Look! God's dwelling place is now among the people, and he will dwell with them"

21:3b—"They will be his people, and God himself will be with them and be their God"

21:4—"'He will wipe every tear from their eyes. There will be no more death' or mourning or crying or pain, for the old order of things has passed away."

21:5—"He who was seated on the throne said, 'I am making everything new!'"

21:6—"To the thirsty I will give water without cost from the spring of the water of life" (also 22:17)

21:9—"Come, I will show you the bride, the wife of the Lamb" (also 19:7)

21:27—"only those whose names are written in the Lamb's book of life" (also 3:5; 5:6; 13:8; 17:8; 20:12, 15)

22:1—"Then the angel showed me the river of the water of life, as clear as crystal" (also 21:6)

22:14—"Blessed are those who wash their robes, that they may have the right to the tree of life and may go through the gates into the city" (also 2:7; 22:2, 19)

Summary Statement: Those who are saved by grace through faith receive both imputed and imparted victory over sin and the kingdom of darkness through Christ. God's redeemed people are given many privileges, including: eternal life, a "victor's crown," a "new name" (2:17; cf. "my new name," 3:12), a "new song," spiritual "worthiness" (3:4); clean garments of righteousness, assurance, spiritual richness, spiritual vision, spiritual authority, spiritual refreshment, comfort, communion with Christ, and the presence of God throughout eternity. Jesus receives those who follow Him as his "bride" (19:7; 21:9); and, we are made "a kingdom and priests" (1:6; 5:10). While many believers will face physical death for their testimony of Christ, none will face "the second death" (2:11; 20:6), i.e., eternal separation from the life of Christ.

> ▶ See also under Anthropology: God's Ultimate Will for Redeemed Humanity Expressed
> ▶ See also under Ecclesiology: God's Promises to the True Church—the Redeemed of All Ages
> ▶ See also under Eschatology: The Resurrection and Eternal Reward of the Righteous

Israelology—The Study of Israel

General References to the Nation of Israel, Jerusalem, the Jewish People, and the Temple

1:7—"every eye will see him, even those who pierced him"

2:9—"I know about the slander of those who say they are Jews and are not, but are a synagogue of Satan" (also 3:9)

7:3—"until we put a seal on the foreheads of the servants of our God"

7:4—"Then I heard the number of those who were sealed: 144,000 from all the tribes of Israel" (also 7:3, 14:1)

7:5—"From the tribe of Judah 12,000 were sealed, from the tribe of Reuben 12,000, from the tribe of Gad 12,000"

7:6—"from the tribe of Asher 12,000, from the tribe of Naphtali 12,000, from the tribe of Manasseh 12,000"

7:7—"from the tribe of Simeon 12,000, from the tribe of Levi 12,000, from the tribe of Issachar 12,000"

7:8—"from the tribe of Zebulun 12,000, from the tribe of Joseph 12,000, from the tribe of Benjamin 12,000"

11:1—"I was given a reed like a measuring rod and was told, 'Go and measure the temple of God and the altar, with its worshipers'"

11:2a—"But exclude the outer court; do not measure it, because it has been given to the Gentiles"

11:2b—"They will trample on the holy city for 42 months"

11:8—"the great city—which is figuratively called Sodom and Egypt—where also their Lord was crucified"

11:13a—"At that very hour there was a severe earthquake and a tenth of the city collapsed. Seven thousand people were killed in the earthquake"

11:13b—"and the survivors were terrified and gave glory to the God of heaven"

12:1—"A great sign appeared in heaven: a woman clothed with the sun, with the moon under her feet and a crown of twelve stars on her head"

12:2—"She was pregnant and cried out in pain as she was about to give birth" (also 12:4, 5)

12:4—"The dragon stood in front of the woman who was about to give birth, so that it might devour her child the moment he was born" (also 12:13)

12:6—"The woman fled into the wilderness to a place prepared for her by God, where she might be taken care of for 1,260 days" (also 12:14)

12:13—"he pursued the woman who had given birth to the male child" (also 12:2, 4, 5)

12:14—"The woman was given the two wings of a great eagle, so that she might fly to the place prepared for her in the wilderness, where she would be taken care of for a time, times and half a time, out of the serpent's reach" (also 12:6)

12:15—"to overtake the woman and sweep her away with the torrent"

12:16—"But the earth helped the woman" (also 12:6)

12:17—"Then the dragon was enraged at the woman and went off to wage war against the rest of her offspring—those who keep God's commands and hold fast their testimony about Jesus" (also 12:4, 11, 13, 14; 14:12)

13:7—"It was given power to wage war against God's holy people and to conquer them" (also 13:10; 21:3; 22:21)

14:1—"and with him 144,000 who had his name and his Father's name written on their foreheads" (also 7:4)

14:20—"They were trampled in the winepress outside the city"

20:9—"and surrounded the camp of God's people, the city he loves"

Summary Statement: The nation of Israel, Jerusalem, the Jewish People, and the Temple are all identified by John in the end time scenario; but, one must not miss the contrasting terms in which they are presented. Early, Jesus speaks distinction between those who "say they are Jews and are not" (2:9; 3:9). Soon we also see dissimilarity between the remnant of 144,000 sealed on their foreheads "from all the tribes of Israel" (7:4; 14:1) and those who are not (in fact, Dan's name is excluded and Joseph is referenced in the place of his son Ephraim). Disparity is then seen when Jerusalem is called "the holy city" (11:2) and yet also identified as "the great city— which is figuratively called Sodom and Egypt—where also their Lord was crucified" (11:8). Great contrast is further seen between God's protection of Israel under the extreme persecution of the Devil—such as when she is provided "the two wings of a great eagle, so that she might fly to the place prepared for her in the wilderness" (12:14)—and God's chastening of Israel, as when the Gentiles are permitted to "trample on the holy city for 42 months" (11:2) and when "a severe earthquake" destroys a tenth of the city of Jerusalem, killing seven thousand (11:13). Finally, contrast is seen in Israel's central role in bringing forth the Christ·child (12:5, 13) and in her identity as "those who pierced him" (1:7; perhaps an allusion to Zechariah 12:10).

▶ See also under Eschatology: Persecution and Martyrdom of Tribulation Saints and of the Jewish People

The New Jerusalem and the "Temple" in Heaven

3:12a—"The one who is victorious I will make a pillar in the temple of my God"

3:12b—"I will write on them the name of my God and the name of the city of my God, the new Jerusalem, which is coming down out of heaven from my God" (also 21:2)

6:9—"I saw under the altar the souls of those who had been slain"

7:15—"they are before the throne of God and serve him day and night in his temple"

11:19—"Then God's temple in heaven was opened, and within his temple was seen the ark of his covenant" (also 15:5)

14:15—"Then another angel came out of the temple and called in a loud voice" (also 14:17)

15:5—"After this I looked, and I saw in heaven the temple—that is, the tabernacle of the covenant law—and it was opened"

15:6—"Out of the temple came the seven angels with the seven plagues" (also 15:8; 16:1)

15:8—"And the temple was filled with smoke from the glory of God and from his power"

16:7—"And I heard the altar respond" (also 6:9; 8:3, 5; 9:13; 14:18)

16:17—"and out of the temple came a loud voice from the throne" (also 16:1)

21:2—"I saw the Holy City, the new Jerusalem, coming down out of heaven from God" (also 3:12; 21:10, 14-16, 18, 19, 21-23; 22:19)

21:12—"On the gates were written the names of the twelve tribes of Israel" (also 21:13, 15, 21, 25; 22:14)

21:22—"I did not see a temple in the city, because the Lord God Almighty and the Lamb are its temple"

22:3—"The throne of God and of the Lamb will be in the city, and his servants will serve him"

22:14—"Blessed are those who wash their robes, that they may have the right to the tree of life and may go through the gates into the city"

Summary Statement: Though John does indicate a rebuilt physical, last day's temple in Jerusalem (cf. 11:1-2), most of his references to "the temple" indicate a temple fashioned for and situated in Heaven. Within "God's temple in heaven" (11:19) is found the Throne of God (where the Father and the Son are seated in authority and in glory), "the altar" (6:9; 8:3; 9:13; 14:18; 16:7), and "the ark of his covenant" (11:19). Also located in the Heavenly temple, are numerous angels—who both worship God and minister God's judgment—and "a great multitude" (7:9) of the redeemed, serving Him there "day and night" (7:15).

Just as there is a perfect "temple" in Heaven, of which the earthly temple seems to be a reflection, so John sees a perfect, heavenly, "new Jerusalem" (3:12; 21:2), "the city of my God" (3:12). Both the earthly and the heavenly Jerusalem are called "the holy city" (cf. 11:2 with 21:2, 10; 22:19). A further parallel and connection is seen in that "on the gates were written the names of the twelve tribes of Israel" (21:12). Though essentially connected, this "new Jerusalem" seems to be distinct from "heaven," for three times John describes it as "coming down out of heaven from God" (cf. 3:12; 21:2, 10). And yet it is clear that—following the Revelation of Jesus to the earth and with the descent of "new Jerusalem"—God's presence, blessings, and provision come to dwell with His redeemed for eternity. It should also be noted that once the "new Jerusalem" descends from Heaven, John no longer sees a detailed heavenly "temple" as before, for now "the Lord God Almighty and the Lamb are its temple" (21:2).

> ▶ See also under Eschatology: Heaven (Where God's Throne Is), The New Heavens and Earth, and The New Jerusalem

Ecclesiology—The Study of the Church

The Constituents and Character of the True Church—the Redeemed of All Ages

1:1—"which God gave him to show his servants" (also 6:11; 7:3; 11:18; 19:2, 5; 22:3, 6, 16)

1:4—"To the seven churches in the province of Asia: Grace and peace to you" (also 1:11, 12)

1:6—"and has made us to be a kingdom and priests to serve his God and Father" (also 5:10; 20:6)

1:9—"I, John, your brother and companion in the suffering and kingdom and patient endurance that are ours in Jesus" (also 12:10; 13:10; 14:12; 17:14; 19:10)

1:11—"Write on a scroll what you see and send it to the seven churches: to Ephesus, Smyrna, Pergamum, Thyatira, Sardis, Philadelphia and Laodicea" (also 1:4; 2:1, 8, 12, 18; 3:1, 7, 14; 22:16)

1:20a—"The mystery of the seven stars that you saw in my right hand and of the seven golden lampstands is this: [...]" (also 1:12; 3:1)

1:20b—"The seven stars are the angels of the seven churches, and the seven lampstands are the seven churches" (also 1:12; 2:1)

2:1—"To the angel of the church in Ephesus write" (also 2:8, 12, 18; 3:1, 7, 14)

2:7a—"Whoever has ears, let them hear what the Spirit says to the churches" (also 2:11, 17; 29; 3:6, 13, 22; 13:9)

2:7b—"To the one who is victorious [...]" (also 2:11, 17, 26; 3:5, 12, 21; 15:2; 21:7)

2:13—"Yet you remain true to my name. You did not renounce your faith in me" (also 3:8; 17:14)

3:4—"Yet you have a few people in Sardis who have not soiled their clothes. They will walk with me, dressed in white, for they are worthy" (also 3:5; 7:9; 19:8; 22:14)

4:4a—"Surrounding the throne were twenty-four other thrones, and seated on them were twenty-four elders" (also 4:10; 5:6, 8, 14; 7:11; 19:4)

4:4b—"They were dressed in white and had crowns of gold on their heads" (also 7:14; 19:8)

5:8—"Each one had a harp and they were holding golden bowls full of incense, which are the prayers of God's people" (also 8:3, 4)

5:9—"and with your blood you purchased for God persons from every tribe and language and people and nation" (also 7:9; 14:4; 19:1, 6)

6:9—"I saw under the altar the souls of those who had been slain because of the word of God and the testimony they had maintained" (also 12:11; 20:4)

6:11—"until the full number of their fellow servants, their brothers and sisters, were killed just as they had been" (also 1:1; 7:3; 11:18; 19:2, 5; 22:3, 6)

7:9—"After this I looked, and there before me was a great multitude that no one could count, from every nation, tribe, people and language" (also 5:9; 15:4; 19:1, 6)

7:14—"These are they who have come out of the great tribulation; they have washed their robes and made them white in the blood of the Lamb'" (also 6:11; 7:9, 13; 12:11; 19:8, 14; 22:14)

11:3—"And I will appoint my two witnesses, and they will prophesy for 1,260 days, clothed in sackcloth" (also 11:10)

11:18—"your servants the prophets and your people who revere your name, both great and small" (also 10:7; 16:6; 18:24; 19:5; 21:14; 22:6, 9)

12:10—"our brothers and sisters" (also 1:9)

12:11—"They triumphed over him by the blood of the Lamb and by the word of their testimony; they did not love their lives so much as to shrink from death" (also 7:14)

12:17—"the rest of her offspring—those who keep God's commands and hold fast their testimony about Jesus" (also 12:11; 13:10; 14:12)

13:7—"It was given power to wage war against God's holy people" (also 16:6; 17:6; 18:24)

14:1—"and with him 144,000 who had his name and his Father's name written on their foreheads" (also 7:4)

14:4—"They were purchased from among mankind and offered as firstfruits to God and the Lamb" (also 5:9)

14:5—"No lie was found in their mouths; they are blameless"

14:12a—"This calls for patient endurance on the part of the people of God" (also 1:9; 13:10)

14:12b—"who keep his commands and remain faithful to Jesus" (also 12:17; 13:10; 17:14)

15:2—"those who had been victorious over the beast and its image and over the number of its name" (also 20:4)

16:6—"for they have shed the blood of your holy people and your prophets" (also 13:7; 17:6; 18:20, 24)

17:6—"the blood of God's holy people, the blood of those who bore testimony to Jesus" (also 12:11; 13:7; 16:6; 18:24)

17:14—"and with him will be his called, chosen and faithful followers" (also 12:17; 13:10; 14:12)

18:4—"Come out of her, my people" (also 22:11, 21)

18:20—"Rejoice, you people of God! Rejoice, apostles and prophets!" (also 10:7; 11:18; 16:6; 18:24; 21:14; 22:6, 9)

19:6—"Then I heard what sounded like a great multitude, like the roar of rushing waters and like loud peals of thunder, shouting: 'Hallelujah! [...]'" (also 7:9; 19:1)

19:7—"and his bride has made herself ready" (also 21:9; 22:17)

19:8—"Fine linen, bright and clean, was given her to wear. (Fine linen stands for the righteous acts of God's holy people.)" (also 6:11; 7:9, 13, 14; 13:7, 10; 22:11, 14)

19:10—"your brothers and sisters who hold to the testimony of Jesus" (also 1:9; 6:9; 12:11, 17; 17:6; 20:4)

19:14—"The armies of heaven were following him" (also 19:19)

21:3a—"Look! God's dwelling place is now among the people, and he will dwell with them" (also 22:21)

21:3b—"They will be his people, and God himself will be with them and be their God" (also 22:21)

21:9—"Come, I will show you the bride, the wife of the Lamb" (also 19:7; 22:17)

21:14—"on them were the names of the twelve apostles of the Lamb" (also 18:20)

22:6—"God who inspires the prophets, sent his angel to show his servants" (also 1:1; 6:11; 7:3; 11:18; 19:2, 5; 22:3)

22:11—"let the one who does right continue to do right; and let the holy person continue to be holy"

22:16—"I, Jesus, have sent my angel to give you this testimony for the churches" (also 1:1)

22:21—"God's people" (also 18:4; 20:9; 21:3)

Summary Statement: In identifying the redeemed of all ages—those who will dwell with God for eternity—within the book of Revelation, we must look beyond the word "church." Here "church" (always *ekklēsia*) is used exclusively in referring to the recipients of this letter, "the seven churches in the province of Asia" (1:4). Apart from Chapters 1-3, the plural "churches" is found only once, in 22:16, reminding us that the entire message was addressed to "the seven churches," i.e., "the seven golden lampstands" (1:12, 20). These together undoubtedly represent all "churches," faithful or compromised from that day until our own. If by the "Church" we mean the entirety of the redeemed of all ages, then we certainly cannot limit its constituents to "the seven churches" proper, for the redeemed encompass "a great multitude that no one could count, from every nation, tribe, people and language" (7:9; cf. 5:9; 19:1, 6).

With this common thread of redemption through Christ's blood always in view, John identifies "God's holy people" (13:7, 10; 21:3; 22:21) with the following terms and descriptions: those "wearing white robes" [made] "white in the blood of the Lamb" (7:9, 13, 14; cf. 6:11; 19:8; 22:14); "a kingdom and priests" (1:6; 5:10); "our brothers and sisters" (12:10; cf. 1:9); "fellow servants" (6:11; cf. 1:1; 7:3; 11:18; 19:2, 5; 22:3, 6); "144,000 who had his name and his Father's name written on their foreheads" (14:1; cf. 7:4); "his called, chosen and faithful followers" (17:14; cf. 13:10; 14:12); and "his bride" (19:7; 21:9; 22:17). By their appearance—for they too are "dressed in white"—and their role and ministry, it is quite certain that the "twenty-four elders" (4:10; 5:6, 8, 14; 7:11; 19:4) are representative of this "Church" of all ages. It is also quite certain that John indicates a spiritual relationship between the faithful of the nation of Israel and gentile believers with the words, "the rest of her offspring—those who keep God's commands and hold fast their testimony about Jesus" (cf. 12:17; 14:12).

The Activities and Experiences of the True Church—the Redeemed of All Ages

1:6—"and has made us to be a kingdom and priests to serve his God and Father" (also 5:10; 19:5; 20:6)

1:9—"your brother and companion in the suffering and kingdom and patient endurance that are ours in Jesus" (also 2:3, 10; 13:10; 14:12; 17:14; 19:10)

2:2a—"I know your deeds, your hard work and your perseverance" (also 2:3, 19)

2:2b—"I know that you cannot tolerate wicked people"

2:4—"You have forsaken the love you had at first"

2:5—"Consider how far you have fallen! Repent and do the things you did at first"

2:7—"Whoever has ears, let them hear what the Spirit says to the churches" (see also 2:11; 2:17; 2:29; 3:6; 3:13; 3:22)

2:9—"I know your afflictions and your poverty—yet you are rich!"

2:10a—"Do not be afraid of what you are about to suffer" (also 12:11)

2:10b—"I tell you, the devil will put some of you in prison to test you, and you will suffer persecution for ten days"

2:13—"Yet you remain true to my name. You did not renounce your faith in me"

2:14—"There are some among you who hold to the teaching of Balaam" (

2:15—"you also have those who hold to the teaching of the Nicolaitans"

2:19—"I know your deeds, your love and faith, your service and perseverance, and that you are now doing more than you did at first" (also 2:2, 3)

2:20—"You tolerate that woman Jezebel, who calls herself a prophet"

2:24—"to you who do not hold to her teaching and have not learned Satan's so-called deep secrets"

2:25—"except to hold on to what you have until I come"

3:2—"Wake up! Strengthen what remains and is about to die, for I have found your deeds unfinished in the sight of my God"

3:3—"Remember, therefore, what you have received and heard"

3:4—"Yet you have a few people in Sardis who have not soiled their clothes. They will walk with me, dressed in white, for they are worthy" (also 3:5; 6:11; 7:9, 13, 14; 13:7, 10; 19:8; 22:14)

3:8—"you have little strength, yet you have kept my word and have not denied my name" (also 2:13)

3:10—"Since you have kept my command to endure patiently, I will also keep you from the hour of trial that is going to come on the whole world to test the inhabitants of the earth"

4:10—"the twenty-four elders fall down before him who sits on the throne and worship him who lives for ever and ever" (also 5:6, 8, 14; 7:11; 11:16; 19:4)

5:8—"Each one had a harp and they were holding golden bowls full of incense, which are the prayers of God's people" (also 8:3, 4; 14:2; 15:2)

5:9—"And they sang a new song" (also 14:3)

5:10—"and they will reign on the earth" (also 1:6; 20:6; 22:5)

6:9—"I saw under the altar the souls of those who had been slain because of the word of God and the testimony they had maintained" (also 6:10)

7:9—"They were wearing white robes and were holding palm branches in their hands" (also 3:4, 5; 19:8)

7:10—"And they cried out in a loud voice: 'Salvation belongs to our God, who sits on the throne, and to the Lamb'"

7:11—"They fell down on their faces before the throne and worshiped God" (also 5:8; 7:15; 15:4; 19:4)

7:15—"they are before the throne of God and serve him day and night in his temple" (also 1:6; 7:9; 22:3)

8:3—"He was given much incense to offer, with the prayers of all God's people, on the golden altar in front of the throne" (also 5:8; 8:4)

11:18—"your servants the prophets and your people who revere your name" (also 15:4; 19:5)

12:11a—"They triumphed over him by the blood of the Lamb and by the word of their testimony"

12:11b—"they did not love their lives so much as to shrink from death"

14:2—"The sound I heard was like that of harpists playing their harps" (also 5:8; 15:2)

14:3a—"And they sang a new song before the throne and before the four living creatures and the elders" (also 5:9)

14:3b—"No one could learn the song except the 144,000 who had been redeemed from the earth"

14:4a—"These are those who did not defile themselves with women, for they remained virgins"

14:4b—"They follow the Lamb wherever he goes"

14:5—"No lie was found in their mouths; they are blameless"

14:12—"This calls for patient endurance on the part of the people of God who keep his commands and remain faithful to Jesus" (also 13:10; 17:14)

14:13a—"Blessed are the dead who die in the Lord from now on"

14:13b—"they will rest from their labor, for their deeds will follow them"

15:2—"those who had been victorious over the beast and its image and over the number of its name"

15:3—"and sang the song of God's servant Moses and of the Lamb" (also 14:3)

15:4a—"Who will not fear you, Lord, and bring glory to your name?" (also 11:18)

15:4b—"All nations will come and worship before you" (also 7:9; 19:1; 21:26)

17:6—"those who bore testimony to Jesus" (also 1:9; 6:9; 12:11, 17; 17:6; 19:10; 20:4)

19:5—"Praise our God, all you his servants, you who fear him, both great and small!" (1:1, 6; 6:11; 7:3; 11:18; 19:2, 5; 22:3, 6)

19:6—"like the roar of rushing waters and like loud peals of thunder, shouting: 'Hallelujah! For our Lord God Almighty reigns [...]'" (also 7:10; 19:1, 3, 4)

19:7—"and his bride has made herself ready"

19:8—"'Fine linen, bright and clean, was given her to wear.' (Fine linen stands for the righteous acts of God's holy people.)" (also 3:4, 5; 7:9)

19:14—"The armies of heaven were following him, riding on white horses"

20:4—"those who had been given authority to judge" (also 3:21)

20:6a—"Blessed and holy are those who share in the first resurrection"

20:6b—"but they will be priests of God and of Christ and will reign with him for a thousand years" (also 1:6; 5:10; 22:5)

21:26—"The glory and honor of the nations will be brought into it" (also 21:24)

22:5—"And they will reign for ever and ever" (also 5:10; 20:6)

22:11—"let the one who does right continue to do right; and let the holy person continue to be holy"

22:14—"Blessed are those who wash their robes, that they may have the right to the tree of life and may go through the gates into the city" (also 2:7; 3:4, 5; 7:9)

22:17a—"The Spirit and the bride say, 'Come!' And let the one who hears say, 'Come!' Let the one who is thirsty come"

22:17b—"and let the one who wishes take the free gift of the water of life" (also 21:6; 22:1)

Summary Statement: The activities and experiences of God's redeemed may best be viewed in the context of this lifetime on earth and then in eternity in Heaven. While on earth, the righteous deeds, love, faith, service, and perseverance of God's people do not go unnoticed by Jesus. Perhaps the greatest commendation of the redeemed is that, "They follow the Lamb wherever he goes" (14:4), remaining faithful to Jesus (14:12). In response to the call of the Lamb to His bride, "I am coming soon," the Church's earnest cry is, "Amen. Come, Lord Jesus" (22:20). In reprisal for this loyalty, deep suffering and persecution, even unto death, is foretold as the common experience of believers at the hands of Satan and his emissaries. Not to be confused with this suffering for faith in Christ is the suffering promised to unrepentant humanity through the wrath of God. Here, the Church hears Jesus' promise to "keep you from the hour of trial that is going to come on the whole world to test the inhabitants of the earth" (3:10).

Nevertheless, it cannot be missed that not all activity in the visible Church is upright. In His messages to the seven churches, apart from Smyrna and Philadelphia, Jesus rebukes compromise and false teaching, calls to repentance, and warns of judgment upon those who refuse to repent.

In Heaven, the first activity of the Church is the worship of God before His throne, which John heard rising from the innumerable multitude of the redeemed "like the roar of rushing waters and like loud peals of thunder" (19:6). Within the gates of the New Jerusalem, the redeemed will forever be refreshed as they drink of "the river of the water of life" (22:1, 17) and partake of "the tree of life" (22:2, 14; cf. 2:7). The service as "a kingdom and priests" (1:6; 5:10)—which began while on earth—reaches through the Millennial Reign of Christ (20:6) and into eternity, for "they are before the throne of God and serve him day and night in his temple" (7:15; cf. 22:3). There, the redeemed "reign for ever and ever" (22:5).

▶ See also under Eschatology: Persecution and Martyrdom of Tribulation Saints and of the Jewish People

God's Promises to the True Church—the Redeemed of All Ages

1:3a—"Blessed is the one who reads aloud the words of this prophecy, […]"

1:3b—"and blessed are those who hear it and take to heart what is written in it" (also 22:7)

1:4—"Grace and peace to you" (also 22:21)

2:7—"To the one who is victorious, I will give the right to eat from the tree of life, which is in the paradise of God" (also 22:14)

2:10—"Be faithful, even to the point of death, and I will give you life as your victor's crown"

2:11—"The one who is victorious will not be hurt at all by the second death" (also 20:6)

2:17a—"To the one who is victorious, I will give some of the hidden manna"

2:17b—"I will also give that person a white stone with a new name written on it, known only to the one who receives it"

2:26—"To the one who is victorious and does my will to the end, I will give authority over the nations"

2:27—"that one 'will rule them with an iron scepter and will dash them to pieces like pottery'—just as I have received authority from my Father"

2:28—"I will also give that one the morning star"

3:5a—"The one who is victorious will, like them, be dressed in white" (also 7:9; 19:8, 14)

3:5b—"I will never blot out the name of that person from the book of life, but will acknowledge that name before my Father and his angels" (also 20:12)

3:10—"I will also keep you from the hour of trial that is going to come on the whole world to test the inhabitants of the earth"

3:12a—"The one who is victorious I will make a pillar in the temple of my God. Never again will they leave it"

3:12b—"I will write on them the name of my God and the name of the city of my God, the new Jerusalem, which is coming down out of heaven from my God"

3:12c—"and I will also write on them my new name"

3:19—"Those whom I love I rebuke and discipline"

3:20—"Here I am! I stand at the door and knock. If anyone hears my voice and opens the door, I will come in and eat with that person, and they with me"

3:21—"To the one who is victorious, I will give the right to sit with me on my throne, just as I was victorious and sat down with my Father on his throne"

5:10—"You have made them to be a kingdom and priests to serve our God, and they will reign on the earth" (also 1:6; 20:4, 6)

6:11—"Then each of them was given a white robe, and they were told to wait a little longer, until the full number of their fellow servants, their brothers and sisters, were killed just as they had been"

7:15—"and he who sits on the throne will shelter them with his presence"

7:16—"'Never again will they hunger; never again will they thirst. The sun will not beat down on them,' nor any scorching heat"

7:17—"For the Lamb at the center of the throne will be their shepherd; 'he will lead them to springs of living water.' 'And God will wipe away every tear from their eyes'" (also 21:4)

11:18—"and for rewarding your servants the prophets and your people who revere your name, both great and small"

12:11—"They triumphed over him by the blood of the Lamb and by the word of their testimony"

14:1—"and with him 144,000 who had his name and his Father's name written on their foreheads" (also 22:4)

14:13a—"Blessed are the dead who die in the Lord from now on"

14:13b—"'Yes,' says the Spirit, 'they will rest from their labor, for their deeds will follow them'"

16:15—"Blessed is the one who stays awake and remains clothed"

19:9—"Blessed are those who are invited to the wedding supper of the Lamb!"

20:4—"I saw thrones on which were seated those who had been given authority to judge"

20:6a—"Blessed and holy are those who share in the first resurrection"

20:6b—"The second death has no power over them"

21:3a—"God's dwelling place is now among the people, and he will dwell with them"

21:3b—"They will be his people, and God himself will be with them and be their God"

21:4—"'He will wipe every tear from their eyes. There will be no more death' or mourning or crying or pain" (also 7:17)

21:6—"To the thirsty I will give water without cost from the spring of the water of life" (also 22:17)

21:7—"Those who are victorious will inherit all this, and I will be their God and they will be my children" (also 21:3)

22:4—"They will see his face, and his name will be on their foreheads" (also 14:1)

22:7—"Blessed is the one who keeps the words of the prophecy written in this scroll" (also 1:3)

22:12—"My reward is with me, and I will give to each person according to what they have done"

22:14—"Blessed are those who wash their robes, that they may have the right to the tree of life and may go through the gates into the city" (also 2:7)

22:17—"Let the one who is thirsty come; and let the one who wishes take the free gift of the water of life" (also 21:6)

22:21—"The grace of the Lord Jesus be with God's people" (also 1:4)

Summary Statement: From the beginning to the end of Revelation, "grace and peace" is promised to God's people (1:4; 22:21). The same is true of the unique blessing that comes to those who read and obey the words of this prophecy (1:3; 22:7). Jesus calls those who follow him "victorious," to which are given a wide range of promises, including: "the right to eat from the tree of life" (2:7; 22:14); "your victor's crown" (2:10); "share in the first resurrection" (20:6), as opposed to "the second death" (2:11; 20:6); "a new name," which is the Father's name (2:17; cf. 3:12; 14:1; 22:4); "authority over the nations" (2:26), while ruling and reigning with Christ (2:27) as "a kingdom and priests" (1:6; 5:10; 20:4, 6); the white garments of righteousness (3:5; 6:11; 7:9; 19:8, 14); invitation to "the wedding supper of the Lamb" (19:9); "the free gift of the water of life" (22:17; cf. 21:6); and, shelter, comfort, and provision for eternity (7:15-17; 21:4). Greatest of all is the promise to dwell intimately with God for eternity as "His people," seated with Him on His throne (3:21; 21:3, 7).

- ▶ See also under Anthropology: God's Ultimate Will for Redeemed Humanity Expressed
- ▶ See also under Soteriology: The Blessings and Privileges of Salvation
- ▶ See also under Eschatology: The Resurrection and Eternal Reward of the Righteous

The Identity and Judgment of the Unrepentant and False Church and Its False Leaders and Teachers

2:2—"that you have tested those who claim to be apostles but are not, and have found them false"

2:4—"If you do not repent, I will come to you and remove your lampstand from its place"

2:6—"You hate the practices of the Nicolaitans, which I also hate" (also 2:15)

2:9—"those who say they are Jews and are not, but are a synagogue of Satan" (also 3:9)

2:14—"There are some among you who hold to the teaching of Balaam, who taught Balak to entice the Israelites to sin so that they ate food sacrificed to idols and committed sexual immorality"

2:15—"Likewise, you also have those who hold to the teaching of the Nicolaitans" (also 2:6)

2:16—"Repent therefore! Otherwise, I will soon come to you and will fight against them with the sword of my mouth"

2:20a—"Nevertheless, I have this against you: You tolerate that woman Jezebel, who calls herself a prophet"

2:20b—"By her [Jezebel] teaching she misleads my servants into sexual immorality and the eating of food sacrificed to idols"

2:22—"So I will cast her on a bed of suffering, and I will make those who commit adultery with her suffer intensely, unless they repent of her ways"

2:23—"I will strike her children dead. Then all the churches will know that I am he who searches hearts and minds, and I will repay each of you according to your deeds"

3:1—"you have a reputation of being alive, but you are dead"

3:9—"I will make those who are of the synagogue of Satan, who claim to be Jews though they are not, but are liars—I will make them come and fall down at your feet and acknowledge that I have loved you" (also 2:9)

3:15—"I know your deeds, that you are neither cold nor hot. I wish you were either one or the other!"

3:16—"So, because you are lukewarm—neither hot nor cold—I am about to spit you out of my mouth"

3:17—"You say, 'I am rich; I have acquired wealth and do not need a thing.' But you do not realize that you are wretched, pitiful, poor, blind and naked"

Summary Statement: A distinction must be seen between those within the true Church who repent of their compromise and those within the visible church who refuse to repent and are condemned. From the start of the seven messages to the churches, Jesus identifies "those who claim to be apostles but are not" and finds them "false" (2:2). Along with such false leaders, Jesus identifies false teachers and prophets, namely, "those who hold to the teaching of the Nicolaitans" (2:15; cf. 2:6); those who "hold to the teaching of Balaam" (2:14); and, "Jezebel, who calls herself a prophet" (2:20). A common theme here is the religious promotion of "sexual immorality" (2:14, 20). Jesus also twice rebukes the deceptive lies of "those who say they are Jews and are not, but are a synagogue of Satan" (2:9; 3:9). Those within the visible church who refuse to repent and walk in righteousness Jesus calls "dead" (3:1) and "lukewarm" (3:16), as well as "wretched, pitiful, poor, blind and naked" (3:17).

We also cannot miss the religious connotations—though evil—attributed to "the dragon" (i.e., Satan), "the first beast," and "the second beast" (i.e., "the false prophet"). Both the "dragon" and "the first beast" receive the awe-filled worship of rebellious humanity (13:4). "The false prophet" appears with "two horns like a lamb" (13:11) and performs "great signs, even causing fire to come down from heaven to the earth" (13:13). Out of the mouths of all three come "spirits of demons performing miraculous signs" (16:14).

- ▶ See also under Eschatology: The Appearance and Nefarious Work of the Antichrist (the Beast) and the False Prophet (the second Beast)
- ▶ See also under Eschatology: The Resurrection and Final Judgment of Unrepentant Humanity, Including the Lake of Fire

Eschatology—The Study of the Last Days

Including:

- The Revelation of Christ in His Second Coming
- The Gathering of the Church To Christ and Into Heaven
- The Great Tribulation—The Wrath of God in Judgment Upon the Unrepentant
- Persecution and Martyrdom of Tribulation Saints and of the Jewish People
- Spiritual Warfare Led by Satan in the Last Days and His Final Demise and Judgment
- The Appearance and Nefarious Work of the First and Second Beasts and Their Final Demise and Judgment
- The Resurrection and Final Judgment of Unrepentant Humanity, Including the Lake of Fire
- The Resurrection and Eternal Reward of the Righteous
- The Millennial Reign of Christ and the Eternal Kingdom of God
- Heaven (Where God's Throne Is), The New Heavens and Earth, and The New Jerusalem

The Revelation of Christ in His Second Coming

1:1—"The revelation from Jesus Christ, which God gave him to show his servants what must soon take place" (also 1:3; 3:11; 22:7, 10, 12, 20)

1:3—"because the time is near" (also 3:11; 22:10)

1:7a—"'Look, he is coming with the clouds,' and 'every eye will see him, even those who pierced him'"

1:7b—"and all peoples on earth 'will mourn because of him'" (also 18:7, 9, 11, 15)

3:11—"I am coming soon" (also 1:1, 3; 22:7, 10, 12, 20)

16:15—"'Look, I come like a thief!' Blessed is the one who stays awake and remains clothed, so as not to go naked and be shamefully exposed" (also 3:3)

17:14a—"but the Lamb will triumph over them because he is Lord of lords and King of kings" (also 15:3; 19:16)

17:14b—"and with him will be his called, chosen and faithful followers" (also 19:14)

19:11a—"I saw heaven standing open and there before me was a white horse, whose rider is called Faithful and True" (also 3:14; 19:14)

19:11b—"With justice he judges and wages war" (also 18:8)

19:12a—"His eyes are like blazing fire, and on his head are many crowns" (also 1:14)

19:12b—"He has a name written on him that no one knows but he himself" (also 2:17; 15:4; 19:13, 16)

19:13a—"He is dressed in a robe dipped in blood" (also 1:5; 5:9; 7:14; 12:11)

19:13b—"and his name is the Word of God" (also 1:2, 9; 20:4)

19:14—"The armies of heaven were following him, riding on white horses and dressed in fine linen, white and clean" (also 17:14; 19:11)

19:15a—"Coming out of his mouth is a sharp sword with which to strike down the nations. 'He will rule them with an iron scepter'" (also 1:16; 2:12, 16, 27; 12:5; 19:21)

19:15b—"He treads the winepress of the fury of the wrath of God Almighty" (also 6:16, 17; 11:18; 14:10, 19, 20; 15:1, 7; 16:1, 19)

19:16—"On his robe and on his thigh he has this name written: king of kings and lord of lords" (also 15:3; 17:14)

22:12—"Look, I am coming soon! My reward is with me, and I will give to each person according to what they have done" (also 16:11; 20:12, 13; 22:7, 10, 20)

22:20a—"He who testifies to these things says, 'Yes, I am coming soon'" (also 1:3; 3:11; 22:7, 10, 12)

22:20b—"Amen. Come, Lord Jesus" (also 22:7, 12)

Summary Statement: Though the major focus of the Book of Revelation is the "Revelation" (*apokalypsis*) of Jesus Christ at the end of this age, surprisingly, this word—used many times in the New Testament for the return of Jesus (cf. 1 Cor. 1:7; 2 Thess. 1:7; 1 Pet. 1:7, 13; 4:13)—is found only once in this book (1:1), and here referring to the entire prophetic message given to John for the Church. Rather, John speaks broadly (1:7, 3:11; 22:7, 12, 20) of Christ's "coming." Yet, even here he uses the common word for "coming" (*erchomai*) rather than *parousia* ("presence" or "coming") used so often by other New Testament writers (cf. 1 Thess. 5:23; 2 Thess. 2:1, 8; 2 Pet. 1:16; 1 John 2:28).

The imminent, sudden, and unexpected nature of Christ's Second Coming is clear; His return is "soon" (1:1; 3:11; 22:7, 12, 20) and "the time is near" (1:3; 22:10)—though not yet, for His Revelation "will take place later" (1:19). Twice He says, "I come like a thief" (3:3; 16:15). He is also coming openly, publicly, and gloriously "with the clouds" for "every eye will see him" (1:7). In completion of His mission, He comes triumphantly as Savior, King, and Judge; He will rule and reign justly "with an iron scepter" [...] as "king of kings and lord of lords" (19:11-16). In His final victory, He—along with "his called, chosen and faithful followers" (17:14; cf. 19:14)—will triumph over His enemies in both the natural and spiritual realms (19:19).

To the unrepentant wicked, the Revelation of Jesus will bring harrowing judgment under God's wrath, for He has promised, "My reward is with me, and I will give to each person according to what they have done" (22:12). Conversely, Christ's Revelation is itself the deep anticipation and blessed hope of every true believer (16:15; 22:20).

▶ See also under Christology: The Current and Eternal Work of Jesus

The Gathering of the Church To Christ and Into Heaven

7:9a—"there before me was a great multitude that no one could count, from every nation, tribe, people and language, standing before the throne and before the Lamb" (also 5:9; 15:4; 19:1, 6)

7:9b—"They were wearing white robes and were holding palm branches in their hands" (also 3:5; 7:13, 14; 19:8, 14; 22:14)

7:10—"And they cried out in a loud voice: 'Salvation belongs to our God, who sits on the throne, and to the Lamb'" (also 12:10; 19:1)

7:14—"These are they who have come out of the great tribulation; they have washed their robes and made them white in the blood of the Lamb" (also 3:5; 7:9, 13; 19:8, 14; 22:14)

7:15a—"they are before the throne of God and serve him day and night in his temple" (also 1:6; 7:9; 22:3)

7:15b—"and he who sits on the throne will shelter them with his presence" (also 21:3)

7:16—"'Never again will they hunger; never again will they thirst. The sun will not beat down on them,' nor any scorching heat" (also 21:6; 22:17)

7:17—"For the Lamb at the center of the throne will be their shepherd; 'he will lead them to springs of living water.' 'And God will wipe away every tear from their eyes'" (also 21:4)

14:1—"there before me was the Lamb, standing on Mount Zion, and with him 144,000 who had his name and his Father's name written on their foreheads" (also 22:4)

14:3a—"And they sang a new song before the throne and before the four living creatures and the elders" (also 5:9)

14:3b—"No one could learn the song except the 144,000 who had been redeemed from the earth"

19:1—"After this I heard what sounded like the roar of a great multitude in heaven shouting: 'Hallelujah! Salvation and glory and power belong to our God'" (also 7:10; 12:10; 19:6, 7)

19:7—"For the wedding of the Lamb has come, and his bride has made herself ready" (also 21:9; 22:17)

19:8—"[...] 'Fine linen, bright and clean, was given her to wear.' (Fine linen stands for the righteous acts of God's holy people)" (also 3:5; 7:9, 13, 14; 19:8, 14; 22:14)

19:9—"Blessed are those who are invited to the wedding supper of the Lamb!'"

Summary Statement: The first view of the Church gathered in Heaven comes in Chapter 7, where John sees an innumerable company of believers "from every nation, tribe, people and language, standing before the throne and before the Lamb" (7:9; cf. 19:1, 6). This gathering is triumphant, joyful, and worshipful, always in celebration of the Father's salvific work through the Son (7:10, 14), reflected in the "white robes" given them to wear (cf. 3:5; 7:9, 13, 14; 19:8, 14; 22:14). These garments of "fine linen, bright and clean" later identify the Church as Christ's "bride" (19:7), who herself has been "invited to the wedding supper of the Lamb!" (19:9). Along with worship, the multitude of believers is also gathered to "serve him day and night in his temple" (7:15). Reciprocating the intimate worship and service of the redeemed, God blesses those He has gathered to Himself with His very own presence, provision, and protection.

To find the gathering of the Church before God's throne in the words of 4:1—"Come up here"—is inconclusive, since here John is called personally to a Heavenly perspective (and that, while still in his natural body). Likewise, to identify the "144,000" of 14:1-4 as distinct from the multitude of 7:9-17 can also not be concluded (the number symbolizing the full reckoning of the redeemed). Certainly, the "new song"—exclusively learned and sung by the redeemed (14:3)—serves to identity them *with* rather than distinguish them *from* the redeemed who sing before God's throne in 7:10 (cf. Ps. 40:3; 149:1). The same connection is seen in that "they were purchased from among mankind and offered as firstfruits to God and the Lamb" (cf. 14:4 with 5:9). And again, that the "144,000" of 14:1 have "his name and his Father's name written on their foreheads" compares with Christ's promise to the Church in 2:17; 3:12; and 22:4.

What is certain is that God's promise to the Church is to "keep you from [*ek*, 'out of'] the hour of trial that is going to come on the whole world to test the inhabitants of the earth" (3:10), which certainly speaks of the coming wrath of God upon a rebellious world (6:17). While the presence and persecution of saints throughout the Last Days Tribulation is clear (13:10; 14:12, 13), it is also clear that the redeemed will return *with Jesus* at His Revelation at the end of the Tribulation—"and with him will be his called, chosen and faithful followers" (17:14; 19:14). They must be first gathered to Him before they can return with Him!

> ► See also under Ecclesiology: God's Promises to the True Church—the Redeemed of All Ages

> ► See also under Eschatology: The Resurrection and Eternal Reward of the Righteous

The Great Tribulation—The Wrath of God in Judgment Upon the Unrepentant

(Note: while the entirety of Chapters 5-19 address the events of the Tribulation, the following verses specifically describe the outpouring of God's wrath upon unrepentant humanity.)

3:10—"the hour of trial that is going to come on the whole world to test the inhabitants of the earth"

5:1—"Then I saw in the right hand of him who sat on the throne a scroll with writing on both sides and sealed with seven seals" (also 5:2-9; 6:1-12; 8:1)

5:5—"See, the Lion of the tribe of Judah, the Root of David, has triumphed. He is able to open the scroll and its seven seals" (also 5:6-9; 6:1)

6:1—"I watched as the Lamb opened the first of the seven seals" (also 6:2-14)

6:2—"I looked, and there before me was a white horse! Its rider held a bow, and he was given a crown, and he rode out as a conqueror bent on conquest" (also 9:16; 16:14, 16; 19:19)

6:3—"When the Lamb opened the second seal, I heard the second living creature say, 'Come!'"

6:4—"Then another horse came out, a fiery red one. Its rider was given power to take peace from the earth and to make people kill each other. To him was given a large sword"

6:5a—"When the Lamb opened the third seal, I heard the third living creature say, 'Come!'"

6:5b—"I looked, and there before me was a black horse! Its rider was holding a pair of scales in his hand"

6:6—"Then I heard what sounded like a voice among the four living creatures, saying, 'Two pounds of wheat for a day's wages, and six pounds of barley for a day's wages, and do not damage the oil and the wine!'"

6:7—"When the Lamb opened the fourth seal, I heard the voice of the fourth living creature say, 'Come!'"

6:8a—"I looked, and there before me was a pale horse! Its rider was named Death, and Hades was following close behind him" (also 20:13, 14)

6:8b—"They were given power over a fourth of the earth to kill by sword, famine and plague, and by the wild beasts of the earth"

6:10—"They called out in a loud voice, 'How long, Sovereign Lord, holy and true, until you judge the inhabitants of the earth and avenge our blood?'" (also 6:9, 11; 16:6; 17:6; 18:24; 19:2)

6:12—"I watched as he opened the sixth seal. There was a great earthquake. The sun turned black like sackcloth made of goat hair, the whole moon turned blood red" (also 11:13; 16:18, 19)

6:13—"and the stars in the sky fell to earth, as figs drop from a fig tree when shaken by a strong wind"

6:14—"The heavens receded like a scroll being rolled up, and every mountain and island was removed from its place" (also 16:20)

6:15—"Then the kings of the earth, the princes, the generals, the rich, the mighty, and everyone else, both slave and free, hid in caves and among the rocks of the mountains" (also 19:17)

6:16—"They called to the mountains and the rocks, 'Fall on us and hide us from the face of him who sits on the throne and from the wrath of the Lamb!'" (also 6:17; 11:18; 14:10, 19; 15:1, 7; 16:1, 19; 19:15)

7:14—"These are they who have come out of the great tribulation" (also 1:9)

8:1—"When he opened the seventh seal, there was silence in heaven for about half an hour"

8:2—"And I saw the seven angels who stand before God, and seven trumpets were given to them" (also 8:7, 8, 10, 12; 9:1, 13; 11:15)

8:5—"Then the angel took the censer, filled it with fire from the altar, and hurled it on the earth; and there came peals of thunder, rumblings, flashes of lightning and an earthquake" (also 6:12; 11:19; 16:18)

8:7a—"The first angel sounded his trumpet, and there came hail and fire mixed with blood, and it was hurled down on the earth"

8:7b—"A third of the earth was burned up, a third of the trees were burned up, and all the green grass was burned up" (also 16:8, 9)

8:8a—"The second angel sounded his trumpet, and something like a huge mountain, all ablaze, was thrown into the sea"

8:8b—"A third of the sea turned into blood" (also 16:3, 4) 8:9—"a third of the living creatures in the sea died, and a third of the ships were destroyed" (also 16:3)

8:10—"The third angel sounded his trumpet, and a great star, blazing like a torch, fell from the sky on a third of the rivers and on the springs of water" (also 16:4)

8:11—"the name of the star is Wormwood. A third of the waters turned bitter, and many people died from the waters that had become bitter" (also 16:3, 4)

8:12a—"The fourth angel sounded his trumpet, and a third of the sun was struck, a third of the moon, and a third of the stars, so that a third of them turned dark" (also 16:10)

8:12b—"A third of the day was without light, and also a third of the night" (also 16:10)

8:13—"As I watched, I heard an eagle that was flying in midair call out in a loud voice: 'Woe! Woe! Woe to the inhabitants of the earth, because of the trumpet blasts about to be sounded by the other three angels!'" (also 8:2; 9:12, 11:14; 12:12; 18:10, 16, 19)

9:1a—"The fifth angel sounded his trumpet, and I saw a star that had fallen from the sky to the earth"

9:1b—"The star was given the key to the shaft of the Abyss" (also 9:2, 11; 20:1, 3)

9:2a—"When he opened the Abyss, smoke rose from it like the smoke from a gigantic furnace"

9:2b—"The sun and sky were darkened by the smoke from the Abyss" (also 11:17; 17:8)

9:3—"And out of the smoke locusts came down on the earth and were given power like that of scorpions of the earth" (also 9:5)

9:4—"They were told not to harm the grass of the earth or any plant or tree, but only those people who did not have the seal of God on their foreheads" (also 7:3)

9:5—"They were not allowed to kill them but only to torture them for five months. And the agony they suffered was like that of the sting of a scorpion when it strikes" (also 9:3)

9:6—"During those days people will seek death but will not find it; they will long to die, but death will elude them" (also 6:16)

9:7—"The locusts looked like horses prepared for battle" (also 9:8, 9)

9:10—"They had tails with stingers, like scorpions, and in their tails they had power to torment people for five months" (also 9:3, 5)

9:12—"The first woe is past; two other woes are yet to come" (also 8:13; 11:14)

9:13—"The sixth angel sounded his trumpet, and I heard a voice coming from the four horns of the golden altar that is before God"

9:14—"It said to the sixth angel who had the trumpet, 'Release the four angels who are bound at the great river Euphrates'" (also 16:12)

9:15—"And the four angels who had been kept ready for this very hour and day and month and year were released to kill a third of mankind" (also 9:18)

9:16—"The number of the mounted troops was twice ten thousand times ten thousand. I heard their number" (also 6:2, 4; 9:17-19; 16:14, 16)

9:20—"The rest of mankind who were not killed by these plagues still did not repent [...]" (also 9:21; 16:9, 11)

10:4—"but I heard a voice from heaven say, 'Seal up what the seven thunders have said and do not write it down'" (also 10:3-7)

11:13—"At that very hour there was a severe earthquake and a tenth of the city collapsed. Seven thousand people were killed in the earthquake" (also 6:12; 11:19; 16:18, 19)

11:14—"The second woe has passed; the third woe is coming soon" (also 8:13)

11:15a—"The seventh angel sounded his trumpet, and there were loud voices in heaven" (also 7:10; 14:2; 19:1)

11:15b—"The kingdom of the world has become the kingdom of our Lord and of his Messiah, and he will reign for ever and ever'" (also 2:27; 12:5; 19:15)

11:18a—"The nations were angry, and your wrath has come" (also 6:16, 17; 14:10, 19; 15:1, 7; 16:1, 19; 19:15)

11:18b—"The time has come for judging the dead, and for rewarding your servants the prophets and your people who revere your name, both great and small—and for destroying those who destroy the earth" (also 20:12,13)

11:19—"And there came flashes of lightning, rumblings, peals of thunder, an earthquake and a severe hailstorm" (also 6:12; 8:5; 11:13; 16:18)

14:8—"A second angel followed and said, 'Fallen! Fallen is Babylon the Great,' which made all the nations drink the maddening wine of her adulteries" (also 16:19; 18:2, 3)

14:9—"A third angel followed them and said in a loud voice: 'If anyone worships the beast and its image and receives its mark on their forehead or on their hand, […]" (also 13:4, 8, 12; 14:11)

14:10a—"[…] they, too, will drink the wine of God's fury, which has been poured full strength into the cup of his wrath" (also 6:16, 17; 11:18; 14:19; 15:1, 7; 16:1, 19; 18:6, 7; 19:15)

14:10b—"They will be tormented with burning sulfur in the presence of the holy angels and of the Lamb" (also 14:11)

14:15—"Then another angel came out of the temple and called in a loud voice to him who was sitting on the cloud, 'Take your sickle and reap, because the time to reap has come, for the harvest of the earth is ripe'" (also 14:16, 17)

14:18—"Still another angel, who had charge of the fire, came from the altar and called in a loud voice to him who had the sharp sickle, 'Take your sharp sickle and gather the clusters of grapes from the earth's vine, because its grapes are ripe'" (also 14:19)

14:19—"The angel swung his sickle on the earth, gathered its grapes and threw them into the great winepress of God's wrath" (also 6:16, 17; 11:18; 14:10; 15:1, 7; 16:1, 19; 19:15)

14:20—"They were trampled in the winepress outside the city, and blood flowed out of the press, rising as high as the horses' bridles for a distance of 1,600 stadia" (also 9:16; 16:14; 19:19)

15:1—"the seven last plagues—last, because with them God's wrath is completed" (also 6:16, 17; 11:18; 14:10, 19; 15:6, 7; 16:1, 19; 19:15)

15:6—"Out of the temple came the seven angels with the seven plagues" (also 15:8; 16:1; 17:1; 21:9)

15:7—"seven golden bowls filled with the wrath of God" (also 6:16, 17; 11:18; 14:10, 19; 15:1; 16:1-17, 19; 19:15)

16:2—"The first angel went and poured out his bowl on the land, and ugly, festering sores broke out on the people who had the mark of the beast and worshiped its image"

16:3—"The second angel poured out his bowl on the sea, and it turned into blood like that of a dead person, and every living thing in the sea died"

16:4—"The third angel poured out his bowl on the rivers and springs of water, and they became blood"

16:5—"Then I heard the angel in charge of the waters say: 'You are just in these judgments, O Holy One, […]" (also 16:6, 7)

16:8—"The fourth angel poured out his bowl on the sun, and the sun was allowed to scorch people with fire" (also 16:9)

16:10—"The fifth angel poured out his bowl on the throne of the beast, and its kingdom was plunged into darkness. People gnawed their tongues in agony" (also 16:11)

16:12—"The sixth angel poured out his bowl on the great river Euphrates, and its water was dried up to prepare the way for the kings from the East" (also 9:14)

16:14—"They are demonic spirits that perform signs, and they go out to the kings of the whole world, to gather them for the battle on the great day of God Almighty" (also 16:13, 16; 17:14; 19:15, 17, 18)

16:15—"'Look, I come like a thief!' Blessed is the one who stays awake and remains clothed, so as not to go naked and be shamefully exposed" (also 3:3, 17)

16:17—"The seventh angel poured out his bowl into the air, and out of the temple came a loud voice from the throne, saying, 'It is done!'"

16:18—"No earthquake like it has ever occurred since mankind has been on earth, so tremendous was the quake" (also 6:12; 11:19)

16:19a—"The great city split into three parts, and the cities of the nations collapsed" (also 11:8, 19; 18:10)

16:19b—"God remembered Babylon the Great and gave her the cup filled with the wine of the fury of his wrath" (also 6:16, 17; 11:18; 14:8, 10, 19; 15:1, 7; 16:1; 18:2; 19:15)

16:20—"Every island fled away and the mountains could not be found" (also 6:14)

16:21a—"From the sky huge hailstones, each weighing about a hundred pounds, fell on people" (also 8:7)

16:21b—"And they cursed God on account of the plague of hail, because the plague was so terrible" (also 16:9, 11)

17:1—"Come, I will show you the punishment of the great prostitute" (also 17:2-7, 15, 16, 18)

17:14—"They will wage war against the Lamb, but the Lamb will triumph over them because he is Lord of lords and King of kings" (also 17:12, 13; 19:19)

17:17—"For God has put it into their hearts to accomplish his purpose by agreeing to hand over to the beast their royal authority, until God's words are fulfilled" (also 18:8)

18:2—"Fallen! Fallen is Babylon the Great!" (also 14:8; 16:19; 18:3)

18:4—"'Come out of her, my people,' so that you will not share in her sins, so that you will not receive any of her plagues; [...]"

18:5—"for her sins are piled up to heaven, and God has remembered her crimes"

18:6—"Give back to her as she has given; pay her back double for what she has done. Pour her a double portion from her own cup" (also 18:7)

18:8—"Therefore in one day her plagues will overtake her: death, mourning and famine. She will be consumed by fire, for mighty is the Lord God who judges her" (also 17:17; 18:4)

18:9—"When the kings of the earth who committed adultery with her and shared her luxury see the smoke of her burning, they will weep and mourn over her" (also 18:16)

18:10—"Terrified at her torment, they will stand far off and cry: 'Woe! Woe to you, great city, you mighty city of Babylon! In one hour your doom has come!'" (also 14:8; 16:19; 18:3, 17, 19)

18:11—"The merchants of the earth will weep and mourn over her because no one buys their cargoes anymore" (also 18:12-16, 23)

18:18—"When they see the smoke of her burning, they will exclaim, 'Was there ever a city like this great city?'" (also 18:17)

18:19a—"They will throw dust on their heads, and with weeping and mourning cry out: 'Woe! Woe to you, great city, where all who had ships on the sea became rich through her wealth! [...]'" (also 18:15, 17)

18:19b—"In one hour she has been brought to ruin!" (also 18:10, 17)

18:20—"Rejoice over her, you heavens! Rejoice, you people of God! Rejoice, apostles and prophets! For God has judged her with the judgment she imposed on you" (also 18:6, 8, 24)

18:21—"Then a mighty angel picked up a boulder the size of a large millstone and threw it into the sea, and said: 'With such violence the great city of Babylon will be thrown down, never to be found again [...]'" (also 14:8; 16:19; 18:3, 10, 17, 19)

18:22a—"The music of harpists and musicians, pipers and trumpeters, will never be heard in you again"

18:22b—"No worker of any trade will ever be found in you again. The sound of a millstone will never be heard in you again [...]" (also 18:23)

19:11—"With justice he judges and wages war" (also 17:14; 19:12-14, 19)

19:15a—"Coming out of his mouth is a sharp sword with which to strike down the nations. 'He will rule them with an iron scepter'" (also 2:27; 11:15; 19:21)

19:15b—"He treads the winepress of the fury of the wrath of God Almighty" (also 6:16, 17; 11:18; 14:10, 19; 15:1, 7; 16:1, 19)

19:17—"to all the birds flying in midair, 'Come, gather together for the great supper of God [...]'" (also 19:21)

19:18—"so that you may eat the flesh of kings, generals, and the mighty, of horses and their riders, and the flesh of all people, free and slave, great and small" (also 6:15; 19:21)

19:20a—"But the beast was captured, and with it the false prophet who had performed the signs on its behalf" (also 13:13-15)

19:20b—"The two of them were thrown alive into the fiery lake of burning sulfur" (also 20:10, 14)

19:21—"The rest were killed with the sword coming out of the mouth of the rider on the horse, and all the birds gorged themselves on their flesh" (also 2:12; 19:11, 15, 17)

Summary Statement: Though the majority of the Revelation is given to detailed description of unprecedented suffering on the earth, the term "the great tribulation" is used only once (7:14) to describe this period of Last Days judgment. "Tribulation" here is *thlipsis*, which refers to the pressing in of distress and affliction, the literal reading being, "the tribulation, the great one" (cf. Matt. 24:21, 29; Mark 13:19, 24). One additional phrase, "the hour of trial" (*peirasmos*; meaning, a trial, adversity, or affliction [here, sent by God]) is used in 3:10 to identify this same period "that is going to come on the whole world to test [*peirazō*, to prove or try] the inhabitants of the earth." Yet, the most consistently used term to describe this coming

Tribulation is "wrath," the translation of the word *orgē* ("anger, wrath, indignation" [Thayer]) in 6:16, 17; 11:18; 14:10; 16:19; 19:15) and *thymos* ("anger forthwith boiling up and soon subsiding again" [Thayer]) in 14:19; 15:1, 7; 16:1. Both words come together in 14:10, 16:19, and 19:15 to describe the "fury" of God's "wrath," which is also often pictured through the metaphor of grapes thrown into a winepress, the wine then being "poured full strength in the cup of his wrath" (14:10, 15-19; 16:19; 18:6; 19:15).

This wrath proceeds from the throne of both the Father and the Son (the Lamb in 6:16). It is only Jesus—"the Lion of the tribe of Judah, the Root of David"—who "is able to open the scroll and its seven seals" (5:5). He alone is qualified to open this Book of Redemption (6:1-14) since He alone "has triumphed" through the shedding of His blood (5:5-8; cf. 17:14). Yet, God also employs holy angels to minister His judgments (e.g., 6:1, 3, 5, 7; 8:2, 5, 7, 8, 10, 12; 9:1, 13; 11:15; 14:10; 15:6-8; 16:1-17; 20:1). God's sovereign will and initiative in carrying out judgment on the earth is found in such verses as 16:17, "and out of the temple came a loud voice from the throne, saying, 'It is done!'"; 17:17, "For God has put it into their hearts to accomplish his purpose [...], until God's words are fulfilled"; and, 18:8, "for mighty is the Lord God who judges her."

The reason for God's wrath is related directly to humanity's continued wickedness and because, "they cursed the name of God, who had control over these plagues, but they refused to repent and glorify him" (16:9, 11; 9:20, 21; 21:8). God will judge those who worship the dragon and the beast (13:4, 8, 12, 14:9, 11) and He will destroy "those who destroy the earth" (11:18). Additionally, God will avenge the blood of his saints (6:9-10; 16:6; 17:6; 18:24; 19:2). The scope of the Tribulation judgments is universal. On earth, God's wrath will "come on the whole world to test the inhabitants of the earth" (3:10) including every stratum of society, "kings, generals, and the mighty, of horses and their riders, and the flesh of all people, free and slave, great and small" (19:18; cf. 6:15). God will judge the wickedness of Babylon, "which made all the nations drink the maddening wine of her adulteries" (14:8; cf. 16:19; 18:2, 3). At the apex of the Tribulation judgments, John states, "the stars in the sky fell to earth, as figs drop from a fig tree when shaken by a strong wind. The heavens receded like a scroll being rolled up, and every mountain and island was removed from its place" (6:13-14; cf. 16:20). Certainly, nothing could be more final.

Of special note is that all of the Tribulation judgments described in the Revelation are contained in "a scroll with writing on both sides and sealed with seven seals" (5:1), which can only be opened by the Lamb. The significance of the seals (historically, placed there by seven witnesses according to Roman law) is that they secure the contents of the scroll until an appointed time. The breaking of each seal (Chapter 6) in turn indicates both the wrath of God, but also the warring of man and the persecution of God's people. Additionally, it is inconceivable that the thorough devastation and finality of the sixth seal (again, see 6:13-14; cf. 16:20) could be followed by sustained life on earth without God's intervention. Thus, it is best to understand the seven "seals" as a panoramic overview of the contents of the scroll, a preface to the book, as it were, before it is opened.

It is only with the opening of the seventh seal in 8:1 that the details of God's judgments are presented from the vantage point of Heaven. These first come in the form of "seven trumpets" (8:1-11:19), which include: worldwide devastation by fire (8:7); global devastation of the seas and sea life (8:8-9); widespread poisoning of the earth's water sources (8:10-11); universal darkening of earth's light sources (8:12); the release of tormenting "locusts" (9:1-11); the death of one-third of humanity at the hands of "200 million mounted troops" (NLT; 9:13-16). The sounding of the "seventh trumpet" announces the triumph of the Father and of His Anointed (11:15-18), opening the way for the pouring out of the final seven "bowl" judgments (15:1-16:21); these are "the seven last plagues—last, because with them God's wrath is completed" (15:1; cf. 15:6-8; 17:1; 21:9).

Poured from these "bowls" are the following: "ugly, festering sores" (16:2); ubiquitous death to all sea life (16:3); water sources turned to blood (16:4); intense heat from the sun (16:8-9); agonizing darkness and pain (16:10-11); preparation and gathering for the final world war (16:12-14; cf. 9:14-16; 19:19); and, a world-wide cataclysmic earthquake (16:18-19; cf. 6:12).

It must be pointed out that no time frame is given in Revelation for the duration of these judgments. A period of 1,260 days (equal to 42 months or 3 ½ years in lunar time) is related to the ministry of the "two witnesses" (11:3) and to God's protective care of "the woman" in the desert (12:6)—parallel to "a time, times, and an half" (12:14; cf. Dan. 7:25; 12:7, 11). Aligned with a period of "42 months" (again, 3 ½ years) is also the trampling of the "holy city" by the Gentiles (11:2) and the exercised authority of the beast (13:5). Yet, no clear and specific time frame aligns with the actual outpouring of God's wrath in the Book of Revelation.

▶ See also under Anthropology: Spiritual and Physical Death, the Consequence of Unrepentant Wickedness

▶ See also under Anthropology: The Effect of Humanity's Sin Upon the Natural/ Physical Earth and World

▶ See also under Hamartiology: God's Call to Repentance & God's Judgment upon the Unrepentant

Persecution and Martyrdom of Tribulation Saints and of the Jewish People

1:9—"I, John, your brother and companion in the suffering and kingdom and patient endurance that are ours in Jesus" (also 2:10)

6:9—"I saw under the altar the souls of those who had been slain because of the word of God and the testimony they had maintained" (also 1:2, 9; 12:11; 20:4)

6:10—"They called out in a loud voice, 'How long, Sovereign Lord, holy and true, until you judge the inhabitants of the earth and avenge our blood?'" (also 6:9, 11; 16:6; 17:6; 18:24; 19:2)

6:11a—"Then each of them was given a white robe" (also 3:4, 5, 18; 7:9, 13, 14; 19:8, 14; 22:14)

6:11b—"[…] and they were told to wait a little longer, until the full number of their fellow servants, their brothers and sisters, were killed just as they had been" (also 16:6; 17:6; 18:24; 19:2)

7:14—"These are they who have come out of the great tribulation" (also 1:9)

11:2—"it has been given to the Gentiles. They will trample on the holy city for 42 months" (also 13:5)

11:7—"Now when they have finished their testimony, the beast that comes up from the Abyss will attack them, and overpower and kill them" (also 11:8-10; 13:7)

12:11a—"They triumphed over him by the blood of the Lamb and by the word of their testimony" (also 1:2, 5, 9; 5:9; 6:9; 7:14; 12:17; 17:6; 19:10; 20:4)

12:11b—"they did not love their lives so much as to shrink from death" (also 6:9; 16:6; 17:6; 18:24; 19:2; 20:4)

12:13—"When the dragon saw that he had been hurled to the earth, he pursued the woman who had given birth to the male child" (also 12:4, 14, 17)

12:15—"Then from his mouth the serpent spewed water like a river, to overtake the woman and sweep her away with the torrent" (also 12:16)

12:17—"Then the dragon was enraged at the woman and went off to wage war against the rest of her offspring" (also 12:4, 13; 13:7; 17:14)

13:7—"It was given power to wage war against God's holy people and to conquer them" (also 13:2)

13:10a—"If anyone is to go into captivity, into captivity they will go. If anyone is to be killed with the sword, with the sword they will be killed" (also 6:4, 8)

13:10b—"This calls for patient endurance and faithfulness on the part of God's people" (also 1:9; 14:12)

13:15—"and cause all who refused to worship the image to be killed" (also 13:14; 15:2; 20:4)

13:17—"so that they could not buy or sell unless they had the mark, which is the name of the beast or the number of its name" (also 13:16)

14:4—"and offered as firstfruits to God and the Lamb"

14:13a—"Blessed are the dead who die in the Lord from now on" (also 1:3; 6:9, 10; 12:11; 16:6, 15; 17:6; 18:24; 19:2, 9; 20:6; 22:7, 14)

14:13b—"'Yes,' says the Spirit, 'they will rest from their labor, for their deeds will follow them'" (also 2:2, 19; 3:8)

15:2—"standing beside the sea, those who had been victorious over the beast and its image and over the number of its name" (also 13:16, 17; 20:4)

16:6—"for they have shed the blood of your holy people and your prophets" (also 6:6, 10; 17:6; 18:24; 19:2; 20:4)

17:6—"I saw that the woman was drunk with the blood of God's holy people, the blood of those who bore testimony to Jesus" (also 1:2, 9; 6:6, 10; 16:6; 17:6; 18:24; 19:2; 20:4)

17:14—"They will wage war against the Lamb, [...] and with him will be his called, chosen and faithful followers" (also 12:17; 13:7; 19:14, 19)

18:20—"For God has judged her with the judgment she imposed on you" (also 16:6; 17:6; 18:24)

18:24—"In her was found the blood of prophets and of God's holy people, of all who have been slaughtered on the earth" (also 6:9, 10; 13:7; 16:6; 17:6; 19:2; 20:4)

19:2—"He has avenged on her the blood of his servants" (also 18:20)

19:19—"Then I saw the beast and the kings of the earth and their armies gathered together to wage war against the rider on the horse and his army" (also 17:14; 19:14)

20:4—"And I saw the souls of those who had been beheaded because of their testimony about Jesus and because of the word of God" (also 6:9; 10; 16:6; 17:6; 19:2)

Summary Statement: While the most common New Testament word for "persecution" (from *diōkō*) is found just once in Revelation (12:13; NIV, "pursued")—and there in regard to the persecution of Israel, "the woman," by the dragon—much attention is given to the suffering of God's people throughout all ages from John's day through to the Revelation of Jesus. John begins his writing by referencing "suffering" (*thlipsis*, the pressing in of distress and affliction), and Jesus acknowledges and warns the Church that "afflictions" (2:9; *thlipsis*), "suffering" (2:10; from *paschō*), and extended "persecution" (2:10; here, *thlipsis*) were already present in John's day. Nevertheless, those who suffer for righteousness sake in every age are considered victorious overcomers (2:11; 7:9).

As pertains to the Last Days and the period of the "Great Tribulation," John several times refers to the shedding of blood and the martyrdom of Christ's followers (also 6:9, 10; 7:14; 12:11; 13:7, 15; 17:6; 19:2; 20:4) and of those prophets and apostles who have gone before (16:6; 18:20, 24). Most vividly, in describing this vast persecution, John sees "under the altar" in Heaven "the souls of those who had been slain because of the word of God and the testimony they had maintained" (6:9). While gathered from all nations is the "great multitude" of those "who have come out of the great tribulation" (7:14), we cannot doubt—especially in consideration of the "144,000 from all the tribes of Israel" sealed on their foreheads as "servants of our God" (7:3) and of the hatred of the dragon for Israel (12:13-17)—that much of this persecution is directed against the faithful of Israel. Whereas no timeframe is attributed to the outpouring of God's wrath itself, the Last Days persecution of God's people is related to a specific period of 3 ½ years, i.e., "42 months" (11:2; cf. 13:5); "1,260 days" (12:6; cf. 11:3); and, "a time, times, and half a time" (12:14; cf. Dan. 7:25; 12:7).

▶ See also under Ecclesiology: The Activities and Experiences of the True Church—the Redeemed of All Ages

Spiritual Warfare Led by Satan in the Last Days and His Final Demise and Judgment

9:11—"They had as king over them the angel of the Abyss, whose name in Hebrew is Abaddon and in Greek is Apollyon (that is, Destroyer)" (also 9:1, 2; 11:7; 17:8; 20:1, 3)

12:3—"Then another sign appeared in heaven: an enormous red dragon with seven heads and ten horns and seven crowns on its heads" (also 12:4, 7, 9, 16, 17; 13:1, 2, 4, 11; 16:13; 17:3; 20:2)

12:4—"The dragon stood in front of the woman who was about to give birth, so that it might devour her child the moment he was born" (also 12:13)

12:7—"Michael and his angels fought against the dragon, and the dragon and his angels fought back"

12:8—"But he was not strong enough"

12:9a—"The great dragon was hurled down—that ancient serpent called the devil, or Satan, who leads the whole world astray" (also 20:2)

12:9b—"He was hurled to the earth, and his angels with him" (also 12:7, 8, 10)

12:10—"For the accuser of our brothers and sisters, who accuses them before our God day and night"

12:11—"They triumphed over him by the blood of the Lamb and by the word of their testimony; they did not love their lives so much as to shrink from death" (also 17:14)

12:12a—"But woe to the earth and the sea, because the devil has gone down to you!" (also 12:9)

12:12b—"He is filled with fury, because he knows that his time is short" (also 11:18)

12:13—"When the dragon saw that he had been hurled to the earth, he pursued the woman who had given birth to the male child" (also 12:4, 17)

12:14—"out of the serpent's reach" (also 12:15)

12:15—"Then from his mouth the serpent spewed water like a river, to overtake the woman and sweep her away with the torrent" (also 12:16)

12:17—"Then the dragon was enraged at the woman and went off to wage war against the rest of her offspring" (also 12:4, 13)

13:1—"The dragon stood on the shore of the sea" (also 12:3, 9)

13:2—"The dragon gave the beast his power and his throne and great authority" (also 13:4, 7)

13:4—"People worshiped the dragon because he had given authority to the beast" (also 13:2, 5, 6, 7)

13:7—"It was given power to wage war against God's holy people and to conquer them" (also 13:2)

13:11—"It had two horns like a lamb, but it spoke like a dragon" (also 13:5)

16:13—"they came out of the mouth of the dragon" (also 13:5, 11)

20:2—"He seized the dragon, that ancient serpent, who is the devil, or Satan, and bound him for a thousand years" (also 12:9; 20:1-6)

20:3a—"He threw him into the Abyss, and locked and sealed it over him" (also 11:7; 20:1, 2)

20:3b—"to keep him from deceiving the nations anymore until the thousand years were ended" (also 13:7, 8; 20:8, 10)

20:7—"When the thousand years are over, Satan will be released from his prison" (also 20:2, 3)

20:8—"and will go out to deceive the nations in the four corners of the earth—Gog and Magog—and to gather them for battle" (also 20:3, 10)

20:10a—"And the devil, who deceived them, was thrown into the lake of burning sulfur, where the beast and the false prophet had been thrown" (also 19:20)

20:10b—"They will be tormented day and night for ever and ever" (also 20:14; 21:8)

Summary Statement: Satan, also identified as "the angel of the Abyss" (9:11); "Apollyon"/"Abaddon"/"Destroyer" (9:11); the devil; the dragon; and, "the ancient Serpent" (12:9, 14) is certainly a major figure in the end time drama. His personage is clearly defined as furious, murderous, accusatory, deceptive, and blasphemous; in fact, he invites the worship of rebellious humanity. It becomes clear by Chapter 12 that Satan is the driving force behind wickedness in the (second) heavens and in the earth. He deceives and leads astray all the nations of the earth (also 20:2, 8, 10) and he directs the evil activities of fallen angels (12:7), the first beast (13:2, 4, 7), and the second beast (13:11). His direct connection with Babylon is seen in that both appear "with seven heads and ten horns" (12:3; 17:3), which also associates him with wicked earthly rulers and end-time kings (17:10-13).

From the ancient past up until a determined period of time, Satan's rule issues from the "heavens" (12:3, 7). With defeat at the hands of archangel Michael and his angels, Satan and his angels are "hurled to the earth" (12:9, 10, 12). As the chief enemy of God, the dragon opposes and persecutes the following: "the woman" and the male child, Jesus, to whom she gives birth (12:4, 13, 15-17); Michael and his angels (12:7); Jesus, the Lamb (17:14; 19:19); and,

God's holy people (12:11, 17; 13:7; 16:6; 17:6, 14; 18:24). Satan, in fact, does not prevail against any of these his foes. At the Revelation of Jesus, the devil will be bound in the Abyss, which is locked and sealed for one thousand years (20:2-6), keeping him "from deceiving the nations anymore" (20:3). At the end of this period, he is released for a short time (20:7), at which he once again leads a global rebellion (20:8, 9), which is immediately met with fiery judgment from Heaven (20:9). Satan is then personally judged by God and eternally consigned to "the fiery lake of burning sulfur" (20:10; cf. 19:20; 21:8).

▶ See also under Angelology: The Names, Essence, Attributes, Appearance, Role, and Activities of Satan (Satanology)

▶ See also under Angelology: The Essence, Attributes, Appearance, Role, Activities, and Judgment of Unholy, Fallen Angels (Demonology)

The Appearance and Nefarious Work of the First and Second Beasts and Their Final Demise and Judgment

6:2—"I looked, and there before me was a white horse! Its rider held a bow, and he was given a crown, and he rode out as a conqueror bent on conquest" (also 13:4)

11:7—"Now when they have finished their testimony, the beast that comes up from the Abyss will attack them, and overpower and kill them" (also 17:8)

13:1—"And I saw a beast coming out of the sea. It had ten horns and seven heads, with ten crowns on its horns, and on each head a blasphemous name" (also 17:3, 9, 10, 12)

13:2a—"The beast I saw resembled a leopard, but had feet like those of a bear and a mouth like that of a lion"

13:2b—"The dragon gave the beast his power and his throne and great authority" (also 12:9; 13:4, 7)

13:3a—"One of the heads of the beast seemed to have had a fatal wound, but the fatal wound had been healed" (also 13:12)

13:3b—"The whole world was filled with wonder and followed the beast" (also 13:4)

13:4a—"People worshiped the dragon because he had given authority to the beast" (also 12:9; 13:2, 7)

13:4b—"and they also worshiped the beast and asked, 'Who is like the beast? Who can wage war against it?'" (also 13:7, 8; 19:19)

13:5—"The beast was given a mouth to utter proud words and blasphemies and to exercise its authority for forty-two months" (also 13:6)

13:7a—"It was given power to wage war against God's holy people and to conquer them" (also 13:2, 15; 20:4)

13:7b—"And it was given authority over every tribe, people, language and nation" (also 13:2; 17:15)

13:8—"All inhabitants of the earth will worship the beast—all whose names have not been written in the Lamb's book of life" (also 13:3, 4)

13:11—"Then I saw a second beast, coming out of the earth. It had two horns like a lamb, but it spoke like a dragon" (also 13:1, 5)

13:12—"It exercised all the authority of the first beast on its behalf, and made the earth and its inhabitants worship the first beast, whose fatal wound had been healed" (also 13:3, 4)

13:13—"And it performed great signs, even causing fire to come down from heaven to the earth in full view of the people" (also 13:14)

13:14a—"Because of the signs it was given power to perform on behalf of the first beast, it deceived the inhabitants of the earth" (also 13:8, 13; 19:20)

13:14b—"It ordered them to set up an image in honor of the beast who was wounded by the sword and yet lived" (also 13:3, 12, 15)

13:15—"The second beast was given power to give breath to the image of the first beast, so that the image could speak and cause all who refused to worship the image to be killed" (also 13:14)

13:16—"It also forced all people, great and small, rich and poor, free and slave, to receive a mark on their right hands or on their foreheads" (also 13:17; 19:20)

13:17—"so that they could not buy or sell unless they had the mark, which is the name of the beast or the number of its name" (also 13:18)

13:18—"This calls for wisdom. Let the person who has insight calculate the number of the beast, for it is the number of a man. That number is 666" (also 13:17)

14:9—"If anyone worships the beast and its image and receives its mark on their forehead or on their hand" (also 13:3, 4, 16; 14:10, 11; 16:2; 19:20)

14:11—"There will be no rest day or night for those who worship the beast and its image, or for anyone who receives the mark of its name" (also 13:3, 4, 16; 14:10; 16:2)

15:2—"those who had been victorious over the beast and its image and over the number of its name" (also 20:4)

16:2—"on the people who had the mark of the beast and worshiped its image" (also 13:14, 16; 14:9-11; 19:20)

16:10—"on the throne of the beast, and its kingdom was plunged into darkness"

16:13—"out of the mouth of the beast and out of the mouth of the false prophet" (also 3:5, 6)

17:3—"a scarlet beast that was covered with blasphemous names and had seven heads and ten horns" (also 13:1; 17:9, 10)

17:7—"the beast she rides, which has the seven heads and ten horns" (also 13:1; 17:3)

17:8a—"The beast, which you saw, once was, now is not, and yet will come up out of the Abyss and go to its destruction" (also 11:7; 13:3, 12; 17:11)

17:8b—"the beast, because it once was, now is not, and yet will come" (also 13:12)

17:10—"They are also seven kings. Five have fallen, one is, the other has not yet come; but when he does come, he must remain for only a little while" (also 13:1; 17:3, 8, 9)

17:11—"The beast who once was, and now is not, is an eighth king. He belongs to the seven" (also 13:12; 17:8, 10)

17:12—"The ten horns you saw are ten kings who have not yet received a kingdom, but who for one hour will receive authority as kings along with the beast" (also 13:1; 17:3, 7)

17:13—"They have one purpose and will give their power and authority to the beast" (also 17:12)

17:14—"They will wage war against the Lamb, but the Lamb will triumph over them" (also 19:19)

17:16—"The beast and the ten horns you saw will hate the prostitute" (also 13:1; 17:3, 7, 10, 12)

17:17—"to hand over to the beast their royal authority, until God's words are fulfilled" (also 17:13)

19:19—"Then I saw the beast and the kings of the earth and their armies gathered together to wage war against the rider on the horse and his army" (also 17:13, 14)

19:20a—"But the beast was captured, and with it the false prophet who had performed the signs on its behalf" (also 13:12, 13)

19:20b—"With these signs he had deluded those who had received the mark of the beast and worshiped its image" (also 13:13, 14)

19:20c—"The two of them were thrown alive into the fiery lake of burning sulfur" (also 20:10)

20:4—"They had not worshiped the beast or its image and had not received its mark on their foreheads or their hands" (also 13:15, 16)

Summary Statement: Authorized and empowered by Satan ("the dragon"; 13:2, 4, 7) are two "beasts" with distinct character and actions, yet the same mission. The "first beast" is seen "coming out of the sea" (13:1), which may by Jewish thought indicate the Gentile world (17:15). Above all else, this "first beast" is associated with unrelenting conquest and war (13:4, 7), which may identify him with the first seal "rider" on a white horse, who John sees holding a bow and wearing a crown—"he rode out as a conqueror bent on conquest" (6:2). His fierceness and boldness are portrayed with the imagery of a "leopard," "bear," and "lion" (13:2). Satan empowers this "beast"—who, also comes up from the Abyss (11:7; 17:8)—to "utter proud words and blasphemies" and to wage war directly against God (12:7; 13:5, 6); against the Lamb (17:13, 14; 19:19; cf. 16:16); and, against "God's holy people" (13:2, 7, 15; 15:2; 20:4). Satan also gives this "beast" "his power and his throne and great authority" (13:2) for a period of "forty-two months" (13:5; parallel to the Gentile trampling of Jerusalem in 11:2). The final war on earth will take place at the Revelation of Jesus, Who returns with "the armies of Heaven" (19:14; both angels and redeemed humanity must be included; cf. 17:14; 19:8 and 2 Thess. 1:7). Though the "beast" marshals "the kings of the earth and their armies" (19:19; 17:14) for battle at "the place that in the Hebrew is called Armageddon" (16:16), it is, in fact, God Himself who has called rebellious humanity to this appointment and final encounter with His wrath.

The extent of the "first" beast's supernatural authority and of his ability to demand worshipful allegiance is global and ubiquitous (13:3, 7, 8, 13, 14; 19:20; 20:4). Equally mysterious is the healing of "one of the heads of the beast," which "seemed to have had a fatal wound" (13:3, 12, 14 ["wounded by the sword"]). This is the same "beast" with "ten horns and seven heads" that, for a time, supports (17:3, 7) and then devours (17:16) the adulterous woman, "Mystery Babylon the Mother of Prostitutes" (17:3-5, 7, 9). His heads and horns then identify him with a long progression of global authorities (17:8, 10-11), with a "seven-hilled" location (17:9), and, with ten kings (cf. Daniel 2:33-34, 41-43; 7:20) who rule in association with the "beast" until the time of Christ's Revelation (17:9-13, 17). While the "first beast" may be identified as a governing system, he is also clearly recognized as an individual person, for he personally is captured and "thrown alive" into "the fiery lake of burning sulfur" under the judgment of the Lamb (19:20).

John also sees a second ("another") "beast, coming out of the earth [*gē*]" (13:11). (Inasmuch as "*ge*" is often translated as "land" in the New Testament, it is feasible that John is contrasting the "sea" of 13:1 with the "land" of Israel [cf. Acts 7:3]). Under the authority and empowerment of both "the dragon" and the "first beast," the mission of the second "beast" is to make "the earth and its inhabitants worship the first beast" (13:12). With supernatural—if not religious ("two horns like a lamb," 13:11; "false prophet," 19:20)—deceptive appeal and global power, the second "beast" "performed great signs [...] on behalf of the first beast" (13:13, 14; 19:20; cf. 2 Thess. 2:9-10). Most mysteriously, he orders the inhabitants of the earth "to set up an image in honor of the beast" (13:14) and then gives "breath to the image of the first beast, so that the image could speak" (13:15). Correlated with the mandated worship of this image, the second "beast" "forced all people, great and small, rich and poor, free and slave, to receive a mark on their right hands or on their foreheads, so that they could not buy or sell unless they had the mark" (13:16, 17). Directly associated with "having the mark" is "the number of the beast," which number is "666" (13:18). Here, God is clear; to receive "the mark" (tantamount to worshiping the "first beast" and its "image") will result in immediate affliction (16:2) and eternal judgment in the lake of fire (14:9-11). Like the "first beast," the "second" ("false prophet") is also personally captured and "thrown alive" into "the fiery lake of burning sulfur" (19:20).

Note: For an overview of the Rise and Fall of the "Babylon" world system, see under Hamartiology: Humanity's Corporate Sin and Rebellion—The Rise and Fall of the Three-Fold "Babylon" World System

---

The Resurrection and Final Judgment of Unrepentant Humanity, Including the Lake of Fire

11:18—"and your wrath has come. The time has come for judging the dead" (also 6:17; 14:10; 20:12)

13:8—"all whose names have not been written in the Lamb's book of life" (also 3:5; 17:8; 20:12, 15; 21:27)

14:7—"He said in a loud voice, 'Fear God and give him glory, because the hour of his judgment has come [...]'" (also 11:18)

14:9—"If anyone worships the beast and its image and receives its mark on their forehead or on their hand" (also 13:14, 15, 17; 14:11; 16:2; 19:20)

14:10a—"they, too, will drink the wine of God's fury, which has been poured full strength into the cup of his wrath" (also 6:17; 11:18)

14:10b—"They will be tormented with burning sulfur in the presence of the holy angels and of the Lamb" (also 19:20; 20:10, 14, 15; 21:8)

14:11a—"And the smoke of their torment will rise for ever and ever" (also 19:3; 20:10)

14:11b—"There will be no rest day or night for those who worship the beast and its image, or for anyone who receives the mark of its name" (also 13:14, 15, 17; 14:9; 16:2; 19:20)

20:5—"(The rest of the dead did not come to life until the thousand years were ended.)" (also 20:6)

20:9—"But fire came down from heaven and devoured them" (also 18:8)

20:11—"Then I saw a great white throne and him who was seated on it" (also 5:1)

20:12a—"And I saw the dead, great and small, standing before the throne, and books were opened" (also 6:15)

20:12b—"The dead were judged according to what they had done as recorded in the books" (also 20:13)

20:13—"The sea gave up the dead that were in it, and death and Hades gave up the dead that were in them, and each person was judged according to what they had done" (also 11:18; 20:12)

20:14—"Then death and Hades were thrown into the lake of fire. The lake of fire is the second death" (also 19:20; 20:6, 10, 13, 15; 21:8)

20:15—"Anyone whose name was not found written in the book of life was thrown into the lake of fire" (also 3:5; 19:20; 20:10, 12, 14; 21:8)

21:8—"But the cowardly, the unbelieving, the vile, the murderers, the sexually immoral, those who practice magic arts, the idolaters and all liars—they will be consigned to the fiery lake of burning sulfur" (also 19:20; 20:10, 14; 21:27; 22:15)

22:19—"God will take away from that person any share in the tree of life and in the Holy City" (also 2:7; 21:27)

Summary Statement: In addition to the wrath of God manifested through Tribulation judgments upon the wicked while still alive on the earth, God has also determined that those who die without repentance from sin will face eternal judgment and punishment. This, too, is described as His "wrath" (11:18; 14:10) and "the hour of his judgment" (14:7). Specifically, those who face eternal judgment will be any one who "worships the beast and its image and receives its mark" (13:14, 15, 17; 14:11; 16:2; 19:20) and "all whose names have not been written in the Lamb's book of life" (13:8). Following the Revelation of Jesus and His subsequent thousand-year reign (20:4-6), John sees the wicked dead "great and small" (20:12) called before "a great white throne" (20:11) as "death and Hades gave up the dead that were in them" (20:13). Those dead whose names are not found in "the book of life" will be judged "according to what they had done as recorded in the books" (20:12, 13). Having rejected Jesus and having refused to repent (21:27; 22:15), they will be "thrown into the lake of fire" (14:10; 19:20; 20:10, 13, 15; 21:8) where already assigned will be the beast, false prophet, and Satan (19:20; 20:10). There they will know suffering for eternity (14:11; 20:10); this John calls "the second death" (20:14; 21:8).

- ▶ See also under Anthropology: Spiritual and Physical Death, the Consequence of Unrepentant Wickedness
- ▶ See also under Hamartiology: God's Call to Repentance & God's Judgment upon the Unrepentant

The Resurrection and Eternal Reward of the Righteous

2:7—"To the one who is victorious, I will give the right to eat from the tree of life, which is in the paradise of God" (also 22:14)

2:10—"Be faithful, even to the point of death, and I will give you life as your victor's crown" (also 3:11)

2:11—"The one who is victorious will not be hurt at all by the second death" (also 20:6, 14)

2:26—"To the one who is victorious and does my will to the end, I will give authority over the nations" (also 19:15; 20:6)

3:5a—"The one who is victorious will, like them, be dressed in white" (also 7:9; 19:8, 14)

3:5b—"I will never blot out the name of that person from the book of life, but will acknowledge that name before my Father and his angels" (also 20:12; 21:27)

3:12a—"The one who is victorious I will make a pillar in the temple of my God. Never again will they leave it" (also 21:22)

3:12b—"I will write on them the name of my God and the name of the city of my God, the new Jerusalem, which is coming down out of heaven from my God" (also 21:2)

3:12c—"and I will also write on them my new name" (also 2:17)

3:21—"To the one who is victorious, I will give the right to sit with me on my throne, just as I was victorious and sat down with my Father on his throne" (also 20:6)

6:11—"Then each of them was given a white robe, and they were told to wait a little longer, until the full number of their fellow servants, their brothers and sisters, were killed just as they had been" (16:6; 17:6; 18:24; 19:2; 20:4)

7:15—"and he who sits on the throne will shelter them with his presence" (also 21:3)

7:16—"'Never again will they hunger; never again will they thirst. The sun will not beat down on them,' nor any scorching heat" (also 21:6)

7:17—"For the Lamb at the center of the throne will be their shepherd; 'he will lead them to springs of living water.' 'And God will wipe away every tear from their eyes'" (also 21:4, 6)

11:11—"But after the three and a half days the breath of life from God entered them, and they stood on their feet" (also 11:7-10, 12)

11:18—"and for rewarding your servants the prophets and your people who revere your name, both great and small" (also 22:12)

14:13a—"Blessed are the dead who die in the Lord from now on" (also 20:6)

14:13b—"'Yes,' says the Spirit, 'they will rest from their labor, for their deeds will follow them'"

20:4—"They came to life" (also 2:8; 20:5, 6)

20:5—"This is the first resurrection" (also 20:6)

20:6—"Blessed and holy are those who share in the first resurrection" (also 14:13; 20:5)

21:3—"They will be his people, and God himself will be with them and be their God" (also 22:4)

21:4—"'He will wipe every tear from their eyes. There will be no more death' or mourning or crying or pain" (also 7:17)

21:6—"To the thirsty I will give water without cost from the spring of the water of life" (also 7:17; 22:17)

21:7—"Those who are victorious will inherit all this, and I will be their God and they will be my children" (also 21:3; 22:4)

22:4—"They will see his face, and his name will be on their foreheads" (also 21:3, 7; 14:1)

22:12—"Look, I am coming soon! My reward is with me, and I will give to each person according to what they have done" (also 11:18; 20:12, 13)

Summary Statement: In stark contrast to the harrowing eternal destiny of the wicked, the redeemed of the Lord are presented with great and blessed eternal promises in the Revelation. Within the letters to the seven churches (Chapters 2 and 3) are varying aspects of our inheritance as overcomers in Christ, which also relate to our blessed future (21:7). Noteworthy amongst these, Christ's followers will have their names included in "the book of life" (3:5; 20:12; 21:27). In so doing they will not experience the "second death" (20:6; 14) nor the "lake of fire" (21:15), neither will they be included with those who die and are called before the "great white throne" judgment (20:11). In great contrast to the curse and dread of the "second death," the redeemed look forward to being included in the "first resurrection" (20:5, 6).

Of great importance to understanding the timing of the resurrection of the redeemed are the simple words, "They came to life" in 20:4. In light of Christ's proclamation in 2:8, "These are the words of him who is the First and the Last, who died and came to life again," we can only conclude that this "life" speaks of the resurrection of the body since the soul and spirit of Jesus remained alive. It appears, then, that John affixes the time of the bodily resurrection of Tribulation martyrs—"They had not worshiped the beast or his image […]"—as being after the Revelation of Jesus and before the commencement of His thousand-year reign (20:4). Further, we can deduce that the "souls of those who had been slain," which John sees under the altar in Heaven in 6:9, are specifically those who have died during the Great Tribulation (for they, comprising the fifth seal, speak of what is contained within the scroll). Additionally, "they were told to wait a little longer, until the number of their fellow servants and brothers who were to be killed as they had been was completed" (6:11). It seems plausible that in comparison with the bodily resurrection of these same saints in 20:4, the "white robes" given to clothe these "souls" in 6:11 are actually a temporary covering as opposed to their permanent resurrected bodies.

We must then make a comparison with the great multitude of 7:9. These saints too are "wearing white robes" (7:9) and are associated with "the great tribulation" (7:14). However, a clear contrast is seen with the "souls" of 6:9, for these comprise an innumerable number "standing before the throne and in front of the Lamb"; they are not found under the altar. Twice more we find the redeemed clothed in "fine linen, bright [or 'white,' v. 14] and clean"—once as a bride (19:7, 8) and once as an army (19:14; cf. 17:14). It would seem, then, that those dressed in white as a great multitude (7:9) "standing before the throne" and "holding palm branches in their hands" are the same as "his bride [who] has made herself ready" (19:7) and "the armies of heaven […] riding on white horses," battling and defeating the physical kings and armies of the earth. Given their activities and clear contrast with the "souls" of 6:9—who are resurrected only after the Revelation of Jesus at the end of the Tribulation (20:4)—it stands to reason that the multitude, bride, and army have already experienced their resurrection. Supporting this further is the bodily resurrection (11:11) and ascension into Heaven (11:12) of the "two witnesses" (11:3) well before the Revelation of Jesus.

The greatest promise to the redeemed is the eternal reward of God's presence (7:15; 21:3; 22:4), which brings His provision (21:6, 7), comfort (7:17; 21:4), and protection as well (7:16, 17; 21:4, 6). The resurrection of the redeemed is also seen as a time of reward (11:18; cf. 22:12)—"for rewarding your servants the prophets and your people who revere your name, both great and small." It is for these reasons that John hears a voice from Heaven saying, "Blessed are the dead who die in the Lord from now on" (14:13; 20:6).

▶ See also under Anthropology: God's Ultimate Will for Redeemed Humanity Expressed

▶ See also under Soteriology: The Blessings and Privileges of Salvation

▶ See also under Ecclesiology: God's Promises to the True Church—the Redeemed of All Ages

▶ See also under Eschatology: Heaven (Where God's Throne Is), The New Heavens and Earth, and The New Jerusalem

The Millennial Reign of Christ and the Eternal Kingdom of God

1:6—"and has made us to be a kingdom and priests to serve his God and Father—to him be glory and power for ever and ever! Amen" (also 1:9; 5:10)

2:26—"To the one who is victorious and does my will to the end, I will give authority over the nations" (also 2:27; 11:15; 12:5; 15:3; 19:15; 20:4, 6)

3:21a—"To the one who is victorious, I will give the right to sit with me on my throne" (also 5:10; 20:6)

3:21b—"just as I was victorious and sat down with my Father on his throne"

4:2—"and there before me was a throne in heaven with someone sitting on it" (also 1:4; 4:3-6, 9, 10; 5:1, 6, 7, 11, 13; 6:16; 7:9-11, 15, 17; 8:3; 12:5; 14:3, 5; 16:17; 19:4, 5)

5:10—"You have made them to be a kingdom and priests to serve our God, and they will reign on the earth" (also 1:6; 20:4, 6)

5:13—"To him who sits on the throne and to the Lamb be praise and honor and glory and power, for ever and ever!" (also 1:6; 10:6; 11:15)

11:15a—"The kingdom of the world has become the kingdom of our Lord and of his Messiah" (also 12:10; 15:3)

11:15b—"and he will reign for ever and ever" (also 11:17)

11:17—"because you have taken your great power and have begun to reign" (also 11:15)

12:5—"who 'will rule all the nations with an iron scepter'" (also 2:27; 15:3; 19:15)

12:10a—"Now have come the salvation and the power and the kingdom of our God" (also 11:15, 17)

12:10b—"and the authority of his Messiah" (also 2:26, 27; 11:15, 17; 12:5; 19:15)

15:3—"Just and true are your ways, King of the nations" (also 11:15; 12:5)

19:15a—"Coming out of his mouth is a sharp sword with which to strike down the nations" (also 2:26, 27; 12:5; 15:3)

19:15b—"He will rule them with an iron scepter" (also 2:27; 12:5)

20:2—"He seized the dragon, [...] and bound him for a thousand years" (also 20:3, 7)

20:3—"to keep him from deceiving the nations anymore until the thousand years were ended" (also 20:7)

20:4—"They came to life and reigned with Christ a thousand years" (also 5:10; 20:6)

20:5—"(The rest of the dead did not come to life until the thousand years were ended.)" (also 20:12, 13)

20:6a—"but they will be priests of God and of Christ" (also 1:6; 5:10)

20:6b—"and will reign with him for a thousand years" (also 3:21; 20:4)

20:7—"When the thousand years are over, Satan will be released from his prison" (also 20:4, 5, 6)

20:11—"Then I saw a great white throne and him who was seated on it" (also 21:5)

21:5—"And he that sat upon the throne said, Behold, I make all things new" (also 20:11)

22:1—"flowing from the throne of God and of the Lamb" (also 22:3)

22:5—"And they will reign for ever and ever" (also 1:6; 3:21; 5:10; 20:6)

Summary Statement: The truth of the Kingdom of God ("the kingdom of our Lord and of his Messiah" [11:15]) is presented, both, in its current expression or realm (1:6, 9; 5:10) and in its eternal, future realm (11:15, 17; 12:10; cf. 5:10). Central to the Kingdom is the glorious presence of its King, both Father and Son, found upon their thrones (4:2; 20:11; 21:5; etc.). We, too, are promised a place, seated with Him there (3:21; cf. Eph. 2:6). All-important to the eternal realm of the Kingdom of God is that His Kingdom will displace "the kingdom of the world" (11:15) and that He will rule with great authority over the nations of the world (2:26, 27; 11:15, 17; 12:5, 10; 15:3; 19:15), and we with him (2:26). Still greater is that, "[H]e will reign for ever and ever" (11:15; cf. 1:6; 5:13), and we with him (1:6; 22:5).

Only in a limited passage of the Book of Revelation do we read of a particular segment of Christ's eternal kingdom; in 20:2-7, we read six times of a period of "a thousand years." At the beginning of this period, Satan is bound "for a thousand years" (20:2, 7) specifically "to keep him from deceiving the nations anymore until the thousand years were ended" (20:3). Throughout this period, believers "who share in the first resurrection" (20:6; also 20:5) [...] "will reign with him for a thousand years" (20:4, 6). A strong point must be drawn that since the wicked and pervasive activity of Satan, "the dragon," is prevalent throughout the Tribulation period on earth—e.g., 12:12; 13:1, 2, 4, 11—the thousand years cannot include this prior period of judgment. Nor can the thousand years include John's day, for even then Satan was active and authoritative (2:9, 13; 3:9); it cannot be said in these earlier verses that Satan is kept "from deceiving the nations anymore." We can only conclude that the thousand years takes place after the Tribulation judgments upon the earth; after the Revelation of Jesus Christ (19:11-16); after "the first resurrection" (20:5); before the final demise and eternal judgment of Satan (20:10); and, before the eternal judgment of the wicked dead (20:11-15).

▶ See also under Christology: The Current and Eternal Work of Jesus

Heaven (Where God's Throne Is), The New Heavens and Earth, and The New Jerusalem

2:7—"I will give the right to eat from the tree of life, which is in the paradise of God" (also 22:2)

3:12—"the city of my God, the new Jerusalem, which is coming down out of heaven from my God" (also 21:2, 10)

4:1a—"After this I looked, and there before me was a door standing open in heaven"

4:1b—"[...] 'Come up here, and I will show you what must take place after this'" (also 11:12)

4:2—"and there before me was a throne in heaven with someone sitting on it" (also 5:1, 13; 7:10; 20:11; 21:5)

4:3—"A rainbow that shone like an emerald encircled the throne"

4:4—"Surrounding the throne were twenty-four other thrones and seated on them were twenty-four elders" (also 4:10; 5:6, 8, 11; 11:16; 19:4)

4:5a—"From the throne came flashes of lightning, rumblings and peals of thunder" (also 8:5; 11:19)

4:5b—"In front of the throne, seven lamps were blazing. These are the seven spirits of God" (also 1:4; 3:1; 5:6)

4:6a—"Also in front of the throne there was what looked like a sea of glass, clear as crystal" (also 15:2; 22:1)

4:6b—"In the center, around the throne, were four living creatures, and they were covered with eyes, in front and in back" (also 4:8, 9; 5:6, 8, 11, 14; 19:4)

5:6a—"Then I saw a Lamb, looking as if it had been slain, standing at the center of the throne" (also 5:9; 7:10; 13:8)

5:6b—"The Lamb had seven horns and seven eyes, which are the seven spirits of God sent out into all the earth" (also 1:4; 3:1; 4:5)

5:11a—"Then I looked and heard the voice of many angels, numbering thousands upon thousands, and ten thousand times ten thousand" (also 5:12; 7:11, 12; 11:15; 14:17; 21:12)

5:11b—"They encircled the throne and the living creatures and the elders" (also 4:4, 6; 5:12)

5:13a—"Then I heard every creature in heaven and on earth and under the earth and on the sea, and all that is in them, saying: [...]" (also 5:3)

5:13b—"To him who sits on the throne and to the Lamb be praise and honor and glory and power, for ever and ever!" (also 7:10, 12)

7:9—"After this I looked, and there before me was a great multitude that no one could count, from every nation, tribe, people and language, standing before the throne and before the Lamb" (also 7:10; 19:6)

7:11—"They fell down on their faces before the throne and worshiped God" (also 5:8, 11; 19:4)

7:15a—"Therefore, 'they are before the throne of God and serve him day and night in his temple'" (also 1:6; 5:10; 22:3)

7:15b—"and he who sits on the throne will shelter them with his presence" (also 21:3)

8:1—"When he opened the seventh seal, there was silence in heaven for about half an hour" (also 5:1)

8:2—"And I saw the seven angels who stand before God, and seven trumpets were given to them" (also 8:6; 11:15; 14:17; 15:1; 21:9)

10:8—"Then the voice that I had heard from heaven spoke to me once more" (also 9:13; 10:4; 11:12)

11:12—"Then they heard a loud voice from heaven saying to them, 'Come up here'" (also 4:1; 21:3)

11:13—"and the survivors were terrified and gave glory to the God of heaven"

11:19—"Then God's temple in heaven was opened, and within his temple was seen the ark of his covenant" (also 15:5)

12:1—"A great sign appeared in heaven" (also 12:3, 7, 8; 15:1)

12:10—"Then I heard a loud voice in heaven say" (also 5:2, 12; 10:4; 11:12; 14:7, 9, 15, 18; 19:5, 17)

13:6—"God, [...] and his dwelling place and those who live in heaven" (also 21:3)

15:5—"After this I looked, and I saw in heaven the temple—that is, the tabernacle of the covenant law—and it was opened" (also 11:19)

15:8—"And the temple was filled with smoke from the glory of God and from his power" (also 21:11)

18:1—"After this I saw another angel coming down from heaven" (also 10:1, 5; 18:2, 4; 20:1)

18:5—"for her sins are piled up to heaven, and God has remembered her crimes" (18:20)

19:1—"After this I heard what sounded like the roar of a great multitude in heaven" (also 7:10; 14:2; 19:6)

19:9—"Then the angel said to me, 'Write this: Blessed are those who are invited to the wedding supper of the Lamb!'" (also 19:1, 6, 7)

19:11—"I saw heaven standing open and there before me was a white horse"

19:14—"The armies of heaven were following him" (also 17:14)

20:4—"I saw thrones on which were seated those who had been given authority to judge" (also 2:26; 3:21)

20:9—"But fire came down from heaven and devoured them"

20:11—"Then I saw a great white throne and him who was seated on it" (also 4:2; 20:12)

21:1—"Then I saw 'a new heaven and a new earth,' for the first heaven and the first earth had passed away, and there was no longer any sea" (also 20:11, 13; 21:5)

21:2a—"I saw the Holy City, the new Jerusalem, coming down out of heaven from God" (also 3:12; 21:10, 22:19)

21:2b—"prepared as a bride beautifully dressed for her husband" (also 19:7; 21:9)

21:3a—"And I heard a loud voice from the throne saying, 'Look! God's dwelling place is now among the people, and he will dwell with them'" (also 7:15; 13:6)

21:3b—"They will be his people, and God himself will be with them and be their God" (also 21:7)

21:4a—"'He will wipe every tear from their eyes. There will be no more death' or mourning or crying or pain" (also 7:17; 22:3)

21:4b—"for the old order of things has passed away" (also 21:5)

21:5—"He who was seated on the throne said, 'I am making everything new!'" (also 21:1, 4)

21:7—"Those who are victorious will inherit all this" (also 2:7; 3:5, 12, 21; 15:2)

21:11—"It shone with the glory of God, and its brilliance was like that of a very precious jewel, like a jasper, clear as crystal" (also 15:8; 19:1; 21:23)

21:12a—"It had a great, high wall with twelve gates, and with twelve angels at the gates" (also 21:17)

21:12b—"On the gates were written the names of the twelve tribes of Israel" (also 21:13)

21:14—"The wall of the city had twelve foundations, and on them were the names of the twelve apostles of the Lamb" (also 21:12, 17, 19)

21:15—"a measuring rod of gold to measure the city, its gates and its walls" (also 21:12, 14, 17)

21:16a—"The city was laid out like a square, as long as it was wide"

21:16b—"He measured the city with the rod and found it to be 12,000 stadia in length, and as wide and high as it is long" (also 11:1)

21:17—"The angel measured the wall using human measurement, and it was 144 cubits thick" (also 21:12, 15)

21:18—"The wall was made of jasper, and the city of pure gold, as pure as glass" (also 21:12, 17, 21)

21:19—"The foundations of the city walls were decorated with every kind of precious stone. The first foundation was jasper, the second sapphire, the third agate, the fourth emerald" (also 21:14, 20)

21:20—"the fifth onyx, the sixth ruby, the seventh chrysolite, the eighth beryl, the ninth topaz, the tenth turquoise, the eleventh jacinth, and the twelfth amethyst" (also 21:19)

21:21a—"The twelve gates were twelve pearls, each gate made of a single pearl" (also 21:12)

21:21b—"The great street of the city was of gold, as pure as transparent glass" (also 21:18)

21:22—"I did not see a temple in the city, because the Lord God Almighty and the Lamb are its temple" (also 3:12; 7:15; 11:19; 15:5, 8; 16:1, 17; 21:23)

21:23—"The city does not need the sun or the moon to shine on it, for the glory of God gives it light, and the Lamb is its lamp" (also 21:11; 22:5)

21:24—"The nations will walk by its light, and the kings of the earth will bring their splendor into it" (also 21:26; 22:14)

21:25—"On no day will its gates ever be shut, for there will be no night there" (also 21:12, 15, 21, 23; 22:5, 14)

21:26—"The glory and honor of the nations will be brought into it" (also 21:24; 22:14)

21:27a—"Nothing impure will ever enter it, nor will anyone who does what is shameful or deceitful" (also 21:8; 22:14, 15)

21:27b—"but only those whose names are written in the Lamb's book of life" (also 3:5; 20:12)

22:1—"Then the angel showed me the river of the water of life, as clear as crystal, flowing from the throne of God and of the Lamb" (also 4:6; 7:17; 15:2; 21:6; 22:2)

22:2a—"On each side of the river stood the tree of life, bearing twelve crops of fruit, yielding its fruit every month" (also 2:7; 22:1)

22:2b—"And the leaves of the tree are for the healing of the nations" (also 21:26)

22:3a—"No longer will there be any curse" (also 21:4)

22:3b—"The throne of God and of the Lamb will be in the city, and his servants will serve him" (7:15)

Summary Statement: With the words, "Come up here, and I will show you what must take place after this" (4:1), John is given an open door to view events of the Last Days from the perspective of Heaven. "Heaven" is the consistent translation of the word *ouranos*—found 38 times in the Revelation—primarily referring to the eternal dwelling of God (13:6). This is most importantly the place of God's Throne (4:2; 5:1, 13; 21:5) and of the Throne of Jesus (1:4; 3:21), Who is also seen standing before the Throne of the Father (5:6, 13; 7:9, 10, 17). The unity of God is seen in 22:1 and 3 where "the throne" of both "God and of the Lamb" is singular (3:21). Surrounding the Throne of God are the "twenty-four elders" (4:4, 10; etc.) and the "four living creatures" (4:6, 8, 9; etc.), which join with angels "numbering thousands upon thousands, and ten thousand times ten thousand" (5:11; etc.) in bowing down in worship before the throne. John also saw "standing before the throne and before the Lamb" an innumerable multitude of the redeemed "from every nation, tribe, people and language" (7:9), whose calling is to worship and serve their God (7:9, 15; 22:3). For eternity in Heaven, these are promised God's presence, comfort, protection, and provision as their inheritance (7:17; 21:4, 7).

Following the thousand-year reign of Christ, a cataclysmic, cosmic event takes place. As the dead are called before the "great white throne" of God's eternal judgment, John sees that "the earth and the heavens fled from his presence, and there was no place for them" (20:11; cf. 6:14 and 2 Pet. 3:7). (Note that the plural of *ouranos* is used only seven times, where "the heavens" refers to the created universe and not to God's dwelling place; cf. also the singular "heaven" in 12:1, 3, 7, 10, 12). Immediately, John sees "a new heaven and a new earth, for the first heaven and the first earth had passed away" (21:1); attending this vision is God's declaration that "the old order of things has passed away" [...] "I am making everything new!" (present tense; 21:4, 5). John further notes another shift from the prior physical world with the words, "there was no longer any sea" (21:1), though there had been throughout the thousand-year reign (cf. 20:5 with 20:13).

Just as importantly, with these astonishing events comes an eternal and elemental shift in God's relationship with His people—"God's dwelling place is now among the people, and he will dwell with them" (21:3), the culmination of God's eternal plan of redemption. It is only at the point of this unspeakable transition in the physical world that John sees "the Holy City, the new Jerusalem, coming down out of heaven from God" (21:2; cf. 3:12; 21:10). Based upon this wording and the descriptions following in Chapters 21 and 22, we may make some careful observations. "The Holy City" is the present eternal dwelling of God—i.e., Heaven, "the city of my God" (3:12). It is this very dwelling that is seen moving ("coming down") toward redeemed humanity in Revelation 21:3. (That the "Holy City" comes down "out of heaven from God" cannot mean that God is separated from that "City" or that Heaven and "the Holy City" are distinctly different. "Out of heaven" most likely means out of the newly created "heaven.") "The Holy City" is, however, distinct from the "new earth," though it seems to be in close proximity to this "new earth" based on the probability that the "mountain great and high," which became John's vantage point, was part of the "new earth" and the message of 21:24-26. Unless "the nations" spoken of in 21:24, 26 and 22:2 specifically indicate the redeemed who have come out of the nations that existed prior to the creation of the "new earth," then a stark implication remains. Now absent of Satan, death, and Hades, a new righteous civilization will inhabit "the nations" of the "new earth" led by "the kings of the earth." The immortality of these citizens—i.e., in resurrected, glorified bodies—is established by the absence of "any sea," which is essential to the survival of our current physical bodies.

Clearly "the Holy City, the new Jerusalem" is a place of unfathomable beauty, for it is "the city of my God" (3:12), designed by God Himself (cf. Heb. 11:10, 16; John 14:2). As a city it is greatly populated with the activity of the righteous (21:8, 27; 22:15) and of holy angels, and is encompassed by "a great, high wall with twelve gates (21:12, 15). The dimensions of the city are vast, laid out in what appears to be a cube "12,000 stadia" (21:16), approximately 1,400 miles, in each direction (perhaps foreshadowed in the cubed dimensions of the Holy of Holies in 1 Kings 6:20). The entire city is fashioned of pure transparent gold; its walls are made of "jasper" (21:18; cf. v. 11, "like a jasper, clear as crystal") and the foundations of its walls (which must be exposed) are "decorated with every kind of precious stone" (21:19), twelve in all (21:19-20). Amazingly, each of the twelve gates is made of "a single pearl" (21:21).

John had earlier seen that "in front of the throne there was what looked like a sea of glass, clear as crystal" (4:6; cf. 15:2). He now sees "the river of the water of life, as clear as crystal, flowing from the Throne of God and of the Lamb" (22:1; cf. 7:17; 21:6), and "on each side of the river stood the tree of life" (singular; cf. 2:7; 22:14). Whereas John had earlier described "God's temple in heaven [...] and within his temple was seen the ark of his covenant" (11:19; cf. 15:5, 8; 16:1, 17), John now sees no temple in "the New Jerusalem" "because the Lord God Almighty and the Lamb are its temple" (21:22). "The Holy City" is illuminated with God's glory alone (21:11, 23; 22:5). This truly is "the paradise of God" (2:7), the eternal home of the righteous.

- ▶ See also under Theology (Proper): The Worship and Praise of God (Inclusive of the Trinity)
- ▶ See also under Angelology: The Role and Activities of God's Holy Angels
- ▶ See also under Anthropology: God's Ultimate Will for Redeemed Humanity Expressed
- ▶ See also under Ecclesiology: God's Promises to the True Church—the Redeemed of All Ages
- ▶ See also under Eschatology: The Gathering of the Church To Christ and Into Heaven
- ▶ See also under Eschatology: The Resurrection and Eternal Reward of the Righteous